The Middle East Enters the Twenty-first Century

Florida A&M University, Tallahassee
Florida Atlantic University, Boca Raton
Florida Gulf Coast University, Ft. Myers
Florida International University, Miami
Florida State University, Tallahassee
University of Central Florida, Orlando
University of Florida, Gainesville
University of North Florida, Jacksonville
University of South Florida, Tampa
University of West Florida, Pensacola

The Middle East Enters
the Twenty-first Century

Edited by Robert O. Freedman

University Press of Florida

GAINESVILLE · TALLAHASSEE · TAMPA · BOCA RATON

PENSACOLA · ORLANDO · MIAMI · JACKSONVILLE · FT. MYERS

Library of Congress Cataloging-in-Publication Data
The Middle East enters the twenty-first century / edited by Robert O. Freedman
p. cm.
Proceedings of a conference held in November 2000 and sponsored by the Center for
the Study of Israel and the Contemporary Middle East, Baltimore Hebrew University.
Includes bibliographical references and index.
ISBN 0-8130-2575-3 (p.: alk. paper)
1. Middle East—Politics and government—20th century—Congresses. I. Freedman,
Robert Owen. II. Baltimore Hebrew University. Center for the Study of Israel and the
Contemporary Middle East.
DS62.8 M54 2002
956.04—dc21 2002071464

The University Press of Florida is the scholarly publishing agency for the State
University System of Florida, comprising Florida A&M University, Florida Atlantic
University, Florida Gulf Coast University, Florida International University, Florida
State University, University of Central Florida, University of Florida, University of
North Florida, University of South Florida, and University of West Florida.

University Press of Florida
15 Northwest 15th Street
Gainesville, FL 32611–2079
http://www.upf.com

498 0 589 2

To my shining jewels—Sharon, Debbie, and David:
May they ever shine brightly!

Contents

III. Egypt and North Africa

IV. The Outside Powers

Preface

As we move into a new century, indeed into a new millennium, it is useful to take stock of where we have been in order to understand where we might be going. For this reason the Center for the Study of Israel and the Contemporary Middle East of Baltimore Hebrew University convened a conference in November 2000 on the topic "The Middle East Enters the Twenty-first Century." This was the eleventh conference hosted by the center since its creation in 1978. Previous conferences have dealt with more limited time frames or with a more narrow focus. Thus the first conference, in May 1978, titled "The Middle East and the Arab-Israeli Conflict," dealt with the situation following the 1967 and 1973 Arab-Israeli wars. Subsequent conferences hosted by the center included "The Middle East after Camp David," "Israel in the Begin Era," "The Middle East after the Israeli Invasion of Lebanon," "The Middle East from the Iran-Contra Affair to the Intifada," "The Intifada: Its Impact on Israel, the Arab World, and the Superpowers," "The Middle East after Iraq's Invasion of Kuwait," "Israel under Rabin," "The Middle East and the Peace Process," and "Israel's First Fifty Years." The proceedings of each conference were published in book form by scholarly presses, after being edited by the director of the center, Robert O. Freedman.

For the 2000 conference, however, the participants were asked to speak about, and later write about, a wider theme. As the Middle East enters the twenty-first century, they were asked to comment on and analyze the key developments in their countries since World War II, when many of the countries of the Middle East gained independence, and particularly to discuss the impact on their countries of the three seminal developments of the latter part of the twentieth century: the Islamic revolution in Iran, the Arab-Israeli peace process, and the Iraqi invasion of Kuwait. This book, which represents the views of scholars of Arab, Israeli, Turkish, Iranian, and American origin, with often differing perspectives, will provide the necessary background for understanding the Middle East as we enter this new century.

In preparing this book, I received help from many sources. My secretary, Elise Baron, did a masterful job in preparing the manuscript; Dr. Steven Fine and his able staff in the BHU Library—Barbara Salit-Mischel, Andrew Johnson, and Elaine Mael—provided invaluable computer and research assistance. I would also like to thank Rabbi Mark Loeb, chairman of the Board of Trustees of Baltimore Hebrew University, and Dr. Rela Geffen, president of Baltimore Hebrew University, for their strong support of the Center for the Study of Israel and the Contemporary Middle East; Stanley and Linda Panitz, who provided a major share of the funding for the conference through a gift from The Stanley and Linda Panitz Fund; and Dr. Arthur Abramson, director of the Baltimore Jewish Council, which was Baltimore Hebrew University's partner in convening the conference. Finally, without the continuing support of my wife, Sharon, and my children, Debbie and David, this book would not have been possible, and I dedicate the book to them.

Introduction

As the Middle East enters the twenty-first century, many of the legacies of the twentieth century continue to dominate the politics of the region. In particular, while most of the countries achieved independence during or soon after World War II, three seminal developments in the latter part of the twentieth century are casting a long shadow into the twenty-first century.

The first development was the Islamic revolution in Iran in February 1979, which led to the rapid growth of political Islam in the region. It was to affect not only the states and peoples of the Middle East but also the United States and Russia.

The second key event, coming one month later, was the peace treaty between Egypt and Israel in March 1979, the first such treaty between Israel and an Arab state. It was to be the beginning of the Arab-Israeli peace process in the region, a process that has had numerous ups and downs since 1979. The peace process has affected the states of the region and the Palestinian people, as well as the United States, which was intimately involved in many of the developments of the peace process.

The third seminal development was the Iraqi invasion of Kuwait in August 1990, an event that was not only to split the Arab world—some commentators attributed to it the death of Arab nationalism—but also to motivate the United States to increase greatly its involvement in the defense of the Persian Gulf.

These themes—the growth of political Islam, the evolution of the Arab-Israeli peace process, and the impact of the Gulf War on the region—are the central themes around which this book has been organized. While the themes affect each of the states of the region differently, overall they form the structure through which the region enters the twenty-first century.

The first section of the book deals with the countries of the Persian Gulf and Turkey, which were affected by all three of these key developments. Since Iraq was responsible for two major wars in the latter part of the twentieth century by invading Iran in 1980 and Kuwait in 1990, events that had major implications for both regional and inter-Arab politics, this section begins with an analysis by Judith Yaphe, of the National Defense University, of the changing role of Iraq in the region and the ruling style of its leader, Saddam Hussein. She notes Saddam's growing dependence on selected Arab tribes, along with the Republican Guard, the Special Republican Guard, the regular army, and his tribal clan, to maintain himself in power. Indeed, she notes that Saddam now rules as a "tribal godfather." She also emphasizes the role of Iraq's history in creating a leader such as Saddam and asserts that even if Saddam is overthrown, Iraqi politics may not change much.

The second chapter deals with Iran, the home of the first Islamic revolution in the twentieth century. Shaul Bakhash, of George Mason University, analyzes the evolution of the revolution since 1979. He deals in detail with the contending forces in the Iranian political arena and, in particular, the battle that erupted in the mid-1990s between so-called reformist and conservative forces that came to a head when Mohammad Khatami became Iran's president in 1997. He also notes the major transformation of the Iranian economy since the days of the shah and the far greater role of the state in the economy under the Islamic Republic. In the area of foreign policy, Bakhash asserts that despite the Islamic rhetoric, Iran, especially in the 1990s, has pursued a cautious and pragmatic foreign policy in which Iranian state interests, rather than Islamic interests, have taken priority except in areas peripheral to Iran such as Lebanon and Israel.

The third chapter deals with the Gulf Arab states. Its author, Gregory Gause, of the University of Vermont, notes that when oil revenues declined in the 1980s and 1990s, after the prosperity of the middle and late 1970s, the compact between rulers and ruled, under which the people would give their rulers a relatively free hand in return for an assured high standard of living, began to erode. He also notes the Islamic challenge to the rulers of Saudi Arabia, who themselves have sought legitimacy from Islam, and the continuing need of the Gulf Cooperation Council states for U.S. help in protecting themselves from the ongoing threat of Iraq and the potential threat of Iran. Gause also notes, however, that sympathy for the people of Iraq (if not their leader, Saddam Hussein) and for the Palestinians during the al-Aqsa intifada have created problems for the Gulf leaders in their

Turkey has been heavily influenced both by the Iraqi invasions of Iran and Kuwait and by the Islamic revolution in Iran. Malik Mufti, of Tufts University, discusses the impact of these events, noting that Turkish foreign policy toward the Middle East in the last forty years has swung back and forth between the isolationist policy of Ismet Inönü and the more activist policies of Adnan Menderes and Turgut Ozal. Just as Menderes in the 1950s wanted Turkey to play a role in confronting the Nasser-led United Arab Republic, so too did Ozal seek to get Turkey heavily involved in the Gulf War against Iraq. Mufti describes the foreign and domestic political pressures that counterbalanced these activist efforts and concludes that although events in the Middle East over the past decade—the growth of Iraqi, Iranian, and Syrian missile technology, the rise of the PKK (Kurdish Workers Party) and its use of bases in Iraq as the Iraqi regime weakened, and so on—have dragged Turkey into a more active role in the region, successive Turkish leaders have not worked out a coherent strategy for dealing with the region.

The next section of the book deals with the core area of the Arab-Israeli conflict: Israel, Jordan, Syria, Lebanon, and the Palestinians. While by the end of the twentieth century Israel had made peace with Jordan, albeit a somewhat tenuous one, it remained in conflict with the Palestinians, Lebanon, and Syria. Ilan Peleg, professor of government and law at Lafayette College, begins this section with a chapter on Israel. He argues that Israel has been beset by four ongoing challenges that are shaking the very foundation of the polity: the occupation of the Palestinian-populated West Bank and Gaza; the challenge by the Arab citizens of Israel for equality and national rights; the role of religion among Israeli Jews—especially the growing conflicts between secularists and the Orthodox; and a culture war (Kulturkampf) between universalism and particularism over the question of whether Israel should continue to be a Jewish state or become a state of all of its peoples, Jewish and Arab. Peleg carefully analyzes the numerous connections between the four challenges Israel faces and concludes that a more democratic Israel is a possible result of the polity's struggle with the four challenges.

Of all the Arab countries and peoples, the Palestinians have posed the greatest existential threat to Israel. Barry Rubin, director of the Global Research in International Affairs Center, contends that the central problem facing the Palestinians, and especially their leader, Yasser Arafat, is that they could never agree to settle for what was a realistic solution to the Israeli-Palestinian conflict. Consequently, their position has deteriorated steadily since 1947, when they could have received, through the same UN vote that created Israel, a Palestinian state on a large part of the former British Mandate over Palestine. Rubin also argues that the al-Aqsa intifada is but one more example of the inability of the Palestinians to separate the ideal from the possible, and he attributes the primary cause of the Palestinian failure to achieve their aims to the poor leadership of Arafat.

Jordan, the only Arab country other than Egypt to have made peace with Israel as the twentieth century came to an end, is discussed by Yehuda Lukacs, director of the Center for Global Education at George Mason University. He analyzes the delicate balancing act, both domestically and in Jordan's foreign policy, that first King Hussein and then his successor King Abdullah II have had to perform to maintain stability in their country. Lukacs points to this balancing act as the reason both for Jordan's support of "functional cooperation" with Israel from 1967 to 1987 and for the king's support of the Iraqi invasion of Kuwait in 1990. When the king then took a risk by signing a peace treaty with Israel in 1994—one that has not brought the promised peace dividend to the Jordanian people —his policy came under sharp attack, especially from Jordanians of Palestinian origin who form more than one-half of Jordan's population. Relations with Israel deteriorated sharply following the election of Prime Minister Netanyahu. Hussein's successor, King Abdullah II, has sought to alleviate the pressure by distancing Jordan from Israel and improving ties with both Syria and Iraq—a trend that accelerated following the outbreak of the al-Aqsa intifada.

Syria, discussed by David Lesch, professor of history at Trinity University, also experienced a leadership transition at the end of the twentieth century as longtime strongman Hafiz al-Assad was replaced by his son Bashar. Lesch analyzes the constantly shifting Syrian strategy since 1970 when Hafiz al-Assad, the pragmatist, replaced the radical Ba'athists who had ruled Syria since 1966 and had lost the Golan Heights in the 1967 war with Israel that they had helped precipitate. With his primary goals the regaining of the Golan Heights and the political and military containment of Israel, Hafiz al-Assad engaged in a series of changing alliances and alignments in the 1970s and 1980s, seeking, above all, to control Lebanon (which Syria occupied in 1975), Jordan, and the Palestinians. Following Egypt's peace agreement with Israel, Assad put particular emphasis on preventing Lebanon, Jordan, and the Palestinians from following Anwar Sadat's example. While he was successful in outflanking Israel in Lebanon following the Israeli invasion of 1982, he proved unable, by the 1990s, to prevent the Palestinians or Jordan from moving to peace with Israel. Consequently, the flexible Assad, looking to improve relations with the United States following the collapse of his main political and military backer, the Soviet Union, began his own peace negotiations with Israel. Lesch also

ЉЉЉ

notes that despite all the diplomatic zigzagging Syria did from 1970 to 2000, the Syrian economy has done very poorly. Consequently, besides maintaining himself in power, reinvigorating the Syrian economy is Bashar's number one domestic priority.

While Syria has been in full occupation of Lebanon since 1975 (except for a brief period from 1982 to 1985 when Israel controlled large parts of the country), many Lebanese, especially the Christians, want the Syrian army to leave, especially since Israel has now withdrawn to the borders approved by the United Nations. Marius K. Deeb, professor of Islamic and Middle Eastern studies at the School of Advanced International Studies of Johns Hopkins University, addresses this theme. He analyzes both the alliance between Syria and Iran and the alliance between Syria and Hizballah (also backed by Iran) and notes how Syria has used Hizballah as a tool in pressuring Israel to return the Golan Heights. Deeb also asserts that a Lebanon free of Syrian control would move toward a peace with Israel, based on mutual mercantile interests, that would rapidly become much warmer than Israel's peace treaties with Egypt and Jordan.

The third section of this book deals with Egypt and the states of North Africa. Egypt has been a pivotal state in the region, and the three main developments in the Middle East in the latter part of the twentieth century have all had a major impact there. Egypt was the first Arab state to make peace with Israel, and it spearheaded Arab forces in the Gulf War against Iraq. The nation also suffered from the impact of the Islamic revolution in Iran as Islamism had become a major political force in Egypt by the end of the century. Louis Cantori, of the University of Maryland, Baltimore County, describes the evolution of Egyptian policy, both domestic and foreign, from the period when Gamal Nasser ruled Egypt (1952–70) through the period of Anwar Sadat (1970–81) and the rule of Hosni Mubarak (1981–). Utilizing the analytic model of corporatism, he defines Egypt as both a strong and weak state during this period and notes that in an era of globalization, Egypt, as a rentier state, is not a major player. Cantori also describes the rise of Islamic influence in Egypt and asserts that Mubarak has been fighting an unsuccessful secularist war to contain it. Finally, while its ties to the United States have resulted in significant economic gain for Egypt, its dependence on U.S. aid has limited its freedom of action in the area of foreign policy, especially in relation to the Israeli-Palestinian conflict.

While Islam had become a major force in Egypt by the end of the century, it was perhaps even more important in North Africa as Islamists rose to be the most important opposition forces in Algeria, Morocco, Tunisia, and Libya. Mary-Jane Deeb, of the U.S. Library of Congress, describes the rise of Islamic opposition groups in all four countries. Inspired by the Islamic revolution in Iran (although there were Islamic groups in each country before 1979), the Islamic groups, often linked to each other across national boundaries, exploited such issues as political stagnation, economic decline (including high levels of unemployment), deteriorating security conditions, a perceived Western cultural invasion, and political attempts to secularize society. The governments of North Africa responded to these challenges by opening up their economies to encourage development (and hence cut unemployment) and banded together to share intelligence, a process that helped bring Libyan leader Muammar Kaddafi out of regional isolation. While no Maghrebi Islamic group has yet seized power on the model of Iran, the Islamists, as Deeb notes, pose major challenges to the governments of the region both domestically and in their foreign policy, especially with regard to Israel.

The final section of the book deals with the outside powers that have had the greatest influence on the Middle East in the latter part of the twentieth century—the United States and the Soviet Union/Russia. The United States, which brokered the Egyptian-Israeli peace agreement, led the allied coalition to free Kuwait after Iraq's invasion and frequently came into conflict with Iran following the Islamic revolution in that country. The United States played a central role in Middle East politics as the century came to an end and, as the world's only superpower, is likely to play a major role in this century as well. Don Peretz, professor emeritus of the State University of New York at Binghamton, discusses U.S. policy in detail, with particular emphasis on the role of the United States in the Arab-Israeli conflict. He analyzes the growing ties between the United States and Israel since 1967 and questions whether, in the twenty-first century, the relationship will remain as strong, due to changes both in the Middle East and in the American Jewish community. Peretz also underlines the strategic relationship between the United States and Gulf states, particularly Saudi Arabia, where the United States provides protection against Iraq (and potentially against Iran), while Saudi Arabia has become a reliable provider of oil to the United States.

The other superpower, the Soviet Union, collapsed in 1991, and its main successor state, Russia, has been in a far weaker position economically, politically, strategically, and diplomatically than was the USSR. Robert O. Freedman analyzes the policies of Russia, compared to those of the USSR, and presents four case studies of Russian policy toward the region: Iran, Iraq, Turkey, and Israel. He notes there has been continuity in

Russia's policy toward Iran, as the two states have developed a tactical alliance. In the case of Iraq, Moscow, while not breaking the UN sanctions, has sought to regain the influence it had in Baghdad in the time of the USSR. Russian policy toward Turkey has been a combination of continued Cold War confrontation and economic cooperation, although by 1998, with Russia's economic collapse, cooperation had taken priority, as symbolized by the multibillion-dollar Blue Stream natural gas pipeline agreement. In the case of Russia's treatment of Israel, the tentative rapprochement that began in the latter part of the Gorbachev era has expanded to include extensive economic, cultural, and even military ties. Freedman concludes that with the advent of Vladimir Putin as Russia's president, Moscow is striving to regain the influence it had when the Soviet Union existed, but a weak economy and a different geopolitical position make this goal difficult to achieve.

Part I

The Persian Gulf and Turkey

The Legacy of Iraq's Past and the Promise of Its Future

JUDITH S. YAPHE

Most observers of Iraq's recent history credit or blame Saddam Hussein, Iraq's self-appointed president since 1979, for every evil perpetrated in or by Iraq, while ignoring or misunderstanding Iraq's turbulent history. A country that has tremendous potential wealth in its people and natural resources, it is also a society stripped of its civil rights and lacking in understanding of the norms that govern most inter- and intrastate relationships. Except for the Arab-Israeli peace process, Iraq was the root cause of or a major participant in the confrontations disrupting regional stability in the late twentieth century: its invasion of Iran in 1980 and the eight-year war that followed, and its invasion and occupation of Kuwait and the ensuing war in 1990–91. During this time Iraq has swung from one extreme to another, experiencing great wealth, making great strides in improving the living standards of its people—and developing indigenous programs for the proliferation of weapons of mass destruction, including nuclear weapons; allowing its society, especially the middle class, to be devastated by ten years of economic sanctions; and reducing a whole society to rule by terror.

Note: Judith S. Yaphe is senior research professor for the Middle East and an expert on Iraq and Persian Gulf security issues at the Institute for National Strategic Studies, National Defense University, Washington, D.C. The comments and opinions expressed here are hers and do not represent policies of the university, the Department of Defense, or any other government agency.

The Legacy of Iraq's History

Saddam Hussein is generally held responsible for the violence and terror that have characterized the thirty years of his rule, for religious and ethnic intolerance, for authoritarian rule, for unrestrained corruption, and for uncontrolled national rage—all characteristics that have marked the thirty years of his dominance in Iraqi politics. Yet, certain of these characteristics were present in Iraq long before Saddam came to power and will probably remain after he has disappeared from the scene.

The Legacy of Political Violence

Iraq has a complicated and violent history.[1] It is both 6,000 years old and 80 years old. Its history begins with that of ancient Mesopotamia and the founding of the first government in 1920 under the British Mandate when three provinces of the Ottoman Empire—Mosul, Baghdad, and Basra—were cobbled together as a state under the imported Hashemite king, Faisal I. Iraq became an independent state in 1932 but remained under British influence until the end of World War II. Some say its borders, like those of all the other Middle Eastern states carved out of the Ottoman Empire after World War I, are artificial, but they reflect the ancient land between the two rivers that was Mesopotamia. This heritage includes being the first agricultural settlement (Kirkuk 6500 BCE) and one of the first centralized, autocratic empires (the Akadians 2400 BCE), inventing the wheel and writing, and having the first written legal code (Hammurabi).

In contrast, Iraqi society and culture have been shaped more by Iraq's Islamic and Arab tribal past. Both these factors give Iraq its modern identity and shape its political character. Baghdad was the capital of the Abbasid Caliphate, the so-called golden age of medieval Arab civilization, from 750 CE until it was devastated by the Mongol invasion of 1258. It contains the shrine cities of Shia Islam—An-Najaf, where the Imam Ali was slain and buried; Karbala, where Ali's son Hussein was martyred and buried; and Kufah and al-Kazimyah (Baghdad), where several of the prominent imams of early Shia Islam are entombed. Iraq inherited from its Ottoman history traditions of military training and Sunni leadership, influences that survived the end of both imperial and republican rule. The conversion of Sunni Arab Iraqis to the political ideology of Arab nationalism began under the Young Turks, although it took the Hashemite monarchy to develop this into a defining force in Iraq.

Iraq has a bloody and violent history of military coups, political violence, and repression of minorities. The origins can be seen in the Assyrian massacres of 1933, the repression common under Prime Minister Nuri al-Said and the regent Abd-illah, the 1958 coup in which the young king was killed and Nuri's mutilated body dragged through the streets of Baghdad in a woman's dress, in the coups and attempted coups of the 1960s, when assassination and repression were commonly used to hunt down opponents, and in the hanging of Jews and regime opponents from the lampposts of Liberation Square in 1969. Sham trials and executions, begun under Abd al-Karim Qassim, intensified under the Ba'ath, as did the use of torture. Iraq's military, created in 1932, played a prominent role in virtually all these events. Ubiquitous intelligence and security services grew apace as did the suppression of dissent. These became institutionalized as the "*mukhabarat* (police) state" took shape.[2]

The Legacy of Tribalism

Iraq has long been dominated by powerful tribal confederations, and its people have long been defined by their *'asabiya,* their loyalties to tribe, clan, and family.[3] Ibn Khaldun, the thirteenth-century Arab historian, defined a tribe as a self-contained and autonomous organization having social, economic, cultural, protective, and political functions. Tribes, he wrote in *The Muqaddimah,* existed separate from cities and civilization, while cities absorbed and conquered the tribes.[4] Through the long period of Turkish rule, tribes in Iraq were mobile mini-states, headed by a patriarch, with their own military force and codes of justice and retribution. The tribe derived its livelihood from pastoralism, trade, raiding, and tribute. The tribe's existence depended on intertribal wars, government campaigns to control them, and the mercy of nature.

In the early twentieth century, when the Turks ruled the three provinces that became modern Iraq, large confederations and extended families dominated the region. Unlike Palestinian and Lebanese Arabs, Iraq's tribes lacked close links to the land and settled villages until modern times. Loyalties to family, clan, and tribe were—and are—more important than fealty to land and village. One prominent historian of ancient and modern Iraq describes the devotion to personal honor, factionalism, and intense individualism that are characteristics of the tribe and of those who resist central authority as legacies of tribalism in Iraq.[5] Despite Ottoman, British, and Ba'athist efforts to break the power of tribal warlords and *shaykh*s, tribalism survived, based on intermarriage, common lineage, collective economic interests, social support structures, and/or common residence. Tribes were encouraged to settle in towns, and the large confederations lost some of their identity as military alliances. They became involved in squabbles over land and water rights. Their chiefs became tax farmers and agents of the state, not the tribe.

While most tribal units claim to trace their roots to a common ancestor or family, tribes in modern Iraq are also formed by disparate urban groups of individuals sharing common needs.[6] The lineage, symbols, and culture of some prominent tribes have been integrated into the state to enhance the status, legitimacy, and power of the ruling elite. In effect, the tribe becomes the state. A second kind of tribe gains power and authority from a state too weak to govern; the tribe replaces the state to some extent in local matters. The tribes resume their tribute collection and judicial powers, becoming in effect an extension of the state itself. Saddam's tribal policy of the 1990s, in which he co-opted the tribes to help him maintain law and order in the countryside and the cities, fits this category.

A third kind of tribalism—based on military necessity as well as ideology—is also present in modern Iraq, especially among its Kurdish and Shia tribal groups. Ethnic and tribal loyalties were important to Iraq's Shia Arab tribes; they fought fierce battles as Iraqis and Arabs against the Persian Iranians in Qurna and the marshes from 1982 through 1985. The Kurds, too, have long honored tribal and family ties, and a militant and military-style tribalism has long defined their sense of loyalty and identity, in particular among the Barzani Kurds. Baghdad, for its part, has for many years hired the services of mercenary tribal Kurdish families, called *jash* or donkeys, to serve as border guards in the north against Iran and occasionally against other Kurdish factions. Baghdad valued these ethnic and tribal ties that separated Persian Shia from Iraqi Arab Shia and Kurd from Kurd. Party circulars during the Iran-Iraq war praised the tribes for their cultural values, stressing valor, honor, manhood, courage, and military prowess.[7] In the 1990s, at the end of the Kuwait war, both Kurds and Shia tribes mobilized to confront an external threat, in this case, Baghdad.

The Mesopotamian Heritage

Tribal loyalties continue, in many instances, to supersede those created by the nationalisms of the twentieth century, even those created by Saddam Hussein. Saddam tried to erase tribal culture and influence and bind all of Iraq's diverse peoples into one new culture by creating a new Iraqi identity, an identity shaped by Iraq's 6,000-year-old culture and traditions and a loyalty that owes all status, benefits, and achievement to Saddam alone.[8] In part, this focused on linking the heroic myths of ancient Iraq, including Hammurabi and Salah al-Din, the Kurdish hero of the Crusades who was born in Tikrit, and the icons of early Islam, particularly the Prophet Muhammad and his son-in-law and successor Ali, to the Arab Sunni clans and tribes related to Saddam. Identity in the new secular Iraq was to supersede outmoded concepts of tribal identification, ethnic solidarity, or religious loyalty. Iraq was part of a historical continuum with ancient Mesopotamia. To reinforce this, Saddam had his name put on all the bricks used to rebuild ancient Babylon. He also had his family lineage written to show descent from the family of the Prophet.

Saddam endorsed the image of the New Iraqi Man and Woman. Tribal ties, however, brought Saddam to power—he was a cousin of President Ahmad Hassan al-Bakr as well as the chief enforcer of the Ba'ath Party's security force. For Saddam, tribal values and loyalties as well as Ba'athist ideology and Arab nationalism were intended to enforce pride in his and the country's uniqueness. More importantly, they gave the Iraqi leader tools to reinforce his own power and control.

Is There a Republican or Democratic Legacy?

Iraq had a relatively short history as a participatory republic. The British included Sunnis, Christians, and Jews in the first government formed in modern Iraq in 1920; only the Shias opted out of a political role. Governments from King Faisal I through the last one formed by Nuri al-Said in 1958 manipulated the prominent Sunni leaders willing to participate in the National Assembly at the same time that they isolated democrats, Communists, tribal elements, and intellectuals. Elections were meaningless, meant to serve as a rubber stamp for a parliament already chosen by Nuri or the so-called republicans who formed the governments between the 1958 revolution and the Ba'athist takeover in July 1968.

The Ba'ath Party, by contrast, was intended by its leaders to appeal to all Iraqis—Sunni and Shia, Arab and Kurd. In the 1950s and 1960s it represented a wide spectrum of Iraqis—Sunni, Shia, and Christian, Arab and Kurd. In theory the party was to provide all with special and equal status—meaning membership brought privileges not available to nonparty members and accorded Arab and Kurd, Sunni, Christian, and Shia in the party with the same access to position, education, and whatever else determined status in the new society. And many from the ethnic and sectarian communities joined the new parties—the Kurds and Shia in particular joined the Iraqi Communist Party as well as the Ba'ath Party.[9]

The new parties provided no easy or democratic solutions for Iraq's ethnic and religious minorities. Communist activities were fixed by Moscow and circumscribed more strictly as relations between the Soviet Union and the Ba'athists grew in the 1970s. Ba'athist ideology presented a different set of problems for non-Sunni, non-Arab Iraqis. Ba'athism as a political philosophy was based on a theory of Arab unity, economic equality, and social justice. As such, it held little appeal for most Shia, who interpreted Arabism as union with Sunni Syria; the Kurds showed a similar lack of interest. Nevertheless, Kurds continued to join the military, and secular Shia and Christians joined the Ba'ath Party, becoming loyalists of Saddam.[10]

Enter Saddam: Republican *Shaykh* and Tribal Godfather

Saddam is the product of a dysfunctional family in a small village and society dominated by tribalism and a patriarchal culture. He has always reflected the tribal characteristics of loyalty to family, clan, and tribe. He used these qualities to build loyalty to himself as the republic's *shaykh*, the father of his people, the essential Iraqi. But he also uses these tribal characteristics to rule as a tribal godfather, the dispenser of wisdom, justice, wealth, and punishment.

Saddam's own history is tied up in tribal values. He was born in a small village near Tikrit in 1937; his official birth date is April 28. His father died before he was born. Saddam was reared first by his mother and a stepfather, who refused to send him to school, and then by his mother's brother, Khayrallah Talfah.[11] In a culture strictly ruled by patriarchy and ancient codes of honor and justice, Saddam was in some ways a social outcast as a young child.[12]

If Saddam did not invent the violence and oppression common in his Republic of Fear, he did refine the methodology, increasing in scope and quality the practices of violence and terror. Saddam began his political career with an assassination attempt on Iraq's leader, Abd al-Karim Qassim. He played the role of security thug and enforcer from the time he joined the nascent Ba'ath Party in the early 1950s, pursuing real and imagined political opponents through his long tenure as party security chief, vice president, and security tsar under President Ahmad Hassan al-Bakr and as self-proclaimed president since 1979.

In the decade between the 1958 revolution, which ended the monarchy, and the July 30, 1968, coup, that brought the Ba'ath Party to power, Iraq experienced four successful coups and a dozen abortive ones. To Saddam and others in the new regime, the lessons of that ten-year period showed that power based solely on the military, party bureaucrats, or government civil servants would not succeed. In the early years, the party had members who were military officers, and party functionaries held high positions in the government and security services.

Reinventing Iraq

In the three decades Saddam has ruled Iraq, through revolutions, coups, countercoups, wars, and UN-imposed sanctions intended to deny him absolute authority over all of Iraq, Saddam has survived by reinventing himself and Iraq. Bakr, Saddam, and the new Ba'athist elite that controlled the party after the 1963 coup came almost entirely from provincial, semi-bedouin small towns and villages, where tribal and family loyalties were and still are strongest. The first "invention" was Saddam's recreation after the 1968 coup of a new Ba'ath Party purged of its intellectuals, leftists, and military heroes. In their place was a new kind of party loyalist who owed his education, position, and wealth to his standing in the party apparatus and proven reputation for loyalty to Saddam. Saddam oversaw the expansion of the party from a membership of several hundred in the 1960s to nearly 2 million by the mid-1970s.[13]

At the same time, Saddam began mobilizing clan and family networks into the military and security services, giving them control of institutions of coercion, violence, and terror. Members of Saddam's tribe, the Albu Nasir, and his clan, the Bayjat, were given preference in joining the sensitive security units—as bodyguards to the inner circle of the regime and to Saddam and his family and as protectors of special sites and programs (such as those for development of weapons of mass destruction). Tribes related to Saddam's clan—the Dulaym, Dur, Jabbur, and Ubayd—were recruited for the Republican Guard, the Special Republican Guard, the bodyguard units, intelligence and security units in the military and the party, the Baghdad garrison, and, on occasion, the Defense Ministry.[14] They replaced the non-Tikritis, the non-Ba'athist military leaders, and party ideologues of dubious loyalty.[15]

The next layer of invention was evident by the early 1980s. Close family members were given senior posts, including Saddam's Ibrahim half brothers—Barzan, Sibawi, and Watban—and his Talfah and al-Majid cousins. By the mid- to late 1980s, members of Saddam's family and tribe dominated all areas critical to Saddam's power. His half brother Barzan was intelligence minister and chief security thug for several years after the revolution, a position later held by his other half brothers, Sibawi and Watban. Cousins Adnan Khayrallah Talfah and Ali Hassan al-Majid (known as Chemical Ali for his use of chemical weapons in the Kurdish repression of 1988) both served as defense minister. Cousins Hussein and Saddam Kamil and Ali Hassan al-Majid would run the first circle of protection around Saddam, including intelligence, security, and the all-important Ministry of Industry and Military Industrialization (MIMI).[16] By the early 1990s, Saddam's family policy had brought in sons Qusay and Uday. Qusay now controls the intelligence and security forces, including the Special Republican Guards, and many Iraqis believe Saddam has chosen him as his successor.

From the early days of their rule, Bakr, Saddam, and their close allies, including Izzat Ibrahim al-Duri and Taha Yasin Ramadhan, oversaw the military bureau of the party, which was in charge of selecting and indoctrinating military cadets. Ramadhan, a Mosuli, was later removed because of his appointment of Mosuli friends and kin to the military academy.[17] Saddam oversaw selection of the members of the security bureau (Maktabat al-Alaqat al-Amm or Bureau of Public Relations). Saddam also established a Committee of the Tribes to work among tribes in the Sunni Arab region. Saddam thus became the patriarch, the dispenser of power, and the source of all influence in the party, the tribe, and the state.[18]

The Legacy of War

Iraqis have known few years of calm under Saddam's rule. In 1980 Saddam began eight years of war with Iran. Although the ostensible reason was to stave off what he and many Arabs saw as danger that the Islamic Republic would spread its revolution to Shia communities in Iraq and the Gulf, he primarily wanted to take advantage of Iranian military weakness and political disarray to regain territory conceded to the shah in the 1975 Algiers Accord. In 1990, he invaded and began the brutal occupation of a second neighbor, Kuwait. Again, the ostensible reason was Kuwaiti refusal to provide financial aid in the reconstruction and rearming of war-damaged Iraq, but Saddam also saw vulnerability in a weak but rich country with few friends in the neighborhood. Through these decades, the thread of opposition to Israel and support for the Palestinians runs through Iraqi foreign policy, with actions ranging from sending military contingents in the 1973 war through the launching of SCUD missiles against Israeli cities during the 1991 Gulf War to a call for a *jihad* (holy war) against Israel at the October 2000 Arab League summit held in Cairo, the first Iraq had been invited to attend since it invaded Kuwait.

In all these developments, certain common threads emerge about Saddam's vision of Iraq, Arabism, and his role in shaping regional events. And without overinterpreting the actions of a ruthless authoritarian with no visible means of opposition, one can see elements of his character that shape his decision-making style:

- A pragmatism and ability to calculate when to withdraw—in accepting the 1975 accord with the shah to end the Kurdish war and Iranian-U.S. backing for the Kurds;
- A willingness to wait until the time for revenge is more propitious—in 1980 when the Islamic extremists in the revolution were trying to consolidate their hold on Iran;
- A tendency to overestimate his powers of persuasion and terror in trying to resolve domestic problems with aggression abroad—the invasion of Kuwait;
- A belief that he can represent all things to all people—defender of the Arabs and especially the Palestinians, the poor and oppressed, the religious, and the secular;
- A near-mystical belief in his and Iraq's destiny to provide leadership in the Gulf and the broader Middle East and to defeat what he perceives to be the intention of the West—particularly the United States—to exploit Iraq and keep it weak, just as in colonial times.

Saddam's Kurdish Solutions: Contained Autonomy and *Anfal*

Iraq's Kurds had been promised equal partnership with the Arabs in the state of Iraq since the 1958 revolution. Mullah Mustafa Barzani, father of Masud, the current leader of the Barzani Kurds, returned to Baghdad from exile in the Soviet Union in 1959, encouraged apparently by a promise that Baghdad would restore administrative and cultural rights to the Kurds. This was the first time Kurds had been offered equal rights in the Iraqi state. The Kurds and the Iraqis soon became disenchanted with their arrangement, however, with the Kurds suspecting correctly that Baghdad was only paying lip service to Kurdish demands for autonomy while Baghdad feared that Kurdish demands for autonomy would only lead to Kurdish independence.[19] War between the Barzani Kurds and Baghdad began in 1961 when Mullah Mustafa sent an ultimatum demanding an end to authoritarian rule, recognition of Kurdish autonomy, and restoration of democratic rights.[20] In a tactic to be used later by Saddam, Baghdad bombed Kurdish villages, including Barzani's home village of Barzan.

Barzani was joined in rebellion by loyal tribal forces, the Kurdish Democratic Party, and Kurdish army officers who deserted the regular army. The war was costly for Baghdad, in money, prestige, and a demoralized military; it was weakened by defections and its inability to defeat a smaller force of Kurdish guerrillas. The Kurds demanded a binational state when the Ba'athists reached agreement in 1963 with Egyptian president Gamal Abdel Nasser on a future pan-Arab union. War began again, with the Kurds in control of the entire northern region and aided by Iranian Kurds. Baghdad's response was to bomb villages, destroy those under Kurdish control, and try to Arabize strategic areas. Over the next seven years and through successive Iraqi governments, Baghdad tried to quell the north; the Kurds aided Baghdad by factional infighting. Barzani himself was drawn into closer alliance with the shah of Iran, with the shah supplying heavy arms to the Kurds by 1965.[21] There were intermittent cease-fires between the Kurds and Baghdad, but by the mid-1960s Baghdad had been drawn into armed clashes with Iran, with Baghdad accusing Tehran of providing arms and safe haven to the rebels and Tehran accusing Baghdad of attacking Iranian border villages. Barzani continued to consolidate relations with the shah and opened contact with Israel.[22]

These were the conditions facing Saddam Hussein when the Ba'ath Party seized power a second time in July 1968. Saddam had come to power under the leadership of his kinsman, Ahmad Hassan al-Bakr, secretary-general of the party and head of the Revolutionary Command Council. Saddam served as chief of the party's underground apparatuses and worked behind the scenes during the process that brought Bakr and the military wing of the Ba'ath Party to power. His loyalty to Bakr was rewarded; by 1969 he had become the second-most-powerful force in Baghdad. By 1973, according to Marr, he overshadowed his mentor, Bakr.[23]

Faced with a more basic need to consolidate power at home and put an end, at least temporarily, to the shah's meddling in northern Iraq, Saddam reversed years of official Iraqi policy and drafted a unique settlement directly with Barzani. On March 11, 1970, Baghdad published its 15-point agreement with the Kurdish leadership. Its terms included:

- recognition of Kurdish autonomy and guaranteed proportional representation for Kurds in a national legislative assembly;
- appointment of a Kurdish vice president to the national government (Taha Muhyi al-Din Maruf remains as Kurdish vice president today), with Kurds or Kurdish speakers to be civil servants in administrative units inhabited by a Kurdish majority;

- a commitment to spend a proportion of Iraq's oil revenues in the autonomous region;
- recognition of Kurdish and Arabic as the official languages in Kurdish Iraq;
- a promise to carry out a census to determine areas where Kurds formed the majority of the population.[24]

Barzani, in turn, agreed to turn in his heavy weapons and integrate his *peshmerga* (the term means those who face death) fighters into the Iraqi army. Implementation of the agreement was to be delayed four years. The government withdrew support for Barzani's opponents, and five Barzani loyalists were put on the Council of Ministers, including Jalal Talabani.[25]

The peace negotiated in 1970 was short-lived. The Iraqis recognized the governates of Irbil, Sulaymaniyah, and Dohuk as comprising the autonomous region; the Kurds claimed much more, including the oil-rich region of Kirkuk, which was not a predominantly Kurdish city. Amid accusations of bad faith, assassination attempts against Barzani and his sons, and government attempts to move Arabs into predominantly Kurdish areas to change the population balance, fighting once again broke out.[26] In mid-1972, the Kurds began receiving aid from the CIA, authorized by President Nixon, as well as the shah.[27] Amid squabbling over the status of Kirkuk and Kurdish rejection of the government's autonomy plan, war resumed in April 1974.

One year later, the shah and Saddam decided on peace. It was to their mutual advantage to resolve their long-standing border dispute, end Iranian assistance to the Kurds and Iraqi efforts to subvert Iran through its dissident, Kurdish, and Arab populations, and institute strict border regulations. The shah obtained most of what he wanted—his abrogation of the 1937 treaty was legalized, with the border set at the thalweg line in the middle of the Shatt al-Arab;[28] both parties agreed to strictly control their borders, thereby ending Iranian aid to the Iraqi Kurds; and Iraq renounced all claims to the Arabic-speaking province of Iranian Khuzistan. Iran removed its weapons from the Kurds, and Baghdad sealed the border—and the fate—of Iraqi Kurdistan. The uneasy peace between Baghdad and Tehran would last until 1980.

During the war with Iran, Iraq's Kurdish Democratic Party, led by the Barzanis, supported Iran. It joined with other anti-Baghdad dissidents, including the Tehran-based Shia Dawa Party and Iraqi exiles based in Damascus, to fight Saddam. In retaliation, Baghdad rounded up nearly

8,000 Barzani Kurdish loyalists between the ages of twelve and eighty who were being held in camps near Irbil. They were almost certainly murdered. Baghdad paid little attention to the Kurdish region and allowed many Kurds who had been deported south to return to the north. Saddam offered amnesty to Kurds accused of antigovernment activities, including Kurdish deserters from the army, and allowed elections (rigged, of course) to be held for the Legislative Council of the Kurdish autonomous region.

The relative calm in Kurdistan was short-lived. In 1988 the KDP (Kurdish Democratic Party) and the PUK (Patriotic Union of Kurdistan), along with several small Kurdish factions, joined together in a common front to overthrow Saddam Hussein's regime, establish democratic government in Iraq, and develop a federal status for Kurds in Iraq. The combined strength of the Kurdish forces has been estimated at about 60,000 *peshmerga* plus an unknown number of anti-Turkish Kurdish dissidents, all armed with antiaircraft missiles and other weapons looted from the Iraqis or obtained from Iran. Fighting in the north escalated in 1987 and early 1988. It was a commonplace observation that the Iraqis controlled the roads by day, but the night belonged to the Kurds. In January 1988 the PUK captured one of Saddam's palaces.[29]

Baghdad's response was the *anfal*.[30] Beginning in April 1987 and continuing through 1988, Iraq conducted a systematic campaign attacking villages in Iraqi Kurdistan suspected of harboring Kurdish dissidents. In June 1987 Baghdad declared a shoot-to-kill policy and allowed army commanders "to carry out random bombardments, using artillery, helicopters and aircraft, at all times of the day or night, in order to kill the largest number of persons present in these prohibited zones." All persons captured were to be detained and interrogated, and executed after any useful information had been obtained from them.[31]

The actual *anfal* began four months after the census, in February 1988. On March 16, 1988, the Iraqi military attacked Halabjah, a Kurdish city of 70,000 located approximately fifteen miles from the border with Iran; the city had recently been captured by *peshmerga* aided by Iranian Revolutionary Guard forces. In what was partly counterinsurgency operation and mostly retaliation for its capture, more than 5,000 civilians were killed in operations using chemical weapons—mustard, nerve, and cyanide gas. Chemical attacks against civilian targets recurred throughout the summer. More than 60,000 Kurdish refugees fled across the Turkish border while Baghdad forced resettlement of Kurdish villagers to camps in southern Iraq. The Middle East Watch estimates that at least 50,000 and possibly as many as 100,000 persons—many of them women and children—were killed between February and September. The killings were part of a systematic plan by the central government to kill as many Kurds as possible and destroy their villages.[32] Baghdad insisted then—and still does today—that its 1970 agreement with the Kurds is still in effect, including the puppet parliament for the so-called autonomous region.

Saddam's *Qadisiyyah* against Iran

Relations between Baghdad and Tehran were never good but were occasionally correct, depending on the regional balance of power and the ability of the two countries to maintain a countervailing level of threat. The issues that divided them—control of the Shatt al-Arab, quarrelsome Kurds on both sides of the border, a Soviet-backed Iraq versus a pro-Western shah—continued through 1979. An Iraq divided by revolution, unstable and short-lived regimes, and internal wars was no match for Iran under an increasingly powerful shah, backed by the United Kingdom and the United States in his quest for strategic domination of the "Persian" Gulf (declared to be the "Arabian" Gulf in 1961 by Baghdad).

The situation would reverse itself in 1980 when Iran, recovering from the overthrow of the shah, the imposition of clerical rule in Iran, and the loss of a superpower backer, was perceptibly weak.[33] Now, Iraq was in a position of strength, following five years of relative peace from internal fighting (Kurdish) and Saddam's successful consolidation of power. Iraqis, increasingly urbanized, were enjoying a newfound prosperity with oil wealth financing educational and health improvements and higher standards of living. A rising middle class, an estimated 35 percent of the population, was emerging, some helped along by party membership or connections to the family and clan of Saddam.[34] And, thinking ahead to the day when Iraq would confront Iran again, Saddam had spent the decade acquiring the technology and expertise to build advanced weapons systems, including the first stirrings of nuclear, biological, and chemical weapons programs.[35]

If Saddam did not have to be overly concerned about potential unrest in the north, he was faced with growing Shia unrest in southern Iraq, especially in the years just prior to the Islamic revolution in Iran. The tensions were particularly evident in the Shia holy cities of An-Najaf and Karbala, where the clerics were primarily of Iranian origin and the unrest was religiously and politically motivated; and in the predominantly Shia sections of Baghdad, slum areas where economic and social woes contributed to a sense of alienation among the newly arrived Shia dispossessed. An underground Shia religious party, the Dawa al-Islamiya (Islamic Call Party) was formed in the late 1960s. It was influenced by Ayatollah Muhammad Baqr Sadr, whose message of a return to rule by Islamic precepts and social justice foreshadowed the Islamic revivalism that was to sweep the region in the 1980s. It also echoed the political philosophy of Ayatollah Khomeini, who spent fifteen years in exile in An-Najaf until Saddam deported him to France in 1979. In 1977, a government crackdown on the Shia practice of self-flagellation during ceremonies commemorating the martyrdom of Imam Husayn (the prophet Muhammad's grandson and preferred political heir for some Muslims) triggered demonstrations. Baghdad also claimed a Syrian agent had been discovered carrying explosives into the shrine in Karbala.[36] Military troops quelled rioting, which had spread to An-Najaf.

The success of the Islamic revolution in Iran and the installation of a militant cleric-dominated government led by Ayatollah Khomeini were cause for grave concern in Baghdad. The army again had to put down riots in the holy cities in 1979, sparked by Ayatollah Muhammad Baqr Sadr's real and suspected links to the new Iranian regime.[37] Several Shia dissident groups backed by Iran were discovered in Iraq, including the Dawa and the Islamic Amal Party, the latter headed by an Iranian cleric. Baghdad responded by arresting and executing Baqr Sadr, his sister, and a number of clerical students and scholars.[38]

Saddam, Kuwait, and the Grand Coalition

Saddam won the eight-year war with Iran in 1988 but had little to show for it. Casualties were estimated to be nearly one-half million, with virtually no family left untouched by the war. The economy was uncertain—the war had been financed by foreign debt, with Saudi Arabia, Kuwait, Qatar, and the United Arab Emirates "loaning" Baghdad approximately $80 billion. The money was intended to allow Iraq to pursue the war and keep Baghdad's civilian economy stable. After the war, cash poor and determined to pursue an aggressive posture in the region while continuing his buildup of special weapons programs, Saddam turned once again to his oil-rich neighbors for new loans. This time, the Kuwaitis balked and may even have had the temerity to ask him for repayment of the previous loans. Saddam's response was to charge Kuwait with stealing oil from oil fields bordering the two countries, accuse Kuwait and the UAE of cheating on OPEC quotas, and threaten Israel with a rain of chemical fire.

Much has been written about Saddam's intentions in invading Kuwait. As in his invasion of Iran, Saddam chose a neighbor that was weaker and seemingly lacking in allies. He assumed no one would care if he intimidated and then eliminated a regime he viewed as illegitimate and restored "proper" rule to a country that was inherently part of historical Iraq.[39] Saddam professed many reasons for invading and occupying Kuwait, including

- restoring the nineteenth province torn away by British colonialism to its rightful place—republican, democratic Iraq;
- eliminating greedy, rapacious, lascivious rulers like the Al Sabah;
- helping the Palestinians to regain their homeland;
- helping the poor defeat the corrupt plutocrats who controlled the wealth of their countries (again, the Al Sabah and the Al Sa'ud);
- boosting the cause of Islam—Saddam was the holy warrior fighting to restore true Islamic rule—the Islamic militants, including the Brotherhood, bought this, if only for tactical reasons, despite Saddam's dismal track record of murdering clerics and his non-Islamic ruling style;
- ensuring fairness in oil production and pricing—he promised to share the benefits of great wealth based on oil with the have-not countries.

Saddam portrayed himself as the republican *shaykh,* the honest broker of the Arabs, the defender of Palestinian and Muslim rights, and the only Arab leader brave enough to stand up to the West to claim what rightfully belonged to the Arabs and Iraq. He calculated that his demands for economic and social justice, coupled with what he perceived to be his impeccable Islamic lineage, would make him popular with the Arab street and untouchable by any Arab regime. He put it more simply to U.S. ambassador April Glaspie in their now-historic first and only meeting on July 25, 1990, one week before the invasion. In essence he told the U.S. envoy that this was an inter-Arab problem and warned the United States not to intervene diplomatically or politically. He was, she noted, willing to guarantee the United States all the oil it wanted, but, as he revealed later, he believed the United States would not challenge him militarily because Americans were still responding to the Vietnam experience, wanting to avoid war and body bags at all costs.[40] Who would care, he must have concluded, if he moved against a vulnerable and unpopular regime in Kuwait.

Saddam won the support of the Arab street, especially in Jordan, Yemen, and North Africa and among the Palestinians. He also had the support of Islamist radicals, such as the Muslim Brotherhood, despite his slaughter over the years of many Arab clerics, their students, and families. He was their hero for standing up to the West, the United States, and their own governments. Arab governments—Egypt, Syria, Saudi Arabia, and the smaller Gulf states—along with Iran and Turkey rejected Saddam's invasion and, with the exception of Iran, joined the international coalition determined to liberate Kuwait. The Palestinians found themselves declared ungrateful pariahs and cast out of the Gulf countries that had long sheltered and employed them. They were ridiculed by Saddam when they failed to give him the kind of assistance (mostly terrorist) that he expected after years of dole and training.

After War: Still Defiant after All These Years

Saddam has survived two devastating wars, rebellions in the north and south, a decade of sanctions, and countless coup attempts. He has also survived, politically speaking, his major antagonists—George H. Bush, Margaret Thatcher, François Mitterrand, Turget Ozal, Mikhail Gorbachev, and Bill Clinton. He calculates he can outwait and outlast any enemies and that his control over the population is sufficient to allow him to risk repeated confrontations with the United Nations, deny access to weapons inspectors, and evade sanctions. He may be correct. The international community, especially the members of the UN Security Council, shows the signs of "Saddam fatigue": exhaustion with the embargo and Saddam's ability to place the blame for Iraqi suffering on the United Nations and the United States; and acceptance of Saddam's survivability and the desire to "get on" with a more normal set of diplomatic and commercial relations.

The period since 1991 has also enabled Saddam to test loyalties and eliminate those who would oppose his continued rule. He brutally suppressed rebellion in the predominantly Shia cities and towns of southern Iraq. By draining much of the marsh area he destroyed the habitat and the protection it afforded rebels at the same time he destroyed a 1,000-year-old culture.[41] The middle class—the bureaucrats, professionals, and civil servants on whom the West has traditionally pinned hopes for the growth of tolerance and civil society—has all but disappeared into poverty or exile. The bases of his regime—the military and security services responsible for his protection, the Republican Guard, the Special Republican Guard, the regular army, his Tikriti-based clan and tribe—remain intact.

Sanctions have worked in denying Saddam sovereignty and unfettered use of oil revenues, in weakening his military, and in denying him the ability to easily acquire components necessary to rebuild his weapons systems or reconstitute programs for the development of weapons of mass destruction. He has not been able to threaten his neighbors. But sanctions have not modified Saddam's behavior; they have not changed his aggressive nature or the brutality of his regime, nor have they made him willing to forgo possession of his weapons of mass destruction. Saddam has not felt the weight of sanctions directly, unless you believe he is touched by their impact on Iraq's poor and its vanishing middle class.

Is There Peace in Iraq's Future?

What are Saddam's priorities and what do they portend for Iraq's future? Saddam's primary concern is his survival and that of his regime. By rejecting the UN-imposed sanctions and their restrictions, he is moving to restore Iraq's political independence, national sovereignty, and territorial integrity free from international observation and control. This will include control of northern Iraq, now under Kurdish control and monitored by Operation Northern Watch. He has encouraged the restoration of air links with Baghdad by opening its international airport, and as of mid-October 2000, nine countries, including Turkey, France, Russia, Jordan, and the UAE, have sent flights into Baghdad. Sanctions are crumbling, although not at the pace or level Saddam would like. Jordan announced in late October that it would no longer allow inspection of goods going into Iraq. And in the three years without UN weapons inspections, Iraq has test-fired a short-range, liquid-fueled ballistic missile—the al-Samoud ("resistance" in Arabic)—that could carry conventional explosives or the chemical or biological weapons that Iraq is still suspected of hiding.[42] U.S. officials said the tests are evidence that Iraq is working to perfect its ballistic missile technology, which could be easily adapted to missiles with a longer range.

Saddam or any successor is certain to demand an end to all sanctions, economic and military. He is certainly likely to resume building Iraq into a strong regional military and political power. Saddam's reaction to the Palestinian-Israeli crisis that began in late September 2000 was to send troops on maneuvers to his western border, announce that 4 million Iraqis were ready to volunteer to battle for Jerusalem, and call for holy war against Israel. He sent food, offered medical treatment in Baghdad to wounded Palestinians, and provided $25,000 to each family of a Palestinian "martyr." In addition, Saddam announced in early December that Iraq would donate $880 million to the Palestinians, with the money to be withdrawn from Iraq's UN escrow account. (The UN disapproved the request.) Saddam, his sons, and the government-controlled press called on the people of Egypt, Turkey, Saudi Arabia, and Kuwait to overthrow their rulers for supporting the United States and opposing jihad against Israel.

The crisis, along with the tight oil market, has helped Iraq partially reenter Arab ranks. While he has not been fully exonerated for his occupation of Kuwait, Saddam has managed to use the crisis to remind Arab leaders of his ability to act the spoiler if denied a role in the Arab arena.

Saddam apparently learned few lessons from his difficulties of the past decade. In a speech to Ba'ath Party members at the end of the Gulf War for Kuwait, he admitted his "mistakes." They included not continuing the attack into Saudi Arabia's oil-rich Eastern Province and mining the oil fields there, releasing the Western hostages before the war in the belief this would placate the Europeans and undermine the coalition (it did not), and not attacking the U.S. forces when they first arrived in the region before the coalition could be formed and additional troops sent. Had he done so, Saddam apparently believed, he would have met with military success, creating pressure on the United States to cut its losses (the Vietnam syndrome again), withdraw, and leave him with Kuwait.

More revealing are remarks Saddam made in speeches to the party faithful in the summer of 2000. On eliminating weapons systems, Saddam told officials of the Military Industrial Organization in June that he was willing to limit weapons on condition that Israel did so first: "If the world tells us to abandon our weapons and keep only swords, we will do that. We will destroy all the weapons, if they destroy their weapons. But if they keep a rifle and then tell me that I have the right to possess only a sword, then we would say no. As long as the rifle has become a means to defend our country . . . then we will try our best to acquire the rifle."[43]

Will Saddam be a good neighbor in the region? In a speech commemorating the end of the Iran-Iraq war—and in tones oddly echoing biblical prescriptions on behavior—Saddam accused Turkey and the Gulf Arabs of "treachery and disgrace" for harboring the planes that kill the men, women, and children of Iraq. He criticized "those rulers and kings who have sold out their souls and appointed [the occupying foreigner] to rule over everything that is dear and precious in the values and wealth of their people." Will he seek revenge? Saddam warned Iraqis "not to provoke a snake before you make up your mind and muster up the ability to cut its head," and in vintage Saddam style, he warned Iraqis, "Do not give your enemy any chance to get the upper hand of you . . . do not exaggerate a promise you cannot fulfill or a threat your ability cannot support . . . keep your eyes on your enemy. Be ahead of him but do not let him be far behind your back."[44]

Sanctions have had remarkable success: they have uncovered weapons programs, weakened Iraq's conventional military, slowed WMD development, prevented new aggressive moves, and generally kept the regime isolated. The scramble for limited/declining resources has fueled rivalries among Saddam's family and between them and other Iraqis, according to defector accounts. Iraq has recognized Kuwait's borders, albeit grudgingly and with harassment, returned some damaged goods, and paid some compensation through the escrow fund. Sanctions have also contributed to weakening Iraq's society more than they have weakened Saddam's regime, creating inflation that is hardest on the poor and virtually destroying the middle class. They have failed in part because policymakers failed to consider the willingness of Saddam to forgo an estimated $120 billion in revenue while he battled UNSCOM (United Nations Special Commission) to retain his WMD capability.

And that is the inherent danger in trying to predict how Iraq will behave in the future and what factors will influence the decisions of Iraq's leaders. If history is a guide—and it usually is—then Iraq under Saddam or a successor will continue in its present course. It will be secular and "liberal" in the sense that it will most likely continue to have an autocratic "president" and a professed belief in some form of social justice and economic equity, even if only for the favored classes. It will be a spoiler state, existing on the fringes of the Arab world, never fully trusted and too dangerous to be ignored. It will have shadows of instability and violence; perhaps there will be blood feuds and tribal-style revenge in the event Saddam or his sons are overthrown.

Indeed, tribalism in some form is likely to remain a force in Iraqi politics. The sanctions imposed on Iraq after its invasion of Kuwait in 1990 strengthened this trend, especially as the state lost much of its economic and military capability. With no oil revenues, the state withdrew social services and was no longer able or willing to provide the subsidies and salaries on which the middle and lower classes depended. Government policies fed inflation that, coupled with low salaries, the downsizing of the military, and the disintegration of the party, virtually eliminated a large percentage of Iraq's middle class in the city and the countryside. In this vacuum, tribalism, based on cultural need as well as family lineage and connections, became more dominant. Moreover, when Saddam felt threatened by the weakening of law and order and the potential threat to his rule after the Gulf War, he resurrected tribal rule. He rewarded the loyalty of tribal leaders by allowing tribal law to prevail in many areas and bestowing on them guns, cars, and privileges. In return, they acknowledged his leadership. Saddam had become *shaykh mashayikh* or chief of chiefs. Will this kind of transparent loyalty be transferred to a successor? Or will the heads of prominent families and clans, who have members in the military and security services, see an opportunity to seize power by marrying their political and military clout to tribal values and clan loyalties? Tribal networks extend the narrow base of the ruling elite, provide manpower to help it control the state and society, and bring a semblance of stability to the power structure. Tribal solidarity and values are a source of cohesion, loyalty, and discipline. Most importantly, they provide the leader with a sense of trust in what is normally a conspiratorial environment where power struggles are the norm. And it is hard to envision an Iraq in the near term without these dark forces.

In any event, this may be too dark a view. Iraq could gradually evolve into a limited democracy with political rights and protections for all Iraqis and the recreation of civil society. But traditional values and custom will have a strong hold on the psyche of many Iraqis. Tribes and tribalism were important factors in Iraqi history, culture, and politics long before Saddam came to power and will be long after he is gone. Just as Saddam has had to make concessions in return for support, a successor regime will probably have to make similar accommodations to prominent tribal leaders in order to gain powerful allies, consolidate its rule, and stabilize large parts of Iraq. The successor to Saddam will have to accommodate the anachronistic demands and visions of power sharing of the prominent tribal and family leaders with the needs of a modern and potentially wealthy state. He will have to ensure the tribes do not challenge the growth of civil society and associational politics for those Iraqis not tribal, not rural, and not dependent on these extralegal groupings for their well-being and survival.

All of this poses a dilemma for those outside Iraq looking for persons inside Iraq willing to try to overthrow Saddam. Any Iraqi willing to try to unseat Saddam would demand proof of support and loyalty from inside Iraq and from backers outside the country. The risk is great, he would argue, and the reward should be unquestioned. Backing elements as roguish as Saddam will make no difference to neighbors and governments looking for *anyone but Saddam* to rule Iraq. If tribalism remains a factor defining Iraqi political and social behavior, then a successful challenger should bring with him, at minimum, the loyalties of the Sunni Arab center and possibly Shia elements as well. If a form of participatory democracy is the goal, then the United States and other democratic countries will have to weigh in with any successor regime to try to soften the dark tendencies and move a new government toward a more enlightened form of rule.

Notes

1. The best accounts of Iraq's modern history and tragic political culture include Phebe A. Marr, *The Modern History of Iraq* (Boulder, Colo.: Westview Press, 1985); Kanan Makiya, *Republic of Fear* (Berkeley and Los Angeles: University of California Press, 1989); and Makiya, *Cruelty and Silence* (Berkeley and Los Angeles: University of California Press, 1993).

2. Phebe Marr, "Iraq's Foreign Policy" (unpublished paper, July 2000), 22.

3. The word *'asabiya* connotes tribal solidarity, clannishness, tribalism, and race as well as national consciousness.

4. Ibn Khaldun, *The Muqaddimah: An Introduction to History,* trans. Franz Rosenthal (Princeton, N.J.: Princeton University Press, 1989).

5. See Marr, *Modern History.*

6. See Faleh Abu Jaber, "Shaykhs and Ideologues: Detribalization and Retribalization in Iraq, 1968–1998," *Middle East Report* 215 (summer 2000): 28–31, 48; and Abu Jaber, "The Reconstruction and Deconstruction of Iraq's Tribes: Tribalism under Patrimonial Totalitarianism, 1968–1998" (unpublished paper, October 1999). See also Judith S. Yaphe, "Tribalism in Iraq, the Old and the New," *Middle East Policy* 7, no. 3 (June 2000): 51–58.

7. See Abu Jaber, "Reconstruction and Deconstruction," 17.

8. The creation of a new nationalism that harks back to ancient and historical glories from the mists of time is similar to Mussolini's glorification of ancient Rome, Hitler's pride in the folk culture of pre-Christian Germanic tribes, Atatürk's vision of Hittite culture, and Reza Shah's vision of the new Aryan nation at Persepolis. Saddam frequently invokes Hammurabi, Salah al-Din, Abraham of Ur, and other hoary figures as well as Islam's pantheon of Muhammad, Hussein, and other saints to embellish his own person as well as Iraqis' pride in their history and culture.

9. See Marr, *Modern History,* for a historical overview of this complex period in Iraqi history.

10. Sadun Hammadi, a secular Shia, and Tariq Aziz, a Chaldean Christian, were early members of the Iraqi branch of the Ba'ath Party and are among the few from the early days who are still with Saddam. Hammadi, educated in the United States, has served as a cabinet minister, was appointed prime minister for a brief period after the Kuwait war, and currently is speaker of the National Assembly. Tariq Aziz, who has long served as Saddam's intermediary with the outside world, was for many years foreign minister; he was appointed deputy prime minister in 1979.

11. Talfah was a staunch anti-British Arab nationalist whose singular contributions to Iraq's history were his role in a 1941 coup attempt, a book, *Three Things God Should Not Have Made: Persians, Flies, and Jews,* and a reputation for venality so excessive that Saddam had to remove him as mayor of Baghdad.

12. Amatzia Baram paints a compelling family history of Saddam and his clan

in *Building toward Crisis: Saddam Husayn's Strategy for Survival,* Washington Institute for Near East Policy Paper no. 47 (Washington, D.C., 1998); Ofra Bengio provides an excellent textual analysis of modern Iraqi history and Saddam's behavior in *Saddam's Word: Political Discourse in Iraq* (New York: Oxford University Press, 1998).

13. See Abu Jaber, "Reconstruction and Deconstruction," 17.

14. Baram, *Building toward Crisis,* 25–30; Abu Jaber, "Reconstruction and Deconstruction," 17.

15. The reports of coup plotting after the war revealed to outsiders the extent to which certain powerful tribal federations and extended families had been recruited into the security and intelligence services as well as key military units in the Republican Guard and Special Republican Guards. These included the Jabburi, the Dulaymi, and the Ubaydi.

16. Saddam's cousin and son-in-law Hussein Kamil headed MIMI until his defection in 1995; MIMI was responsible for developing programs for weapons of mass destruction.

17. Abu Jaber, "Reconstruction and Deconstruction," 9.

18. In 1976, the government ordered Iraqis to drop their tribal/family names. No longer would they be identified as at-Tikriti, al-Mosuli, or ad-Duri. The change was intended primarily to mask how many Tikritis, Dulaymis, and others close to Saddam's clan were in key positions. Israeli scholar Amatzia Baram believes this "loss" of identity succeeded to the extent that many Iraqis, especially those who were urbanized and in the military or government, did not know their tribal roots. While this may be true of a small group of urbanized, well-educated Sunni Arabs, it is not true of the majority of Iraqis, for whom family, clan, and tribal identification always remained strong. Amatzia Baram, "Neo-Tribalism in Iraq: Saddam Hussein's Tribal Policies, 1991–96," *International Journal of Middle East Studies* 29, no. 1 (February 1997): 1–31.

19. Phebe Marr notes that Qassim brought Barzani back primarily to act as a counterforce to the Arab nationalists (*Modern History,* 177).

20. For a brief history of Kurdish struggles for self-rule in Iraq, see Marr, ibid. Longer and fuller treatments include David McDowall, *A Modern History of the Kurds* (London: Tauris, 1997), and Mehrdad R. Izady, *The Kurds* (Washington, D.C.: Crane Russak, 1992).

21. Marr, *Modern History,* 197–99.

22. Ibid., 222; Edmund Ghareeb, *The Kurdish Question in Iraq* (Syracuse, N.Y.: Syracuse University Press, 1981), 142–45.

23. Ibid.

24. Marr, *Modern History,* 220.

25. Under subsequent legislation, Iraq's Turkmen and Assyrian communities were accorded similar "rights," that their language would be the language of instruction in the primary schools, that cultural rights for writers and intellectuals would be preserved, and that special studies programs would be established in

schools of higher education. See RCC Decree 288 of March 11, 1970; Act 33. The Iraqi Kurdistan Regional Autonomy Act of March 11, 1974; RCC Decree 89 of November 24, 1970, for the cultural rights of Iraq's Turkmen community; and Decree 251 of February 20, 1972, for the cultural rights of Iraq's Syriac-speaking citizens. Report submitted by the Government of Iraq to the UN Committee on the Elimination of All Forms of Racial Discrimination, CERD/C/240/Add.3, 124 June 1996, pars. 2–7.

26. For the complete text of the March 1970 Manifesto, see Michael M. Gunther, *The Kurds of Iraq: Tragedy and Hope* (New York: St. Martin's Press, 1992), 14–16.

27. Baghdad expelled approximately 40,000 Shia (Fayli) Kurds who had lived for generations in Baghdad and near Khanaqin, on the grounds they were Iranian nationals. See Gunther, *The Kurds of Iraq,* 17.

28. For information on the CIA role, see portions of the Pike Report that appeared in New York's *Village Voice,* February 16, 1976, 72–92; Gunther, *The Kurds of Iraq,* 26–29.

29. Gunther, 43–45.

30. The word, meaning "spoils," is the name of the eighth *sura* of the Quran and the official military code name used publicly by the Iraqi government to refer to its actions against the Kurds.

31. For additional details on the *anfal* campaign, see Middle East Watch, *Genocide in Iraq: The Anfal Campaign* (New York: Human Rights Watch, 1993). It documents the *anfal* from conception to completion based on documents uncovered by the Kurds in 1991, interviews with survivors of the *anfal,* and forensic research on remains found in the mass graves. For an examination of Iraq's historic human rights record, see Judith S. Yaphe, "Iraq: Human Rights in the Republic of Fear."

32. The definition is that of the Convention on the Prevention and Punishment of the Crime of Genocide, 78 UNTS 277, approved by UN General Assembly Resolution 2670 on December 9, 1948; cited in *Genocide in Iraq,* 5.

33. Revolutionary Iran's hostility toward the United States was marked by the student occupation of the U.S. Embassy in Tehran and the holding of U.S. diplomats hostage for more than a year. Khomeini's dictum of "neither East nor West" precluded Iran from seeking overt assistance from either superpower during this period.

34. See Marr, *Modern History,* for the best account of Iraq's history in this period.

35. See Phebe A. Marr, "Iraq and the Nuclear Non-Proliferation Treaty: The Case of a Nuclear Cheater," in *The Diffusion of Advanced Weaponry: Technologies, Regional Implications, and Responses,* ed. W. Thomas Wander, Eric H. Arnett, and Paul Bracken (Washington, D.C.: American Association for the Advancement of Science, 1994), 297–325.

36. Marr, *The Modern History of Iraq,* 237.

37. Ibid. Marr claims that Baqr Sadr wanted to lead a procession to Iran to congratulate Khomeini but was denied permission by Baghdad.

38. Iraq's Shias are not one community united in faith and action. Iraqi Shia scholars describe three communities: those who live in the shrine cities and are religious but not influenced by Iranian clerics; those who live in the south and are more Arab and tribal-oriented than they are religious; and those who moved to Baghdad and other Iraqi cities and are secular in outlook, many of whom joined the Ba'ath Party in the early days. See Abu Jaber, "Reconstruction and Deconstruction," 17; *Iraq's Shia Community,* presentations by Dr. Laith Kubba at National Defense University, July 1999, July 2000.

39. Iraq's claims to Kuwait date back to the period of the Ottoman Empire, when Kuwait was ruled by an Ottoman governor from the *wilayat* of Baghdad; in 1920 one of the candidates proposed by the British to rule Iraq was the *shaykh* of Muhammarah, then part of what became Kuwait. Iraqi leader Abd al-Karim Qassim made similar claims to Kuwait in 1961 when he moved troops to the border.

40. See Thomas L. Friedman, "After the War: Envoy to Iraq, Faulted in Crisis, Says She Warned Saddam Sternly," *New York Times,* March 20, 1991, A6.

41. "Saddam Hussein's Iraq," *http://usinfo.state.gov/regional/nea/iraq/iraq99.htm* (September 13, 1999).

42. The range of the missile was less than 150 kilometers (95 miles) and not in violation of UN Security Council resolutions banning missiles with a range greater than 150 kilometers. See Steven Lee Meyers, "Flight Tests Show Iraq Has Resumed a Missile Program," *New York Times,* July 1, 2000, A1.

43. Speech to the Military Industrial Organization carried on Republic of Iraq Television, June 12, 2000, and translated by FBIS, GMP200006120000293.

44. See the text of the Iraqi president's speech on the anniversary marking the end of the Iran-Iraq war, August 8, 2000.

2

Iran

Slouching toward the Twenty-first Century

SHAUL BAKHASH

When Iran marked the twentieth anniversary of the Islamic revolution in February 1999, the country appeared to be embarked on a far-reaching experiment in democratic transition. Two years earlier, Mohammad Khatami had been elected president, after campaigning on a platform that emphasized the need to strengthen the rule of law and the institutions of civil society, protect the civil rights of Iranians, tolerate a variety of views, and open Iran to new ideas and to the outside world. Over 80 percent of the electorate voted. Khatami received 70 percent of the vote. The first three years of Khatami's presidency witnessed a revival of political life, the rise of a vigorous daily press, serious public discussion of fundamental questions of governance, some curbs on the fearsome security agencies, and improved relations with foreign states. In 1999, the Khatami government successfully carried out the Islamic Republic's first elections for village, district, and town councils, creating hundreds of local representative bodies throughout the country, although the effectiveness of the councils remained to be demonstrated in practice. In parliamentary elections in 2000, a loose coalition of groups supporting Khatami won a solid majority to the new Majlis, or parliament, and seemed poised to implement an ambitious legislative agenda designed to ensure expanded political and press freedoms, an independent judiciary, and government accountability.

But within a year of the Majlis elections, the reform movement was in deep trouble. A severe conservative backlash closed down the reformist press. Dozens of journalists, intellectuals, clerics, and political activists associated with the reform movement were in jail. Novel interpretations of the constitution threatened to curtail the prerogatives of the Majlis.

The civil society movement that took shape around the figure of Khatami (but whose beginnings preceded his candidacy), and the attempts to suppress it, underlined the formidable obstacles to bringing about fundamental change in Iran; demonstrated the enduring strength of the conservative and status quo forces; and graphically illustrated a recurrent pattern in the politics of the Islamic Republic. Repeatedly since 1979 there had been attempts to temper the radical forces unleashed by the revolution and to steer domestic political, economic, and foreign policy in a centrist direction. Repeatedly, these efforts proved abortive or met with limited success. The conservative response evoked by the civil society movement was at one level a replay of this familiar pattern. Having rapidly gained momentum, the movement was suddenly thwarted. But the civil society movement also represented a major new departure in the twenty-year history of the Islamic Republic, suggesting the intriguing possibility of a democratic political life in Iran. Although the conservatives appeared to have temporarily prevailed, the civil society movement provided a glimpse into the powerful new intellectual and political currents stirring in Iran and the widespread desire among millions of Iranians for a greater degree of freedom, accountable government, and the rule of law. Along with elections in 1996 and 1997, it suggested a rejection by a large majority of Iranians of the existing political order, or at least a desire for extensive change within it, and revealed deep divisions between society and the state and within the ruling elite itself.

The Internal Struggle: Radicals, Conservatives, Pragmatists, and the Proponents of Civil Society

The Islamic revolution was made possible by a broad coalition of forces: clerics and laymen; Islamic and secular political movements; centrist parties and radical left-wing guerrilla movements; bazaar merchants, shopkeepers, and industrial workers; middle-class civil servants and the urban unemployed; organized political groups and the unorganized citizenry. But the movement was dominated by the towering figure of Ayatollah Khomeini; and in the postrevolution struggles among the various elements of this unwieldy coalition, the clerics most closely associated with Khomeini, and the radicals among them, emerged in control of the state and its institutions.[1] In confrontation after confrontation, the secular parties lost out to the clerics, and the moderates lost out to the radicals. Clerical radicals in the early years repeatedly prevailed in debates within the inner circle over key issues of policy: to continue or to halt executions of officials of the Shah's regime (1979); to expand or limit the role of the revolutionary courts, committees, and guards (1979–81); to hold on to or release the American hostages (1980); to end or pursue the war against Iraq once Iraqi troops had been expelled from Iranian territory (1982); to expand or limit the role of the state in the economic sphere (throughout the 1980s).

Mehdi Bazargan, the first prime minister of the Islamic Republic and a centrist, tried to rein in the revolutionary committees and courts, to end large-scale arrests and executions, and to moderate the wave of nationalization and expropriation that followed on the heels of the revolution. But he ended up describing the country as "a city with a hundred sheriffs" and his own prime ministership as "a knife without a blade." He was forced to resign in November 1979, nine months after taking office. Abol-Hassan Bani-Sadr, Iran's first president, a populist before he took office, nevertheless became a law-and-order man once elected. He declared his presidency would usher in "the year of order and security." He, too, tried to curb the revolutionary organizations and to limit clerical influence in the government. He was impeached in June 1981, only eighteen months after being elected with a large majority. The overthrow of Bani-Sadr marked the definitive defeat of the secular and (relatively) moderate forces and the domination of the new regime by the radical clerical parties.

Even before the fall of Bazargan and Bani-Sadr, the radicals had set about dismantling the old order and establishing the new one. Hundreds of officials of the old regime were sent before the firing squad. Hundreds, perhaps thousands, more were jailed. Waves of purges and dismissals virtually eliminated the upper and middle ranks of the Shah's senior civil service; men of the new order moved in to fill the vacated posts. A parallel government of revolutionary courts, revolutionary committees, and revolutionary guards rivaled, then overshadowed, the judiciary, police, and military forces of the old regime. The pillars of the Shah's power, such as the army, the security services, and the police, were eviscerated before being reconstituted under new leadership. The political and economic weight of the entrepreneurial classes and prominent families of the old regime was eroded through expropriation and nationalization and by an exodus of these classes to Europe. The exodus, in turn, further fueled property seizures.

The new constitution, approved in a national referendum in April 1980, institutionalized the dominance of the clergy over the state. The constitution vested supreme authority and extensive powers in the *faqih*, or Islamic jurist (later designated as *rahbar*, or Leader), who was to be chosen from among the leading clerical scholars of the day; reserved certain offices, including the office of chief of the judiciary, to the clergy; required all laws and institutions of the state to be in accordance with Islamic principles; and gave the Council of Guardians, a body dominated by clerics, veto power over the laws. Clerical domination over the key institutions of the state was maintained in practice even where not written into law and survived into the second decade of the Islamic Republic. After Bani-Sadr, the presidency was always held by a cleric. Technocrats gradually became more prominent in the cabinet, especially in the economic ministries, but the ministers of interior and intelligence (state security) and the senior judiciary officials and judges were almost invariably clerics. The number of clerics in the Majlis fell dramatically after the 1996 and 2000 parliamentary elections. But the position of speaker of the Majlis and key Majlis leadership posts continued to be held by clerics. The laws were interpreted to ensure that virtually all the members of the Assembly of Experts, a body that selects the Leader, would be clerics. Clerical domination of the state was reinforced by amendments to the constitution approved in 1989.

The ascendancy of the radicals was also evident in the economic sphere. Laws were passed immediately after the revolution for the nationalization and expropriation of banking and insurance and the largest private sector industries and enterprises. Additional sectors of the economy were subsequently nationalized. Other laws provided for takeover by the state of the management (not ownership) of large private enterprises and companies that were allegedly experiencing economic or managerial problems. In time these, too, slipped under full state control. The expansion of state control over the economy, with some exceptions, continued in the 1980s. Clerics of a more conservative cast of mind had reservations about this trend. Conservative clerics on the Council of Guardians, for example, arguing that an Islamic state had limited authority to tamper with private property, to monopolize economic activity in specified sectors, or to regulate economic relations between consulting adults, blocked laws for large-scale land distribution or measures aimed at strengthening workers' wage and bargaining rights.

However, with advocates of state control and distributive justice dominating the Majlis and the cabinet, and given the exigencies created by revolutionary turmoil and the Iran-Iraq war, state controls that could not be secured by legislation were often secured by administrative fiat. The Council of Guardians, for example, vetoed a law nationalizing foreign trade. But the government adopted emergency and foreign exchange measures that placed over 80 percent of foreign trade in the hands of the state anyway. The Council of Guardians vetoed a law that permitted the government to seize the property of "fugitives"—Iranians living abroad who did not return home in a specified period of time. But after a temporary halt, seizure of the property of "fugitives" resumed, on instructions of the Leader and actions taken by the revolutionary courts. A modified labor law made it extremely difficult for employers to lay off workers.

The consolidation of clerical control was also effected through the often ruthless elimination of rival or opposition parties. The radical left-wing parties and former guerrilla organizations, including the Mojahedin-e Khalq, the Fadayan-e Khalq, Paykar, and the Union of Communists, were crushed in 1981–82 in a new wave of arrests and executions. According to the most conservative estimates, 3,000 adherents of these organizations were sent before the firing squads and thousands more jailed.[2] A decree by Ayatollah Khomeini in December 1982 brought an end to wholesale executions, but it did not altogether end judicial killings or other forms of political repression. The Tudeh (Iranian Communist) Party was proscribed and its leaders and hundreds of its members arrested in 1983. The centrist Iran Liberation Movement was prevented from holding meetings, publishing its newspaper, or participating in elections. Thousands of supporters of the Mojahedin and smaller left-wing organizations, already in jail, were executed following secret summary trials in 1988, in a renewed wave of revolutionary terror. The rationale for this new wave of executions has never been satisfactorily explained. But the end of the Iran-Iraq war on terms humiliating to Iran, Khomeini's advanced age, a Baghdad-backed Mojahedin military excursion across the Iraqi border into Iran, and general fears for the regime's stability and durability may have triggered the killings.[3]

The ruling clerics were also intolerant of serious criticism or dissidence within their own ranks. Ayatollah Kazem Shariatmadari, who had reservations about the powers claimed for the *faqih*, or Leader, and the involvement of the clergy in politics, was defrocked, publicly humiliated, and placed under house arrest in 1982. Ayatollah Hosain Ali Montazeri, who grew critical of the behavior of the revolutionary courts and the treatment of political prisoners, and who criticized the mass execution of prisoners in 1988, was forced to step down as Khomeini's designated successor, prevented from speaking publicly, and in time also placed under virtual house arrest. Several other senior clerics, critical of property seizures, political repression, or the activities of the revolutionary courts, were over the years cowed into silence, prevented through censorship from airing their views, or restricted in their movements.

Rafsanjani and the Limits of Pragmatism

The end of the Iran-Iraq war in 1988, Khomeini's death in 1989, and the election of Ali-Akbar Hashemi-Rafsanjani to the presidency that same year allowed a turn toward more pragmatic policies. The end of the war redirected government energies and attention to the long-neglected economy. The death of Khomeini gave his lieutenants greater room for maneuver. Having consolidated its hold on the country, the regime felt less need for another wave of revolutionary terror. The new president, Rafsanjani, displayed a penchant for pragmatism and appeared ready to downplay ideology in favor of practical achievements.[4] During his first term (1989–93) Rafsanjani used the cover of the 1990–91 Gulf War to restore diplomatic relations with Saudi Arabia, Jordan, and Morocco and to attempt a partial rapprochement with Egypt. He used Iran's influence to help secure the release of American hostages in Lebanon. These were considered controversial measures. At home, even before Khomeini's death, Rafsanjani obtained the Leader's approval for a development plan that allowed for foreign loans and a much larger role in the economy for the domestic and foreign private sectors. These measures, too, challenged the prevailing revolutionary ideology. As president, Rafsanjani also emphasized the need to eschew sloganeering and to focus on postwar reconstruction, job creation, economic development, and measures for economic rationalization.

Rationalization measures included privatization of state-owned enterprises; unification of foreign exchange rates; reduction in state subsidies and more realistic prices for essential goods; reform of laws and regulations to improve the climate for private investment; and reduced state control over foreign trade. Rafsanjani also reined in the morals police. Women secured a little more freedom in matters of dress, and Iranians felt slightly more secure in the privacy of their homes, less fearful that members of the Revolutionary Committee would suddenly appear at their doorsteps. Censorship of theater, film, the arts, book publishing and the press eased.

Rafsanjani engineered or acquiesced in measures that led to the virtual exclusion of the radical wing of the clerical hierarchy from the Assembly of Experts, after elections held in 1990, and from the Majlis, after elections held in 1992.[5] The ruling clerics were organized in a number of loosely structured associations. The two most important of these were the similar sounding Combatant Clerics of Tehran (Ruhaniyyat-e Mobarez-e Tehran) and Society of Militant Clerics (Jaam'eh Ruhaniyyun-e Mobarez). Iranian newspapers described the Combatant Clerics as conservatives and the Militant Clerics as left leaning, or radical. The Militant Clerics favored state control of the economy, measures for advancing distributive justice, restrictions on the private sector, and militancy in foreign policy. The Combatant Clerics, the clerical conservatives, favored the bazaar merchants, shopkeepers, and small businessmen and had begun to accept a more tempered foreign policy. The Combatant Clerics were social conservatives, particularly on the issue of women's dress and mixing between the sexes and in their attitude to music, film, theater, and the arts. The Militant Clerics were somewhat more liberal on these issues. The conservatives endorsed and sought to bolster the authority of the Leader. The radicals favored a diminution in his authority and stressed the primacy of the Majlis.[6]

Rafsanjani was himself a leading member of the Combatant Clerics, the conservative clerical association. But, as noted, at least on some issues, Rafsanjani had come to represent a centrist position within the conservative clerical camp. Nevertheless, in 1990–92, he joined hands with the conservatives to marginalize the radicals, blunting the radical temper in domestic and foreign policy and denying the radicals platforms from which to snipe at his economic and foreign policy initiatives. The radicals dominated the Majlis and the cabinet in the 1980s; after 1989, Rafsanjani and his centrist technocrats dominated the cabinet, while conservatives dominated the Fifth Majlis (1992–96).

Rafsanjani, relatively liberal in economic and social policy, showed little inclination, however, to ease restrictions on political activity. He had played a key role in the repressive political policies of the 1980s. During his early presidency, elections continued to be closely controlled. Although some easing of censorship occurred, restrictions on the political press remained considerable. Even centrist political groups unacceptable to the narrow ruling coalition could barely operate. More ominously, several Iranian dissident politicians and opposition figures in exile were murdered in Paris, Berlin, Geneva, and elsewhere in Europe during Rafsanjani's first term. These killings were thought to be the work of the security agencies, and evidence that surfaced in subsequent years appeared to bear out these suspicions.

But Rafsanjani, having curbed the radical left, proved unable or unwilling to stand up to conservatives on the right, who grew increasingly assertive during Rafsanjani's second presidential term (1993–97). The conservative majority in the Majlis forced the resignation of Rafsanjani's minister of culture and also the head of national broadcasting. Both officials were charged with excessively liberal policies. The Leader, Ayatollah Ali Khameini, spearheaded a campaign against the so-called Western cultural onslaught, encouraging a crackdown on the press and the arts. The morals police reemerged in force to harass women and the young. Rowdy club-wielders broke up lectures by reformist thinkers like Abdol-Karim Soroush and attacked bookstores and publishing houses. In 1994, a prominent writer died while in police custody. A number of other intellectuals and writers were mysteriously killed in 1995–96.[7] Many observers suspected complicity of the intelligence agencies in these murders. Rafsanjani did nothing to investigate them, nor did he forthrightly condemn them.

Rafsanjani's privatization program also failed to get off the ground, due to economic mismanagement, the resistance of the *bonyads*, or parastatal foundations that controlled hundreds of expropriated enterprises, and fear of the economic dislocation and unemployment that privatization or price rationalization might cause. Bureaucratic red tape, the insecurity of private property, and tangled laws and regulations did not encourage large-scale private sector investment. By the end of Rafsanjani's second term, the Majlis and, with rare exceptions, the press were quiescent; political life, defined in terms of genuine competition and debate over ideas and policies, was virtually nonexistent, even within the ruling group. In foreign affairs, Rafsanjani's shift to centrist policies was uneven and repeatedly undercut by the government's own actions and missteps. Rafsanjani's close association with Khamenei, his insider status, his preference for backroom deals and backroom politics, and the extensive business interests of his family meant he would not risk an open split with the conservative faction. In his second term, Rafsanjani's centrist policies were in retreat, and the conservatives were once again in the ascendant.

Khatami and the Civil Society Movement

Two events in 1996–97 sparked the second major attempt in the post-Khomeini decade to set the revolution on a different course.[8] First, on the eve of the 1996 Majlis election, the Rafsanjani technocrats, who controlled the cabinet and government, failed to reach an agreement with their traditional allies, the conservative Combatant Clerics members, who controlled the Majlis, on a common slate of candidates to contest the all-important 30-seat Tehran constituency. A small group of ministers and high-ranking officials closely associated with Rafsanjani (and no doubt with Rafsanjani's blessing) broke away to form a new association, the Executives of Construction. They contested the election on a separate slate, stressed their commitment to efficient management and to the industrial and entrepreneurial sector rather than to the bazaar, and won nearly 30 percent of the 270 Majlis seats. The election thus unexpectedly led to a significant split within the dominant, conservative clerical camp; indicated substantial public support for a centrist, pragmatic politics; lent respectability to the idea of a political faction not centered on clerics and religious issues; and made possible a debate on policy alternatives within the ruling establishment.[9] These trends accelerated in the 1997 presidential election.

The second event was the surprise election of Mohammad Khatami to the presidency in 1997.[10] Khatami, as noted, galvanized voters by emphasizing the rule of law, expansion of freedoms for Iranians, the need for a society-wide dialogue on problems before the country, the idea of civil society, and dialogue rather than confrontation with the West. Once in office he provided an opening for expanded press and political activity.

The civil society movement that took shape around Khatami differed fundamentally from the more limited attempt at change under Rafsanjani. First, Rafsanjani and his technocrats defined a sluggish economy, unemployment, poor productivity, and a low level of investment as the principal problems facing the country. They accorded the highest priority to getting the economy moving and a low priority, if any, to political liberalization. By contrast, Khatami and the men around him believed that the basic problem facing the country was political. Economic revival, they argued, could not occur without the institutions of civil society, the rule of law, and participation in politics by the citizenry. They accorded the highest priority to opening up the political system.

Second, a pragmatic turn of mind aside, the Rafsanjani reforms were not informed by any overarching or big ideas. The civil society movement that took shape around the Khatami presidency was propelled by powerful new ideas, initially cultivated by a small group of intellectuals writing in limited-circulation journals of opinion. These journals included *Kiyan, Rah-e Now, Goftogu,* and *Iran-e Farda* and the women's magazine *Zanan.* Soroush, writing in *Kiyan,* showed it was possible to subject religion and religious belief, including Islam, to dispassionate but also pointed and critical analysis; to distinguish between religious ideology and reason; to question the privileges and power amassed by the clergy; and to conceive of an Islam that was tolerant, democratic, and open to reinterpretation. Other Islamic and secular intellectuals, building on the concept of civil society, promoted the idea of democracy, not in populist terms or as mass politics but as a system based on checks and balances, freedom of association, political competition among a multiplicity of civic, political, and professional associations, pluralism, and transparency and accountability in government.[11] Khatami drew on these ideas in his presidential campaign, but he also helped give them wider currency. They began to reach an even wider audience through the reformist press that proliferated in the Khatami era.

Third, although Rafsanjani's more pragmatic approach appealed to many Iranians weary of years of political turmoil and revolutionary ideology, he evoked little personal enthusiasm or loyalty among the public. He was regarded, rather, as a clever and wily politician who, it was hoped, would curb the excesses of the extreme right and the extreme left. Khatami, by contrast, was hugely popular. He proved to have a winning personality; more importantly, his ideas resonated with the public. While he did not create a civil society movement, he provided it with a symbol and a leader; and both during the campaign and as president, he acquired the platform to address a national audience.

Fourth, the Rafsanjani presidency witnessed the decline of organized political competition and sparked little popular interest or participation in the political process. By contrast, numerous new political factions and groups were formed during the first three years of the Khatami presidency, and they helped make the 2000 Majlis elections a genuine (if limited) contest between competing factions and ideas. Already in the 1996 Majlis elections, the split between the Executives and the Combatant Clerics, and the availability of choice, had drawn voters to the polls. Voter participation greatly increased when Khatami ran for president in 1997 and during the 2000 parliamentary elections. While membership in political parties and movements remained limited, in the Khatami years Iranians became avidly engaged in political issues as voters, newspaper readers, and participants in informal debate and discussion on questions before the country.

As president, Khatami did not control the main instruments of power. The judiciary, the security agencies, the military, the Revolutionary Guards and the paramilitary Basij forces, the broadcast media, and the Council of Guardians all remained in the hands of the conservatives, and all these bodies were ultimately answerable to the Leader, Khamenei. But Khatami's first minister of interior, Abdollah Yazdi, and his minister of culture, Ayatollah Mohajerani, were able to use their departments effectively to expand the space for political activity. Yazdi permitted new political and professional associations to be established and allowed dormant ones to revive. Mohajerani made possible a flourishing reformist press by liberally granting licenses for publication of newspapers and magazines. The reformist newspapers played a vital role in a number of areas. Along with conservatively inclined newspapers, they provided a forum for serious discussion of political issues; in the absence of political parties they served as unofficial organs for political movements of various persuasions, and, although highly partisan, they created a better-informed readership. The reformist newspapers also served in a watchdog role, exposing excesses of government officials and organizations, including the judiciary and the security agencies.

From the beginning of the Khatami presidency, the conservatives used the institutions under their control, particularly the judiciary and the security agencies, to crush or at least neutralize the reform movement. Tehran mayor Gholam Hosain Karbaschi, who helped engineer Khatami's electoral victory, was tried on corruption charges in 1998. He was sentenced to five years in jail and barred for twenty years from public service. In June 1998, the conservative-dominated Majlis forced interior minister Nuri out of office on a no-confidence vote. When Nuri went on to publish an outspoken and popular newspaper, the judiciary banned his newspaper, put him on trial, and sentenced him to a five-year prison term for violating Islamic principles.[12] Conservatives in the Majlis tried, but failed, to muster a majority to oust Mohajerani as well. The Islamic thinker Mohsen Kadivar was sentenced to eighteen months in prison for articles questioning the extensive powers and prerogatives claimed for the Leader. Several newspapers were closed down. Club-wielding vigilante groups attacked meetings addressed by reformist intellectuals. In the winter of 1998, in what came to be known as the "serial murders," several writers and opposition political figures were mysteriously killed, often in their own homes. When Tehran University students protested the closure of another reform newspaper in July 1999, the student dormitories were trashed and students beaten by police and club-wielding thugs. In March 2000, an attempt was made to assassinate Said Hajjarian, a key Khatami adviser and reformist thinker. He survived the attempt but, incapacitated, could not resume his official duties.

The Khatami government and the reform movement displayed considerable resilience in the face of these attacks during the first three years of Khatami's presidency. Nuri's successor at the Interior Ministry continued his predecessor's policies. Thanks to Mohajerani's liberal license-granting policy, newspapers that were shut down quickly reappeared, under different mastheads but with the same editorial staff, reporters, and editorial policy.[13] Student and reformist political associations remained engaged in political activity, and public support for the president and the reform movement remained strong. These factors made possible the sweeping victory of the pro-Khatami coalition in the 2000 Majlis elections.

The Conservative Response

The election results greatly disturbed the conservatives. The reform coalition performed consistently well throughout the country and appeared to have a comfortable majority. The reform coalition, for example, took 29 of the 30 Tehran seats and swept elections in other major cities as well. Equally striking was the rout of the conservatives. Fewer than 30 incumbents were reelected to a Majlis that now numbered 290 members. Fewer than 40 of those elected were clerics. Several of those who lost their seats were among the leading lights of the conservative movement and had served three or four consecutive terms. They included the deputy leader of the conservative majority in the outgoing Majlis, the powerful secretary of the National Security Council, and the Leader's personal representative in the Revolutionary Guards.

Equally threatening was the projected agenda of the reformists. Reformist leaders indicated they would push for legislation to expand freedom of the press, association, and assembly and to ease the formation of political parties; exercise Majlis oversight of the Ministry of Intelligence and national radio and television, another conservative stronghold; seek transparency and accountability of the parastatal foundations; look into the sources of wealth amassed by high officials (many of whom were clerics); conduct independent investigations into the 1998 serial killings and the assassination attempt against Hajjarian; and review the sentences passed on Nuri and other targets of political trials. The new Majlis was also expected to attempt to depoliticize the judiciary; to do away with the specialized clerics court and press court that had put on trial and imprisoned reformist journalists and intellectuals; and to restrict the authority of the Council of Guardians to disqualify candidates running for office.

Conservatives were also troubled by articles in the reformist press by Akbar Ganji, Emad ad-Din Baqi, and other journalists implicating shadowy elements in the Ministry of Intelligence, other security agencies, and the Revolutionary Guards, as well as unnamed senior officials and clerics, in the 1998 serial murders and earlier assassinations of intellectuals and dissident politicians both at home and abroad. Ganji indirectly implicated Rafsanjani in these killings and implied that senior clerics had issued religious decrees endorsing them.[14] Finally, early in the Khatami presidency, student leaders, journalists, and a number of Islamic thinkers had discussed the desirability of restricting, or defining more precisely, the Leader's extensive powers and of subjecting the Leader's conduct in office to closer scrutiny. Public discussion of this subject was quickly silenced, but there was now a danger that reformist newspapers or politicians would revive it.

After an initial period of confusion, conservative leaders appear to have concluded that the reform movement posed a serious threat to their hold on power and to the entire clerical domination of the state. The crackdown that followed the parliamentary elections was severe. On April 27, 2000, using a highly restrictive press law enacted by the outgoing Majlis, the judiciary shut down eight dailies, four weeklies, and one monthly. Further closures followed in the ensuing months. By March 2001, more than forty publications, comprising the entire reformist press and the country's leading intellectual and political journals, were silenced. In addition, several of the country's most prominent editors and political commentators were arrested, tried, and sentenced to long prison terms. Baqi, for example, was sentenced to five and one-half years, Ganji to ten years in jail and a further five years in internal exile (an appeals court subsequently quashed all but a few months of Ganji's sentence, but Ganji continued to be held in prison on other charges). In a clear warning to the entire intellectual community, judiciary officials ordered the arrest and then tried over a dozen intellectuals who had participated in a conference at the Heinrich Böll Institute in Berlin. Two translators, a publisher, a women's rights lawyer, a student leader, and two others were subsequently sentenced to terms of four to ten years in prison. The reason: the Islamic Republic had been criticized and insulted at the conference. The cleric, Hassan Yusefi Eshkevari, was tried separately, by the clerics court, for participation in the same conference and for his writings and was found guilty of insulting Islam and "waging war against God," crimes that carried the death sentence.

In March 2001, authorities arrested over forty intellectuals and politicians associated with the moderate Iran Liberation Movement and the "religious-nationalist union." The Iran Liberation Movement was banned, and judicial authorities suggested that some of the arrestees would be charged with serious political crimes, including plotting to overthrow the state. That same month, Mostafa Tajzadeh, the Ministry of Interior undersecretary in charge of elections, was tried and found guilty of election irregularities. The reformist press suggested Tajzadeh was being penalized for defending the integrity of the 2000 Majlis elections. He was sentenced to one year in prison and was barred from holding public office for thirty months. The prison sentence was suspended on appeal, but the ban on holding public office was allowed to stand. It meant Tajzadeh could play no role in the 2001 presidential elections or the 2004 Majlis elections.

The conservatives accompanied this crackdown with an ideological offensive against the reformers. In newspaper articles, sermons, and statements by officials, conservatives accused the reformist press of undermining the people's faith in religion and in the institutions of the state, giving encouragement to internal enemies of Islam, and seeking to destroy the revolution in order to open the door to foreign domination. Leader Khameini helped shape and set the themes for this ideological campaign. In an unmistakable reference to the reformist press, he said some newspapers were serving as "bases for the enemy"; he accused unspecified opponents of the revolution and "spy networks" of adopting reformist slogans to mislead the people, defended the judiciary against its critics, and cast doubt on the sincerity of reformers who, he noted pointedly, were being applauded by Iran's foreign enemies.

The Council of Guardians and Khamenei, meantime, advanced novel interpretations of the constitution designed to limit the legislative and oversight powers of the new Majlis. In April 2000, the council ruled that the Majlis had no authority to look into the affairs of institutions that come under the purview of the Leader. If allowed to stand, this implied that the Majlis lacked authority to scrutinize the activities of the judiciary, the armed forces, the Revolutionary Guards, the Expediency Council, the broadcast media, or the *bonyads*—all organizations whose chief officers are appointed by the Leader. A member of the council asserted the council could disqualify a sitting member of parliament from holding office if it decided he had acted against the interests of Islam or the Islamic Republic. In what appeared to be a violation of the principle of parliamentary immunity, judicial officials, meantime, summoned a number of deputies for questioning for remarks they made in or outside the Majlis; in one instance, a deputy was even briefly detained.

In August 2001, Khamenei, citing dangers to Islam and the state should newspapers fall under foreign influence and control, intervened to prevent the new parliament from revising or overturning the repressive press law enacted by the outgoing Majlis.[15] Khamenei was presumably acting on the basis of his authority to set the broad policies of the Islamic Republic, and also on the authority claimed for him to protect the highest interests of the state. On the other hand, the power of the Leader to dictate to the Majlis the issues it could debate or enact into law was by no means an established principle; and Khameini's intervention, in which the Majlis reluctantly acquiesced, appeared to establish a precedent that could gravely curtail the parliament's prerogatives. If the results of the 2000 Majlis election had demonstrated strong popular support for the idea of reform and the rule of law, the aftermath had also demonstrated the continuing strength of the conservative forces, employing the authority of the Leader and the instruments of judicial and coercive power under their control.

The Economy: Swollen State, Embattled Private Sector

The economy under the Islamic Republic was shaped by the interventionist philosophy of Iran's new rulers, the consequences of the war with Iraq, the Islamic Republic's commitment to the "disinherited" and its underlying hostility to the private sector, the general disorder resulting from the revolution, and a number of other, lesser factors.[16]

The wave of expropriation and nationalization that followed on the heels of the revolution shifted very considerable private sector assets—industries, banks, insurance companies, trading, contracting and construction firms, office and residential buildings, urban and agricultural land—from the private to the public sector.[17] The massive shift of assets was further fueled by other factors: the general hostility of the revolutionaries to the modern propertied classes (as against the traditional bazaar and shopkeeper class); revolutionary turmoil; the flight of wealthy and propertied families; the "temporary" takeover, in the early months following the revolution, of residential buildings, factories, business enterprises, and agricultural land by squatters, workers, peasants, and revolutionary organizations—takeovers that in time became permanent; and the pronounced propensity of the courts, well into the second decade after the revolution, to rule in favor of the state and the revolutionary organizations in property dispute cases.

The bulk of the expropriated enterprises were assigned to the Foundation for the Disinherited (later renamed the Foundation for the Disinherited and War Veterans) and, to a smaller extent, to the Martyrs Foundation. The foundations, or *bonyads*, which later used their revenues to invest in additional areas of the economy, came to control a significant part of industrial and commercial activity. Nationalized industries and enterprises were assigned to the National Iranian Industries Organization and, at times, to individual ministries. Enterprises whose management was taken over by the state but whose ultimate fate remained undecided were assigned to various ministries. The large majority of these enterprises remained in government hands and were never returned to their original owners.

The eight-year Iran-Iraq war resulted in considerable physical destruction of cities in the war zone, including Iran's main port at Khorramshahr and its largest refinery at Abadan. The war drained financial and material resources that might otherwise have been invested in economic development and disrupted oil exports and trade. At the end of the war, a UN team calculated the replacement costs of the direct physical damage resulting from the war, at 1988 prices, at $97.2 billion.[18] Iranian estimates were much higher. For eight years, very little attention could be paid to internal economic development. The human cost of the war was also considerable; several hundred thousand young men lost their lives or were physically disabled. The war led to rationing and government distribution of essential goods; price controls; restrictions on foreign exchange transactions; and an elaborate system of government licensing of imports and other economic activities. In these ways, the war considerably reinforced the state's propensity to intervene in the economy.

The new regime's ideological commitment to the poor and to distributive justice led to a series of measures with important consequences for the economy. The government expanded subsidies and price supports for essential foods; turned a blind eye to takeovers of residential property by squatters; required the income of the Foundation for the Disinherited and the Martyrs Foundation to be used to assist the poor, war veterans, and families of "martyrs"; reserved places at universities for war veterans, members of the Revolutionary Guards, and the families of martyrs; inflated the rolls in the civil service and the revolutionary organizations to create employment for urban youth; and made it extremely difficult for both government and private commercial enterprises to lay off staff.

Economic problems were exacerbated by a rapid increase in population. Encouraged by the government's own policies, population growth rates jumped from an average of 2.7 percent a year before the revolution to 3.5 percent annually, straining resources and increasing the need for housing, schools, and jobs.[19] U.S.-imposed sanctions on arms sales to Iran during the war forced the government to purchase weapons at much higher prices from other suppliers; and various U.S. sanctions and attempts to isolate Iran in the 1980s and 1990s made access to World Bank loans and international credit and investment more difficult.

Despite the immense difficulties created by revolution, war, sanctions, and the exodus of middle and professional classes, the government managed to expand electrification, the supply of piped water, and the road network in rural areas. School and university places rapidly increased. No starvation or extreme deprivation was reported. Nevertheless there was also much evidence of economic mismanagement and increasingly intractable problems.

The overstaffed bureaucracy was inefficient and red-tape ridden, and inadequate government salaries encouraged moonlighting and taking of bribes. Many of the industries run by the state and the parastatal foundations operated at a loss, requiring hidden subsidies in order to remain in operation. Despite the huge assets at their disposal, as well as the budget transfers, preferential-rate foreign exchange, and other forms of assistance they received from the government, the *bonyads* provided no public accounting of their operations. Subsidies may have helped low-income groups, but they distorted the real price of essential foods, fuel, and other oil products and skewed consumption. By the early 1990s, the cost of these subsidies was estimated at $10 billion annually.

The economy remained overly dependent on oil for foreign exchange earnings, and fluctuations in oil income tended to lend a boom/bust character to the performance of the economy. Unusually high oil prices permitted profligacy in the years immediately following the revolution; declining revenues in the mid-1980s imposed new stringency in foreign exchange expenditure. The mini economic boom of 1990–92 was made possible partly by very high imports, financed by oil income. When oil prices fell in 1994–97, the government was forced to cut back severely on imports. The resulting shortage of spare parts, raw materials, and machinery left many industries operating at well below capacity, and several infrastructure projects could not be completed. Tangled laws and regulations, and the continued propensity of the courts arbitrarily to order, or sanction, property seizures, discouraged private investment. A complicated system of import and manufacturing licenses, and state-controlled goods distribution, resulted in corruption and preferential treatment for businessmen with links to the ruling clerics. An equally complicated system of exchange rates put in place during the war (twelve different rates were in operation up to 1989); unrealistic official rates at nearly all levels; and preferential rates accorded to various government organizations encouraged black market foreign exchange dealings, rather than productive investment.

In 1990–91, more than a decade after the revolution, the gross domestic product was 6.3 percent below total output in 1977–88. Per capita income was 38 percent lower for the same period. Housing construction had declined, and housing remained in severely short supply. Residential units completed in 1989–90 were just over one-fifth of the number completed in 1976–77; the stock of housing units had declined from 16 per 1,000 inhabitants before the revolution to under 3 per 1,000 inhabitants ten years later. Unemployment and underemployment were widespread.[20] The poor performance of the economy and the inability, or unwillingness, of the government to collect taxes meant revenues were inadequate to cover domestic spending. With isolated exceptions, the government resorted each year to deficit spending, borrowing from the Central Bank to cover expenditures. The increase in money supply was rapid. Double-digit inflation was a common feature of the post-revolution era. The value of the rial in relation to the U.S. dollar declined rapidly. Before the revolution, when official and open-market exchange rates were roughly equal, the dollar traded at around 70 rials. In 1994, the open-market exchange rate stood at 2,400 rials to the dollar, and, in 2000, at over 8,000 rials to the dollar.

Free-Market Reforms

Upon becoming president, Rafsanjani and his team of technocrats attempted to put in place an economic reform program based on privatization and deregulation and greater reliance on private enterprise and the free market.[21] The Structural Adjustment Program (SAP), as it was called, coincided with the beginning of the first five-year development plan (1989–94). The program involved fundamental structural adjustments and met with some initial successes. Rationing on most goods was abandoned. Price controls were removed on all but seven essential food items. Subsidies were reduced. A start was made at reunifying exchange rates, with the twelve different rates reduced to three. Slightly more realistic prices were adopted for state-subsidized goods and services, including fuel, airline tickets, and utilities. Import and credit controls eased. Some 391 light industries under the control of state organizations were offered for sale, and, by 1994, about half were partially or fully privatized. In the first two or three years of the five-year plan, farm output, industrial production, social indicators, and GDP growth rates all improved, and a number of infrastructure and industrial projects were completed.

However, problems quickly developed. The rise in growth rates had been fueled primarily by a substantial rise in imports. By 1994–95, coupled with a fall in oil revenues, foreign exchange reserves had been depleted and Iran had accumulated a short- and medium-term foreign debt of nearly $30 billion, requiring a successful, but difficult, debt rescheduling. A severe curtailment of imports undercut industrial production. Growth rates plunged in the last three years of the development plan. The project for exchange rate unification had to be abandoned due to renewed balance of payments difficulties. The sale of state-owned factories was suspended due to irregularities, while the *bonyads* remained untouched by the privatization program. In the push for economic growth, thousands of projects had been launched that could not be efficiently managed or even completed. In the Majlis, resistance developed to further reductions in subsidies or rationalization of the prices of state-supplied goods and services. The government continued to borrow from the Central Bank to finance budget deficits. Inflation ran at an average annual rate of 23 percent in 1991–93, rose to 35 percent in 1994–95, and climbed higher in 1995–96.[22]

In his first term as president (1997–2001), Khatami attempted to continue his predecessor's policies, with somewhat more emphasis on social justice. The new government also committed itself to privatization, deregulation, and liberalization and also emphasized the need to reenergize the private sector and encourage private sector investment. The result— partial success and partial failure—was about the same.[23] The government succeeded in slowing the rate of inflation, reducing foreign debt, completing a number of infrastructure projects, and prioritizing and bringing some order to the thousands of projects launched under Rafsanjani. It also successfully concluded a number of agreements with foreign firms for oil and gas projects in Iran. On the other hand, GDP hardly grew, unemployment remained high, and privatization hardly advanced. State involvement in the economy was little reduced, while major, long-term private sector investment did not materialize.

A decade of effort and limited success at economic reform suggested the problems were structural and fundamental. Government councils remained divided between advocates of the private sector and of state control of the economy, and between the advocates of a welfare state committed to the cause of the poor and those who hoped for trickle-down benefits for all, once the private sector got the economy moving again. Fear of popular unrest meant nothing could be done about the overstaffed civil service, state-owned industries, and numerous other state-affiliated organizations. The powerful *bonyads* continued to be an obstacle to economic reform but could not be touched because they served powerful political and vested interests. Reduction of the regulatory apparatus of the state was proving to be highly difficult. The courts, applying the law arbitrarily, did not create a secure climate for investments. Management remained weak because of emigration by the professional classes and because politics, rather than ability, often determined appointments to government and managerial positions. Political conflicts generated by the civil society movement diverted attention away from economic problems and made cooperation between various political factions more difficult. In the economic sphere as in the political, the obstacles to fundamental change proved formidable.

Foreign Policy: Years of Upheaval

The revolution brought about radical changes in the orientation of Iran's foreign policy.[24] Under the Shah, Iran regarded the United States as a principal ally, maintained discreet but close military and intelligence-sharing relations and trade ties with Israel, identified with the monarchies and conservative states of the Persian Gulf and the Middle East (Saudi Arabia, Kuwait, Jordan, Egypt), and helped maintain the status quo in the Persian Gulf.

By contrast, under the Islamic Republic, America was labeled the "great Satan," the U.S. embassy was seized, and American diplomats were taken hostage. Diplomatic relations between Tehran and Washington were broken in 1979 and still had not been reestablished twenty years later. All ties with Israel were ended and Iran took a very strong stand against Israel. Iran in time labeled Israel an illegitimate state, called for its extermination, strenuously opposed the Madrid/Oslo Arab-Israeli peace process, and became the principal patron of Hizballah, Israel's Lebanese adversary.

The radical temper engendered by the revolution, the idea of a revolution for export, hostility to conservative Arab regimes and monarchies, the taking of the American hostages, the war with Iraq, the involvement of Iranian agents in assassinations and terrorism abroad, ruling-group factionalism, and a generally confrontational attitude on issues of diplomacy exacerbated Iran's relations with other states, even past the first decade following the revolution.

Diplomatic relations with Morocco, Jordan, and Egypt were ruptured within a year of the revolution and with Saudi Arabia in 1987. Over a decade passed before diplomatic relations were resumed with the first three of these countries, and four more years before diplomatic relations were resumed with Saudi Arabia. Two radical Middle East states shunned by the Shah, Libya and Syria, became Iran's principal Arab allies. Various incidents exacerbated and disrupted diplomatic relations with England, France, and Germany.

Periodically, during the first decade of the revolution, there were attempts to rein in Iran's more radical foreign policy inclinations and to normalize Iran's relations with European and Middle East states. But the persistence of forces unleashed by the revolution, and actions by the Iranian government itself or its officials, repeatedly undermined these efforts. For example, as early as 1984, in what came to be known as the Open Window policy, Iran's Leader, Ayatollah Khomeini, sanctioned good relations with the international community. At the time, this was considered a controversial policy; to justify it, Khomeini cited the practice of the Prophet in the seventh century. It led to an attempt to repair relations with Saudi Arabia, Kuwait, France, Turkey, and Pakistan and to forge stronger ties with China and Japan. But within three years, in 1987, Iran was again implicated in bombings in Kuwait. Syria's chargé d'affaires in Tehran was abducted due to a factional struggle within the ruling elite. Britain's second-ranking diplomat in the Iranian capital was beaten on a Tehran street after an Iranian consular official was arrested in Manchester on shoplifting charges. Relations with France were badly disrupted when menacing mobs surrounded the French embassy in Tehran, after French authorities announced they sought to question an employee at the Iranian embassy in Paris in connection with a series of bombings in the French capital. The arms-for-hostages deal secretly negotiated between Iran and the United States in 1985–86, which came to be known as "Irangate," became public when a radical faction in the Iranian ruling group revealed the details to a Beirut weekly.

In 1989, Ayatollah Khomeini wrecked months of careful fence mending with the European Community countries—fence building he himself had sanctioned—by issuing a death sentence against the British writer Salman Rushdie for passages in his novel *The Satanic Verses,* which Khomeini considered insulting to Islam. It was not until 1997 that the Iranian government was able to overcome internal hard-line opposition and give a written guarantee to the EU states that it would not attempt to kill Rushdie, permitting resumption of full diplomatic relations. Hashemi Rafsanjani was considered a pragmatist when he became president in 1989; in office he pursued a markedly more moderate course in foreign policy. Yet in 1991, France's president François Mitterrand canceled an official visit to Iran—the first by a European head of state to the Islamic

Republic—after Iran's former prime minister, Shapour Bakhtiar, was assassinated in his Paris home, almost certainly by agents of the Iranian government. A year later, the leader of Iran's Democratic Party of Kurdistan and three associates were assassinated in a Berlin restaurant, again by agents acting for the Iranian government. In April 1997, a German court found an Iranian and two Lebanese associates guilty of these assassinations.

Earlier, the German federal prosecutor had issued a warrant for the arrest of Iran's minister of intelligence (state security) for involvement in the assassinations. At the trial, the judge implicated Iran's highest officials in the murder. The European Union suspended its "critical dialogue" with Iran and, Greece aside, all member states withdrew their ambassadors from Tehran in protest; the ambassadors returned only seven months later. After the 1996 bombing of the Khobar Towers military housing complex in Saudi Arabia, in which nineteen American airmen were killed, American publications, citing official sources, repeatedly referred to evidence of Iranian involvement in the attack.

New Foreign Policy Priorities

Beginning in the mid-1990s, Iran's foreign policy appeared gradually to settle on a steadier course, reflecting exhaustion from the eight-year Iran-Iraq war, internal economic pressures, lessons learned from missteps during the previous fifteen years, and greater cohesion within the leadership on matters affecting foreign affairs. There emerged a clearer set of foreign policy priorities that were pursued with greater consistency. First, the Iranian leadership agreed on the need for stability along Iran's borders and good relations with Iran's neighbors. An early indication of a more cautious attitude and reluctance to get enmeshed in the internal affairs of neighboring states came during the Shiite uprising in southern Iraq in 1991, following the second Gulf War and the expulsion of Iraq from Kuwait. Although the revolt by fellow Shiites was cruelly suppressed and Shiism's holiest shrines were bombed by the Iraqi government, Iran's support for the uprising was muted and limited. Subsequently, concerned lest foreign intervention lead to the disintegration of Iraq, Iran joined Turkey and Syria in emphasizing a commitment to uphold Iraq's territorial integrity. When he assumed the presidency in 1997, Mohammad Khatami continued his predecessor's policy of careful fence building with the Arab states of the Persian Gulf. Saudi Arabia's Crown Prince Abdullah attended the Islamic summit in Tehran in December 1997, and in 2001 the two countries signed an agreement for cooperation in security matters, includ-

ing the control of terrorism, money laundering, smuggling, and drug traf-
ficking.

There were other indications in the 1990s of a newfound desire for
order along the country's borders. Iran did not attempt to stir up Islamic
sentiments in the newly independent republics in the Caucasus and Central Asia. It increasingly confined support for Islamic movements to the
"far abroad," to countries like Lebanon, Sudan, and Bosnia, distant from
Iran's own borders. It refrained from taking sides in the Indo-Pakistani
quarrel over Kashmir, although the Kashmir dispute might easily have
been viewed in Tehran as a matter requiring solidarity with fellow Muslims. Iran did not allow mistreatment of Shiites in Pakistan to disrupt
relations with Islamabad. Relations with Turkey remained correct, despite
the growing military cooperation between Turkey and Israel and steps
taken by the Turkish government to suppress the Islamic Welfare Party.
Criticism of Kuwait, Saudi Arabia, and other Gulf states for providing the
U.S. military with land and port facilities remained muted.

On the other hand, viewed from the perspective of Tehran, serious
regional threats to Iran's security persisted into the 1990s. Iraq remained
an uncertain and menacing presence. Instability was endemic along Iran's
borders with Afghanistan and Pakistan. India and Pakistan emerged as
nuclear powers. Saudi Arabia and Kuwait were acquiring large quantities
of advanced weaponry. The U.S. military presence in the Persian Gulf and
Israel's military cooperation with Turkey and its growing commercial
presence in Central Asia reinforced the Islamic Republic's perennial fear of
encirclement by hostile powers. A second pillar of foreign policy as it took
shape in the mid-1990s was a limited military buildup, including medium-
and long-range missiles, enhanced naval power, and, possibly, pursuit of
an elusive nuclear option.

Third, Iran consciously and deliberately cultivated relations with major
powers other than the United States, particularly Russia and China, but
also the EU states, Japan, and India: as counterweights to the United
States, as sources of arms and military technology, and as trade partners,
potential investors, and diplomatic allies who might blunt the edge of
U.S.-imposed sanctions and efforts to isolate Iran. Fourth, Iran cautiously
opened up its oil and gas sector to foreign investment. The policy was
controversial; independence from foreign control in the energy sector had
become a tenet of revolutionary ideology. But by the 1990s a flagging
economy, widespread unemployment, long neglect of the oil sector, and
the huge investments required to revive it dictated otherwise.

Fifth, Iran raised its opposition to Israel and the Arab-Israeli peace process to a matter of high policy. There were a number of reasons for this. The conservatives in Iran's leadership appear to have concluded that Iran's interests would be better served by tension rather than peace between Israel and the Arab states. Iranian support for Palestinian opponents of the peace process, such as Hizballah in Lebanon or Hamas and Islamic Jihad in the Palestinian territories, was a means of creating difficulties for two countries, Israel and the United States, who were deemed hostile to Iran. Iran's stance coincided with that of its most important Arab ally, Syria. Iran also hoped to enhance its standing with Muslims in the region and worldwide by championing the cause of the Palestinian refugees, opposing compromise on such issues as ceding control of the Temple Mount or Palestinian land to Israel, and steadfastly opposing the very existence of the Jewish state.

The claim, or aspiration, to a kind of worldwide Islamic leadership formed a sixth and major pillar of foreign policy. Ever since the revolution, Iran's leaders had sought to present Iran as the exemplary Islamic state, a model to be emulated by all other Islamic countries. During his lifetime, Khomeini's lieutenants claimed for him leadership not only for Iran's Muslims but for Muslims everywhere. Khomeini's successor as Leader, Ali Khamenei, aspired to the same status. By championing Islamic movements elsewhere in the world, speaking out on causes important to Muslims, opposing U.S. and Great-Power influence in Muslim states, preventing the "plundering" of the resources of Muslim countries by outside powers, and resisting the West's so-called cultural onslaught against the Muslim world, Iran was seeking to bolster its leadership credentials. The failure of attempts at a rapprochement between Iran and the United States in the late 1990s was due in part to the fear of appearing, as Khamenei once put it in another context, "soft" on America.

In January 1998, half a year after assuming the presidency, Mohammad Khatami invited Americans to "a thoughtful dialogue" with Iranians as a means of breaking down the "wall of mistrust" between the two countries. At the time, it was widely assumed that unofficial dialogue and exchanges between scholars, athletes, and artists would lead eventually to an official dialogue and even to the resumption of diplomatic relations. However, by the end of Khatami's first term, which coincided with the beginning of the Bush presidency, such a dialogue had not materialized. The United States continued to object to Iran's weapons program, its opposition to the Arab-Israeli peace process, and its support for groups that used violence to disrupt the peace process. Iran took the position that dialogue was not possible as long as U.S.-imposed sanctions remained in place and the United States insisted on designating Iran as a country supporting terrorism.

The Future

The second decade of the Islamic Republic witnessed attempts to shift political, economic, and foreign policy in a more centrist direction. Although some success was achieved in all three areas, the task proved immensely difficult. The obstacles, stemming from attitudes engendered by the revolution, divisions within the ruling elite, conflicting state and vested group interests, and the very intractability of long-festering problems, proved to be formidable.

While these problems and internal conflicts were long-standing, the civil society movement that preceded the Khatami presidency and rapidly gained momentum once he came to office represented a new development in the history of the Islamic Republic. Rooted in the idea of the rule of law, individual rights, freedom of speech and association, pluralism, and politics based on competition between organized associations of citizens, it represented a strikingly different way of thinking about government. Not surprisingly, the civil society movement evoked a powerful conservative backlash, revealing the tensions and strains within society, within the ruling elite, and between the state and society. As Iran entered the twenty-first century, it appeared that the future course of the Islamic Republic would be shaped by the manner in which these tensions are resolved.

Notes

1. For developments in the early years of the revolution, see Shaul Bakhash, *Reign of the Ayatollahs: Iran and the Islamic Revolution,* rev. ed. (New York: Basic Books, 1990), and Dilip Hiro, *Iran under the Ayatollahs* (London: Routledge and Kegan Paul, 1985). For a brief analytic overview for the period up to 1997, see David Menashri, *Revolution at a Crossroads: Iran's Domestic Politics and Regional Ambitions* (Washington, D.C.: Washington Institute for Near East Policy, 1999).

2. Bakhash, *Reign,* 221–22.

3. This new wave of killings is graphically described in Ervand Abrahamian, *Tortured Confessions: Prisons and Public Recantations in Modern Iran* (Berkeley and Los Angeles: University of California Press, 1999), 209–22.

4. Rafsanjani's policies are described in Shaul Bakhash, "Iranian Politics since the Gulf War," in *The Politics of Change in the Middle East,* ed. Robert B. Satloff (Boulder, Colo.: Westview Press, 1993), 63–84.

5. On the 1992 Majlis elections, see Menashri, *Revolution at a Crossroads,* 24–26.

6. Divisions between the radicals, conservatives, and pragmatists are described in more detail in Menashri, 27–32.

7. For further reading on this wave of repression, see Menashri, 64–68, and Bakhash, "Iran since the Gulf War," in *The Middle East and the Peace Process: The Impact of the Oslo Accords,* ed. Robert O. Freedman (Gainesville: University Press of Florida, 1998), 254–56. Both the more open cultural environment of the early Rafsanjani years and the repression that followed are also covered in Robin Wright, *The Last Great Revolution: Turmoil and Transformation in Iran* (New York: Knopf, 2000), 77–99.

8. On the early Khatami period, see Wright, *The Last Great Revolution.* For a brief overview of the early Khatami period, see Mohsen M. Milani, "Reform and Resistance in the Islamic Republic of Iran," in *Iran at the Crossroads,* ed. John L. Esposito and R. K. Ramazani (New York: Palgrave, 2001), 96–104.

9. On the 1996 Majlis elections, see Menashri, *Revolution at a Crossroads,* 39–44.

10. On the Khatami election, see Bakhash, "Iran's Remarkable Election," *Journal of Democracy* (January 1988): 80–94; Elaine Sciolino, *Persian Mirrors: The Illusive Face of Iran* (New York: Free Press, 2000), 75–84; and Wright, *The Last Great Revolution,* 25–28, 63–75.

11. The ideas of Soroush and other reformist thinkers are covered, in part, in Wright, 32–63, 75–76; and in Daniel Brumberg, *Reinventing Khomeini: The Struggle for Reform in Iran* (Chicago and London: University of Chicago Press, 2001), 185–229. Khatami's own ideas are described in Bakhash, "Iran's Unlikely President," *New York Review of Books,* November 5, 1998.

12. On the arrest and trial of Karbaschi and Nuri, see Sciolino, *Persian Mirrors,* 300–310, and Wright, *The Last Great Revolution,* 104–6.

13. On the expansion and suppression of newspaper publishing under Khatami, see Sciolino, 249–60, and Wright, 106–10.

14. Akbar Ganji's articles on the serial killings were published as a book, *Tarik-khaneh-ye Ashbah* (The dark house of ghosts) (Tehran: Tarh-e Now, 1378/1999). For a summary of the charges made by Ganji and an interview with him, see Robert Fisk, "The Untold Story of President Rafsanjani of Iran and the Killing of Intellectuals," and Fisk, "Revealed: Role of a President in the Murder of His People," *Independent,* March 8, 2000.

15. Text of Khamenei letter in *Hamshahri,* August 7, 2000.

16. On the economy after the revolution, see Jahangir Amuzegar, *Iran's Economy under the Islamic Republic,* rev. ed. (London: I. B. Tauris, 1997).

17. These measures of expropriation and nationalization are described in Bakhash, *Reign,* chaps. 7 and 8 and pp. 246–55.

18. Amuzegar, *Iran's Economy,* 304–5.

19. Ibid., 289.

20. Ibid., 277, 285. Amuzegar provides an overall balance sheet for the performance of the economy under the Islamic Republic in chapter 14 of the book, pp. 269–309.

21. These free-market reforms are described in Amuzegar, *Iran's Economy*, 314–20, 335–36, and in Khajehpour, "Iran's Economy: Twenty Years after the Islamic Revolution," in *Iran at the Crossroads*, ed. Esposito and Ramazani, 96–104.

22. See table in Khajehpour, 102.

23. For preliminary assessments of Khatami's economic policies, see Khajehpour, 114–21; Amuzegar, "Iran Nascent Democracy in Retreat," *Middle East Economic Survey* 43, no. 45 (November 6, 2000): D2–D3; Amuzegar, "Iran's Post-Revolution Planning," *Middle East Policy* (March 2001).

24. On the Islamic Republic's foreign policy, see R. K. Ramazani, *Revolutionary Iran: Challenge and Response in the Middle East* (Baltimore: Johns Hopkins University Press, 1986); Ramazani, "Iran's Foreign Policy: Contending Orientations," in *Iran's Revolution: The Search for Consensus*, ed. R. K. Ramazani (Bloomington: Indiana University Press, 1990), 48–68; and Shireen T. Hunter, ed., *Iran and the World* (Bloomington: Indiana University Press, 1990).

3

The Arabian Peninsula Monarchies
from Camp David I to Camp David II

F. GREGORY GAUSE III

The political agenda in the monarchical states of the Arabian Peninsula (Saudi Arabia, Kuwait, Bahrain, Qatar, the United Arab Emirates, and Oman) has shifted markedly during the past two decades. From the late 1970s through 1991, foreign and security policy challenges dominated. These small (in population and, except for Saudi Arabia, in area), rich, vulnerable states had to navigate the splits in the Arab world caused by the Egyptian-Israeli peace treaty of 1979, the regional ferment produced by the Iranian revolution of 1978–79 and the upheaval of two regional wars, the Iran-Iraq war of 1980–88, and the Gulf War of 1990–91. Their relations with their primary security ally, the United States, fluctuated through these regional crises and, at the end of the period, the end of the Cold War. The almost simultaneous defeat of Iraq and the collapse of the Soviet Union in 1991 substantially altered their security environment, ushering in a period of almost unparalleled stability for these states.

Since 1991 their political agenda has increasingly focused on domestic political and economic issues. All of these oil-dependent states have had to deal with the long-term decline in the real price of oil from its peak in 1980–81. Their populations, growing at among the fastest rates in the world, have become accustomed to a level of government-provided services that are increasingly difficult to sustain. The combined factors of economic stringency, increased literacy and educational levels among the population, global trends toward democratization and greater openness, and the intense experience of the 1990–91 Gulf War all pushed the issue of political participation to the forefront in these states in the 1990s. The governments reacted in different ways, but each acknowledged these pressures by creating new channels for popular participation in politics.

These domestic political and economic issues remain on the agenda as the Gulf monarchies enter the twenty-first century. Increased oil prices in 1999–2000 have lessened the immediate economic pressures but have not solved the long-term problem of economic restructuring to meet the needs of growing populations. The political activism of the immediate post–Gulf War period has abated, but the question of how to integrate new or revived institutions for popular participation in politics into monarchical decision making remains. The security honeymoon of the 1990s also appears to be ending. The Arab-Israeli peace process, which helped to stabilize the Middle East region in the 1990s, has for the foreseeable future collapsed. Iraq has taken advantage of renewed Arab-Israeli tensions and the fraying of the Gulf War international coalition to push for the lifting of sanctions and reintegration into regional politics. Both of these trends have added new tensions to these states' relations with the United States, which during the 1990s vastly increased its military presence in the Gulf region. Decision making on all these questions is complicated by uncertainty at the top of many of these political systems. In Bahrain and Qatar, sons replaced their fathers as rulers in the latter part of the 1990s. But in Kuwait, Saudi Arabia, and the United Arab Emirates increasingly old and enfeebled leaders hamstring systems where decision-making authority still flows from the top.

The 1980s: From Camp David I to the Gulf War

The 1970s were a good decade for the monarchical states of the Arabian Peninsula. Independence from Great Britain came to Bahrain, Qatar, the United Arab Emirates, and Oman in 1971, just as revolutionary changes in the world oil market were increasing both the price of oil and the control that governments had over their oil industry. All six states became fabulously rich with the quadrupling of oil prices in 1973–74 and then their doubling in 1979–80. The divisive split between Arab progressives and reactionaries in the 1960s, which placed the monarchies under severe regional and domestic stress, faded into the background with Israel's defeat of the Arab armies in 1967 and the death of the leader of the pan-Arab movement, Egyptian president Gamal Abdel Nasser in 1970. New leaders in Egypt (Anwar Sadat) and Syria (Hafiz al-Assad) sought to build more constructive relations with the Peninsula monarchies. The leading role taken by Saudi Arabia, Kuwait, and the UAE in the Arab oil boycott directed against the United States during the 1973 Arab-Israeli war not only contributed to the surge in oil prices but also gave these states an unprecedented stature and acceptance in the regional and international arenas.[1]

In the Gulf itself, the monarchs were suspicious of the ultimate intentions of both the Shah's Iran and Ba'thist Iraq, both of which had also become very rich, militarily more powerful, and politically more ambitious with the oil price increases. During the 1970s, however, Baghdad and Tehran balanced each other, and both sought (most of the time) to maintain good relations with the Gulf monarchies as part of their contest for influence with each other. The 1970s also saw a strengthening of relations between the Gulf states and their ultimate security guarantor, the United States. After the crisis of the oil embargo of 1973–74, Washington, recognizing the new importance of oil in world politics and the Gulf monarchies in regional politics, not only repaired relations but took them to unprecedented levels in terms of arms sales and military cooperation. This was most apparent in Saudi-American relations, as Saudi Arabia was the largest and richest of the states and the one with the longest history of close relations with the United States. But even in the smaller monarchies, all former British protectorates, the United States made a concerted effort to improve military, political, and economic ties.

As the 1970s came to an end, this comparatively idyllic security situation began to come apart. The first cracks appeared in the Arab-Israeli arena. The signing of the Egyptian-Israeli peace treaty in 1979 split the Arab world, as Iraq and Syria moved to mobilize an Arab boycott of President Sadat's regime. This split threatened a renewal of the kind of bitter inter-Arab struggles that characterized the 1950s and 1960s. The Gulf monarchies had benefited greatly from the moderation in inter-Arab disputes during the 1970s, maintaining good relations with all their Arab neighbors. Now Baghdad and Damascus were pushing them to break relations with Egypt, warning them in only slightly veiled terms of the possible domestic and regional consequences of supporting a pro-Israel peace and abandoning the Palestinian cause. Meanwhile Cairo was reminding them of the political benefits that good relations with the Arab world's largest state had brought them in the past decade. The United States, which had brokered the peace treaty, also leaned heavily on the Gulf states to back it.

The Saudi reaction was the most important. If Saudi Arabia, the richest

Arab state and home to the Muslim holy cities of Mecca and Medina, endorsed Sadat's peace policy, Egypt could not be isolated in the Arab world. There is indirect evidence of a serious debate within the ruling family in Saudi Arabia over which course to take. Then Crown Prince Fahd, identified as the most pro-American and pro-Egyptian member of the ruling circle, left the country for a period of months after the decision was made to break diplomatic relations with Egypt and join the Iraqi-Syrian-sponsored Arab boycott.[2] U.S.-Saudi relations were badly, if temporarily, frayed. Only Oman among the smaller Gulf monarchies maintained its ties with Egypt. Kuwait, with its substantial Palestinian population (until the Gulf War Palestinians made up nearly 20 percent of the total population of Kuwait), moved before the Saudis did to condemn the Egyptian-Israeli peace treaty and join the anti-Sadat front led by Baghdad and Damascus.

As the Egyptian-Israeli treaty was being negotiated, a second regional upheaval confronted the Gulf monarchies. In February 1979 the regime of the Shah of Iran was toppled in a massive popular revolution, bringing to power the Iranian Shia clerical establishment under the leadership of Ayatollah Ruhallah Khomeini. Iran, one of the oldest monarchies in the world, had become a revolutionary Islamic republic. The Iranian revolution challenged the Gulf states on a number of levels. While none of the Arab monarchs particularly liked or trusted the Shah, he was a fellow monarch who did not question their form of government or their right to rule. He was, as they were, a close ally of the United States. Conversely, the leader of the new Iranian regime explicitly denounced monarchy as an un-Islamic form of government and called on Muslims throughout the Gulf to bring down their monarchical rulers as the Iranians had done. The Iranian revolution had particular resonance among the Shia populations in the Gulf monarchies—the Shia majority in Bahrain and the important Shia minorities in Kuwait, Saudi Arabia, and the UAE. In the years immediately following the Iranian revolution there were a number of demonstrations, assassination attempts, and plots aimed against the governments by local Shias, encouraged and aided by the new Iranian government.[3] Finally, the new Iranian leadership castigated the United States as the world's "great Satan" and sought out confrontation with it through the hostage crisis of 1979–81. This anti-American stance increased the domestic and regional pressure on the Gulf monarchies to distance themselves from the United States. At least part of the Saudi decision not to support the Egyptian-Israeli peace treaty can be attributed to fears of seeming too close to the United States immediately after the Iranian revolution.

The third security challenge for the Gulf states emerged in September

1980, with the Iraqi invasion of Iran. None of the Gulf states wanted to see Iraq emerge as the undisputed military power in the Gulf, because they knew that they would be Baghdad's next targets. On the other hand, if the Iranians could defeat Iraq and replace the Ba'athist regime with an Islamic republic, the momentum for Islamist political upheaval in their own countries would be unstoppable. In an immediate and direct way, the Iran-Iraq conflict threatened their own economic lifeline—oil exports through the Persian/Arabian Gulf. At the outset of the war the two sides struck at each other's oil facilities and their oil shipments in the Gulf. The prospect that the war might spread to other Gulf shipping and even to the oil facilities of the Gulf monarchies could not be discounted. The beginning of the Iran-Iraq war also contributed to a further splintering of the Arab world. Iraq and Syria, which had briefly joined forces against the Egyptian-Israeli peace treaty, had fallen out by mid-1980. Syria opposed the Iraqi attack on Iran, developed close political relations with the new Iranian regime, and encouraged other Arab states to stay neutral in the conflict.[4]

These three interrelated security challenges—an Arab world splintered over the proper response to the Egyptian-Israeli peace treaty, the domestic repercussions of the Islamic revolution in Iran, and the Iran-Iraq war—dominated the politics of the Gulf monarchies for the rest of the 1980s. Their responses to these challenges involved actions on the regional, international, and domestic levels.

The first, and in many ways most difficult, decision that the Gulf monarchies had to make was how to respond to the Iraqi attack on Iran. Neutrality was not an option, as both Iran and, particularly, Iraq pressed the Gulf states for support. Reluctantly, but importantly, the Gulf states backed Iraq from the outset of the war. The threat posed by Iran's vision of Islamic revolution was seen as more immediate and damaging than the threat posed by Iraq's geopolitical strength. The degree of support for Iraq varied among the states. Saudi Arabia and Kuwait, closest to the battle-field, were the most involved in providing immediate material support to Baghdad; they offered money primarily but also access to facilities in both countries for Iraqi imports and exports. Oman and the UAE, farthest from the battlefield, maintained the most distance from Iraq politically and continued to have correct relations with Iran throughout the war. However, all of the Gulf states supported Iraq politically, through votes in the Arab League and at the United Nations and through their public statements. After 1982, when Iranian forces had expelled the Iraqi army from Iranian territory and carried the battle into Iraq itself, the hesitations in Saudi Arabia and Kuwait about supporting an offensive Iraq disappeared.

Billions of dollars from Saudi Arabia and Kuwait (and lesser amounts from the UAE) funded the Iraqi war effort.[5]

The second, and more enduring, regional response to these challenges was the formation by the six monarchical states in 1981 of the Gulf Cooperation Council (GCC). The GCC was an institutional expression of the belief by the leaders in that perilous time that they must all hang together if they were not to hang separately. The smaller states, indicating how seriously they viewed their security situation, put aside decades-long fears about Saudi dominance in agreeing to join the group. Neither Iraq nor Iran was particularly pleased by this move, as both contended that no Gulf organization should exclude them. However, there was little they could do, mired in their conflict with one another, to prevent the GCC's formation. The formation of a regional grouping within the Arab world—in essence, the six asserting an identity other than their all-Arab identity— was a telling reflection of the fragmentation of Arab politics at that time. The founding documents of the GCC emphasized economic and cultural cooperation among the members, but it was in the political and security fields that the GCC took its most important and substantive steps during the 1980s. The six cooperated on internal security matters and took common positions on the regional crises they confronted.[6] The GCC has endured beyond the crises that sparked its formation. It has had its ups and downs, to be certain, but it provided an important institutional support for Kuwait during the 1990–91 Gulf crisis.[7] The GCC states have recently taken some tentative steps toward economic integration, including a commitment made at the 1999 GCC summit to unify their tariffs.[8] At the 2000 GCC summit the members signed a new defense agreement, though it remains unclear what new commitments they have undertaken in this agreement.[9]

At the international level, the most important step the monarchical states took was to repair their relations with the United States, which had been frayed by their response to the Egyptian-Israeli peace treaty. Oman signed a facilities agreement with the United States in 1980, allowing American forces access to Omani bases in exchange for U.S. military assistance and political support. At the beginning of the Iran-Iraq war the United States sent a squadron of jet fighters to Saudi Arabia as a public manifestation of Washington's commitment to Saudi security. In 1981, the United States sold Saudi Arabia a sophisticated air defense system based on AWACS (airborne warning and control system) planes. In that deal the Saudis not only purchased military hardware but also an American commitment to maintain an air defense umbrella over the kingdom. As the

Iran-Iraq war spread to the waters of the Gulf, in 1987 Kuwait and Saudi Arabia requested the U.S. Navy to protect their ships from Iranian attack. In response, Washington dispatched its largest naval deployment since the Vietnam War to the Gulf and engaged in a number of skirmishes with Iranian naval forces. That escalation culminated in the accidental shooting down of an Iranian civilian aircraft by the USS *Vincennes* in July 1988, which in turn led Iran to accept a cease-fire in its war with Iraq.[10] The naval deployment in 1987 represented a quantum leap in military cooperation between the United States and the Gulf monarchies. All of the GCC states, even those like Kuwait which publicly professed a neutral stance in the U.S.-Soviet Cold War competition, opened their ports, airports, and airspace to American military ships and planes.

Domestically, the six Gulf monarchies worked during the 1980s to insulate their societies from the military and ideological spillover of the Iran-Iraq war. On the political side, that involved maintaining the already strict limits on political expression and political rights. The only Gulf monarchy to have an elected parliament, Kuwait, had closed that parliament in 1976. The government announced in August 1980 (one month before the Iran-Iraq war started) that the parliament would reopen after new elections the following year. Kuwait's rulers followed through on that promise, despite the heightened political sensitivities caused by the war. In July 1986 they closed the parliament once again, citing security concerns and the need for unity in the face of the war.[11] In the other Gulf states there were no formal representative institutions (Bahrain's parliament was closed in 1975) and no moves to expand political participation during the 1980s.

The second part of the "domestic insulation" strategy, meant to balance the political crackdown, was an economic strategy of providing benefits to the population. That was not hard at the outset of the 1980s. The combination of the Iranian revolution and the beginning of the Iran-Iraq war had sent oil prices soaring once again, to over $30 per barrel. The Gulf monarchies had plenty of money to spend on everyone, including their Shia populations. However, maintaining that policy of economic largesse grew more difficult as the 1980s wore on. Profound changes on both the supply and demand sides of the world oil market pushed prices down, at one point in 1986 below $10 per barrel. Gulf states saw their revenues fall precipitously (in Saudi Arabia, from over $120 billion in 1981 to approximately $30 billion in 1986). With their populations growing and demand for state-supplied services and subsidies increasing apace, the Gulf monarchies by the mid-1980s were facing a serious choice: cut government spending on both the domestic and military-security fronts, or draw down financial reserves and go into debt to maintain current levels of expenditure.

All of the six states chose the second option. They would not cut arms purchases and other security expenditures (most importantly for Saudi Arabia and Kuwait, financial support for Iraq) at a time of serious regional instability. They could not impose austerity on their populations at a time of political ferment, for fear that their citizens would turn against their regimes. They therefore engaged in a sustained period of deficit spending, postponing for a more secure time in the future the inevitable economic readjustments they would have to make.

Many in the Gulf thought that a more secure future had arrived by 1990. The Iran-Iraq war ended in August 1988. Oil prices had recovered somewhat from their 1986 lows. After the death of Ayatollah Khomeini in 1989 Iran took a much less aggressive position on the export of its Islamic revolutionary political model. The Cold War itself seemed to be winding down, with the profound changes in the U.S.-Soviet relationship and in Eastern Europe. Very few suspected that 1990 would see the most serious political-military-security challenge to the Gulf monarchies in their histories.

The causes of the Iraqi invasion of Kuwait on August 2, 1990, continue to be debated.[12] The effects on the Gulf monarchies were immediately obvious. One of their number had been swallowed whole by an ambitious regional neighbor, who subsequently challenged the legitimacy of all of the GCC governments. The choice facing Saudi Arabia in particular was immediate and momentous: to accept the Iraqi occupation of Kuwait and, indirectly, Iraqi dominance over the Arab side of the Gulf, or to invite into the kingdom American and other international forces with the intention of undoing the Iraqi invasion, either politically or militarily. The Saudis chose the latter path and were supported in that decision by all the other members of the GCC. Once that choice was made, the dynamics of the Gulf crisis were out of the hands of the Gulf rulers and in those of the United States and Iraq. What remained for the Gulf states was to pay for the war (particularly Kuwait and Saudi Arabia) and await its consequences.

Those consequences, on the security side, were overwhelming and positive for the Gulf monarchies. Iraq was expelled from Kuwait and defeated militarily. The Al Sabah were restored as the rulers of Kuwait with the practically unanimous support of Kuwaitis. The GCC remained politically united during the crisis. The Kuwaiti and Saudi leaders would certainly have liked to see the regime of Saddam Hussein fall and probably would have supported a continuation of the war until Saddam himself collapsed. But in 1991 he seemed unlikely to be able to threaten any of his neighbors, and his downfall was considered by most to be a matter of time. Iran had, from the Gulf states' perspective, acted with enormous restraint during the Gulf crisis. The crisis was a turning point in the course of Iranian-GCC relations, which had been severely strained during the Iran-Iraq war. Most importantly, Saudi Arabia and Iran resumed diplomatic relations shortly after the war and began a political dialogue that continued throughout the 1990s. Other important Arab states, most notably Egypt and Syria, had supported the GCC states politically and militarily during the crisis. Regionally, the GCC states left the Gulf crisis in the most secure position of their independent existences.

The Gulf crisis also cemented the strong security relations between the Gulf monarchies and the United States. The GCC states' reluctance (with the exceptions of Oman, which had a facilities agreement with the United States from the late 1970s, and Bahrain, which was headquarters for the small U.S. naval force stationed in the Gulf since World War II) to have a direct military tie to the United States was a thing of the past. The end of the Cold War made that close military tie to the United States less controversial than it would have been in the past, as did the revival of the Arab-Israeli peace process with the Madrid Conference of 1991 and the Israeli-PLO Oslo agreement of 1993. The regional security issues that had dominated the Gulf states' political agenda of the 1980s had been, at least temporarily, solved.

The 1990s: The New Domestic Agenda of Gulf Politics

If the Gulf War of 1990–91 solved, at least for a decade, the external security problems facing the Gulf monarchies, in many ways that war and its consequences exacerbated domestic issues that had, for the previous decade, been pushed to the back of the political agenda. During the rest of the 1990s the twin domestic challenges of economic change and political reform dominated Gulf states' politics.

The Gulf War was very costly for the Gulf states, particularly for Kuwait and Saudi Arabia. As was mentioned above, this financial burden came at a time when the GCC states were already drawing down their financial reserves in order to maintain high levels of government spending as oil revenues declined from their high point in the early 1980s. Estimates of Kuwaiti expenditure during and immediately after the Gulf crisis range as high as $65 billion; the International Monetary Fund estimated the direct costs of the Gulf War for the Saudis at $55 billion, a figure that Saudi officials have not challenged.[13] In essence, the combination of lower oil prices in the 1980s, the costs of supporting Iraq in the Iran-Iraq war, and the costs of the Gulf War reduced the financial reserves of the Gulf governments to the point that they could no longer cover continued government deficits from their own resources. The only exception was the United Arab Emirates, which largely avoided the political burdens taken on by Kuwait and Saudi Arabia and maintained a healthy financial reserve. The other Gulf monarchies had to face a new fiscal situation in the 1990s.

The first response of the Gulf states to this new fiscal stringency was not to cut government expenditures but rather to take on debt. In fact, in the three Gulf monarchies most affected by the Gulf war—Kuwait, Saudi Arabia, and Bahrain—the governments increased subsidies and lowered prices on a range of government-supplied goods and services in the wake of the crisis.[14] In Saudi Arabia the domestic economy was large enough to allow the Saudi government to fund its debt by issuing government bonds to local banks and to government social insurance agencies (much as the U.S. Social Security Administration buys U.S. Treasury bills). Kuwait, Qatar, and Oman turned mostly to international creditors for their debts. Bahrain, the first "post-oil" Gulf monarchy, looked to Saudi Arabia for financial assistance. The Saudis responded by transferring on a permanent basis the revenue from one of their offshore oil fields to Bahrain.[15]

Borrowing to meet current expenditures is a stopgap measure, and the Gulf monarchies soon ran up against the limits of prudence in terms of debt. By 1998 the Saudi government's domestic debt reached 116 percent of GDP, above the levels recommended by international financial institutions.[16] In January 1996 the Kuwait Investment Authority reported to the Kuwaiti parliament that official reserves had fallen to $47 billion from $117 billion before the Gulf War and that Kuwait had foreign debts of $30 billion. The authority warned that if current trends continued, Kuwait would soon become a net debtor.[17] In 1994 the IMF and the World Bank warned Oman that it risked a fiscal crisis if it continued to run government deficits.[18] Much of both Oman's and Qatar's debt went to building the natural gas and oil infrastructures of the countries and thus promised payoffs in the long term, but the immediate impact of the loans was to highlight the precariousness of the governments' financial picture at a time of comparatively low oil prices.

The drop in world oil prices in 1998, with prices going as low as $10 per barrel in December 1998, was the shock needed to jolt the Gulf states into taking more seriously the need to reform their economies and get a handle on government spending. All the Gulf states took more serious steps toward privatization of state-owned (and usually money-losing) enterprises. Saudi Arabia and Oman made a serious push to enter the World Trade Organization, which will require significant domestic economic reforms (the other Gulf states were already members). In Saudi Arabia and Kuwait the governments reduced subsidies on consumer goods and increased the price of government-supplied services like telephones, water, and electricity. In August 1999 Saudi Arabia created a new Supreme Economic Council meant to provide high-level direction to economic reform and cut through bureaucratic red tape.[19] All the states, even Saudi Arabia, have altered their tax and regulatory systems to encourage foreign investment.

At the same time, Saudi Arabia worked with other major oil producers to push oil prices up. Saudi Arabia was the linchpin in the March 1999 agreement among major OPEC and non-OPEC producers to take 2 million barrels of daily oil production off the market. Riyadh absorbed 25 percent of the total cut itself. As oil prices rose during 1999, thanks to the production cuts, growing American demand for imported oil, and a faster-than-expected recovery in the economies of East Asia, Saudi production fell by over a million barrels per day. By the middle of 2000 oil prices had nearly tripled from their December 1998 low, and Saudi Arabian oil policy was a major reason for the increase.[20] The increase in oil revenues has helped all the Gulf governments to improve their shaky fiscal positions. The bigger question is whether this improvement will dull their appetites for the long-term economic reform measures that they began to adopt in the mid- and late 1990s.

The political consequences of economic reform are immense for the Gulf states. In the long term it is clear that they cannot rely on the old formulas of oil revenues and debt to meet the needs of fast-growing populations. All of the Gulf monarchies have population growth rates above the average for non-OECD countries; Saudi Arabia and Oman have growth rates over 3 percent per year, among the highest in the world.[21] The strains placed on the GCC states' welfare systems by burgeoning populations are manifold. Longer life expectancies mean greater health care costs. Higher birth rates mean more schools. Larger populations mean greater demand for water, electricity, and telephone services. More school graduates means more demand for jobs, particularly in the public sector, which for the past two decades has absorbed almost all the citizen (as opposed to foreign labor) workforce in these countries. If the states cannot deliver these goods and services, more of their citizens might demand political change. But for the states to deliver in the long term, they have to cut some benefits in the short term and encourage a new economic logic among their citizens—one of cutting costs, accepting higher prices, and looking more to the private sector for jobs.

Negotiating these changes is more complicated now, as Gulf state populations have the potential to be more politicized than was the case in the past. The Gulf War certainly was a catalyst for this politicization, but long-term social trends have also contributed. Gulf citizens are more likely to be educated, literate, and urban than at any time in the history of Arabia.[22] In other societies these kinds of changes have presaged upsurges in political activism. The irony is that these social changes have occurred in large measure as a result of state policy. The Gulf governments used their oil money to build schools and expand literacy programs. The growth of government has meant the growth of cities, and many Gulf states have actively worked to settle previously rural and nomadic populations in urban areas.

In the period during and immediately after the Gulf War, there was an upsurge in political activism throughout the Gulf states. The most widespread manifestation of new political activism during and immediately after the crisis was the circulation of petitions. In Kuwait, Saudi Arabia, Bahrain, and Qatar, citizens of various political inclinations addressed requests to their rulers for more responsible government and greater popular participation in decision making. The nature of the demands differed from country to country. In Kuwait and Bahrain, the call was for restoration of constitutions that mandated elected legislatures. In Saudi Arabia and Qatar, there were more modest requests for an end to arbitrary practices, more freedom of speech, and more formal avenues of consultation between the government and the people. In Saudi Arabia petitions reflected different political agendas, with ad hoc groups of liberals, Islamists, and members of the minority Shia population all proposing their own reform recommendations to the rulers.[23]

In some of the Gulf states, political activism took to the streets and turned to violence. In Bahrain in the mid-1990s a low-level popular uprising, concentrated in the country's Shia population, called into question the stability of the regime.[24] The Omani government in June 1994 arrested over 200 people implicated in a plot organized by the Muslim Brotherhood to overthrow the government.[25] The Saudi government took the unusual step of publicly acknowledging the arrest of 157 people in September and October 1994 for organizing a demonstration against the government in the town of Burayda, north of Riyadh. Included among those arrested were two prominent Islamists, Salman al-Awda and Safar al-Hawali, who had since the Gulf War been writing and preaching against the regime.[26] In November 1995 and June 1996 bomb explosions at U.S. military facilities in Riyadh and Dhahran killed twenty-four Americans and wounded hundreds of Americans and Saudis. Four Saudi Islamists were executed for their involvement in the Riyadh bombing.[27] Despite an intensive investigation by both Saudi Arabia and the United States, no one has been convicted for the Dhahran bombing. America's most notorious international foe, Osama Bin Laden, whom the United States holds responsible for the bombings of the American embassies in Kenya and Tanzania in 1998 and for the attack on the USS *Cole* in the port of Aden, Yemen, in October 2000, is a member of one of Saudi Arabia's richest families. He was stripped of his Saudi citizenship in April 1994 for his increasingly virulent criticisms of the Saudi regime and the United States.

Gulf governments have been harsh in their reactions against violent manifestations of opposition. However, the Gulf leaders have also recognized that to react to the growing politicization of their populations in times of difficult economic decisions, they need to expand the opportunities for political participation. In the 1990s every Gulf state except the UAE (the only Gulf state able to avoid serious economic problems) took important steps in this direction. Kuwait after liberation reopened its elected parliament. A variety of Islamist, liberal, tribal, and independent factions have vied for seats in elections in 1992, 1996, and 1999.[28] The ruler of Kuwait in 1999 issued a decree extending the right to vote to Kuwaiti women, but the parliament elected that year reversed his decision.[29] Oman established a consultative council in 1990 and over the decade increased its membership and the number of members chosen through indirect election rather than by appointment by the sultan. Saudi Arabia and Bahrain also formed appointed consultative councils in 1993 and 1992, respectively. In December 2000 the ruler of Bahrain accepted the recommendation of a constitutional drafting committee to form a two-house legislature, with the lower house to be directly elected. Elections are scheduled for 2004.[30] Qatar established a directly elected municipal council in March 1999, with women permitted to vote and to run for office, and is in the midst of preparing a permanent constitution for the country.

Gulf governments are also less heavy handed than they have been in the past in managing the information that their citizens receive. To some extent, this is simply a recognition that new technologies—satellite television, fax machines, the Internet—make it easier for their people to find out what is going on in the world and in their own countries. The state-controlled newspapers in Saudi Arabia, Qatar, and Oman have become marginally more open. Qatar even went so far as to abolish its Ministry of Information. The Kuwaiti press remains feisty. The Internet is slowly making inroads into all the Gulf countries. Qatar plays host to the most influential and open Arab satellite news channel, *al-Jazeera*. Its straightforward news reporting and freewheeling discussion programs have created a number of diplomatic incidents between Qatar and other Arab governments who feel aggrieved by the station's treatment of their politics.[31]

These new institutional avenues for political participation and manifestations of political freedom in the Gulf states are important, but their impact should not be exaggerated. Ultimate decision-making power still rests with the ruling families, acting through their government ministers (many of whom remain, in all the Gulf states, members of the ruling family). After the upsurge in political activity after the Gulf War and through the mid-1990s, the "street" in the Gulf countries became quieter in the late 1990s (though the regimes have allowed their citizens to voice support for the al-Aqsa intifada of 2000–2002 in very public ways). The Gulf media are freer than they used to be but are by no means free. They are simply less controlled. But all these developments in the 1990s are reflections of the changes that are occurring in the Gulf states, at the political, economic, and social levels. They complicate the political scene and provide at least a tacit check on the ability of rulers to make arbitrary decisions. On the economic front, they underline the fact that the Gulf governments have to respond not simply to changes in the world economy and the price of oil but also to the expectations of their citizens. This makes it harder for the Gulf governments to pursue economic reform plans that reduce economic benefits to citizens, but it also encourages those governments to engage in a more honest dialogue with their societies about the economic realities they face.

Into the New Millennium: Domestic and Security Politics in the Gulf States

During the 1990s, the Gulf monarchies enjoyed an unusual respite from serious security issues. Iraq was defeated and isolated, relations with Iran were improving (except for the UAE, for whom the issue of Abu Musa and the Tunbs islands remained a major irritant in relations with Iran), the Arab-Israeli peace process was progressing, and the American role in the Gulf was basically unchallenged. As these new states entered the new millennium, however, security issues were reemerging onto the political agenda.

The issues on this new security agenda are not nearly as threatening as those the Gulf states have faced in the past. There is no immediate threat of military attack, no regional power with substantial domestic followings actively working to undermine the ruling regimes. But the elements that made for the security honeymoon of the 1990s are unraveling. Iraq is no longer isolated in the region. Popular sympathy for the plight of the Iraqi people has been growing, even in the Gulf states themselves. That sympathy has pushed Arab governments toward a reopening of relations with Baghdad, a reopening that many were moving toward for their own strategic reasons. If anything, it is now the United States and Great Britain that are isolated on the issue of Iraq. That isolation is made starker by the collapse in 2000 of the Arab-Israeli peace process. The inability of the Clinton administration to broker deals on the Syrian-Israeli and Palestinian-Israeli fronts led to new regional tensions and to a new Palestinian popular uprising, the al-Aqsa intifada. Citizen populations in the Gulf states, increasingly disposed against the United States on the Iraq issue, now have another reason to oppose American policy. As 2000 drew to a close, the increasing momentum of popular calls for Gulf citizens to boycott American products and companies reflected the growing public disenchantment with the United States.[32]

This turn in Gulf public opinion complicates the foreign policy choices of the Gulf leaders. The past ten years have seen a deepening of the political-military relationship each GCC state has with the United States. Kuwait, Qatar, and Oman now host U.S. prepositioning facilities, where large amounts of equipment are stored. The American Southern Watch operation of aerial surveillance of southern Iraq is based in Saudi Arabia. The headquarters of the expanded U.S. fleet in the Gulf has been brought onshore in Bahrain. The UAE hosts thousands of U.S. service personnel on rest and relaxation leave.[33] The Gulf governments are not about to abandon their American security link because of changes in public opinion. However, these changes in public opinion cannot be ignored by leaders who are aware of the growing importance of political participation in their systems and who are working to implement economic reforms that will impose, at least in the short term, some hardships on their citizens.

At a minimum Gulf governments will feel the need to distance themselves from the United States, in a public way, over some issues—certainly Arab-Israeli issues and policy toward Iraq (all the Gulf states save Kuwait and Saudi Arabia have already restored diplomatic relations with Baghdad), and possibly oil issues. In the worst case, radical groups in the Gulf states will look to replicate the bombings of U.S. military targets. The Gulf governments are used to managing tension in their relations with the United States; Washington, however, is less used to this. Since Desert Storm, Gulf governments have been closely aligned with Washington on a whole range of Middle East issues and have allowed the United States to base substantial military assets on their territory. Can the American government learn to live with a level of tension and disagreement with those governments?

The American connection is not just a foreign policy issue for the Gulf states; it is also on the domestic agenda. Maintaining that connection at a time when public sentiment in the Gulf is turning against the United States affects the Gulf leaders' willingness to pursue other controversial and difficult policy courses domestically. Two issues in particular bear watching in this regard. The first, discussed above, is economic reform. With the immediate threat of fiscal crisis removed with higher oil prices, will the Gulf governments continue with their policies of privatization, reduction of subsidies, and limitations on government spending, despite the short-term costs of these policies for their citizens? So far, the indications are that the Gulf governments will continue along this path. The second issue is the role of women in the Gulf societies. An increased role for women in the economy and society in the Gulf states could reduce dependence on foreign labor, increase productivity, and make productive use of the talents of half of the Gulf citizens. Gulf leaders recognize this fact. However, many traditionalists and Islamists see changes in the status of women as just another example of the Americanization of the Gulf and will fight government efforts to expand the economic and social options for women. How Gulf governments deal with the women's issue will be a good indication of their willingness to take political risks.

Notes

1. For a more detailed account of the international politics of the Gulf area during the 1970s and 1980s, see F. Gregory Gause III, "Gulf Regional Politics: Revolution, War, and Rivalry," in *Dynamics of Regional Politics: Four Systems on the Indian Ocean Rim,* ed. W. Howard Wriggins (New York: Columbia University Press, 1992).

2. Nadav Safran, *Saudi Arabia: The Ceaseless Quest for Security* (Cambridge: Harvard University Press, 1985), 306.

3. Joseph Kostiner, "Shia Unrest in the Gulf," in *Shiism, Resistance, and Revolution,* ed. Martin Kramer (Boulder, Colo.: Westview Press, 1987); R. K. Ramazani, *Revolutionary Iran: Challenge and Response in the Middle East* (Baltimore: Johns Hopkins University Press, 1986), chaps. 6–9.

4. On Syrian-Iranian relations, see Anoushiravan Ehteshami and Raymond A. Hinnebusch, *Syria and Iran: Middle Powers in a Penetrated System* (New York: Routledge, 1997).

5. King Fahd, in a public speech during the Gulf War, listed the amounts of aid to Iraq (*Al-Sharq al-Awsat,* January 17, 1991, 4). On Gulf-Iraq relations during the Iran-Iraq war, see Gerd Nonneman, *Iraq, the Gulf States, and the War* (London: Ithaca Press, 1986).

6. On the origins of the GCC, see Emile Nakhleh, *The Gulf Cooperation Council: Policies, Problems, and Prospects* (New York: Praeger, 1986).

7. For post–Gulf War developments in the GCC, see Michael Barnett and F. Gregory Gause III, "Caravans in Opposite Directions: Society, State, and the Development of Community in the Gulf Cooperation Council," in *Security Communities,* ed. Emmanuel Adler and Michael Barnett (Cambridge: Cambridge University Press, 1998).

8. *Al-Hayat,* November 29, 1999, 1, 2, 6.

9. "Six Gulf Nations Sign Defense Pact," *New York Times,* December 31, 2000.

10. On the Iran-Iraq war, see Majid Khadduri, *The Gulf War: The Origins and Implications of the Iraq-Iran Conflict* (New York: Oxford University Press, 1988); Shahram Chubin and Charles Tripp, *Iran and Iraq at War* (Boulder, Colo.: Westview Press, 1988); and Ramazani, *Revolutionary Iran.*

11. Jill Crystal, *Oil and Politics in the Gulf: Rulers and Merchants in Kuwait and Qatar* (Cambridge: Cambridge University Press, 1990), 100–109.

12. The best book on the Gulf War remains Lawrence Freedman and Efraim Karsh, *The Gulf Conflict, 1990–91* (Princeton, N.J.: Princeton University Press, 1993).

13. For war expenditure figures, see F. Gregory Gause III, *Oil Monarchies: Domestic and Security Challenges in the Arab Gulf States* (New York: Council on Foreign Relations Press, 1994), 147–48.

14. Gause, *Oil Monarchies,* 61–62.

15. Christine Hauser, "Saudi Aid Will Ease Bahrain Budget Squeeze," Reuters (on-line), April 15, 1996.

16. Saudi American Bank, "The Saudi Economy: Mid-Year 2000 Update," August 2000, 1. Available at www.samba.com.sa.

17. William Maclean, "Kuwaitis Angry at Asset Fall, Weigh Deficit Cut," Reuters (on-line), January 18, 1996.

18. Randall Palmer, "Oman May Be Overdoing Expansion, Economists Say," Reuters (on-line), January 19, 1995.

19. *Al-Hayat,* August 30, 1999, 9.

20. F. Gregory Gause III, "Saudi Arabia over a Barrel," *Foreign Affairs* 79, no. 3 (May–June 2000).

21. Population Reference Bureau, "2000 World Population Data Sheet," www.prb.org.

22. See discussion on this point in F. Gregory Gause III, "The Gulf Conundrum: Economic Change, Population Growth, and Political Stability in the GCC States," *Washington Quarterly* 20, no. 1 (winter 1997): 156–58.

23. For a discussion of the "petition fever" in the Gulf during 1990–92, see Gause, *Oil Monarchies,* 78–101.

24. Louay Bahry, "The Opposition in Bahrain: A Bellwether for the Gulf?" *Middle East Policy* 5, no. 2 (May 1997): 42–57, and Munira A. Fakhro, "The Uprising in Bahrain: An Assessment," in *The Persian Gulf at the Millennium,* ed. Gary G. Sick and Lawrence G. Potter (New York: St. Martin's Press, 1997).

25. *Al-Hayat,* August 29, 1994, 1, 4; September 5, 1994, 1, 4; November 13, 1994, 1, 4.

26. *Al-Hayat,* September 27, 1994, 1, 4; October 17, 1994, 3. For the background on Saudi Islamist opposition, see R. Hrair Dekmejian, "The Rise of Political Islamism in Saudi Arabia," *Middle East Journal* 48, no. 4 (autumn 1994), and Mamoun Fandy, *Saudi Arabia and the Politics of Dissent* (New York: St. Martin's Press, 1999).

27. For an interesting discussion of the background of one of those executed, see Ethan Bronner, "In a Bomber's Life, Glimpse of Saudi Dissent," *Boston Globe,* July 7, 1996, 1.

28. For accounts of the Kuwaiti parliamentary elections, see Gause, *Oil Monarchies,* 101–5; Shafeeq Ghabra, "Kuwait and the Dynamics of Socio-economic Change," *Middle East Journal* 51, no. 3 (summer 1997); Ghanim Alnajjar, "The Challenges Facing Kuwaiti Democracy," *Middle East Journal* 54, no. 2 (spring 2000).

29. *Al-Hayat,* December 1, 1999, 1, 6.

30. *Al-Hayat,* December 20, 2000, 1, 6.

31. For a discussion of *al-Jazeera,* see Edmund Ghareeb, "New Media and the Information Revolution in the Arab World: An Assessment," *Middle East Journal* 54, no. 3 (summer 2000). In that same issue, Deborah Wheeler examines how these new media are affecting national identity in Kuwait ("New Media, Globalization, and Kuwaiti National Identity").

32. Donna Abu-Nasr, "Calls to Boycott U.S. Sweep Gulf," Associated Press (on-line), November 30, 2000.

33. An excellent discussion of the new American military role in the Gulf states can be found in Rachel Bronson, "United States Policy toward the Persian Gulf: A New Focus for a New Administration," *Orbis* (spring 2001).

4

From Swamp to Backyard

The Middle East in Turkish Foreign Policy

MALIK MUFTI

Turkey's foreign policy since the end of the Cold War has been far more assertive than at any previous time in the Republic's history. Nowhere is this widely noted fact more in evidence than in Turkey's relationship with the countries of the Middle East. During the past decade Turkey has established an almost continuous military presence in northern Iraq, come close to fighting a war with Syria, and witnessed a serious deterioration in its relations with Iran. At the same time, it has entered into unprecedented security relationships with Israel and, to a lesser extent, Jordan. Nevertheless, this deepening involvement has occurred in the absence of a coherent overall strategy—it was, as Alan Makovsky wrote, "largely reactive, somewhat in the old mold."[1] In the apt words of another close observer, Henri J. Barkey, "The orientation of Turkish foreign policy increasingly exhibits the same level of confusion as its domestic approach to the question of identity."[2] This chapter builds on Barkey's insight by arguing that the current incoherence of Turkey's Middle East policies arises from a disjunction between the objective factors necessitating activism—most particularly the effects of regional developments on Turkey's domestic political order—and the subjective impact of a strategic culture that has traditionally been averse to involvement with the Middle East.

A Tale of Two Paradigms

Turkish attitudes toward the Middle East—like all other aspects of Turkey's strategic culture—are rooted in the traumatic experiences of the

Ottoman Empire's collapse and the subsequent emergence of the Republic after World War I. A number of enduring legacies were forged in that crucible.

One of the legacies is a strong antipathy toward the East in general and the Arabs in particular. There was an intellectual tradition that for decades had shied away from Eastern influences and turned instead to the West as the model for social progress. The republican elite led by Mustafa Kemal Atatürk grew out of this tradition, and once in power it implemented a series of revolutionary changes ranging from the subordination of Islam to secularism as a key tenet of state ideology, to the replacement of Arabic script by Latin script. In addition, the decision by Arab nationalists to cast their lot with Britain and to revolt against the Ottoman Empire during World War I—a revolt in which thousands of Ottoman soldiers were killed—left a residue of bitterness and gave rise to a view of the Arabs as unreliable and treacherous.[3] For the new republican elite, then, the Middle East came to be seen as a backward and unwholesome swamp to be avoided as far as possible.

A second enduring legacy of that period arises from the fact that the discrepancies between the self-proclaimed boundaries of the new Turkish state—as set out in the 1920 National Pact *(Misak-i Milli)*—and the actual territorial disposition following the war of independence lay mainly to the south. Specifically, Turkey claimed the territories of Hatay, controlled by the French based in Syria, and Mosul, controlled by the British based in Iraq. In Turkish eyes, moreover, both territories served as potential springboards for further imperialist aggression. France, after all, had swept north from Hatay to invade Cilicia during the war of independence in a bid to set up a client Armenian state. And Britain—which had entertained similar ambitions for the Kurds of southeast Anatolia—was suspected of sponsoring Kurdish uprisings within Turkey even after the peace settlement in an attempt to thwart Turkish claims on Mosul. As it turned out, Mosul remained a province of Iraq as a result of an agreement reached between Britain and Turkey in 1926, while Hatay was ceded by France to Turkey in 1939—an outcome never accepted by Syria. Although Turkey's leaders considered the territorial questions thereby formally and finally resolved, they were left with an acute sense of the vulnerability of their southern frontiers to aggression and subversion. Their preexisting antipathy toward the Middle East, therefore, was now compounded by a certain wariness as well.

Nor was there much in the way of material interests. Turkey's economy remained largely inward oriented during the global downturn of the interwar years, and its main trading partners were in any case European. With nothing much to be gained, and with powerful historical reasons to remain aloof, it is not surprising that the Turkish Republic during the first decades of its existence had very little to do with its southern neighbors.

The dominant Turkish attitude toward the Middle East that flows from all these considerations can be summarized by four cardinal principles:

(1) Reserve: pursuing correct relations with all Middle Eastern states and eschewing interference in their domestic affairs;
(2) Neutrality: not becoming identified too closely with any single Middle Eastern state and avoiding being dragged into regional conflicts;
(3) Maintenance of the status quo: opposing attempts to alter the regional balance of power, and especially revisionist bids for regional hegemony (for example, through pan-Arabism);
(4) Compartmentalization: avoiding linkage between Turkey's Middle East policies and its relations with the Western powers—a stance arising from the suspicion that Turkish and Western interests are unlikely to coincide in the region, as well as the desire not to be viewed as the West's "gendarme" by local actors.

Together, these four elements of Turkey's dominant security paradigm as it relates to the Middle East may be titled the Inönü Doctrine after Ismet Inönü, second president of the Republic and the doctrine's most consistent practitioner.

But there has been from the beginning a counterparadigm, reflecting an alternate strand in Turkish political culture. Like the dominant paradigm, its roots stretch back to Ottoman days and to the debates about how best to effect social progress. However, it is less elitist and therefore more open to the cultural influences—Islamic and Middle Eastern—prevalent among the masses. For a variety of reasons, which are beyond the scope of this chapter, it is also less inclined to be suspicious of the Western powers and therefore more willing to consider collaborative ventures with them. Finally, it is a paradigm more disposed to viewing the cultural porousness of the country's frontiers as an opportunity to project Turkish power outward than as a liability making possible external aggression and subversion.

This counterparadigm first shaped Turkish foreign policy toward the Middle East during the Democrat Party governments of 1950 to 1960, under Prime Minister Adnan Menderes and Foreign Minister Fatin Rüştü Zorlu. In order to overcome British objections to Turkey's NATO membership (London wanted Ankara to focus on helping it to defend its Middle East interests), the Democrats decided to participate in whatever regional security initiatives the Western powers devised.[4] The first of these, a 1951 proposal for a military alliance attached to NATO called the Middle East Defense Command, foundered due to Egypt's refusal to join. On February 24, 1955, however, Turkey signed an accord with Iraq that eventually grew into the Baghdad Pact, an American-backed military alliance that also included Britain, Iran, and Pakistan. Inevitably, Turkey soon found itself embroiled in a bitter conflict with radical Arab nationalists who opposed the pact, led by Egypt's president Gamal Abdel Nasser.

In 1956, Turkey voted against Arab efforts to bring the Algerian question before the United Nations General Assembly. In 1957, Turkish troops massed on the border with Syria in an attempt to destabilize the coalition of Nasserists and pro-Communists in power there, and some low-level skirmishes reportedly ensued.[5] Two more times in 1958—first during the unfolding unification of Syria and Egypt into Nasser's United Arab Republic (UAR) in January, then after overthrow of the Hashemite monarchy in Iraq by radical military officers in July—Turkey threatened military action. Also in 1958, Turkey abandoned its aloof stance toward Israel by joining it in a covert axis known as the Periphery Pact. And in 1959 Turkey threatened to intervene militarily in Iraq again, this time to prop up the regime of Abd al-Karim Qassim against the supporters of Nasser, with whom he had fallen out.

Although the government's domestic critics lambasted these policies as pandering to American interests at the expense of Turkey's own interests—and in the process needlessly incurring the enmity of the Arab world's newly emerging dominant forces—the evidence does not support the contention that Menderes and Zorlu were simply carrying out Western bidding. Indeed, it suggests quite the opposite. In every crisis during the decade, it was usually the Turks who sought more vigorous responses to regional upheavals, and it was usually the Americans who held them back.

Throughout the 1956–57 crisis in Syria, for example, the United States —anxious though it was to reverse the rise of anti-Western elements there—made it a top priority to discourage any Turkish intervention.[6] Similarly, when Menderes warned that the establishment of the UAR threatened Turkish interests and mandated urgent action, U.S. Secretary of State John Foster Dulles insisted that "if there is any reaction it must be initiated by Arabs and not Turkey or Western powers."[7] In any event all the Baghdad Pact Council could agree on was to pressure Iraq into a hasty counterunion with Jordan. This hardly sufficed to stem the radical tide, and Turkey's regional policy suffered an even more devastating blow five months later with the overthrow of the Iraqi Hashemites. Convinced that Nasser was behind the coup, Menderes and Zorlu again adopted an assertive posture, initiating military deployments along the Syrian and Iraqi borders and urging the Americans to join them in a vigorous response—in vain. Frustrated, Turkey's leaders in late August joined their Israeli counterparts—themselves alarmed at the regional trend of events—in an attempt to enlist American backing for a Periphery Pact that would also include Iran, Sudan, and Ethiopia.[8] Yet again, however, the United States held back. Finally, in the 1959 power struggle between Nasser and Qassim, Turkish threats to intervene on behalf of the latter ran up against Washington's preference for the former.[9]

A divergence of opinion about Nasser's role in the Middle East lay at the root of this growing alienation between Ankara and Washington. For the Americans, Nasser and his brand of pan-Arab nationalism—distasteful as it was in its own right—constituted the most promising firewall against the spread of Communist influence in Syria and Iraq.[10] For the Turks, the alternatives were not so clear-cut. Menderes and Zorlu appear to have calculated that the consolidation of the Arab world under Nasser's leadership could only have negative consequences—either he would simply align with the Soviet Union, leaving Turkey encircled by hostile forces, or he would continue successfully playing off Washington against Moscow, blackmailing the Americans into basing their entire regional policy on keeping him happy and thereby leaving Turkey marginalized and isolated. More positively, however, Menderes and Zorlu also viewed Middle East developments as opportunities to enhance Turkish influence and power—not just in the region, but vis-à-vis the Great Powers in the context of Turkey's overall security strategy as well.

No less than their predecessors, then, Menderes and Zorlu formulated policies they thought best served Turkish national interests. Unlike their predecessors, however, their inclination was to pursue those interests beyond Turkey's frontiers rather than to hunker down in a defensive and reactive posture. The innovativeness of the Democrats' policy in the Middle East is made apparent by the ways in which it diverged from each of the cardinal principles of the Inönü Doctrine:

(1) Engagement rather than reserve: a willingness to use coercion against and even to intervene in the internal affairs of neighbor-

ing countries (such as Syria and Iraq) in order to influence their behavior;

(2) Alignment rather than neutrality: a willingness to form alliances (such as the Baghdad Pact and the Periphery Pact) that include some neighboring states but antagonize others;

(3) Flexibility rather than rigid adherence to the status quo: a readiness to consider alternatives to the existing political or territorial disposition when necessary (such as Ankara's willingness to go along with the 1958 Hashemite Union of Iraq and Jordan);

(4) Linkage rather than compartmentalization: a conviction that Turkey's overall strategic interests are inextricably connected with its Middle East policies, and a consequent readiness to actively either support or oppose the regional initiatives of great powers—as evidenced by each of the crises discussed above.

Together, these elements of Turkey's alternative security paradigm as it related to the Middle East may be titled the Zorlu Doctrine after the Democrat Party foreign minister who was its chief architect.

This first attempt to implement the Zorlu Doctrine must be judged to have failed, with Turkey's influence and prestige in the Middle East in tatters by 1960. Three explanations may be offered for this failure. Two were external factors beyond Turkey's control: the strategic decision taken by the United States to support Nasser as the preferred alternative to Communism; and the Arab-Israeli conflict, which undermined efforts by Turkey—and its Hashemite allies in Iraq and Jordan—to forge a pro-Western regional alliance. The third explanation was internal: the absence of a military capability that would allow Turkey to undertake serious cross-border operations—and that surely contributed to the lack of enthusiasm for military action displayed by the Turkish armed forces during this period.[11]

At any rate, this chapter in Turkish foreign policy came to an abrupt end on May 27, 1960, with the military coup that overthrew the Democrat Party government and led to the execution by hanging of both Menderes and Zorlu, along with Finance Minister Hasan Polatkan. Once again, the İnönü Doctrine came into play. In the words of Ismail Soysal, a senior Turkish diplomat who had been stationed in Damascus during the mid-1950s and an authority on Turkish-Arab relations: "The general view in Turkey was that the Baghdad Pact had been a fiasco and the disappointment following the coup d'etat was so great that the Turkish rulers admitted with bitterness in their inner circles the impossibility of any political cooperation with the Arabs for a collective defense of the Middle East."[12] And as another analyst added, "For the next three decades Turkish policy towards the region was markedly more cautious, even to the point of meekness."[13]

Retrenchment: 1960–1980

External developments contributed to the change in direction after Menderes and Zorlu. Détente between the superpowers, a less aggressive stance by Moscow, and the growing differences between Ankara and Washington on the Cyprus question all combined to revive neutralist tendencies. Turkey's Ministry of Foreign Affairs (MFA) in particular led the way in arguing for closer relations with Europe and a rapprochement with the Soviet Union.[14] The idea was that Turkey would be able to balance the United States, Europe, and the Soviet Union against each other, thereby maximizing its security without having to subordinate its foreign policy to the interests of any one partner. In the Middle East context, this led to continued close ties with Iran, but a reversal of Democrat Party policies on all other fronts: a gradual rapprochement with radical and nonaligned Arab regimes and a downgrading of relations with erstwhile allies—such as Jordan and Israel—to the minimum level possible without provoking an American backlash.

The 1967 Arab-Israeli war rendered Turkey's new regional orientation still more tenable. On the one hand, by smashing and atomizing Arab power so completely, it eliminated any remaining possibility of a consolidated military threat to Turkey from the south. On the other hand, it gave Turkish leaders the opportunity to win favor among the Arabs by offering them strong rhetorical support. Foreign Minister Ihsan Sabri Çağlayangil set the tone immediately after the war, declaring that his government opposed the acquisition of land by force. During the 1973 Arab-Israeli war, Turkey refused permission to American planes to use Turkish air bases to resupply Israel, even as it allowed Soviet planes on the same mission on behalf of the Arabs to fly over its airspace.[15] And in 1975, Turkey voted for the United Nations General Assembly resolution equating Zionism with racism. The following year, a PLO office was allowed to open in Ankara. Finally, after the Israeli Knesset passed a law in 1980 affirming the whole of Jerusalem as Israel's capital, Turkish parliamentarians passed an unprecedented no-confidence motion that forced Foreign Minister Hayrettin Erkmen, who was judged to be too soft on Israel, out of office. Bülent Ecevit of the CHP joined Necmettin Erbakan's Islamic-oriented National

Salvation Party in supporting the motion, which passed by 203 votes to 2 with 180 abstentions.[16]

The lack of support for Erkmen underlines the important point that the general principles of the Inönü Doctrine were adhered to by all Turkish governments during the 1960s and 1970s—those formed by the CHP as well as those formed by Süleyman Demirel's Justice Party, which aspired to be the Democrat Party's successor. The principle of reserve was assured through correct—that is to say, diplomatic—relations with all of Turkey's southern neighbors. Neutrality entailed affirming the right of the Palestinians to statehood while upholding Israel's own legitimacy as a state in the region, and refusing to take sides in inter-Arab conflicts such as the one between Jordan and Syria. Maintaining the territorial status quo did not pose much of a problem during this period, due to the absence of major revisionist designs. And compartmentalization, finally, was scrupulously observed. As Ecevit, Inönü's successor at the helm of the CHP, declared in 1974: "We have shown that we will not accept the role of the West's agent in the Middle East."[17] This determination went so far that, when the United States lost its anti-Soviet monitoring stations in Iran following the 1979 Islamic revolution, Turkey refused to allow replacements to be installed on its territory.

Seeds of Change: 1980–1989

The Turkish junta that seized power in the September 12, 1980, military coup confronted a Middle East undergoing profound changes. Egyptian president Anwar Sadat's decision to sign a peace accord with Israel on March 26, 1979, isolated Egypt among the Arabs in the short run—but also initiated a new dynamic that bore the promise of an overall Arab-Israeli settlement in the longer run. Almost simultaneously, the Shah's overthrow transformed Iran's status from one of Turkey's most reliable regional allies into a rival with a potent ideology it was keen to export. An added complication arose just ten days after the Turkish coup when Iraq's leader Saddam Hussein launched his war against Iran. On the plus side for Turkey, Iraq thereby emerged as the primary barrier against Iranian expansionism. Moreover, as its exports to both countries soared, Turkey would reap considerable economic benefits during the eight-year conflict. On the negative side, however, both Iraq and Iran would emerge with greatly enhanced military capabilities. Even worse, from Ankara's perspective, the retreat of central authority during the war promoted a revival of Kurdish nationalism in northern Iraq that spilled over into Turkey as well. Indeed, the most serious and prolonged Kurdish rebellion in the Turkish Republic's history broke out in the early 1980s.

The radically new character of these developments for Turkey needs to be emphasized. In the past, the challenges to Turkey's interests arising from the Middle East were primarily indirect, significant only in the ways they affected its relations with the United States, the European states, or the Soviet Union. Now, all that was changing. Many of Turkey's southern neighbors were acquiring potent arsenals. Many of them possessed economies in which Turkey had a growing stake. And, in a most unprecedented and critical development, many of them were now capable of threatening the two central pillars of Turkey's domestic political regime: national unity (through sponsorship of Kurdish nationalism) and secularism (through sponsorship of Islamist radicalism).

It is therefore not surprising that voices dissenting from the Inönü Doctrine orthodoxy that had gone unchallenged for two decades would now begin to be heard. At various points in the war between Iraq and Iran, when the tide appeared to be turning in favor of the latter, for example, arguments were made that Turkey ought to intervene in order to prevent oil-rich northern Iraq from falling into Iranian hands.[18] But the majority of the Turkish elite, both military and civilian, continued to adhere to the Inönü Doctrine. Even before the coup, on April 19, 1980, the Ministry of Foreign Affairs announced that Turkey would not join the embargo against Iran organized by the United States. The military leadership continued that policy because—despite the general improvement in Turkish-American relations after the Soviet invasion of Afghanistan—it remained equally suspicious of American designs in the region. As one high-ranking Turkish security officer noted in an interview in the early 1980s, "The Americans are trying to push us into a war with Iran, but we won't fall for it." General Kenan Evren, the chief of staff who became head of state after the coup, wrote in his diary in August 1982 concerning ideas being floated about a Turkish-Jordanian-Egyptian alliance against Iran: "I believe the United States would also support such an alliance. But this would insert us into inter-Arab disputes, and that would not be good."[19] In the event, the failure of Iran's counteroffensive allowed Ankara to maintain its policy of neutrality until the end of the war.

Still, Turkey's Kurdish problem remained unresolved. Kurdish Workers Party (PKK in its Kurdish acronym) guerrillas fighting government forces in southeast Turkey had established cross-border bases in northern Iraq. With the Iraqi government unable to assert its authority over the region, the Turks found themselves obliged to step in. Ankara, which remained committed to the legitimacy of the existing borders, and Baghdad, anxious to maintain Turkish goodwill as it battled Iran but also unwilling to cede sovereignty in the north, accordingly signed a five-year Border Security and Cooperation Agreement in early 1983 that gave both sides the right of hot pursuit after infiltrators into each other's territory. Turkish air and ground forces then launched an assault on PKK bases in northern Iraq in late May, and such operations became a regular occurrence during the ensuing years. After the end of the Iran-Iraq war in 1988, however, Saddam Hussein moved to consolidate his control over the north and the hot-pursuit agreement was not renewed. Turkish cross-border operations ceased for the time being.

Syria also harbored hostile elements during the 1980s. Turkish complaints prompted Damascus to expel some PKK and Armenian militants (mostly to the Beqa' Valley in Lebanon or to Iraq), but Syrian sponsorship of these groups continued. In 1987 the Turks tried a new tack, offering to guarantee Syria 500 cubic meters per second of Euphrates water in return for a security cooperation agreement.[20] Once again, however, Syria's actions failed to satisfy Ankara, and on October 1, 1989, Turkish prime minister Turgut Ozal for the first time publicly accused Damascus of not living up to the agreement. Tensions increased still further three weeks later when Syrian MIG-21s shot down—Damascus later claimed accidentally—a Turkish land registry plane over Hatay province, killing five people.

Despite Ozal's growing impatience with both the Syrians and the Iraqis, the attitude of the Turkish security establishment as a whole toward the Arabs did not change throughout most of the 1980s. General Kenan Evren, who remained head of state until 1989, and İlter Türkmen, foreign minister during the first years of the military regime, both proved consistent proponents of the İnönü Doctrine. Turkey avoided involvement in regional disputes, advocated a settlement of the Arab-Israeli conflict that would respect the rights of all parties, and at the same time cultivated correct relations with the Arabs by criticizing Israel's policies in Lebanon and toward the Palestinians. By mid-decade, as a result, one Turkish analyst described Turkish-Israeli relations as being "at the lowest level" consistent with continued diplomatic relations.[21] At the same time, the old antipathy toward Arabs continued to permeate the attitudes of many Turkish leaders and ensured that Turkey maintained its distance from them.

Even as external developments (revolution in Iran, retreat of central authority in Iraq) coincided with and exacerbated the resurgence of Islamist and Kurdish challenges to Turkey's domestic political order during the 1980s, the strategic thinking of the Turkish military and civilian establishment remained rooted in the inward-looking worldview of the Inönü Doctrine. It was not until Turgut Ozal was able to impose his own foreign policy vision that the growing tension between Turkey's strategic reality and its strategic culture found a new resolution.

Revolutions: 1989–1993

Turgut Ozal had become prime minister after winning the first postcoup parliamentary elections in 1983, to the chagrin of a military command that distrusted him and had its own preferred candidates. With Kenan Evren occupying the presidency, it took Ozal a while to move from under the military's shadow and begin asserting his own leadership. This process reached its culmination in 1989: Evren retired, Ozal himself became president, and Ozal's Motherland Party—led by his lieutenants—maintained its absolute majority in parliament. Henceforth there could be no doubt about the locus of political authority in Turkey.

As it happened, the underlying geopolitical transformations of the 1980s were also coming to a head at the turn of the decade. Even before the collapse of the Soviet Union, it had become clear that Turkish strategists needed to reassess their security priorities. On December 13, 1989, the following item appeared in the Turkish press: "Brigadier General Hürşit Tolon, secretary general of the general staff, has stated that although the threat against Turkey from the north, that is, from the Soviet Union and Bulgaria, has significantly decreased, the threat from the south, that is, from Syria, Iraq, and Iran, has increased. General Tolon said that the missiles in the hands of the countries beyond Turkey's southern border, which have a range of 1,000 km, constitute a serious threat to Turkey."[22]

These concerns were amplified in an influential study subsequently prepared by Sitki Egeli of the Turkish Defense Ministry titled *Tactical Ballistic Missiles and Turkey.*[23] In it, Egeli reviewed the efforts by Syria, Iraq, and Iran since the late 1980s to develop ballistic missile programs as well as chemical and biological weapons of mass destruction; pointed to the collaboration between Syria and Iran in these fields since mid-1991; and raised the most troubling consideration of all: the possibility that all three southern neighbors would succeed in obtaining nuclear weapons within five to ten years.[24] Given Turkey's deteriorating relations with all three countries, and given new doubts about the Western interest in Turkey's security following the end of the Cold War, Egeli concluded by calling for an immediate enhancement of Turkish long-range air attack capabilities.[25]

If Turkey's security establishment found itself forced by external pressures to divert its attention toward the Middle East, however, President Ozal had always had his eye on the region. As a mid-level bureaucrat in 1973 he had written a letter to then Prime Minister Süleyman Demirel arguing that Iran's growing assertiveness toward its Arab neighbors (manifested by its seizure of three islets claimed by the United Arab Emirates) necessitated a forceful Turkish response: "Turkey ought to develop good relations with the Persian Gulf states, and make them feel that they are not alone against the Iranian threat. We need to reorder our relations with Iran. We must gradually bring out the fact that there is a large population of Turkish origin in Iran. If necessary we must build a big radio station in Van from which to broadcast Azeri-language programs."[26] The radicalism of Ozal's suggestion is rendered all the more remarkable by the fact that Turkey enjoyed good relations with the Iranian monarchy at the time. And when oil prices reached $35 a barrel in 1981, according to a respected journalist, he made an even more daring suggestion—to occupy northern Iraq: "Ozal expressed this desire to me in a conversation on condition that I not report it. But his suggestion was rejected by the coup's generals."[27]

Certainly Ozal himself denigrated the dominant tradition in Turkish foreign policy—which he identified with the person of Ismet Inönü—as "extraordinarily conservative" and devoted "merely to maintaining the status quo."[28] But he pointed to an exception: "Except for the era of the Democrat Party's Fatin Rüştü Zorlu. . . . This may even have been the reason for Zorlu's execution. . . . Otherwise why would a foreign minister be executed? . . . It is evident that Zorlu pursued quite an active foreign policy."[29] For Ozal, the new security environment of 1990 mandated a similar activism. Conservatism was no longer an option because, whether Turkey liked it or not, the status quo was dissolving all around it. And of all the perils unleashed by this dissolution, the one Ozal singled out as the most ominous was the easing of Cold War tensions. He explained this rather counterintuitive conclusion to a group of reporters on August 11, 1990: "Let me put it this way. Unfortunately—the reason I say unfortunately is not because I don't like the development; I do like it—the softening of East-West relations, the spread of world peace, is a development we very much desired and we very much supported but which also, from our perspective, entails an important point: Turkey's significance within NATO is decreasing."[30]

Surrounded by instability—but also new opportunity—on all sides, Turkey in Ozal's view could not allow its old allies to drift away. From this conclusion flowed a central imperative of his foreign policy: "It is absolutely necessary that the West be made to understand that Turkey is an indispensable country. It is necessary that this be achieved."[31] And for Ozal there was only one arena in which such indispensability could be demonstrated at that time:

> We must go to the Arab and Muslim countries one by one to talk with their leaders and to show them that we stand by them. Because, in the new balances that are being created, Turkey must show that it is not merely an important base of the West in this region but also a country with an Islamic identity willing to act as a bridge and to establish good relations with these states. . . . Because in the balances of the future . . . we will hold two cards. One is the card we hold with the Western countries, and the other is the card we hold with these Islamic and Arab countries. Turkey is obliged to carry both these cards. Its weight in the West is commensurate with its weight in the East. The greater our weight in the East, the greater it will be in the West as well.[32]

Here then lies the crux of Ozal's interest in the Middle East. Unlike most members of the Turkish security establishment at the turn of the decade, he was not simply reacting to the new threats originating in the region—he was also actively looking for opportunities to augment Turkey's overall strategic "weight."

This crucial distinction became most apparent during the crisis precipitated by Iraq's invasion of Kuwait on August 2, 1990. Ozal viewed the invasion as a golden opportunity to reap strategic benefits. He immediately adopted a strong anti-Iraqi stance, announcing Turkey's compliance with a UN Security Council decision to impose an embargo on Iraq and closing the pipeline that carried Iraqi oil through Turkey to the Mediterranean. On August 12, he asked parliament to grant him authority to declare war, to send troops to other countries, and to invite foreign troops to Turkey. In part due to the opposition of deputies from his own Motherland Party (including Mesut Yilmaz), however, Ozal's request was watered down: he would be given "permission"—not "authority"—to take those measures only in the event of an attack on Turkey by Iraq. Indeed, although Ozal ultimately succeeded in his overall objective of earning Turkey a central role in the calculations of Washington's regional policymakers, his every step came under withering domestic criticism.

One set of concerns revolved around his practice of making decisions by himself after consulting a small group of close advisers rather than the institutional hierarchies of the security establishment—in particular, the Ministry of Foreign Affairs (MFA) and the Turkish Armed Forces (TAF). Ozal's go-it-alone approach appears to have played a part in the resignations of Foreign Minister Ali Bozer on October 11, Defense Minister Safa Giray on October 19, and Chief of Staff Necip Torumtay on December 3, 1990.

Administrative or turf resentments were not the only issue, however. The TAF and the MFA also opposed Ozal's desire to deploy the Turkish Second Army along Iraq's borders and to send a contingent of Turkish forces to join the coalition army massing around Kuwait. Partly the reservations were due to technical reasons: the TAF was still in the early stages of the military modernization drive initiated in the late 1980s and was not fully prepared for an offensive deployment.[33] On a deeper level, however, they reflected the conviction that Ozal's ultimate aim was to invade and occupy Iraq's Mosul province—a conviction that aroused all the underlying antipathies and anxieties of the İnönü Doctrine.

General Torumtay, for example, insisted that Ozal had raised the issue of an intervention into Iraq repeatedly during the Kuwait crisis.[34] In two books he wrote after retiring, Torumtay described that idea as "a gamble, an adventure" that threatened to drag "our country into the Middle Eastern swamp"[35] and "a kind of bait that would lure Turkey into the Middle East's bottomless problems and would drain our nation's blood and resources."[36] But, he assured his readers, "the Turkish nation and its commanders have not forgotten how we were dragged into World War I and its tragic outcome, a historical example of an adventurist enterprise arising from individual decisions and reckless ambitions."[37] Torumtay's use of the word "bait" suggested the influence of dark forces seeking to manipulate Turkey. Kemal Yavuz, commander of the Second Army during the crisis, elaborated on this point: "We opposed Ozal's position in its entirety. . . . The most important reason was that his policy was inimical to our national interests . . . that it did not arise from a national outlook . . . that it was derived from the ideas of another country [the United States]."[38]

Most of Turkey's opposition politicians also accused Ozal of sacrificing Turkish interests for those of the United States. Erdal İnönü, Ismet's son and leader of the Social Democrat Populist Party, did so during an early parliamentary debate on the Kuwait crisis in words that vividly evoked his father's outlook: "Turkey should carefully and scrupulously avoid interfering in disputes between Arab states; we must not interfere in their internal affairs. . . . We must keep away from the appearance of taking the side of any party in regional disputes, and we especially must never give the impression that we are a vehicle of the West in solving such disputes."[39] Inönü's deputy, Deniz Baykal, added: "We are not the nightclub bouncers of the Middle East. . . . The Turkish soldier who was not deployed on behalf of Palestine should not be used to install the Shaikh of Kuwait in his palace. . . . They want to reduce us to the position of the West's agent in the Middle East. We are not the gendarmes of the Middle East. We are not accountable to the United States."[40] Bülent Ecevit of the Democratic Left Party also joined the chorus, complaining sometime later: "Turkey, which unfurled the world's first banner of resistance against Western imperialism during the 1920's, has now become Western imperialism's go-between and agent on its territory and in its region. This is our history's most bitter contradiction."[41]

Nor were such sentiments confined to the left wing of the political spectrum. Süleyman Demirel also harkened back to the dark days surrounding World War I, at one point comparing Ozal to the Young Turk leader Enver Pasha.[42] Two days later he asked his colleagues in parliament: "If Iraq occupies Kuwait, why is Turkey threatened? . . . Look gentlemen, let me speak quite plainly; we lost martyrs in those deserts for 400 years. Therefore take care. It's a shame, it's a sin. Nobody has the right to insert Turkey into the wrong alliance at the wrong time." He reminded his listeners of insects that fly too near the flame: "Stay away from the flame. Flying around a flame is not a question of courage, it's an adventure."[43] In private he was more explicit about his concerns, telling a Turkish journalist: "The United States is pushing for war, and is determined to involve Turkey as well. If Turkey remains outside this event, tomorrow it will emerge as a great power in the Middle East. The West does not want Turkey to grow so powerful."[44]

Most of Turkey's mainstream center-left and center-right political leaders, then, joined the majority of their counterparts in the civilian and military bureaucracies in opposing Ozal. As individuals many of these people may well have been influenced by administrative sensitivities, political rivalries, or even personal resentments. But it would be a disservice to a number of them as well as an analytical mistake to reduce their opposition to such considerations. The criticisms leveled at Ozal derived their coherence and intensity from the underlying strategic culture in which they were embedded, and in the discourse in which they were articulated. The differences between Ozal and his critics really were, at root, doctrinal.

Did Ozal in fact entertain grandiose ambitions toward Iraq as his critics suspected? In public, he restricted himself to lamenting the technical consequences of the failure to send a small contingent of troops to the Gulf: "We would have gained experience. . . . Our officers would have been able to study the century's most advanced [military] technologies up close."[45] In private, however, he appears to have been less guarded. According to Hüsamettin Cindoruk, leader of the Democratic Turkey Party, Ozal told him in late 1991 or early 1992 that "Turkey lost an opportunity, but that opportunity still exists" and added that occupying the area around Arbil and Mosul in northern Iraq would be a "very easy operation . . . and it would rescue Iraq from Saddam, strip it of its weapons, and on top of that make Turkey sovereign [egemen] over the oil region. I was unable to make either the [Turkish] military or the government accept this idea. But this chance is not yet lost."[46]

It was "not yet lost" because dramatic new conditions had arisen in northern Iraq as a consequence of the war. The massive influx into Turkey of Iraqi Kurdish refugees, the creation of a de facto autonomous entity in Iraqi Kurdistan, and the ability of the PKK to take advantage of the ensuing chaos to consolidate its presence there, all confronted Turkey with a situation it could not walk away from. Once again, as with the missile scare of the late 1980s, there were two sets of Turkish responses to the new external challenge. Ozal and his associates viewed the retreat of Iraqi sovereignty and the emergence of Kurdish nationalism as an opportunity to project Turkish power outwards—perhaps by presenting Ankara as a more attractive power center than Baghdad to the Iraqi Kurds. Their opponents viewed those developments as a threat to Turkey's domestic order and cast about for ways to restore the status quo ante. At first, Ozal had the initiative: the magnitude of the coalition victory, the widespread opprobrium in which Saddam Hussein's regime was now held, and the evident determination of the United States to prevent him from regaining control over Iraq all seemed to vindicate Ozal and served—at least temporarily—to put his critics on the defensive.

Immediately after declaring on March 2, 1991, that "Turkey should leave its former passive and hesitant policies and engage in an active foreign policy,"[47] Ozal began reaching out to the Iraqi Kurds. He invited their representatives to Turkey for official talks; issued Turkish diplomatic passports to the two main Iraqi Kurdish leaders, Masud Barzani of the Kurdish Democratic Party (KDP) and Jalal Talabani of the Patriotic Union of Kurdistan (PUK); and allowed both the KDP and PUK to open liaison offices in Ankara.[48] On April 7, Ozal called for the creation of a UN-administered Kurdish zone in northern Iraq. This statement, in the words of one analyst, "meant going back on what had hitherto been a fixed point in policy towards Iraq—that is, firm opposition to any sort of partition of the country, either implicit or explicit."[49] The TAF, by contrast, reportedly argued that Turkey should cooperate with Saddam Hussein's government to crush Kurdish separatism in northern Iraq.[50]

On the ground, meanwhile, the PKK's escalating campaign necessitated a military response. Following an attack that killed nine Turkish soldiers, the TAF on August 5, 1991, launched the first military operation against PKK positions across the border since the expiration of the Turkish-Iraqi hot-pursuit agreement in 1988. It was therefore also the first such operation undertaken without Baghdad's consent. Turkish military and intelligence units established offices in northern Iraqi towns such as Dohuk, Zakho, Arbil, and Salahaddin, and several more military incursions ensued, culminating in a major operation involving 15,000 troops in October 1992. Here was the dilemma confronting the Turkish generals and their political allies: even as they opposed what they viewed as Ozal's imperial ambitions, they found themselves pulled—precisely because of their overriding concern with domestic order—into escalating military interventions in northern Iraq as well as political intrigues with the KDP, PUK, and a growing list of other Iraqi actors.

While Ozal's opponents viewed the reimposition of central control over Iraqi Kurdistan by Saddam Hussein—or any equally authoritarian successor—as the only way out of their dilemma, Ozal continued to seek more radical changes of the status quo. He pursued a two-pronged strategy: initiating a public dialogue about multiculturalism at home in an attempt to transform Kurdish identity from a threat to the domestic order into an asset in foreign policy, and keeping up the pressure for change in Iraq. As late as February 8, 1993, at a meeting with President George Bush in the White House, he called for Saddam Hussein's overthrow and the establishment of a "democratic [and presumably less centralized] regime" in Iraq.[51] Just two months later, however, the Turkish president died of a heart attack.

His death tilted the balance of power within the security establishment, and Turkey's foreign policy once again fell under the dominance of the Inönü Doctrine during the rest of the 1990s. Nevertheless, far from permitting any disengagement from the Middle East, the geopolitical dynamics of the region continued to pull Turkey into a spiral of ever-escalating involvement.

Confusion: 1993–2000

This central paradox—the objective necessity of activism within the sub-jective ideological framework of the Inönü Doctrine—dominated Tur-key's relations with the Middle East throughout the remainder of the de-cade. It confused and subverted in turn the pro-Western liberalism of Prime Minister Tansu Çiller and her team from 1993 to 1995, the cautious inward orientation of the military commanders who sidelined Turkey's civilian officials from 1996 to 1998, and the ultranationalism of Prime Minister Bülent Ecevit's governing coalition since 1999.

Ozal's death brought Süleyman Demirel to the presidency and Demi-rel's protégé Tansu Çiller to the leadership of the True Path Party (DYP). Çiller enjoyed a good working relationship with the military at the outset: she quickly proved to be a hawk on security issues, approving tough (and occasionally extralegal) measures against the PKK insurrection and adopting an equally uncompromising stance toward Turkey's foreign protagonists. A revision in 1992 of the "National Security Policy Docu-ment"—the basic blueprint of Turkish security strategy—had already placed Kurdish separatism at the top of the list of threats confronting Turkey and thereby confirmed the replacement of Russia and Greece by Syria, Iraq, and Iran (in their capacity as the PKK's main havens) as Turkey's primary external protagonists.[52] At the same time, Turkish se-curity planners continued to point to the weapons of mass destruction and ballistic missile capabilities of those countries as threats in their own right.

The difficulty, however, was that the predominant conviction within the security establishment that Turkey could not trust the motives of other countries, either in the region or in the West, tended to rule out multilat-eral or cooperative solutions to these problems. A study prepared by four colonels at the Turkish Armed Forces Academy in 1993, for example, speculated that the United States—and its oil companies—might stand to gain from the creation of a Kurdish state in northern Iraq.[53] Another colo-nel went even further, writing in a book published by the Turkish General Staff that the United States also supported the PKK and that it, "under the pretext of protecting human rights, is assisting the formation of a Kurdish state in northern Iraq which will eventually demand land from Turkey."[54] Given such suspicions, given Baghdad's inability to resolve the dilemma by successfully reimposing its own authority, and, finally, given the fact that the military modernization drive had by mid-decade given the TAF a greatly enhanced offensive capability, Turkey's leaders saw no option but to act on their own. On March 19, 1995, accordingly, 35,000 Turkish troops backed by jets, tanks, and artillery launched the biggest operation in northern Iraq to date (and the biggest overall since the 1974 Cyprus operation).

This incursion was very much the TAF's brainchild, conceived and presented—without operational details—to the prime minister months before. Indeed, no formal decision to proceed was required, since parliament had authorized the cabinet to send troops abroad at its discretion in January 1991 (in response to Ozal's demands), and the cabinet had subsequently in its turn authorized the Office of the Chiefs of the General Staff to determine whether and when such deployments were necessary. In short, the TAF had had a standing authorization for foreign interventions since 1991.[55] Consequently, neither the Foreign Ministry nor the rest of the cabinet received advance warning in 1995, learning about the operation only as it actually got under way. Despite accusations by opposition leaders such as Mesut Yilmaz that the operation was "imposed" on a reluctant government by the TAF, however, the truth seems to be that Çiller was enthusiastic and maintained a good working relationship with the military leadership throughout the crisis.

But to what end? As it rapidly became clear that most PKK elements had escaped the onslaught and that the incursion by itself would not suffice to eradicate permanently their presence in northern Iraq, various suggestions were put forward. One, made by Defense Minister Mehmet Gölhan on March 21, was the creation of a security zone south of the border, similar to the one maintained by Israel in Lebanon at that time. DSP leader Bülent Ecevit supported the idea, although he took care to specify that the security zone should only be set up with Baghdad's acquiescence and only until such time as Iraqi sovereignty could be restored to the region.[56] Nevertheless, the MFA vigorously opposed any infringement on Iraqi sovereignty, and the TAF backed away from the idea as well.[57]

A second suggestion—raised by Prime Minister Çiller and President Demirel as the incursion was winding down—was to effect minor border revisions that would transfer some strategic heights to Turkish control. Although Çiller and Demirel both stressed that such revisions would not be undertaken unilaterally, violent criticisms from Iraq, the Arab League, and Iran forced Turkey's ambassador to the United Nations to issue a formal denial that Turkey intended to change its frontier with Iraq.[58] In fact, it was evident to all that such a step would not suffice to resolve Turkey's fundamental problem with the PKK presence in Iraq.

More ambitious was the suggestion that Operation Provide Comfort, the U.S.-led airborne effort to safeguard the northern Iraqi safe haven, be given a ground operations component as well. This would have entailed the deployment of a multinational force including Turkish troops and thereby, not coincidentally, also have provided an umbrella for a more institutionalized TAF presence against the PKK. The idea, which emerged during a visit to Washington by Çiller's adviser, Emre Gönensay, in late April, immediately provoked a storm of protest back home. Newly appointed Foreign Minister Erdal Inönü and Deputy Prime Minister Hikmet Çetin, both of the CHP wing of Çiller's coalition government, denounced the proposal and insisted that the only solution was the restoration of Iraqi sovereignty over the north. Çetin went on to call for a lifting of the embargo on Iraq and pointed out that, in contrast to the United States and Britain, "France is very close to our thinking. Moved by its own interests, Russia seems to hold a similar opinion."[59] DSP leader Bülent Ecevit, meanwhile, warned that the United States might be manipulating Turkey in order to realize its own ambitions of creating an American mandate in northern Iraq.[60] More than a year later, he elaborated on this theme: "My personal opinion is that the Americans have a three-stage plan wherein first autonomy is granted to northern Iraq, then a federation is established, then an independent state under an American mandate. . . . Then they'll start saying to us: 'you give some land as well.' This is what I think . . . but of course I have no documents to prove it. . . . Either that, or the Americans really have no policy at all."[61]

Such suspicions sustained the aversion within the security establishment to any radical revision of Turkey's Middle East strategy and therefore—whether or not the ultimate ambitions concerning Iraq of Çiller's team paralleled those of Ozal, as many believed—doomed any possibility of a prolonged presence in northern Iraq in concert with the United States. Emre Gönensay was forced to backtrack, declaring that the suggestion was merely his personal opinion and not an official proposal to the United States.[62] On May 4, 1995, Defense Minister Gölhan announced that all Turkish troops had left northern Iraq.

This episode illustrates the main characteristics of Turkey's Middle East policy under Çiller: a civilian government willing to take bold action but lacking a coherent overall regional policy and in any case increasingly marginalized in the decision-making process; a military leadership reluctantly dragged into an escalating spiral of cross-border operations; and a foreign ministry whose cadres (with some exceptions, most of them Ozal protégés) continued to view their role as one of countering foreign policy "adventurism."

A second illustrative development in Çiller's regional policy was the considerable improvement in relations with Israel. The signing of the Declaration of Principles between Israel and the PLO on September 13, 1993, eased the stigma on close association with the Jewish state and made possible a flurry of contacts leading up to Çiller's visit to Israel in November 1994. Among the more positive reasons for the rapprochement was Turkish concern about the growing political and even military coordination between Greece, Syria, and Iran, culminating in the 1995 news reports that Greece and Syria had gone ahead and concluded a military agreement on the wartime use of each other's air bases. In addition, the Turks hoped to tap into advanced Israeli military technology for their own ongoing military modernization program, and also to benefit from the influence of the Jewish lobby in Washington.

As so often in the past, however, the broad consensus brought about by these considerations masked a dichotomy between those who viewed the rapprochement with Israel as a necessary response to external pressures that nevertheless ought not upset Turkey's traditional Middle East policy, and those who viewed it as an opportunity for an entirely new departure in the region. This dichotomy was apparent even within Çiller's closest circle of advisers. Volkan Vural, for example, articulated the MFA's desire to maintain a degree of neutrality between Israel and its Arab opponents: "I participated in many of these talks; I went to Israel with Çiller. We always made it clear that our cooperation cannot be against any Arab country . . . cannot hurt the Arabs. . . . We urged them to be less intransigent . . . to be fair to the Palestinians." Emre Gönensay, by contrast, seems to have been ready to contemplate a more exclusive alliance between Turkey and Israel as well as Jordan.[63] It is noteworthy that at the same time that this debate was going on, Jordan's King Hussein proposed to Israeli prime minister Shimon Peres a strategic partnership between Jordan, Israel, Turkey, and a post-Saddam Iraq—in short, an updated Baghdad Pact.[64]

Çiller herself certainly broke with Turkish diplomatic tradition—for example, by referring to Israel as the "Promised Land"—to such an extent that one knowledgeable observer concluded: "Her warm regard for Israel appears to be personal as well as strategic."[65] Nevertheless, whatever her true sentiments, Çiller failed to effect any significant changes in Turkish policy toward the Middle East. This was due to three important differences between her and Ozal: first, she never formulated a coherent regional strategy; second, she rarely enjoyed the free hand of governing without coalition partners; and third, she lacked Ozal's skill in knowing how far to buck the Turkish security establishment. This last factor led to her downfall domestically as well: her decision to join a coalition government led by Necmettin Erbakan's Islamist Welfare Party after the December 1995 national elections earned her the bitter and permanent enmity of the country's secular-minded military and bureaucratic elites.

Although Erbakan and Çiller served as prime minister and foreign minister respectively for almost exactly one year beginning June 28, 1996, neither played a significant foreign policy role. Erbakan's early attempt to reorient Turkey toward the Muslim world came to an end after the fiasco of his trip to Libya in October 1996, when he was harangued on Kurdish rights by the Libyan leader Muammar Kaddafi. And Çiller was so engrossed in domestic political intrigues that she paid almost no attention to foreign affairs, rarely visiting the Foreign Ministry and rarely reading the briefings prepared for her. Instead, foreign policy formulation once again fell under the control of the institutions most closely associated with the Inönü Doctrine: the TAF as the dominant force and the MFA as its junior partner.

Nevertheless, a quick review of developments might suggest that a fundamental transformation in Turkish policy toward the Middle East took place during this period. TAF operations in northern Iraq assumed a regular and routine character while the efforts of Turkish officials to deal with the various factions there pulled them deeper and deeper into the region's internal politics. As the Turkish campaign against the PKK widened, moreover, Turkish attention to Syria increased, with tensions beginning to rise during the first half of 1996 and nearly culminating in a war during the fall of 1998. Relations with Iran deteriorated as well, particularly after the Turkish National Security Council identified "religious reaction" as the number one threat to Turkey's security in February 1997.[66] By contrast, Turkey's relationship with Israel was significantly enhanced by the signing of a Military Cooperation and Training Agreement on February 23, 1996. And Jordan drew closer as well, participating (as an observer) in the American-Israeli-Turkish Operation Reliant Mermaid naval maneuvers of January 1998 and holding joint military exercises with Turkey on a regular basis.

Can it then be concluded that Turkey's security establishment was abandoning its traditional commitment to stay out of the Middle East as much as possible? Did the more assertive tone struck by Turkish officials signify a change in basic doctrinal outlook as well? Once again, the crucial distinction is between a tactical and reluctant response arising out of necessity—the imperative of combating Kurdish and Islamist challenges to the domestic political order—and an affirmative choice to take advantage of new conditions in order to reorient the country's overall security strategy.

In the case of Iraq, the dominant attitude within the TAF and MFA remained a nostalgia for the pre-Kuwait invasion days before Kurdish nationalism reignited and the north fell away from Baghdad's control. The implications of this attitude were spelled out by a Turkish diplomat in the following manner: "Our top priority is Iraq's territorial integrity. . . . We are against a Kurdish state [in northern Iraq]. . . . Our policy on Iraq diverges from that of the United States because the Americans want Saddam out while we do not index our policy to [the presence of] Saddam."[67] In practice, according to a well-informed analyst, this translated into Turkish support—conveyed by an official delegation that traveled to Baghdad—both for the rapprochement between Saddam Hussein and the KDP and for the subsequent joint Iraqi-KDP assault on Arbil at the end of August 1996 that wiped out much of the American-backed Iraqi opposition infrastructure.[68] After that debacle, the situation stabilized into a stalemate in which the United States allowed Turkey a free hand against the PKK in southeastern Turkey and northern Iraq in return for Turkish acquiescence in the maintenance of sufficient American pressure to prevent Saddam Hussein from completely retaking the north.

The same frustrated desire to reestablish correct but aloof relations characterized policy toward Syria. Tensions arising from that country's continuing support for the PKK and Turkey's expansion of its dam network in southeastern Anatolia approached the boiling point in 1996. Following increasingly severe warnings by Turkish politicians throughout April, a series of mysterious explosions shook Damascus—one reportedly targeting PKK leader Abdullah Ocalan's apartment—and other Syrian cities in May. Mutual military buildups and small-scale border skirmishes ensued in June. But a showdown was averted in large part due to the resistance of the Foreign Ministry, which feared a messy conflict that would incur the enmity of much of the Arab world.

Two years later, however, the TAF overrode MFA objections and initiated a more determined campaign. A National Security Council meeting on September 30, 1998, ratified a plan of action drawn up by Chief of Staff General Hüseyin Kivrikoğlu, and troop buildups along the border ensued. Kivrikoğlu declared the next day that "an undeclared state of war" already existed between Turkey and Syria, and a week later the Turkish cabinet reportedly issued a final forty-five-day ultimatum to the Syrian government. The outcome was a complete success: Damascus ca-

pitulated, expelling Ocalan and closing down PKK activities on its territory in accordance with an agreement signed with Turkey on October 20.
What is striking about this episode is how quickly bilateral tensions subsequently evaporated, demonstrating that the TAF's anti-Syrian stance—
far from heralding an ambitious new regional strategy—was driven entirely by concern for domestic security. When the PKK lost its salience as
an issue of contention, Turkish-Syrian relations returned to normal.

The absence of any serious strategic reorientation is even more clearly
visible in Turkey's relations with Iran. Ankara repeatedly accused Tehran
of providing support to both the PKK and radical Turkish Islamists during
this period, but these accusations never brought the two countries to the
brink of military conflict. Indeed, they did not even interrupt bilateral
economic relations. The signing by Erbakan's government on August 12,
1996, of a $20 billion deal to purchase Iranian natural gas, although
strongly opposed by the United States, enjoyed the full support of Turkey's
foreign policy establishment. As one MFA official put it: "We seek good
relations with Iran. We do not feel as threatened by Iran as the United
States does."[69] Bilateral relations rebounded to their cool but correct norm
in 1998 from the nadir of the previous year: Iran's foreign minister talked
of a "new era" between the two countries,[70] and in June Turkey and Iran
signed a security agreement to cooperate against terrorism and crime.

On the other hand, it is true that during the 1996–98 period the TAF if
anything strengthened its ties to Israel and that this did indeed constitute
a radical departure from past practice. Even here, however, it is instructive
to note the tension between the realpolitik considerations underlying the
relationship and the normative sentiments still prevalent within the Turkish military.

In the first place, as M. Hakan Yavuz has pointed out, a major factor in
the rapprochement was the desire to thwart Israel's long-standing sympathy for Kurdish nationalism—a sympathy arising from a common concern
about Arab nationalism.[71] The 1993 study prepared by the Turkish Armed
Forces Academy cited earlier, for example, described Israel as one of the
countries providing "direct assistance and support" to Kurdish separatists
in Turkey.[72] More generally, the exaggerated assessment of Israel's global
influence has cut both ways, making Israel seem an even more desirable
partner while at the same time exacerbating apprehensions about it.[73] This
is illustrated in a comment made by Kemal Yavuz, the Second Army commander who went on to head the War Academy before his retirement
and who remains an influential spokesman for the military viewpoint:
"Israel has always—but always—directed America's Middle East policy.

. . . [Turkish-Israeli cooperation] is a correct choice . . . on condition that some distance is maintained. Because not even America knows what Israel intends to do."[74]

Further exacerbating such suspicions was the lukewarm stance adopted by Israel during Turkey's two crises in 1998: the conflict with Syria discussed earlier and a dispute over the attempt by Greek Cypriots to deploy Russian S-300 missiles on the island. In the Syrian case Israel went so far as to reduce its military presence on the Golan Heights in order, according to Israeli defense minister Yitzhak Mordechai, "to preclude the slightest suspicion of any Israeli involvement."[75] And in the words of an analyst citing an Israel Defense Forces (IDF) Radio news report on September 7, 1998: "Israel diplomatically rebuked Turkey . . . when Turkey inquired whether Israel would support it in a possible war with Cyprus."[76] This manifest reluctance to get embroiled in Turkey's conflicts has certainly been noted by security planners in Ankara.

The Turkish-Israeli relationship remains significant and is likely to be enduring, but the evidence so far suggests that neither side views it as anything more than a marriage of convenience. From the Turkish perspective during the 1996–98 period, it no more heralded a sea change in the underlying doctrinal outlook than did the increased tensions with Iraq, Syria, and Iran. For most Turkish military officers and diplomats, interaction with Israelis and Arabs alike remained more a matter of necessity than choice.

By the beginning of 1999 the most urgent of the security issues confronting Turkey had eased. Syria's crackdown on the PKK and the subsequent capture of Abdullah Ocalan by Turkish agents led to a suspension of Kurdish guerrilla activity. At the same time, the other main threat perceived by the Turkish establishment—the threat of an Islamist electoral takeover—also receded following Necmettin Erbakan's ouster in June 1997 and his subsequent banishment from political activity. In the national elections of April 1999, the Islamist party fell to third place, its votes dropping from 21 percent to 15 percent of the total. As a result of these developments, and also as a reflection of new chief of staff Kivrikoğlu's more low-key style, the TAF allowed elected civilian politicians to begin reasserting themselves.

Turkey's new coalition cabinet was composed of the two biggest election winners, Bülent Ecevit's Democratic Left Party (DSP) and the ultrarightist National Action Party (MHP), along with the fourth-place Motherland Party. Prime Minister Ecevit, whose nationalism had become increasingly prominent during the previous decade, and fellow DSP member Foreign Minister Ismail Cem both came into office calling for Turkey to play a more self-confident role on the world stage. The MHP, for its part, had always favored a bold stance in foreign affairs and was the only major party to back Turgut Ozal during the Kuwaiti crisis. Yet in practice Ecevit's government has so far failed to devise any new approaches toward the Middle East and has in fact implemented regional policies closer to the principles of the Inönü Doctrine than was the case with any previous government since the time before Ozal.

Thus, Ecevit's government followed up its calls for the lifting of sanctions against Baghdad by deciding in October 2000 to upgrade its diplomatic mission there and to resume rail links and limited air flights between the two countries. Turkey has also been urging Iraqi Kurdish leaders to negotiate with Saddam Hussein in order to reach a settlement that preserves Iraq's territorial integrity.[77] Relations with Damascus, meanwhile, have improved even more dramatically, particularly after President Necdet Sezer surprised the Syrians by attending Hafiz al-Assad's funeral on June 13, 2000. The two countries signed a security cooperation agreement in September, and Syrian vice president Abd al-Halim Khaddam traveled to Ankara the following month in order to "turn over a new leaf" in bilateral relations.[78] President Bashar Assad is expected to visit Turkey in order to sign a comprehensive declaration of principles between the two countries. Finally, on August 13, 1999, Turkey signed a security cooperation agreement with Iran as well. And although Ankara still voices occasional complaints about Tehran's support for the PKK, some officials express more understanding. Ambassador Vural, for example, argues: "There can never be complete satisfaction. . . . They always have the desire not to allow anything detrimental to Turkey's interests . . . but power is so diffuse there. . . . We need a more sophisticated approach toward Iran."[79]

Turkey's improving relations with its Arab and Muslim neighbors have been paralleled by a noticeable cooling toward Israel. President Sezer on October 25, 2000, criticized Israel's reaction to the latest Palestinian intifada by declaring that "the violent acts perpetrated against our Palestinian brothers following Friday prayers at . . . the Haram al-Sharif, which is one of Islam's most holy sites, has deeply wounded the Islamic world."[80] While Ankara is unlikely to sever its military links with Israel altogether, it did postpone the annual Reliant Mermaid joint naval maneuvers scheduled for December 2000—reportedly in order not to offend Arab sensibilities during the ongoing Israeli-Palestinian conflict.[81] In this respect as well, then, there has been a steady retreat since April 1999 toward the correct but aloof and neutral postures of the past.

Nothing illustrates this retreat better than current Turkish thinking about a strategic axis with Israel and Jordan and possibly other Arab states. MFA undersecretary Faruk Loğoğlu states unambiguously: "No. We don't view such a thing positively. . . . We don't want new divisions in the region."[82] Or, in General Yavuz's characteristically candid words, "Ismet Inönü put it very well: 'Getting into a sack with the Arab is like getting into a sack with a snake. You never know when it will bite you.' . . . It is not possible to enter into such an agreement with Arabs . . . they kiss you on both cheeks and then stab you in the back."[83]

Conclusions

It seems indisputable that there can be no complete reversion to the Inönü Doctrine in the foreseeable future. As another influential security analyst, retired General Sadi Ergüvenc, points out, the Middle East has become Turkey's "backyard" because developments there directly affect Turkey's domestic and foreign interests. Turkey therefore does not have the luxury of abandoning the region to other actors with interests of their own.[84]

At the same time, however, there is no sign on the horizon of a new overall strategy to guide Turkey's inescapable involvement in the Middle East. Despite their very different outlooks, each of the regimes since Ozal's has failed to formulate such a strategy. Until a leadership emerges that is capable and willing to do so, therefore, Turkey's regional policies will continue to be ambivalent, ad hoc, and reactive.

Notes

1. Alan Makovsky, "Israeli-Turkish Relations: A Turkish Periphery Strategy?" in *Reluctant Neighbor: Turkey's Role in the Middle East,* ed. Henri J. Barkey (Washington, D.C.: United States Institute of Peace Press, 1996), 147.

2. Henri J. Barkey, "Under the Gun: Turkish Foreign Policy and the Kurdish Question," in *The Kurdish Nationalist Movement in the 1990's,* ed. Robert Olson (Lexington: University Press of Kentucky, 1996), 70.

3. See, for example, Kemal H. Karpat, "Turkish and Arab-Israeli Relations," in *Turkey's Foreign Policy in Transition: 1950–1974,* ed. Kemal H. Karpat (Leiden: E. J. Brill, 1975), 110.

4. Mehmet Gönlübol and Halûk Ülman, "Türk Diş Politikasinin Yirmi Yili:

1945–1965," *Ankara Üniversitesi Siyasal Bilgiler Fakültesi Dergisi* 21, no. 1 (March 1966): 168.

5. Karpat, "Turkish and Arab-Israeli Relations," 122.

6. See, for example, the White House OCB memorandum "Preparation of Courses of Action against Communism in Syria," dated January 26, 1956, encl. 1, p. 2. USDD, 1993: microfiche 002954 (Washington, D.C.: Carrollton Press, later Research Publications International, 1975–). (Note: USDD refers to the U.S. Declassified Documents Reference System.)

7. Cable from Secretary of State Dulles in Ankara to President Eisenhower, January 29, 1958. *USDD, 1987:* 003223. See Malik Mufti, *Sovereign Creations: Pan-Arabism and Political Order in Syria and Iraq* (Ithaca, N.Y.: Cornell University Press, 1996), 99–108.

8. Amikam Nachmani, *Israel, Turkey, and Greece: Uneasy Relations in the East Mediterranean* (London: Frank Cass, 1987), 74–76. See also "Text of a Letter by Prime Minister Ben-Gurion to the President of the United States of America," July 24, 1958. *USDD,* 1989: 00518.

9. Mufti, *Sovereign Creations,* 131–32.

10. For an extended treatment of this point, see Malik Mufti, "The United States and Nasserist Pan-Arabism," in *The Middle East and the United States: A Historical and Political Reassessment,* ed. David W. Lesch (Boulder, Colo.: Westview, 1999), 163–82.

11. At the height of the 1957 Syrian crisis, for example, Undersecretary Christian Herter wrote to Secretary of State Dulles: "Our telegram of inquiry to Ambassador Warren [in Ankara] brought a somewhat disquieting answer in its implications that the political planners of the Turkish government wanted to go it alone in Syria whereas there were doubts and hesitations on the part of the military": "Memorandum for the Secretary," October 14, 1957, p. 2. *USDD,* 1985: 00357. On Menderes's inability to intervene in Iraq following the overthrow of the monarchy in July 1958, one analyst writes: "However much he may have wanted to make the move, his forces were not prepared for attack from this angle and could not have been deployed rapidly in numbers sufficient to accomplish this objective, given the difficulties of terrain and lack of roads in the vicinity of the Iraqi-Turkish border": George S. Harris, *Troubled Alliance: Turkish-American Problems in Historical Perspective, 1945–1971* (Washington, D.C.: American Enterprise Institute for Public Policy Research, 1972), 66.

12. Ismail Soysal, "The 1955 Baghdad Pact," *Studies on Turkish-Arab Relations* 5 (1990): 83.

13. Philip Robins, *Turkey and the Middle East* (London: Royal Institute of International Affairs/Pinter Publishers, 1991), 27.

14. Kemal H. Karpat, "Turkish-Soviet Relations," in *Turkey's Foreign Policy in Transition: 1950–1974,* ed. Kemal H. Karpat, 73–107; Feroz Ahmad, *The Turkish Experiment in Democracy: 1950–1975* (Boulder, Colo.: Westview Press, 1977), 407.

15. Ismail Soysal, "Turkish-Arab Diplomatic Relations after the Second World War (1945–1986)," *Studies on Turkish-Arab Relations* 1 (1986): 259–62.

16. M. Hakan Yavuz, "Turkish-Israeli Relations through the Lens of the Turkish Identity Debate," *Journal of Palestine Studies* 27, no. 1 (autumn 1997): 35n.10.

17. From a speech reproduced in Bülent Ecevit, *Diş Politika* (Ankara: Ajans-Türk Matbaasi, 1976), 76.

18. Birol A. Yeşilada, "Turkish Foreign Policy toward the Middle East," in *The Political and Socioeconomic Transformation of Turkey,* ed. Attila Eralp, Muharrem Tünay, and Birol A. Yeşilada (Westport, Conn.: Praeger, 1993), 181; Suha Bölükbaşi, *Türkiye ve Yakinindaki Orta Doğu* (Ankara: Diş Politika Enstitüsü, n.d.), 33, 75.

19. Kenan Evren, *Kenan Evren'in Anilari,* 6 vols. (Istanbul: Milliyet Yayinlari, 1990–92), 3:226.

20. Michael M. Gunther, *The Kurds and the Future of Turkey* (New York: St. Martin's Press, 1997), 93.

21. Soysal, "Turkish-Arab Diplomatic Relations," 265.

22. *Milliyet* newspaper, December 13, 1989, 14, in FBIS-WEU-89–241 (December 18, 1989), 22–27.

23. Sitki Egeli, *Taktik Balistik Füzeler ve Türkiye* (Ankara: Milli Savunma Bakanliği Savunma Sanayii Müsterşarliği, 1993).

24. Ibid., 71–76, 140.

25. Ibid., 84–87, 141–42.

26. Quoted in Mehmet Barlas, *Turgut Özal'in Anilari* (Istanbul: Sabah Kitaplari, 1994), 181.

27. Yavuz Gökmen, *Özal Yaşasaydi* (Ankara: Verso Yayincilik, 1994), 319n.8.

28. Quoted in Barlas, *Turgut Özal'in Anilari,* 118.

29. Quoted ibid., 127–28.

30. "President Turgut Ozal's Press Conference at the Çankaya Palace on the Iraq-Kuwait Crisis," August 11, 1990. Transcript provided to the author by Kaya Toperi.

31. "President Turgut Ozal's Discussion Session on the Gulf Crisis with Press Representatives," August 18, 1990. Transcript reproduced as appendix 1 in Mahmut Bali Aykan, *Türkiye'nin Kuveyt Krizi (1990–1991) Politikasi: 1998 Yilindan Geriye Yönelik Bir Yeniden Değerlendirme* (Ankara: Diş Politika Enstitüsü, 1998), 103.

32. Ibid., 104–5.

33. Serhat Güvenç, "TSK'nin Sinirötesi Girişim Yetenekleri: Ulusal Güvenlik Politikasinda Yeni Boyut," in *En Uzun Onyil: Türkiye'nin Ulusal Güvenlik ve Diş Politika Gündeminde Doksanli Yillar,* ed. Gencer Ozcan and Şule Kut (Istanbul: Boyut Kitaplari, 1998), 135–67.

34. See his comments quoted in Cüneyt Arcayürek, *Kriz Doğuran Savaş* (Ankara: Bilgi Yayinevi, 2000), 139–40.

35. Necip Torumtay, *Org. Torumtay'in Anilari* (Istanbul: Milliyet Yayinlari, 1994), 117, 133.

36. Necip Torumtay, *Değişen Stratejilerin Odağinda Türkiye* (Istanbul: Milliyet Yayinlari, 1996), 245–46.

37. Torumtay, *Org. Torumtay'in Anilari,* 126.

38. Kemal Yavuz, interview with author, Istanbul, July 3, 2000.

39. *Türkiye Büyük Millet Meclisi [TBMM] Tutanak Dergisi,* August 12, 1990, 445.

40. *Hürriyet* newspaper, August 18, 1990, 14.

41. Quoted in Arcayürek, *Kriz Doğuran Savaş,* 371.

42. *Hürriyet,* August 11, 1990, 15.

43. *TBMM Tutanak Dergisi,* August 12, 1990, 450, 458.

44. Quoted in Arcayürek, *Kriz Doğuran Savaş,* 19.

45. Quoted in Barlas, *Turgut Özal'in Anilari,* 119.

46. Quoted in Arcayürek, *Kriz Doğuran Savaş,* 137.

47. Quoted in Philip Robins, "Turkish Policy and the Gulf Crisis: Adventurist or Dynamic?" in *Turkish Foreign Policy: New Prospects,* ed. Clement H. Dodd (Huntingdon, U.K.: Eothen Press, 1992), 70. See pp. 70–87.

48. See Kemal Kirişçi, "Turkey and the Kurdish Safe-Haven in Northern Iraq," *Journal of South Asian and Middle Eastern Studies* 19, no. 3 (spring 1996): 21–39.

49. William Hale, "Turkey, the Middle East, and the Gulf Crisis," *International Affairs* 68, no. 4 (October 1992): 679–92.

50. Ufuk Güldemir, *Texas-Malatya* (Istanbul: Takin Yayinevi, 1992), 410.

51. Transcript of the conversation between Presidents Ozal and Bush, shown to the author by Kaya Toperi.

52. Gencer Özcan, "Doksanli Yillarda Türkiye'nin Değişen Güvenlik Ortami," in *En Uzun Onyil,* ed. Özcan and Kut, 19.

53. Ismet Kurtulan, Tuğlu Erol, Yilmaz Ecer, and Mehmet Sari, *Güneydoğu Anadolu'da Devam Etmekte Olan Bölücü Hareketin Gelecekteki Muhtemel Seyri ve Türkiye'nin Bütünlüğüne Etkileri* (Istanbul: Harp Akademileri Basimevi, 1993), 1, 7–8, 26.

54. Mehmet Kocaoğlu, *Uluslararasi Iliskiler Isiğinda Ortadoğu* (Ankara: Genelkurmay Basimevi, 1995), quoted in Kemal Kirişci and Gareth M. Winrow, *The Kurdish Question and Turkey: An Example of a Trans-State Ethnic Conflict* (London: Frank Cass, 1997), 178.

55. Gencer Özcan, "Doksanlarda Türkiye'nin Ulusal Güvenlik ve Diş Politikasinda Askeri Yapinin Artan Etkisi," in *En Uzun Onyil,* ed. Özcan and Kut, 69–70.

56. *Cumhuriyet* newspaper, March 22, 1995, 4.

57. Volkan Vural, interview with author, New York, June 12, 2000. Vural was one of Çiller's top foreign policy advisers at the time. TAF sources informed the press that in their assessment a security zone might lead to a "Vietnam-type quagmire" (*Cumhuriyet,* March 25, 1995, 9).

110 | Malik Mufti

58. *Turkish Daily News* (Ankara), June 17, 1995, A4.

59. Çetin interview in *Türkiye* newspaper (Istanbul), April 3, 1995, 16.

60. *Milliyet,* March 26, 1995, 16.

61. Bülent Ecevit, interview with author, Ankara, August 12, 1996.

62. *Cumhuriyet,* March 31, 1995, 1.

63. Volkan Vural and Emre Gönensay, interviews with author.

64. See Anat Lewin, "Turkey and Israel: Reciprocal and Mutual Imagery in the Media, 1994–1999," 252, in the special issue on "Turkey: A Struggle between Nation and State" of the *Journal of International Affairs* 54, no. 1 (fall 2000): 239–61.

65. Makovsky, "Israeli-Turkish Relations," 152, 169.

66. Özcan, "Doksanli Yillarda Türkiye'nin Değişen Güvenlik Ortami," 19.

67. Mehmet Akat, interview with author, Ankara, August 6, 1996.

68. Ümit Özdağ, "Turkey, the PKK, and Northern Iraq" (unpublished manuscript), 27.

69. Ethem Tokdemir, interview with author, Ankara, August 6, 1996.

70. FBIS-WEU-98-075, March 16, 1998.

71. M. Hakan Yavuz, "Turkish-Israeli Relations," 35n.23.

72. Kurtulan et al., *Güneydoğu Anadolu'da Devam Etmekte Olan Bölücü Hareketin Gelecekteki Muhtemel Seyri ve Türkiye'nin Bütünlüğüne Etkileri,* 7–8.

73. "Perversely, as noted by Zvi Elpeleg, Israel's former ambassador in Ankara, it is helpful that Turks believe in the *Protocols of the Elders of Zion* and other conspiratorial anti-Semitism, for this leads them to think that Israel has vast powers." Amikam Nachmani, "The Remarkable Turkish-Israeli Tie," *Middle East Quarterly* 5, no. 2 (June 1998): 21.

74. Kemal Yavuz interview.

75. FBIS-WEU-98-276, October 3, 1998.

76. Lewin, "Turkey and Israel," 258.

77. "Ankara Wants Barzani to Continue Dialog with Baghdad," *Turkish Daily News* (internet edition), October 6, 2000.

78. Metehan Demir, "Syria, Turkey Move to Normalize Ties," *Jerusalem Post* (internet edition), October 29, 2000.

79. Volkan Vural interview.

80. Quoted by Mustafah Kinali, "Sezer: Kutsal Yerlerde Şiddet Kabul Edilemez," *Hürriyet* (internet edition), October 26, 2000.

81. Selcuk Gültaşli, "Eastern Med Exercises Postponed in Face of Mideast Tensions," *Turkish Daily News* (internet edition), November 11, 2000.

82. Faruk Loğoğlu, interview with author, Ankara, June 27, 2000.

83. Kemal Yavuz interview.

84. Şadi Ergüvenc, interview with author, Istanbul, June 28, 1999.

Part II

The Arab-Israeli Core Area

5

Israel Enters the Twenty-first Century

Hegemonic Crisis in the Holy Land

ILAN PELEG

Israeli politics are known, above all, for their complexity, volatility, and contradictions. The political system is a unique combination of parliamentary and newly introduced presidential features; it is influenced by powerful internal and international pressures; and the numerous political forces within the country seem to push and pull in diametrically divergent directions, producing a system dominated by increasing polarization.

Despite the remarkable systemic complexity, it is possible, indeed necessary, to develop a coherent thesis about the overall conditions of Israeli politics as Israel enters the twenty-first century. The contemporary Israeli polity, it is argued here, is currently in the midst of a multidimensional hegemonic crisis that is likely to further intensify in years to come. While this crisis (the essence of which will be detailed below) could in principle be resolved, such resolution could not occur without a major transformation, indeed a Copernican revolution, of the Israeli polity. Moreover, the multidimensionality of the challenge to the system may doom it to eventual failure and decay, especially since the time for constructive resolution of most problems may already have passed.

The core of the Israeli political crisis is that long-time, existing patterns of hegemony, deeply linked to the fundamental values of the Israeli society, are no longer accepted by a large number of individuals or even significant groups living under the control of the polity. Particularly significant, in terms of this multidimensional challenge to hegemony, are four conditions, trends, and processes:

(1) The challenge to Israel's thirty-five-year control over the West Bank and Gaza could lead, in all likelihood, to the termination of Israeli hegemony over these territories and their populations or, alternatively, to a serious escalation in Israeli-Palestinian tension;

(2) A related crisis of hegemony is the challenge thrown by Israeli Arabs (or Palestinians in Israel, as they now prefer to call themselves) to Israeli Jews: it is the demand for full civic equality (as individuals), recognition as an autonomous national group, and even the restructuring of the country's constitutional order;

(3) The third challenge to the polity deals with the status of religion within the Israeli political system: while significant political groups are trying to increase their own power, based on their own religiosity, other groups demand, more vehemently than ever before, a liberal solution based on separation between religion and state;

(4) The fourth hegemonic challenge evolving within the Israeli polity is the most general, abstract, and deep of all: it is the debate over the very essence of the Israeli polity. This debate, a genuine Kulturkampf,[1] is focused on the question of whether Israeli citizenship—that is, the privilege of participating in determining the Israeli public good—should be ethnic and primordial (namely, limited to Jews, as it has traditionally been) or civic and equal (that is, open to all Israelis, and only Israelis). A related issue is whether the state should be "Jewish" (ethnically or religiously) or "Israeli," belonging to all its citizens and/or inhabitants.[2] Further it is a debate on whether Israel should maintain its traditional ethnocentric order or become a liberal, pluralistic democracy.

This chapter will proceed by analyzing these four issues, especially against the background of increasing economic polarization in Israel that makes these issues even more difficult than they otherwise would have been.[3] The chapter will then assess the overall character of the traditional Israeli "rights regime," privileging certain segments of the population, against an alternative regime that might replace it in the future: the status quo versus the revisionist camps in Israel will be examined. The following section will evaluate the difficulties that the Israeli polity has (and is likely to have) in meeting the challenges, while the concluding section will raise ideas for resolving the political dilemmas via the transformation of the system.

In analyzing the Israeli society of the early twenty-first century, it is essential to recognize that it is a society in flux. The prolonged occupation of the West Bank and Gaza, accompanied by continuous conflict with their Palestinian populations, has created deep instability within Israel itself. This instability is not merely, or even mainly, political. It is conceptual, moral, and psychological. Thus, Israelis are currently debating fiercely how to teach the history of the Zionist movement and the formative years of the State of Israel. Similarly, those involved directly in the political process describe it as a great struggle between societal forces, not a normal political competition. Thus, Benjamin Netanyahu, Israel's former prime minister, introduced the notion of "old elites" into the Israeli discourse, arguing that the essence of his regime was the replacement of these elites by new forces.[4]

Israel's Hegemonic Crises

The Territorial Issue

Of the four hegemonic crises faced by Israel and analyzed in this chapter, none is more urgent, intense, and violent than the *territorial issue*. At the time of writing (March 2001), it is unclear whether Israel's hegemonic control over most of the territories captured during the 1967 war is about to end. Moreover, the exact manner in which the occupation might eventually be terminated is still unknown.

The occupation of the West Bank and Gaza caught the Israeli leadership and public unprepared. It presented the young Israeli ethnic democracy with a serious and to a large extent unprecedented challenge.[5] Ben-Gurion's limited notion of democracy, emphasizing majority rule and periodic elections,[6] was easier to defend with a marginalized Arab population of about 15 percent within Israel proper than it is in the face of a sizable Arab population under occupation.

While early Israeli governments, led by the Labor Party, tried to create the semblance of normalcy in the newly acquired territories, a pattern of serious human rights violations developed.[7] Some of these violations emerged as part of a punitive Israeli policy designed to quell Palestinian resistance to the occupation; deportations, house demolitions, and administrative detentions became quite common. Moreover, only several months after the June 1967 war, the government began permitting and even encouraging civilians to settle in the West Bank, a policy that further radicalized the local population.

As a result of a prolonged resistance by the Palestinian population (including the intifada of 1987 and the al-Aqsa intifada of 2000) and following an extended albeit volatile peace process, the Israeli polity is reluctant to relinquish its control over most of the occupied territories. The continuation of complete Israeli hegemony over all of western Palestine, including the West Bank and Gaza, means, therefore, an uncertain future. The Israeli political system is suffering today from a serious trauma. Despite the fact that the military, economic, and technological power available to Israel is a lot larger than that possessed by the rebellious Palestinians, the internal cohesion and will to sacrifice may work in favor of the weaker party.[8]

Ironically, while the occupation energized the Palestinians, it has weakened the Israelis; it has created a deep political division in Israel and a widespread sense that the country has lost its way. The resolve of the Israelis declined especially after the first intifada broke out in December 1987: it led to the Madrid Conference (1991), the Oslo Accords (1993), and, eventually, to the progressive termination of the occupation.

The eventual emergence of an independent Palestinian state on the West Bank and in Gaza will return the historical clock to its original position. The Palestinians lost the two areas as a result of the 1948 war. They found themselves dominated by the Israelis, the Jordanians (in the West Bank), and the Egyptians (in Gaza). The West Bank was quickly annexed by the Hashemite Kingdom of Jordan, with Israel's acquiescence. Yet, Israel's 1967 takeover of the areas reenergized the Palestinian population, which demanded total (or near total) Israeli withdrawal and true independence.

From the perspective of this chapter, it is important to emphasize that by and large the legitimacy of the occupation within the Israeli political system has been seriously challenged. Nowhere else was it as clear as in the case of conscientious objection, a phenomenon that continues to be of important significance at the time of writing.

Fundamental changes are often reflected in the emergence of new political culture, and changes in attitudes toward conscientious objection are indicative of interesting developments in this regard. The Israel Defense Forces (IDF) (*Tzhal* in Hebrew) have always been a symbol of Israeli Jewish nationalism. The vast majority of Israeli Jews have viewed the service in the IDF not only as a duty but as a privilege. The level of volunteerism has always been extremely high.

One of the effects of the occupation, and the human rights violations that it entailed, was the appearance, for the first time, of conscientious objection on the Israeli political scene, resulting especially from the war in Lebanon (1982) and the intifada (1987), a phenomenon analyzed by Ruth Linn and others.[9]

Conscientious objection in Israel is an indication of the decline of the communal spirit and increase in the assertion of individual prerogative in a society that originally was strongly communal and decidedly non-individualistic. Second, many believe that conscientious objection is a fundamental human right, and the pursuit of that option by a growing number of Israelis is, in itself, a measure of increasing awareness of human rights. Although the Israeli authorities never accepted conscientious objection as legitimate, they have dealt with it quite liberally, imprisoning objectors for relatively brief periods or releasing them from military duty altogether.

During the critical era of the al-Aqsa intifada, the phenomenon of conscientious objection came back to haunt Israeli society, weakening its resolve in the face of a grave challenge. It reflected the decline of unity within Israeli Jewish society, traditionally marked by its high level of cohesion.

In view of the traditional hegemonic role of the IDF within Israel, the issue of unwillingness to serve is emblematic of an overall decline in social cohesion and support for an agreed-upon national agenda.

Soldiers and officers refusing to serve in the IDF declared in newspaper interviews, and in military courts, that their conscience would not allow them to serve beyond Israel's pre-1967 borders. Such selective objection (as against general objection, which rejects service in the IDF altogether) is seen by the objectors themselves as highly political. It is, in effect, a declaration of war against the occupation. Most of the objectors are organized in Yesh Gvul (There Is a Limit), an organization that emerged as part of the opposition to the war in Lebanon in 1982, but similar organizations emerged in response to the al-Aqsa intifada.

It is not easy to assess the exact number of conscientious objectors in Israel today. In early 2001, the *Jerusalem Report* mentioned that there were twenty-eight soldiers "who have recently refused service, four of whom have been jailed," and the number grew to more than 400 by early 2002. Moreover, there were indications that for each "refuser" who went to jail, a large number of soldiers found alternative ways around serving. According to some estimates, during the Lebanon war 180 soldiers were jailed,[10] and many other refusers were released or reassigned. During the 1987 intifada, over 2,500 reserve soldiers signed a refusal petition, and about 180 were jailed for refusal to serve.[11] The meaning of the refusal to serve in the IDF is far reaching. First, most of the refusers come from Zionist families and from a centrist social, political, and cultural position. They are people who in the past would not even have entertained the idea of refusing to serve but have changed their position as a result of the occupation.

Second, the appearance of *groups*—not merely individuals—who promote refusal to serve indicates that this action has now become legitimate in the Israeli political discourse, at least among liberal circles.

Third, the dimensions of this new phenomenon are important. Since we are dealing with a large number of individuals, all with families, thousands of people are actively linked. While in the short run, the numbers are too small to have significant impact on the effectiveness of the IDF, the long-term implications for the country's morale are a lot larger.

The impact of a possible Israeli withdrawal from the territories is, of course, a lot larger than the question of military refusal. The territorial issue has divided the Israeli society for over thirty years, is still highly controversial, and is likely to remain such even if a major territorial withdrawal is completed. Two camps have emerged, "territorial compromisers" and "annexationists," and they are likely to be sustained following a political settlement through a dovish and a hawkish political coalition.

The leading force among the annexationists, a camp that had been on the losing end of the debate between Oslo (1993) and the 2001 elections, has been the Jewish settlers on the West Bank, especially those who could be identified as religious nationalists. This camp produced Gush Emunim, the ideological movement, as well as the Jewish Underground. Yigal Amir, the assassin of Yitzhak Rabin (November 1995), and other radical activists have also identified with that camp.

The National Challenge

The State of Israel is facing today not only a challenge to its continued hegemony over Palestinians in the West Bank and Gaza but an equivalent and, in the long run, even more serious challenge from Palestinians residing in Israel and holding Israeli citizenship.

While Israel's Declaration of Independence tried to "reconcile the national character of the Jewish state with universalistic civil equality,"[12] in practice Israel's Arab citizens have been discriminated against from the very beginning. In no other area has this been so clear as in the establishment of a military government.

Lasting for eighteen years (1948–66), the military government was applied to all Arabs in the Galilee, the occupants of the "Triangle" (along the Jordanian border), and the Bedouin of the Negev. By the time of its elimination, the military government covered 220,000 of the 260,000 Israeli Arabs. It controlled all aspects of Arab lives: travel, land development, business activity, employment, and so on. While the totality of the control normally assured the good behavior of the Arab population, in some cases the authorities had to resort to severe penalties such as internal exile and administrative detentions without trial.

The domination of the Arabs, achieved by paying a huge price in civil rights violations, was part of a national effort to establish, sustain, and strengthen the newly formed ethnocentric order after 1948, a policy that to a large extent is still being carried out today (although in the face of increasing opposition). The military government not only marked the Arabs as second-class citizens; it declared them to be a minority that could not be integrated into Israeli society, people of a different kind, the "ultimate other."[13]

In general, the regime, established in Israel in 1948 and lasting substantially until quite recently—when increasing challenges began to emerge— had a number of distinct characteristics:

(1) Although it was generally democratic, its notion of democracy was, and to a large extent remains, rather narrow. For Ben-Gurion and most of his successors, "democracy" meant majoritarian rule via periodic elections, not minority protection and individual rights.[14] Although often not recognized as such, Israel's traditional democracy has been seen by some observers as "illiberal."

(2) The overall design of the regime has been ethnic. The Israeli sociologist Sammy Smooha coined the term "ethnic democracy" in describing the regime,[15] a rather problematic term and condition.[16] The meaning of ethnic democracy Israel-style has been that the state has defined itself as Jewish, has given Jews some exclusive legal rights (e.g., immigration, citizenship, and land purchase), and has discriminated against Arabs in numerous areas.[17]

(3) While the fundamental democratic order has been enhanced through the years—via legislation (e.g., two important basic laws in 1992), supreme court rulings (on freedom of expression, religious equality, and recently even equality in land allocation) and practice—a full-fledged constitution or a bill of rights, instruments that could have improved significantly the conditions of the Arabs, have not been enacted to date.

(4) In general, the Israeli system has traditionally emphasized the rights of the collective over those of the individual, the prerogative of the state over that of private interests, and the centrality of the core nation over any other group.[18] The dominance of that collective-ethnic-statist approach resulted in the absence of civil

rights as a fundamental element of Israeli political life, culture, and institutionalized system, a condition that may have begun to change in recent years.

Those generally negative characteristics of Israel's traditional "rights order" were further exacerbated as a result of the all-important 1967 war. Israel's decisive victory over the Arabs resulted in further marginalization of the Palestinians inside Israel. The expansion into the Biblical lands of Judea and Samaria further strengthened the power of religious elements within the Israeli regime, weakening the power of liberal circles supportive of enhanced liberties and freedoms.

Nevertheless, in a paradoxical way, the 1967 occupation of the West Bank and Gaza has increased attention among Israeli Jews to civil and human rights, strengthening the challenge to the existing and largely deficient rights order in the country. Thus, it may prove in the long run to be a positive force from the perspective of Israeli Arabs.

The traditional Israeli political system was developed in response to the perceived need of the Israeli Jewish majority to deal with the Arab states' threat to its existence. The Israeli Arabs were marginalized to prevent the emergence of an effective Arab challenge to the exclusive control of the polity by the Jewish majority. While the occupation of the West Bank signaled the apex of Jewish domination and strength, it simultaneously strengthened the demands of Arabs and others for protection, rights, and eventually power.

Thus, the 1970s witnessed the intensification of an organized political struggle for civil equality of the Israeli Arabs, for the first time under the leadership of a national body, the National Committee of the Heads of Arab Local Municipalities.[19] Oren Yiftachel believes, as does Smooha, that this type of political activity led to a "certain moderation of governmental control" over the lives of Arabs.

The overall result of these developments was positive from the perspective of human rights, but their causes were quite varied:

(1) Increasing assertiveness and higher sophistication by the Israeli Arabs in formulating demands for equal treatment;

(2) Growing dependence of Israeli politicians and parties on the electoral support of Israeli Arabs, resulting in increased leverage for the Arabs;[20]

(3) Recognition by some Israeli leaders, especially on the Left, that as part of the Oslo peace process between Israel and the PLO, there should be an equivalent reconciliation process between Arabs and Jews inside Israel.

The last factor explains the positive human rights developments that occurred during the administration of the Labor government in 1992–96.[21] In introducing his government to the Knesset, Prime Minister Rabin committed himself to "full equality of all citizens," stating that he was "ashamed that there is still discrimination against Arabs."[22] He emphasized that the State of Israel is the state of all its citizens, a legal formula that most Israeli Jews have refused to accept. Echoing the prime minister, the state ombudsman warned against the continuous discrimination against the Arabs and called for full equality, stating that "when there is no integration, there is polarization."[23]

Despite the growing awareness among high-ranking Israeli officials, the actual implementation of equality for the Arabs progressed slowly. While budget allocations to Arab localities increased in the 1990s, few Arabs were hired by government ministries, especially for high positions. The macroissues of Israel's ethnic democracy have remained unresolved both in terms of the overall character of the state as primarily a Jewish republic and in terms of the status of the Arabs as a minority within the self-defined ethnic polity. Under the Barak government (1999), some observers suggested that a "quiet revolution" in the status of Arabs had begun.[24] This did not prevent major, unprecedented, and extremely violent clashes between Israeli Palestinians and Israeli security forces in the fall of 2000. Those clashes reflected the identification of many Palestinians in Israel with their West Bank and Gaza brethren, as well as the double standard of Israel's police in dealing with Arab demonstrations.

It is important to note that, despite the growing Arab-Jewish violence inside Israel (and not only in the occupied territories), a very large number of civil and human rights organizations in Israel dedicate themselves to the fostering of understanding and tolerance between Arabs and Jews (Van Leer Institute and Givet Haviva are among the largest organizations of that type; others are Interns for Peace, Sikkuy, Beit Hagefen, the Open House, and so on). This duality is striking and is likely to remain in years to come.

Israeli society faces several challenges at the start of the twenty-first century, the most immediate and serious of which is the country's relations with the Palestinians, both in the occupied territories and in Israel proper. While a negotiated settlement with the Palestinians on the West Bank and Gaza and a termination of the occupation could ease the pressure, the challenge for Arab-Jewish relations inside Israel is likely to remain as serious as ever. Despite some improvements in the situation of Arab citizens of Israel, the degree of resentment among them toward the state and its Jewish majority remains high. The Arab challenge to the Jewish republic is at least threefold: a demand for equality of all citizens, recognition of minority rights, and a redefinition of the polity as the state of all its citizens.

It seems that the traditional Israeli policy of total domination over the Arabs—inside and outside Israel—has backfired. It has not only galvanized Arab resistance inside Israel but has also led to extensive condemnation of Israeli human rights policy in the occupied territories and even inside Israel.

The debate over civil and human rights has now expanded into a fundamental debate on the very nature of the Israeli polity. The single most important question has now become the following: can Israel be both Jewish and democratic, or, in the language of some analysts, is the notion of "ethnic democracy" oxymoronic? While there is a consensus today that the relationship between Israel's Jewishness and democracy in Israel is the key for the country's civil rights status and the quality of its democracy (a consensus reflected in a 1996 volume edited by Dafna Barak-Erez),[25] there is a serious debate over the solution to that dilemma.

It is likely that a solution for the West Bank–Gaza Arabs in the form of an independent Palestinian state would result in the intensification of Palestinian demands for full equality inside Israel. The demand for national minority rights and even a change in the character of the state would likely become more dominant. It is essential to recognize, in this context, that the redefinition of the civil rights agenda in Israel is not merely about individual equality; it has a complicated and far-reaching communal dimension that is as yet unresolved. The reaction of Israeli Jews to the Arab challenge has already assumed a dual character.

The recent demonstrations (October–November 2000) among Israeli Arabs, held in identification with the Palestinians in the West Bank and Gaza, brought to the fore in a dramatic way the tense relationships between the Jewish majority and the Arab minority in Israel. For many years, most Jews have ignored the Arabs, a marginalized and deferential minority. Today, however, such a position has become untenable; the Arab society in Israel has gone through a transformation and is significantly more assertive in demanding its rights.[26] After fifty-four years of systematic discrimination in education, housing, development, budget allocations, and numerous other areas, the Arabs now demand full equality, and they are supported by a large number of Jews (see, for example, the *Ha'aretz* editorial "Equal Partners," December 13, 2000).

The Barak government announced in response to the Arab demonstrations of 2000 that it intended to spend billions of dollars in the "Arab sector." Furthermore, new initiatives were being taken to recruit more

Arabs for positions in government offices. An inquiry commission to investigate the riots (in which thirteen Israeli Arabs were killed) was appointed, following massive pressure on the prime minister. It remains to be seen whether these actions will change the interethnic situation, but it is possible and even likely that Israel has reacted too late to the internal Arab challenge.

The unmistakable mood today among Israeli Arabs is to cut off their links to the Jewish parties. "The sectarian, disjointed, and ethnic reality in Israel has pushed the Arabs to close themselves within a differentiated political entity of their own."[27] This development could prove negative in the long run. At the same time, there are indications that elements within Israel's political elite have begun to focus on the issue of Arab rights in Israel.[28]

State and Religion

When Israel was established, the political elite could have established, at least gradually, a Western-style liberal democracy. Instead, the leadership chose to establish an ethnically based Jewish republic.[29] Between liberal and organic nationalism,[30] Ben-Gurion and his associates preferred the latter as an overall design for nation building.[31] This political architecture destined Israel to develop a flawed rights order that has affected the polity ever since.

The flaws of the rights order were reflected in several crucial areas. None was as important, in the long run, as the decision not to adopt a constitution for the new state. The birth of the state was accompanied by a formal commitment, domestic and international, to elect a constituent assembly, not a regular parliament, that would adopt a constitution.[32] The Declaration of Independence stated that a constitution would be adopted "no later than October 1, 1948." The document was to include all the principles contained in the declaration itself, such as "complete social and political equality." Yet a short time after the first Israeli elections in 1949, Ben-Gurion suddenly announced that there was no need for a constitution.

Why has the leadership abandoned its commitment? According to Chaim Zadok, a close aide to Ben-Gurion and later Israel's justice minister, Ben-Gurion had a "desire to govern without constitutional restrictions, taking whatever action he deemed best to put the State on a firm footing."[33] Ben-Gurion himself, facing the aftermath of Israel's war for independence, argued that a constitution would give too much power to minorities and would not allow the government to take action. In view of what was to quickly follow, for example, the establishment of military government in areas inhabited by Arabs and the large-scale expropriation of Arab lands, Ben-Gurion's words were ominous.[34]

But the effect of the nonadoption decision was not limited to negatively affecting Jewish-Arab relations. The same Declaration of Independence that promised all Israelis full equality also promised to protect their "freedom of religion and conscience." Yet, such freedom was never established. Already the 1947 so-called Status Quo Agreement, reached between the Jewish Agency under Ben-Gurion's leadership and the ultra-Orthodox Agudat Israel, promised the religious parties exclusive Orthodox control over a large number of important issues, including personal status matters, ultra-Orthodox (Haredi) education, the Sabbath, and so on. Additional concessions, such as exemption from military service for religious students, quickly followed; they exacerbated the situation after the establishment of the state and determined the future of the polity for generations to come.

Rather than separating religion and state or, alternatively, creating other arrangements that would guarantee for all Israelis freedom of and from religion, the state became an instrument of religious coercion and illiberality. Adopting the old Ottoman tradition of defining all individuals as members of religious communities *(millets)*, the state transferred control over important areas of people's lives to the hands of religious establishments, mainly the Chief Rabbinate. By not adopting a liberal constitution—which would have secularized public life, privatized religion, and guaranteed religious freedom—the Ben-Gurionist system endorsed the violations of civil rights with which Israelis are still struggling today.

Although Arabs have been the main victims of the overall character of the Israeli regime, others have been marginalized as well: in order to guarantee Orthodox support for state action, religious circles have been accorded preferential treatment in numerous areas, thus discriminating against the nonreligious.

Relations between the religious and the secular segments of the Israeli society have further deteriorated over the last few years. Thus, on February 14, 1999, two huge demonstrations were held in Jerusalem, one opposing the Israeli High Court of Justice and the other supporting it, an unprecedented set of events.

Several trends have contributed to the deterioration of secular-religious relations:

(1) Secular Israelis have come to believe that the real and perceived increase in power of the religious parties (especially Shas) and movements (especially the West Bank settlers) may change the character of the polity and society; and

(2) The ever-increasing Israeli middle class, better off and more liberal than ever before, has begun to resist the demands of the religious parties more vigorously, often in the name of civil rights.[35]

A series of popular books document the increase in the power of the religious element and the intense resentment against it. Seffi Rachlevsky's *Messiah's Donkey* (1998), Yair Sheleg's *The New Religious: A Contemporary Look on Israel's Religious Community* (Keter, 2000), and Shahar Ilan, *Haredim Ltd.* (2000) are but examples of the increasing centrality of this issue in Israel.

The confrontational relationships between religious and secular Jews, as an overall trend, are likely to continue and even intensify in the future. The rise in power of Shas, a Haredi-Sephardi party, has been in the center of this phenomenon. Shas emerged as an internal event within the Haredi camp, a reaction to the blatant discrimination against talented Sephardi youth in the Ashkenazi Yeshivot and the refusal of the Ashkenazi religious leaders to recognize the religious authority of Ovadia Yossef, the Sephardi rabbi.[36]

This internal Haredi event, however, quickly affected the entire Israeli polity. The inability of Shas to change the Haredi world from within led it to intense activity within the wider Israeli political system. First Shas formed itself as a separate political party, initially under the auspices of the Ashkenazi rabbi Eliezer Schach (1984) and then independently (1988). Second, it emphasized its *mizrahi* (Sephardi, oriental) origins, thus attracting not merely religious Jews but also secular Jews of Middle Eastern origin. It took full advantage of the often-justified frustration among these people. Third, while the Ashkenazi Haredi parties focused merely on receiving state benefits and funds for their communities, Shas developed a much more ambitious platform, designed to remake Israeli society in its own image.

The increasing power of Shas and its success in obtaining resources from the state (such as large budget allocations for its independent educational system) have generated powerful resentment from the secular public. While the initial reaction to Shas was mainly suspicion, sometimes with racist overtones, today there is a real fear of and hatred toward Shas.

The attacks of Shas on the High Court of Justice, the criminal behavior of several of its leaders, and the radical language of its head (Rabbi Ovadia Yossef) have contributed to this attitude.

The response of the secular public to the increase in religious power has found political expression in numerous ways:

(1) In the 1999 elections, for the first time, an exclusively anti-Haredi party (Shinui) ran for the Knesset; it received six mandates, an impressive showing. Other parties (e.g., Meretz) have also adopted a strong anti-Haredi position.

(2) In August 2000, following a particularly repugnant analysis of the meaning of the Holocaust by Rabbi Yossef, a group of eight Israelis announced that it intends to establish an Israeli colony abroad, calling it "New Israel."

(3) Israel's prime minister, Ehud Barak, announced toward the end of his term in office that he would implement in Israel a "secular revolution"—civil marriage, a constitution, educational reforms, separation of state and religion, and so forth.

In assessing potential future developments, it is crucial to note that the conflict between the secular public and the religious one (especially Shas) is as much cultural as it is political. Many members of the secular public want an Israeli culture reflective of the old Sabra character; at the same time, due to more recent social and economic developments, this public is increasingly liberal, modern, and Western. It tends to view Shas as racist in its attitude toward the Arabs, the Russians, and the foreign workers; moreover, many secular Israelis believe that Shas wants to establish an Israel with a Middle Eastern, religion-dominated culture.

It is interesting to note that the hatred of Shas is substantially more powerful than that of Agudat Israel, the Ashkenazi Haredi party (today the United Torah Judaism Party). Agudat Israel was resented because of its seclusion, anti-Zionist stance, rejection of Israeli institutions (including the IDF and the Hebrew language), and what was perceived as its *galut* (exile) mentality. Shas is hated for the opposite reasons: it is a successful Israeli (not merely Jewish) party, integrated within the society, and Zionist (in its own way), and its people serve in the IDF and speak Hebrew fluently. Shas is hated because it is feared: it challenges the accepted narrative of Israel's secular community in a way that the Agudah never did.

The religious-secular divide is not limited to the relationships between Shas and Israel's secular majority. Since the 1967 war, the relationship between the secular camp and all religious forces has deteriorated. A source of stability of these relationships prior to the war was the so-called Historic Covenant between the Labor Party, Israel's dominant secular party, and the National Religious Party, the country's most prominent religious force. After the war, however, the NRP quickly moved to the right and became highly hawkish. The Historic Covenant thus came to an end. Moreover, since 1967, an association between hawkishness on the territorial issue and religiosity has emerged, separating all religious parties from Israel's liberal and intellectual elites. The religious-secular cleavage has thus been on the rise.[37]

Israel's Kulturkampf

The fundamental choice faced by the Israeli body politic today, as it enters the twenty-first century, is the one that was faced by the early Zionists and by the Founding Fathers of the State of Israel: should Israel follow a universalistic political model or a particularistic political model? A universalistic model in its pure form would mean that Israel has a supreme commitment to comprehensive democracy, including equal rights for all of its citizens (regardless of their nationality, ethnicity, or religion). A particularistic model would mean that Israel continues to promote, above all, the interests of its Jewish majority, however Jewishness and Judaism are defined.

The central question for Israel is still that of defining the boundaries of the Israeli collectivity and, in particular, determining the criteria for admission into full-fledged membership in that collectivity. The universalistic option calls for individual membership in the collectivity, and its implications are complete equality among all Israeli citizens regardless of their ethnic, national, or religious affiliation. The particularistic option believes that primary attention ought to be given to the groups that constitute the Israeli polity, especially in terms of their ethnicity, nationality, and religion. Specifically, the particularistic camp emphasizes what it sees as the necessity of distinguishing between Arabs and Jews in Israel. Many of the particularists also emphasize the need to recognize the religious obligations of the Israeli collectivity or state (e.g., by recognizing the privileged status of religious groups and organizations) and, in general, maintain the Jewish character of the State of Israel.

The debate over the essence of Israel as a polity comes down to the question of whether the State of Israel is to be an ethnonational state or a democratic-pluralistic polity. If Israel is to be an ethnonational state, as the particularlists would argue, then it "belongs" to its Jewish majority, and possibly to all Jews, wherever they may reside. Such a polity may strive to be purely Jewish or it may recognize one group (Jews) as the majority and another group (Arabs) as a minority. It should, logically, adopt policies (and not only symbols) to perpetuate its own ethnonational character.

If Israel is to be a full-fledged pluralistic polity, as some universalists prefer, it could (a) declare that it belongs to its two inhabiting nations, Jews and Arabs (and develop, for example, a federal government to deal with its binational character); (b) view itself as the national state of a unified Arab-Jewish Israeli nation (a solution supported by the movement known in the past as the Canaanites); or (c) ignore altogether its ethnic composition and allow membership and participation in the body politic on an individual basis only. Less radical pluralist solutions (e.g., guaranteeing material equality but maintaining the Jewish symbols of Israel) are also possible.

To date, Israel has chosen not to choose formally between these "models of essence." In reality, however, it has tended to vigorously pursue an *ethnonational model* along with imperfect, and some would even say minimalist, democracy. It has offered its citizens what might be considered (and is in fact) a contradictory, oxymoronic solution, that of a Western, ethnic state. Thus, while adopting many modern, liberal, and even progressive principles of governance and increasingly following the example of Western Europe and the United States, Israel has also adopted distinct ethnocentric and religious values and policies.

The peace process has made the choice between the alternative models necessary and probably urgent, since certain issues (e.g., the territorial one) touch directly on questions of essence. In making a choice, the Israeli polity could witness, for the first time in its history, a physical, violent confrontation between the universalist-democratic-liberal camp and the particularist-nationalist-ethnic faction, since the gap between the two is considerable.

In general, the universalist orientation in Israel is consistent with the political attitudes developed in Western Europe and the United States over the last 50–100 years. Although many Israeli universalists, like Western universalists, are not necessarily committed to socioeconomic equality, they are opposed to formal, legal, and political discrimination against individuals or groups within society and are significantly more ready than the particularists to recognize the rights of competing national groups.

The particularist camp in Israel represents a different, and possibly more complex, set of positions. Thus, the split within the camp between particularist-nationalistic and particularist-religious is and could become quite important, as shown in the reactions to the July 1995 rabbinical decision regarding the removal of IDF bases from the occupied territories and the exclusive identification of people accused of involvement in the Rabin assassination with the religious camp. Nevertheless, there is an essential unity within the particularist camp to warrant its identification as a coherent ideological group.

What are the main components of particularism in contemporary Israel?

(1) There is a belief that Jews in Israel should enjoy special and preferential rights, both as a group and as individuals. One particularist element was formally adopted in Israel in the form of the Law of Return (a result of the Holocaust), a law that automatically grants Israeli citizenship to every Jew. Other elements of particularism—in the form of preferential treatment in housing, employment, education, and so forth—affect many aspects of Israeli life.

(2) Particularists were slow to adopt the position that the Palestinians have a right to establish their own state in the West Bank and the Gaza Strip. Moreover, they oppose the idea that Palestinians who reside in Israel have rights as a group within the Jewish state or that they should even be dealt with as equals. Thus, spokesmen of the Right have stated repeatedly that an Israeli government, which relies on Arab votes in the Knesset, cannot decide to return parts of the occupied territories. The meaning of this position is that a vote of an Arab is not equal to that of a Jew, clearly a particularist position.

(3) Although the core of Israeli particularism is to be found in its political stance on Arab-Jewish relations, its belief system is based on a deeper philosophical and historical position. Particularists are notoriously suspicious of normalcy: they emphasize the impossibility of normal Jewish existence (thereby negating one of Theodor Herzl's most fundamental beliefs), cherish the concepts of chosenness and separation ("a nation who dwells alone"), and see the Jewish-Gentile conflict as a permanent historical fixture. Events such as the Holocaust are viewed by particularists as final proofs for abnormalcy, chosenness, and permanent struggle. A final Arab-Jewish peace is considered an impossibility for people who see conflict as their raison d'être— "we fight, therefore we are!" in the words of Menachem Begin in his book *The Revolt*. In a nutshell: for a true particularist, an

Arab-Israeli peace is not only politically unlikely; it is, histori-
cally, an absurdity.

(4) Particularists tend to be against any reforms that may undermine
the ethnic and religious advantage given to Jews in Israel. Therefore, the strongest forces against the enactment of a constitution
have always been particularistic, as are forces who oppose the
strengthening of the Israeli High Court of Justice, extension of
the Court's judicial review, and so forth. Particularist forces
worked tirelessly to prevent the appointment of Aharon Barak as
chief justice, especially since Barak has become the leader of judicial activism in Israel.

The split between universalists and particularists goes much deeper
than a bitter debate over concrete political issues such as the future of the
territories. The split is rooted in different approaches to political life, the
centrality of the nation in one's position, the reading of history, and
more. Thus, over the last quarter of a century or so, Israel has seen, for
the first time, the emergence of a genuine network of human and civil
rights organizations, a civil society representing a universalistic position.
Parties such as Ratz in the past and Meretz or Shinui today, the Association for Civil Rights in Israel (ACRI), and B'Tselem are but a few examples of that impressive organizational effort. A number of lawyers
have made a name for themselves defending fearlessly the civil and human rights of their clients. The emergence of an independent human
rights movement—focusing on the rights of the individual and groups
vis-à-vis the power of the state—is a sign that genuine universalism may
have arrived, at last, in Israel. It is likely to remain a significant force, in
opposition to the traditional dominance of the state, as Israel enters the
twenty-first century.

An Emerging Alternative Order?

Israeli society today is a deeply divided and overburdened polity.[38] The
four issues discussed above describe some of the fundamental cleavages
within the contemporary Israeli political system. It is clear from this analysis that Israel's traditional order is under extensive and intensive challenge.
Can this order be redefined and what forms might this redefinition assume?

It seems that in contemporary Israel there are two major camps, two
publics, and two agendas regarding the character of the polity:

(1) The communal, ethnic, nationalist camp of the Likud and the religious parties, which speaks the language of primordial tribalism, a language that rejects the demand for equal civil rights as unimportant, peripheral, or, at best, secondary.

(2) The liberal, secular, Westernized public of Labor, Meretz, Shinui, and others, which increasingly uses the language of equal civil rights, not only or even mainly in regard to the Arab issues. For this camp, rights have become the central litmus test for the quality of Israel's democracy.

The split in Israeli society is reflected institutionally, not only in terms of political parties. Certain groups (such as artists, academics, jurists, and journalists) are in the forefront of the movement toward greater civil rights. Other groups (e.g., the religious establishment) have taken an opposite position. To argue that "the Israeli public is not homogeneous in its support" of civil and human rights is to understate the case: the division is extremely deep.[39]

While the future of civil rights and democracy in Israel remains unclear, it is reasonable to argue that the possible establishment of a Palestinian state in the West Bank and Gaza will have a profound impact on everything political in Israel, including the status of civil rights and democracy. Nevertheless, the direction of the impact is unclear. It is possible that the emergence of a Palestinian state would ease some of the Arab frustrations vis-à-vis the Jewish state. On the other hand, it may lead to significant deterioration of Arab-Jewish relations.

The reaction of Israeli Jews to the Arab challenge has already assumed a dual character, a duality that is likely to intensify. On the one hand, the internal Palestinian challenge is likely to lead many Israeli Jews to the conclusion that Israel must further emphasize its Jewishness and reject outright the Arab demands for full individual and, especially, communal equality. If Israel adopts that line, it will follow the footsteps of other ethnicized polities such as Sri Lanka or India (that have become increasingly Sinhalese or Hindu, respectively).

On the other hand, prorights forces in Israel are likely to push the country in the direction of at least some acceptance of its binational character. There are already numerous signs that the Israeli political establishment has begun to move, for the first time, toward the equalization of Palestinian rights, at least on an individual basis. It remains to be seen whether the core nation in Israel, that is, Israeli Jews, who have assumed for decades that the state belongs to them exclusively, will be capable of accepting the presence of another nation in Israel. Several countries have changed their character from uninational entities to bi- or multinational ones (Canada in the 1960s, Spain in the 1980s, and Northern Ireland today are relevant examples).

In general, a civil rights focus in the Israeli political arena has become legitimate and even respectable. Large numbers of Israelis, especially members of the middle and upper-middle class, professionals, and intellectuals, are increasingly committed to civil rights. Most importantly, the overall political pattern suggests that activity in one area of rights (e.g., human rights violations in the occupied territories) is likely to spill over into other areas of human rights (such as women's issues or state-religion relations).

Nevertheless, despite the increasing acceptance of rights issues in Israel in the 1990s, the progress of civil and human rights in Israel has not been linear, consistent, or unambiguous. A major reason for the uneven progress is that civil and human rights are part of the much larger, murkier, and more conflictual political picture of the country.

Entering the twenty-first century, the Israeli political system has to deal with this complicated reality, which is based on historical legacy. Can Israel do it successfully? If yes, how? If not, what could be the consequences? Those questions call, by their very nature, for some speculation and tentative analysis.

There are several serious problems that Israel faces in trying to solve the four dilemmas described earlier:

(1) The combination of so many fundamental challenges at one time produces a polity that is incredibly overburdened. Israel of the year 2001 is a multicleavage society that is going through a major crisis due to the multiplicity of problems and their severity. Compare Israel today with France of the early 1960s. At the time, France had a serious territorial problem with Algeria, similar to the one Israel has with the West Bank/Gaza today. But France, in 1960, did *not* have a fundamental identity crisis (Kulturkampf) or religious strife (the status of Catholicism was settled decades before), nor did it have a large and problematical minority. Nevertheless, France's withdrawal from Algeria was highly traumatic, accompanied by several assassination attempts on the president (de Gaulle), and a military revolt. This quick comparison might shed some light on the gravity of Israel's multiple problems today.

(2) The second problem facing Israel is that, in trying to deal with any of the four issues, the Israeli leadership will aggravate (necessarily and inevitably) most other issues. Thus, the four dilemmas can hardly be resolved sequentially.

Several examples can demonstrate this second point:

(1) Ehud Barak's courageous attempt to solve the Israel-Palestinian territorial issue ended with an internal *Arab-Jewish confrontation.* The continuation of this effort will further escalate the orthodox-secular clash and will deepen Israel's cultural divide.

(2) Similarly, Barak's call for a secular revolution—civil marriage, constitution, separation of state and religion, and so forth—if successful would lead inevitably to aggravation of several of the other conflicts.

(3) Even if Israel focuses on solving its Arab dilemma, it could (and in all likelihood will) aggravate other dilemmas. Barak, for example, promised a $4 billion investment in the Arab sector. Such a major effort could generate bitter attacks from Israel's large Sephardic community, which feels that it has been neglected for generations.

Possible Solutions

As a historical force, Zionism has been uniquely successful among modern political movements. It created a sovereign state against all odds and in the face of fierce opposition. It did so by striking a delicate balance between nationalism, a relatively egalitarian society with powerful socioeconomic institutions, and genuine democracy within the dominant ethnic group. Israel's commitment to the national imperative, however, meant a sacrifice in terms of comprehensive democracy. Since 1948 Israeli Arabs have had limited access to political power. Until 1966 most Arabs lived under a military government, and since 1967 large numbers of Palestinians have lived under military occupation, enduring the systematic negation of their human rights.

Peace—if and when it is established—is unlikely to eliminate the tensions between ethnicity and democracy in Israel overnight. The Zionist traditions and Judaism itself are too strongly ingrained in Israel to foster an ethnic-blind system of governance and power. Yet, peace, if it prevails, could mean a powerful drive toward genuine democracy at the expense of unlimited ethnicity. The interrelationship between nationalism and democracy, on the background of transition from war to peace, is unmistakable.

If an Israeli-Palestinian peace settlement is eventually achieved, the emergence of a somewhat limited liberalism in Israel is possible. The main elements of such limited liberalism will be as follows:

(1) Jews will continue to be the clear majority in Israel, and the Law of Return, possibly in an amended form, will continue to be in existence (balanced by a Palestinian Law of Return in an adjacent Palestinian state).
(2) All citizens will be equal in terms of both rights and obligations (with Arabs obligated to do national service).
(3) The symbols of the state will be mostly Jewish, but non-Jewish symbols could also be officially recognized (e.g., Muslim and Christian holidays, a holiday for 9/13—Oslo Day (!), or the creation of a verse in *Hatikvah* celebrating Jerusalem's sanctity as a symbol of universal peace).

Under conditions of comprehensive peace in the Middle East, a genuinely mixed universalist/particularist model for Israel could be found. The emergence of such a model could be a surprising and beneficial by-product of a new situation in the region.

Notes

1. Zvi al-Peleg, "Arabs' Rights," in *Report of the Association of Civil Rights in Israel*, ed. Ann Swersky (Tel Aviv, 1988), 94–108 (in Hebrew).

2. Myron J. Aronoff and Pierre M. Atlas, "The Peace Process and Competing Challenges to the Dominant Zionist Discourse," in *The Middle East Peace Process: Interdisciplinary Perspectives,* ed. Ilan Peleg (New York: State University of New York Press, 1998), 41–60.

3. Uri Ram, "The Promised Land of Business Opportunities: Liberal Post-Zionism in the Golden Age," in *The New Israel: Peacemaking and Liberalization,* ed. Gershon Shafir and Yoav Peled (Boulder, Colo.: Westview Press, 2000), 217–40.

4. Gayil Hareven, "No, So Atlas Shrugged," *Jerusalem Report,* September 25, 2000, 54.

5. Sammy Smooha, "Minority Status in an Ethnic Democracy: The Status of the Arab Minority in Israel," *Ethnic and Racial Studies* 13, no. 3 (1990): 389–413. See also Oren Yiftachel, "The Ethnic Democracy Model and Its Applicability to the Case of Israel," *Ethnic and Racial Studies* 15 (1992): 125–37.

6. Ilan Peleg, "Israel's Constitutional Order and Kulturkampf: The Role of Ben-Gurion," *Israel Studies* 3, no. 1 (1998): 237–61.

7. David Grossman, *The Yellow Wind* (New York: Farrar, Straus, Giroux,

1988); Ilan Peleg, *Human Rights in the West Bank and Gaza: Legacy and Politics* (Syracuse, N.Y.: Syracuse University Press, 1995).

8. Danny Rabinowitz, "A Simple Story," *Ha'aretz,* November 2, 2000.

9. Ruth Linn, *Conscience at War: The Israeli Soldier as a Moral Critic* (New York: State University of New York Press, 1996).

10. Yosef Elgozi, "End to the Occupation: The Next Generation," *Ha'aretz,* December 1, 2000, 17.

11. However, after the series of Palestinian suicide bombings in early 2002, support for refusal to serve dropped.

12. Erik Cohen, "Israel as a Post-Zionist Society," in *The Shaping of Israeli Identity: Myth, Memory, and Trauma,* ed. Robert Wistrich and David Ohana (London, 1991), 203–14.

13. Ilan Peleg, "Otherness and Israel's Arab Dilemma," in *The Other in Jewish Thought and History,* ed. Laurence J. Silberstein and Robert L. Cohn (New York: New York University Press, 1994), 258–80, ch. 11; see also Ilan Peleg, "The Arab-Israeli Conflict and the Victory of Otherness," in *Books on Israel,* vol. 3, ed. Russell Stone and Walter Zenner (New York: State University of New York Press, 1996), 227–43.

14. Michal Shamir and John Sullivan, "The Political Context of Tolerance: The U.S. and Israel," *American Political Science Review* 73 (1983): 92–106.

15. Smooha, "Minority Status," 389–413.

16. Yiftachel, "Ethnic Democracy Model," 125–37. See also Yoav Peled, "Ethnic Democracy and the Legal Construction of Citizenship: Arab Citizens of the Jewish State," *American Political Science Review* 86 (June 1992): 432–43; Asad Ghanem, Nadim Rouhana, and Oren Yiftachel, "Questioning 'Ethnic Democracy': A Response to Sammy Smooha," *Israel Studies* 3, no. 2 (1998); and Ilan Peleg, "Culture, Ethnicity, and Human Rights in Contemporary Biethnic Democracies: The Case of Israel and Other Cases," in *Negotiating Culture and Human Rights,* ed. Lynda Bell, Andrew Nathan, and Ilan Peleg (New York: Columbia University Press, 2001).

17. David Kretzmer, *The Legal Status of the Arabs in Israel* (Boulder, Colo.: Westview Press, 1990); and Nadim Rouhana, *Palestinian Citizens in an Ethnic Jewish State* (New Haven: Yale University Press, 1997).

18. Rogers Brubaker, *Nationalism Reframed: Nationhood and the National Question in the New Europe* (Cambridge: Cambridge University Press, 1996).

19. Zvi al-Peleg, "Arabs' Rights," 94–108; Ghanem et al., "Questioning 'Ethnic Democracy.'" See also Jacob Landau, *The Arab Minority in Israel 1967–1991: Political Perspectives* (Tel Aviv: Am Oved, 1993) (in Hebrew).

20. Ian Lustick, "Stability in Deeply Divided Societies: Consociationalisation vs. Control," *World Politics* 31, no. 3 (April 1979): 325–44.

21. Sarah Ozacky-Lazar and Asad Ghanem, "Between Peace and Equality: The Arabs in Israel in the Midterm of Labor-Meretz Government," Institute for the Study of Peace, Givet Haviva, January 23, 1995 (in Hebrew).

22. *New York Times,* July 14, 1992.

23. *Ma'ariv*, December 16, 1994.

24. Deborah Sontag, "Israel Is Slowly Shedding Harsh Treatment of Arabs," *New York Times*, April 7, 2000, A1, A12.

25. Dafna Barak-Erez, ed., *A Jewish and Democratic State* (Tel Aviv: Tel Aviv University School of Law, 1996) (in Hebrew).

26. Gideon Levy, "The Arabs Are Not the Same Arabs," *Ha'aretz*, November 12, 2000.

27. Ada Oshprz, "If We Are an Enemy," *Ha'aretz*, December 8, 2000.

28. Alexandre Kedar, "A First Step in a Difficult and Sensitive Road: Preliminary Observations on Quaadan v. Katzir," *Israel Studies Bulletin* 16, no. 1 (March 3–11, 2000); Gerald Steinberg, "The Poor in Your Own City Shall Have Precedence: A Critique of the Katzir-Qaadan Case and Opinion," *Israel Studies Bulletin* 16, no. 1 (March 3–11, 2000): 12–18.

29. Baruch Kimmerling, "Religion, Nationalism, and Democracy in Israel," *Zmanim* (winter 1996): 50–51, 116–31; Yonathan Shapiro, "Where Has Liberalism Disappeared in Israel?" *Zmanim* (winter 1996): 91–104.

30. Zeev Sternhell, *Nation Building or Model Society: Nationalism and Socialism in the Israeli Labor Movement 1904–1990* (Tel Aviv: Am Oved, 1995) (in Hebrew).

31. Ilan Peleg, "Israel's Constitutional Order and Kulturkampf: The Role of Ben-Gurion," *Israel Studies* 3, no. 1 (1998): 237–61.

32. Yonathan Shapiro, *Politicians as an Hegemonic Class: The Case of Israel* (Tel Aviv: Sifriyat Poalim Publishing House, 1996), esp. ch. 2 (in Hebrew); Philippa Strum, "The Road Not Taken: Constitutional Non-Decision Making in 1948–1950 and Its Impact on Civil Liberties in the Israeli Political Culture," in *Israel: The First Decade of Independence*, ed. S. Ilan Troen and Noah Lucas (New York: State University of New York Press, 1995), 83–104.

33. Strum, "The Road Not Taken," 92.

34. Sabri Jiryis, *The Arabs of Israel* (Beirut: Institute of Palestine Studies, 1969); Ian Lustick, *Arabs in the Jewish State: Israel's Control over a National Minority* (Austin: University of Texas Press, 1980).

35. Peleg, "Biethnic Democracies."

36. Ofer Shelach, "No Covenant and No History," *Yediot Ahronot* (August 11, 2000); and Seffi Rachlevsky, *Messiah's Donkey* in *Yediot Ahronot* (Tel Aviv, 1998).

37. Shmuel Sandler, "The Religious-Secular Divide in Israeli Politics," *Middle East Policy* 4, no. 4 (June 1999), and Chaim Waxman, "Religio-Politics and Social Unity in Israel: Israel's Religious Parties," in *Israel's First Fifty Years*, ed. Robert O. Freedman (Gainesville: University Press of Florida, 2000), 162–79.

38. Dan Horowitz and Moshe Lissak, *Trouble in Utopia* (Hebrew version) (Tel Aviv, 1990).

39. Rita J. Simon and Jean M. Landis, "Trends in Public Support for Civil Liberties and Due Process in Israeli Society," *Social Science Quarterly* 71, no. 1 (spring 1990): 93–104.

6

The Palestinian National Movement

From Catastrophe to Disaster

BARRY RUBIN

The history of the Palestinian nationalist movement from its inception to the present day is a remarkable, almost unprecedented, mixture of success and failure. While the successes are merely sustaining—allowing the movement to continue to exist—the failures are destructive, preventing it from ever accomplishing anything and repeatedly returning to its beginnings in both material and ideological terms. This reality may be ignored, romanticized, or justified, but it is the core reality without which the Middle East's twentieth-century experience makes no sense at all.

The story of the Palestinians is intimately tied up with that of the Palestine Liberation Organization (PLO), and the tale of the PLO is inescapably intertwined with the personality and mind of Yasser Arafat. What can be said is that the movement, the PLO, and Arafat succeeded in building a broad-based and popular cause that survived many disasters. But it has failed because it has been the main author of those disasters and unable to reach its ultimate goal. Simultaneously, then, the movement has been the Palestinian people's greatest hope and biggest problem.

During the 1948–67 period, the Arab side never considered implementing a two-state solution by turning the Jordanian-ruled West Bank and the Egyptian-controlled Gaza Strip into a Palestinian state. After Israel captured those lands, almost all Arab states as well as the PLO rejected a wide range of peace plans—Israel's 1967 offer to trade captured territories for peace, the 1978 Camp David Accords, the 1982 Reagan plan, and many others—which might have been adopted, and adapted, toward this end.

In overcoming this impediment, it has taken almost half a century to arrive back at a situation approximating the one offered at the very start. The basic concept of the 1990s peace process—to create an Arab Palestinian state alongside an Israeli Jewish state—was the UN's original 1947 plan that had been accepted by Israel but rejected by the Arabs, who insisted that the only acceptable outcome was an Arab state on all the land between the Jordan River and the Mediterranean.[1]

The only option offered to Israel was to abandon national existence altogether, a clear roadblock to any political solution. Yet it was the Arab side whose strategic position steadily worsened. By 1948, the Palestinians could have obtained half of what they might have received in 1939; and by 1967, 1979, or 1993 their opportunities were halved again. Suffering the most in the long conflict, they were also the party that most perpetuated it, explicitly preferring deadlock to a solution requiring any real compromise.

The PLO's basic strategy was in line with the 1971 statement of Abu Iyad, the PLO's most powerful leader next to Arafat, that it had "no right" to negotiate a settlement but must keep struggling, "even if they cannot liberate a single inch," in order to preserve the option to regain all of Palestine some day. In 1984, he still thought the same: "Our steadfastness and our adherence to our land is our only card. . . . We would rather be frozen for ten more years than move toward treason."[2] No matter the justice of the Palestinian claim, it was simply not realizable. Consequently, trying to achieve it prevented the Palestinians from getting anything at all for a very long time. Indeed, even today, the Palestinian public has difficulty revising this worldview.

The PLO's strategy also arose from a specific analysis of Israel. Assuming that Israel's existence was an aberration, Palestinian leaders were sure the state would collapse. They urged Arab states to go to war; they staged terrorist attacks to demoralize Israelis, thinking the Israelis would ultimately flee or surrender; and they continued to fight on, believing that time was on their side.

All Arab states rejected Israel's creation in 1948 and maintained a position of total hostility toward it throughout the next thirty years. During that time permanent rejection of peace with Israel was the most fundamental principle of inter-Arab politics. Breaking this taboo was extremely dangerous—Jordan's King Abdullah was assassinated in 1951 by the Palestinian leadership, which feared he might make peace with Israel. Egypt changed this situation by entering into a treaty with Israel in 1979. But despite some secret contacts (mainly with Jordan), no other Arab country followed Egypt's example for another fifteen years. Meanwhile, Egypt was isolated, boycotted, and ejected from the Arab League. President Anwar al-Sadat, who had decided to end Egypt's war with Israel, was assassinated in 1981. Lebanon's 1983 agreement with Israel was terminated due to pressure from Arab states and domestic forces. The man who made that deal, Lebanese president Amin Gemayel, was forced to renounce it by Syria.

The Arab stance was originally based on an expectation of total victory. By the 1970s and 1980s, when this prospect seemed increasingly unlikely, most Arab regimes were still constrained from making peace by ideology, public opinion, and material interests. Obeying the Arab commandment of enmity toward Israel enhanced each regime's stability and ostensibly improved its position in the domestic and inter-Arab contest for power and survival.

For these reasons, the Arab-Israeli conflict was no typical international dispute that might be easily settled by some ingenious formula to split the difference. Equally, the decades-long deadlock was due not to a misunderstanding or mutual hostility but to the Arab side's rejection of compromise. As long as the Arabs viewed Israel's destruction as the only solution, there could be no serious negotiation.

The conflict's burdens did, however, wear down Arab eagerness, and perhaps even willingness, to pursue it. Arabs were frustrated at the inability to destroy Israel and the lack of any reason to believe that the situation would change in the Arabs' favor; likewise, they were frustrated and worn down by defeat in the 1956, 1967, 1973, and 1982 wars with accompanying losses of territory, money, prestige, and stability. Israel was strong enough to defend itself and to impose heavy costs on those who attacked it. Jordan expelled the PLO to end that group's threat to its stability and to avoid conflict with Israel. Syria barred direct terrorist attacks on Israel from its territory lest these provoke reprisals. Iraq saw its nuclear reactor destroyed; Saudi Arabia worried about possible attacks on its oil fields.[3]

Israel, Syrian foreign minister Farouk Sharaa warned, was more powerful than all the Arab states combined. The United States supplied Israel with advanced weapons from rifles to rockets and planes, plus gigantic computers that even the Europeans did not have. It was making advanced weapons of its own, exporting them even to China. New German-made submarines had arrived that could be equipped with nuclear missiles.[4] At the same time, Sharaa and his audience knew, Syria could not afford to pay top prices for the kind of weapons and spare parts it had previously been able to obtain from the USSR, paying discounted Soviet prices with aid from Saudi Arabia.

Equally, Arab leaders and intellectuals could no longer entirely ignore other problems that competed for attention or were worsened by the conflict. These included lagging economic development and growing domestic opposition groups, the threat from Iran, and the danger of radical Islamism. Inter-Arab quarrels continued unabated and sometimes exploded, causing dangerous crises. The oil producers had less money to finance military spending. The gap between rhetoric and action was also increasingly visible, as evidenced during the Lebanon war and the Palestinian intifada, when Arab states remained passive.

At the start of the 1990s these trends intensified due to both global and regional developments. Iraq's annexation of Kuwait showed just how dangerous the old game could be for Arab countries. By endangering regional stability, the Arab-Israeli dispute could be considered for the first time in history as undermining rather than reinforcing the regimes' hold on power. The Cold War's end and the USSR's collapse made the United States the world's sole superpower, weakened radical Arab regimes, gave moderate ones an incentive to improve relations with Washington, and reduced U.S. constraints on using its own power. For Arab states needing to ensure U.S. protection and aid, limiting the conflict and even making peace with Israel seemed a necessity.

Reflecting these historical lessons, Egypt's President Mubarak told an interviewer in 1989, in the most cogent critique of the traditional Arab view ever given, "God has granted us a mind with which to think. We fought for many years, but where did we get? We also spent 100 billion [sic] on wars, apart from thousands of martyrs until we reached the present situation from which we are now suffering. I am therefore not ready to take more risks. . . . Wars have generally not solved any problem. Regardless of the difficulties or obstacles surrounding the present peace process, our real effort focuses on removing these obstacles and bringing viewpoints closer."[5]

The PLO, too, has suffered from its misadventures during the long conflict and the changing conditions. For the PLO, the Arab states have been both blessing and curse. They have been an indispensable base of support without which the movement might have collapsed or been ignored, but they have also injured and tried to dominate it. While Western observers insisted that the Arabs passionately supported the Palestinian cause, Palestinians themselves felt "that virtually every Arab state has stabbed them in the back at one point or another," as Yezid Sayigh wrote in 1984.[6] A PLO intelligence chief estimated the Arab states were responsible for slaying three-quarters of the Palestinians killed in the struggle.[7]

Arab financial pledges have often gone unpaid. A 1978 inter-Arab agreement promised $250 million a year to the PLO and $150 million to a Jordan-PLO committee. Only Saudi Arabia has paid its share. Nor have Arab states given much to the UN relief effort for Palestinian refugees. The United States paid over 40 percent of its budget. During the 1970s and 1980s, Saudi Arabia was the PLO's most reliable source of aid. But apart from a short-lived 1973 oil embargo, the Saudis and other Gulf Arab monarchies have refrained from direct involvement in the conflict. In the latter 1980s, Saudi aid dwindled as Saudi Arabia spent more money at home and diverted funds to help Iraq in its war against Iran. As well, Saudi investments in the West have discouraged actions against Western interests.

The real crisis came when Arafat backed Iraq's seizure of Kuwait, provoking a strong, bitter Saudi response. All aid to the PLO and Palestinian institutions was cut off. Kuwait, whose many Palestinian residents had always made it so sympathetic to the PLO, went even further. After Iraqi forces retreated, Kuwait expelled most Palestinians from the country and virtually boycotted the PLO thereafter.

Arab states stood by, or even pushed, as the PLO was chased from Amman to Beirut, and from Beirut to Tunis. In this context, voting on UN resolutions, donating money, or even secretly abetting terrorism were low-risk propositions. But a PLO trying to drag them into another losing war with Israel or endangering their links to the West was a nuisance. A sympathetic historian wrote, "Few independence movements have been so heavily dependent on external assistance," making the PLO's survival require "unity at any price."[8]

Buffeted by constantly changing Arab policies, Arafat has tried to avoid becoming any ruler's enemy or puppet. This has been a hard chore, as evidenced by the 1970 Jordan-PLO war, the post-1975 Syria-PLO feud, and entanglements with Lebanon's civil war, Iran's revolution, and Saddam Hussein's takeover of Kuwait. The PLO also internalized the Arab world's fragmentation. The PLO is, after all, a loose umbrella organization, and Arafat has never made a serious effort to impose his will on the different ideologies, fiefdoms, and loyalties that simultaneously keep the PLO together while also ensuring its weaknesses and divisions. Constantly toiling for consensus with Arab states and Palestinian groups, Arafat has often given veto power to the most militant ones, blocking any realistic policy.

Even without pressure from those more radical then he, Arafat has repeatedly brought his cause to the brink of disaster. While he escapes each time, Arafat has never even gotten close to the brink of success. In 1970 the PLO was driven out of Jordan. A dozen years later, first Israel and then Syria threw him out of Lebanon. The Palestinian intifada of the late 1980s stirred up a great deal of enthusiasm but produced no real results. Refusing to condemn terror, Arafat threw away his first dialogue with the United States, then backed Iraq in its losing aggression. There was a slow trend in Palestinian debates toward realizing that some compromise with Israel was needed, but no decisive steps were taken.

After Saddam, Arafat's latest patron, suffered such a devastating defeat and discredit among the Arabs, Arafat needed to find a way out of the mess. In the 1990s, one could believe that a majority of Arab rulers were sick of the conflict. Rather than being useful in demagogic and financial terms, maintaining the old battle at its old intense level was clearly dangerous to the survival of some regimes as well as to the prosperity and stability of the countries involved, making them less likely to sacrifice themselves for the Palestinians.

For these and other reasons, Arab states and the PLO began talks with Israel in 1991. In 1993, the PLO signed an agreement with Israel that brought the PLO to the West Bank and Gaza as an interim government, the Palestinian Authority (PA), with the goal of reaching a solution to all the remaining issues. Next, Jordan signed a peace treaty with Israel. Once the PLO signed its own agreements with Israel, it could no longer deny other Arabs the right to do the same thing.

Arab leaders saw the decision as freeing them to choose whether to make peace with Israel, consider their obligation to the Palestinian struggle as ended, or condemn Arafat as a sell-out. Syrian defense minister Mustafa Tlass called Arafat "the son of 60,000 whores" for making too many concessions.[9] Other Syrian leaders used less rude words but also showed their disdain. Most Arab governments took the opportunity to withdraw even further from the conflict and to reduce help for the Palestinians. Only about 5 percent of money pledged to the PA came from the Arab world. Indeed, Israel and the United States were now in the strange position of urging Arab states to help Yasser Arafat.

Meanwhile, moderate Arab states complained about Arafat's policies in order to excuse their minimal help for the PA; radical regimes denounced the peace process. The 1996 Arab summit's final communiqué demonstrates this principle. The Arab leaders urged Europe, Japan, and other countries "to continue providing political and economic support to the Palestinian people and their National Authority." But there was absolutely no Arab pledge—not even a nonbinding recommendation—to organize their own aid program for the Palestinians.[10]

Still, by June 1996, the Arab summit's final resolution called peace with Israel "a strategic decision."[11] Mubarak urged Israel's government "to cooperate with us so as to complete the peace process without slackness or hesitation." King Hussein noted that the Arabs always knew peacemaking would be hard, but the current process was "the only available option . . . [and] possible means to bring the conflict to a just and lasting solution that can endure."[12]

Many thought that a solution would be reached because it fulfilled Arab interests. The question remained, though, which set of interests would be paramount. Some people argued, for example, that progress in Arab-Israeli peacemaking would help place the extremists on the defensive and increase their isolation. This was an overly optimistic assessment, since accusing one's own or a neighboring ruler of selling out Arab nationalism or Islam to Western imperialism continued to prove a useful tool for domestic insurgents and regimes alike. The incumbent governments knew they were being asked to give up an issue that provided their best way of mobilizing internal support, ensuring national unity, and deflecting attention from local problems.

Others contended that when governments, freed by the peacemaking process from engaging in hostilities, would concentrate on the economic well-being of their people, then they would feel more secure in meeting their citizens' demands for greater political participation and accountability.[13] Yet, as rulers felt pressed by economic problems or citizens' demands, they were likely to become more—not less—authoritarian. "Political participation" sounded like a recipe for creating more opposition and internal conflict; "accountability" was a nice way to imply that the leaders would be blamed for their incompetence and corruption.

The history of the 1993–2000 peace process was extremely complex, full of intricate details, agreements, and violent incidents. Yet in the end, it is not accurate to claim that this effort's collapse—an effort so many decades in the making—came about merely because of small issues involving timing and personalities, the precise location of borders, or the exact degree of control over holy sites. The ultimate problem was that the Arab world failed in practice to come to terms with making peace. Even those people, including Arab leaders, who wanted to do so were blocked by their own interests as well as by the framework of regional maneuvering and public opinion they had done so much to create. Can one really conclude that for Lebanon, Syria, and the Palestinians alike, peace agreements were impossible because of a dispute over 1 percent of the land when Israel was ready to turn over the equivalent of 99 percent?

In the Palestinian case, Arafat was ready to sacrifice hundreds of lives and the chance to have an independent state, nominally because of a dispute over a few square blocks in Jerusalem, at a time when Israel was ready to hand over the equivalent of all of the West Bank, Gaza, and most of East Jerusalem. Clearly, the impediment was not these issues but something far deeper and broader: the difficulty of making peace at all and the problems it entailed, the risks involved, and the need to give up all the domestic and regional advantages of having the conflict continue.

For the Palestinians, who have the most to lose, a large element in any outcome is Arafat's problematic leadership. Whether due to a miscalculation in the balance of forces or a failure of nerve, a fear of transforming himself from revolutionary to statesman, or an unwillingness to give up the idea of getting everything in the future, the result is the same. It is one more example, Fouad Ajami wrote, of the Palestinian "refusal to bow to the logic of things that can and cannot be, in its sublime confidence that some force would come to their rescue and a sense of exemption from the historical laws of gravity. . . . The practical always yields in Palestinian thought and practice. It loses out to the wrath, to the persisting idea that the land as a whole . . . is still there to be claimed."[14]

Abdallah Laroui gave a haunting depiction of this sensibility that the hope of ultimate victory is too priceless to compromise for material betterment. "On a certain day," Palestinians believed, "everything would be obliterated and instantaneously reconstructed and the new inhabitants would leave, as if by magic, the land they had despoiled; in this way will justice be dispensed to the victims, on the day when the presence of God shall again make itself felt."[15]

A leader would have to tell his people that this kind of utopian outcome is not going to happen. Arafat will not do this any more than his counterparts might openly call for abandoning the Arab national or Islamist dream. Indeed, he has followed the opposite course, building up further the hope of a right of return for the Palestinians. Even if he were to achieve a state, he would not agree that a two-state solution would end the conflict. Arafat has never made the kind of speeches that are routine for leaders elsewhere in the world, preaching the virtues of education and economic enterprise, preparing the ground for democracy, or encouraging civil society. Somehow, like his fellow Arab leaders, no disaster wrought by his decisions has ever damaged his power. As Ajami notes, Arafat has "done so well for himself by sending his people down so many blind alleyways, so many historical dead ends."[16]

The Arab states did act in reaction to Arafat's decisions to reject the peace proposals presented in 2000 by Israeli prime minister Ehud Barak and President Bill Clinton and then to carry out a war on Israel. Arafat's analysis of Israel and its withdrawal from Lebanon made him expect Israel would make more concessions or even pull out of the West Bank and Gaza Strip unilaterally. Observing earlier events in Kosovo, he also seemed to expect that the violence would cause international intervention to send peacekeeping forces and eventually turn over the territory to the Palestinians.

If Arafat had signed a treaty with Israel, he would have been criticized by many in the Arab world and among his own people. If he had simply refused to make an agreement, his people would be frustrated by the lack of change and he would be criticized in the West for blocking peace. By rejecting peace and mobilizing violence, though, he became a hero to the Arab world and a victim, at least for a while, to the West. Domestic criticism has been silenced. His support in the Arab and Islamic world has hit an all-time high. The choice was politically brilliant on one level, but the price has been the needless sacrifice of a thousand lives, much of the Palestinian infrastructure, and the chance of achieving Palestinian statehood on good—if not ideal—terms.

Even while Arafat seriously contemplated a compromise solution during the Oslo process, he never really challenged the basic goals and ideas that had shaped the movement over many years. Even as he met with Barak at Camp David, the constitution of his Fatah group continued to proclaim its goal to be the "complete liberation of Palestine and eradication of Zionist economic, political, military and cultural existence. . . . Armed public revolution is the inevitable method to liberating Palestine . . . a strategy and not a tactic. . . . This struggle will not cease unless the Zionist state is demolished and Palestine is completely liberated." Even as its leader negotiated, Article 22 of the constitution opposed "any political solution offered as an alternative to demolishing the Zionist occupation in Palestine."[17]

These concepts are not merely relics of the past; they continue to influence the thinking and strategy of Palestinian leaders and activists. PA minister of information Yasir Abd Rabbu told his people over *Voice of Palestine* radio that Barak's offer to turn over the West Bank, Gaza, and parts of East Jerusalem to the Palestinians was a trick intended to "perpetuate their rule over us and turn us into a satellite state of Israel, which will come out of the settlement as the leading power in the region. No one can agree to that."[18] Yet one could equally conclude that any conceivable negotiated solution would arguably leave Israel as "the leading power in the region."

The only thing that could prevent that outcome was the lack of any diplomatic settlement to the Arab-Israeli conflict.

The Clinton administration may have gone further than any previous American government to help the Palestinians, but to Arafat's own Fatah movement Clinton's effort to create a Palestinian state with its capital in East Jerusalem merely proved that "the Zionist group of the White House and the Zionist lobby are controlling the future of the Palestinian people's cause." Making clear its real objection to the Camp David and Clinton proposals, Fatah explained that the right of all Palestinians to return (and, in a newly invented additional demand, to be allowed both to return and to receive compensation "for the years which the occupation used these properties) would bring about the real solution. The right of return does not aim to destroy Israel as Zionists claim; the right of return seeks to help Jews get rid of the racist Zionism that wants to impose their permanent isolation from the rest of the world."[19] In other words, the only outcome it would consider would be one that eliminated Israel on the basis of the PLO's 1974 program, which continued to dictate Palestinian strategy a quarter-century later.

As for the alleged willingness of Arafat's forces to suppress the radicals who would continue to attack Israel and continue the conflict after a Palestinian state was established, Fatah saw this possibility as still another reason to oppose Clinton's plan. This proposal was in fact "the biggest trick" because accepting it "means moving the conflict into an internal Palestinian-Palestinian conflict that will destroy the Intifada."[20]

Rather than oppose the radicals, Arafat's lieutenants want to join them in their strategy and goals. For Fatah's young leaders suicide bombing and terrorism are not just by-products but the very essence of the new strategy to overcome Israel's military superiority. They see that their key advantage is "the ability to transfer the battle into the enemy's territories."[21] Precisely because they are unable to take on Israel's army, their optimal advantage is an ability to blow up and shoot Israel's civilians until that country gives up.

Some Palestinian leaders view violence as a clever tactic to gain more Israeli concessions, yet they do not seem to realize how these actions are destroying any chance for a negotiated solution. Thus, Hani al-Hassan, a Fatah Central Committee member and adviser to Arafat, told a Gaza symposium in October 2000, "The present Intifada enabled the Palestinians to change the old rules of the game, and thwarted Barak's attempt to place the responsibility for the stalemate in the peace process on them."[22] As hundreds of Palestinians were being killed, the PA infrastructure was being destroyed; as terror tactics alienated the world and squandered all the gains of the 1990s, al-Hassan could maintain that the intifada had strengthened the PA. As Israel easily won the military conflict and Israelis came to totally disbelieve Arafat as a partner for peace and move toward electing Ariel Sharon as prime minister, Hassan proclaimed, "What we have witnessed in the Palestinian territories these past few days obliges our negotiators to raise the level of demands in the negotiations."[23]

Arafat in particular tried to incite the region to the height of nationalist and Islamic passion at the October 2000 Arab summit. Speaking of Israeli opposition leader Ariel Sharon's one-hour visit to the Temple Mount in which he entered no buildings, Arafat thundered, "Sharon desecrated the al-Aqsa mosque and its compound. A new, religious, dimension was added to the Arab-Israeli struggle." He said that Israel's government was carrying out a "mass extermination campaign against our people," which it had been plotting for over a year. He accused Israel of using internationally banned weapons. Rather than negotiating with Israel, he said the problem could be solved only if Israel "is forced to submit to international legitimacy, implement the signed agreements, stop aggression," and so on.[24]

There was a curious contradiction in the Palestinian explanation of this struggle. On one hand, it was the Palestinian war of independence, an offensive fought by heroic warriors to force Israel to yield to all of their demands. On the other hand, it was a defensive battle waged by helpless victims that was only made necessary by an unprovoked, carefully planned Israeli aggression intended to force Palestinian submission.

Many Palestinian leaders could not conceal their absolute certainty that they would defeat Israel. PA communications minister Imad al-Faluji was different from other leaders in that he came from an Islamist background, but his views were typical. Speaking at Ein al-Hilwe refugee camp in Lebanon during March 2001, he explained why the Palestinians could ignore the kinds of considerations that other political forces had to take into account: "The Palestinian people are the strong half of the international equation. It is the secret code and the key to any stability and peace not only in the Middle East, but in the world. . . . You can be sure that your stay here is temporary. We will not allow any force to raise any issue detrimental to the Right of Return to Palestine."[25]

Faluji's intoxication with exaggerated expectations of victory is not so different from the ideas expressed by Saddam Hussein, Bashar al-Assad, and many others among the Arab world's politicians, intellectuals, and average people alike. As Faluji put it, "Just as the national and Islamic

Resistance in South Lebanon taught [Israel] a lesson and made it withdraw humiliated and battered, so shall [Israel] learn a lesson from the
Palestinian Resistance in Palestine. The Palestinian resistance will strike in
Tel Aviv, in Ashkelon, in Jerusalem, in every inch of the land of natural
Palestine. . . . We will return to the early days of the PLO, to the 1960's and
1970's. . . . A new stage will continue until the rights are returned to their
owners."[26]

This absolute hatred was not just a propaganda ploy that could be
shrugged off. Each accusation and distortion of Israel beyond its very real
faults made it harder for Palestinians to envision any possible compromise
and for Israelis to believe they would ever do so. The official Palestinian
news agency, Wafa, for example, published stories claiming that Israel had
started a new genocide against the Palestinian people by dropping poi-
soned bags of candy into Gaza from airplanes.[27]

Nader Tamimi, the mufti of the Palestinian Liberation Army, stated on
al-Jazeera television that "the Jews have a sadistic mentality derived from
the Torah which they have distorted as saying that man is 'a creature born
from the seed of a horse.' The Torah says that all peoples that are not Jews
must be killed." Suicide bombers were martyrs who would be married in
heaven to seventy-two virgins. "I, the Mufti of those forces fighting in
Palestine, say to them: your hand is blessed, brothers, when you kill; your
hand is blessed, mother, who nurses this child who will one day become a
martyr; your hands are blessed when you kill the enemy, blessed be you in
Heaven, with the prophet Muhammad."[28]

Abu Ali Shahin, a veteran Fatah official who served in Arafat's cabinet,
stated that "accepting the Oslo Accords was for the Palestinians, a be-
trayal of the historical legitimacy of the Arab right to Palestine." It was
legitimate only because it was done "in order to gain a better position and
to continue in liberation of the land." Syria's Vice President Khaddam
portrayed the intifada as the "countdown for the destruction of Israel."[29]
And a Lebanese leader claimed that the present time offers "an excep-
tional historic opportunity to finish off the entire cancerous Zionist project."[30] "We were forced to leave Jaffa, Haifa and Tel Aviv," said a Hamas
leader, "and recovering from that can only be achieved when war returns
and forces the invaders out."[31]

It was the return of the old PLO slogan "revolution until victory" that
guided the organization through so many defeats, miscalculations, and
setbacks.[32] Muhammad Dahlan, a young favorite of Arafat who com-
manded the Preventive Security force in Gaza and represented the next
generation of Palestinian leadership, explained in October 2000, "The

release of some Hamas people [imprisoned for past terror attacks against Israel] is an ordinary, natural, and simple step, compared to the steps we are going to take in the future. . . . The Intifada will continue until victory."[33] Similarly, a communiqué published that same month by the Supreme Supervisory Committee of the Nationalist and Islamist Forces, signed by twelve groups including Arafat's Fatah, proclaimed, "The Intifada will continue until the aggression is repelled and the realization of all its goals." It called for a united struggle to "disarm the settlers, expel them, and destroy the settlements."[34]

Yet not one settlement was dismantled nor a single settler expelled. By December 2001, Arafat was forced to announce, though not necessarily to implement, an unconditional cease-fire. One of the few public critics of the intifada strategy was Salah Abdel Jawad, chairman of the political science department of Bir Zeit University. No Palestinian newspaper would publish his op-ed piece warning that Palestinians were unprepared for such a military confrontation, that there was an enormous gap between the two sides' capabilities, and that Palestinian leaders simply did not understand the situation.[35]

Younger Palestinian militants, who did not remember the 1960s, 1970s, or 1980s, repeated their fathers' mistakes. Muhammad Dhamrah, deputy commander of Arafat's bodyguards, Force 17, echoed assertions of the intifada's potential for success. The Arabs must "force Israel to end its occupation of the Arab lands, without the smallest [Arab] concession on any right whatsoever." The proper method was to fight relentlessly: "Kill your enemies wherever you may find them. This is a life and death conflict between you and them" until the enemy surrenders. Independence would be achieved "through sacrificing. We have prepared thousands, tens of thousands, of martyrs in order to regain our land and for the return of the refugees. . . . I am not worried. I am very optimistic that victory will come."[36]

There was no limit to the Palestinians' military capacity: "I promise that the number of shootings at the occupation will increase to 500 to 1,000 [incidents] per day. . . . The Palestinians have trained themselves to attack the Israeli tanks and explode their bodies that will be loaded with a belt of explosives. . . . The Palestinians have nothing to lose, while the Israelis have a lot to lose. We can live on olives and za'tar [thyme] and continue our struggle until the liberation of our land."[37]

A good example of this gap between theory and practice could be seen after a brief incursion by Israeli forces into Jenin in August 2001. After the Israeli army pulled back, Palestinian media and discussion revolved around how the "heroic resistance" of armed Palestinian fighters had forced the Israeli tanks to retreat. Tayeb Abd al-Rahim, Arafat's top aide, stated that the Israeli forces had seized seventy collaborators who were being held prisoner and killed two or three Palestinians. In fact, no one had died, no one had been freed from the local prison, and the Israelis had left when they completed their mission. The police had fled when the Israeli troops arrived. "Of course, I ran," said a police lieutenant. "I have nothing with which to oppose them. . . . We're not afraid of them, but we don't have the means. We don't have the weapons."[38] This was the kind of thing that happened when misjudgment led leaders of the weaker side to launch a war based on wrong claims of superiority and inevitable victory.

Remarkably, the statements of Arab leaders and writers during and after 2000—including the younger generation of Palestinian activists— were often identical to explanations of strategy made thirty years earlier that had proven wrong. In 1970, for example, Arafat had explained, "The Israelis have one great fear, the fear of casualties." He intended "to exploit the contradictions within Israeli society." Killing enough Israelis would force the country's collapse, or at least its surrender to Palestinian demands or—the new aspect of the argument during the more recent period—unilateral withdrawal from the West Bank and Gaza. A PLO official in 1970 said that the Jews could not long live under so much tension and threat: "Zionist efforts to transform them into a homogeneous, cohesive nation have failed," and so they would run away or give up. "Any objective study of the enemy will reveal that his potential for endurance, except where a brief engagement is concerned, is limited." The 1968 Palestine National Council meeting concluded: "wearing down Israel will inevitably provide the opportunity for a decisive confrontation in which the entire Arab nation can take part and emerge victorious."[39]

The goal of Palestinian violence, Arafat said in 1968, was to destroy tourism, prevent immigration, weaken the Israeli economy, "to create and maintain an atmosphere of strain and anxiety that will force the Zionists to realize that it is impossible for them to live in Israel." Each Israeli, said the PLO's magazine in 1970, would come to feel "isolated and defenseless" against Arab forces that would be everywhere. Each Israeli would then be bound to value more highly "the life of stability and repose that he enjoyed in his former country" compared with the "life of confusion and anxiety he finds in the land of Palestine. This is bound to motivate him towards reverse immigration." In the 1980s, too, similar themes were expressed in PLO documents. The enemy's "greatest weakness is his small population." Attacks against civilians in the streets would demoralize the Israelis.[40]

Younger Palestinians simply did not remember, and had not been taught, that these ideas had never worked. Islamists especially took up the notion that their readiness to become martyrs would make the difference. The relatively recent immigration of most Israelis was no longer a factor; now the Israeli withdrawal from Lebanon and alleged decadence of Israeli society were supposed to explain why the Palestinians would win a war of attrition. Arguably, the first intifada of the late 1980s and early 1990s had also been based on similar failed notions, though the great propaganda around these events concealed the fact that the uprising had faded away and Israel had actually won that round, also.

The case of Palestinian and, to some extent, Arab strategy, was one of the greatest proofs in modern times of the dictum that those who do not remember history are fated to repeat it. This was not a new pattern in Middle East history. The Palestinians repeatedly, as a moderate Jordanian pointed out, missed opportunities and failed to learn the resulting lessons because their leaders feared "being accused of leniency and negligence [of Palestinian rights]." Since "the Arabs will never agree to be defeated, and the Jews will never allow the shattering of the State of Israel," the only way out was a pragmatic solution involving "mutual concessions from which both sides benefit."[41] Many Palestinian leaders understood this in private but would not speak out in public. At any rate, to whatever extent Arafat understood this reality, he did not act in the manner required to implement it successfully.

Notes

1. After fifty years of struggle, the size of the Palestinian state under discussion was smaller than could have been easily achieved in 1948.

2. Abu Iyad, January 9, 1971, *International Documents on Palestine, 1971* (Beirut, 1972), 352; *al-Majalla*, March 10, 1984. Arafat used almost precisely the same words in December 1977.

3. For an overview of the conflict and Arab politics during these years, see Avraham Sela, *The Decline of the Arab-Israeli Conflict: Middle East Politics and the Quest for Regional Order* (Albany: State University of New York Press, 1997).

4. An interesting example of Arab perceptions was Syrian foreign minister Sharaa's claim that Israel's arms spending was twenty times that of Syria's budget. In fact, according to the Stockholm International Peace Research Institute (SIPRI), Israel's 1998 defense budget was $8.5 billion while Syria's was $3.1 billion. Even this gap, however, is misleading since a large portion of spending was for soldiers'

wages and benefits that were far lower in Syria. In proportion to their gross domestic products, the two countries have a similar level of military spending: 9.5 percent for Israel compared to about 8 percent for Syria.

5. Interview, *Middle East News Agency,* January 24, 1989, in FBIS-USSR (January 25, 1989), 15.

6. Yezid Sayigh, "Fatah: The First Twenty Years," *Journal of Palestine Studies* 13, no. 4 (summer 1984): 115.

7. Ibid.; Walid Kazziha, *Palestine in the Arab Dilemma* (London: n.p., 1979), 15–19.

8. Alain Gresh, *The PLO: The Struggle Within* (London: n.p., 1985), 246. See also Walid Khalidi, "The Asad Regime and the Palestinian Resistance," *Arab Studies Quarterly* 6, no. 4 (fall 1984): 265.

9. Syrian defense minister Mustafa Tlass as quoted in the Lebanese newspapers *al-Safir* and *Daily Star,* August 3, 1999.

10. Official text of the resolution declared at the Arab summit. See "Final Communiqué," FBIS-USSR (June 23, 1996), vol. 2, 13; CNN web site, *http://www.cnn.com/WORLD/9606/23/summit.transcript* (June 23, 1996).

11. "Final Communiqué."

12. Text of June 22, 1996, speech from Egypt's Ministry of Information, State Information Service.

13. Despite Nasser's credible 1967 threat, he did not actually attack Israel. Anwar Sadat's 1973 strategy was to fight in order to gain leverage for negotiations. Saddam Hussein attacked Israel only when the Kuwait war had already begun and he was in a desperate situation.

14. Fouad Ajami, *U.S. News & World Report,* January 8, 2001.

15. Cited in Fouad Ajami, "The Sentry's Solitude," *Foreign Affairs,* December 2001.

16. Ajami, *U.S. News & World Report,* January 8, 2001.

17. Fatah's constitution, *http://www.fateh.org.*

18. *Voice of Palestine,* October 9, 2000.

19. *http://www.pna.gov.ps/peace/44 reasons.htm*; *http://www.pna.gov.ps*; "Forty-four Reasons Why the Fatah Movement Rejects the Proposal Made by U.S. President Clinton," *Our Opinion* (Fatah Movement Central Publication).

20. Ibid.

21. Ibid.

22. *Al-Ayyam,* October 12, 2000, translated in Middle East Media and Research Institute (MEMRI), no. 135 (October 13, 2000).

23. Ibid.

24. Speech at the Arab summit in Cairo, October 21, 2000 (translated in FBIS).

25. Alan Dowty and Michelle Gawerc, "The Intifada: Revealing the Chasm," *Meria Journal* 5, no. 3 (September 2001).

26. *Al-Safir,* March 3, 2001, translated in MEMRI, no. 194 (March 9, 2001).

27. Official Palestine News Agency, "Israel Is Poisoning the Palestinians' Candies," *http://www.wafa.pna.net/EngText/21–05–2001/page4.htm* (May 15, 2001).

28. Al-Jazeera television, May 23, 2001, translated in MEMRI, no. 245 (July 23, 2001).

29. Abdel Halim Khaddam, Agence France-Presse, July 25, 2001.

30. *Financial Times,* April 25, 2001.

31. Reuters, May 16, 2001.

32. Barry Rubin, *Revolution until Victory: The Politics and History of the PLO* (Cambridge: Harvard University Press, 1993).

33. *Al-Jazeera,* October 12, 2000; *al-Ayyam,* October 12, 2000, translated in MEMRI, no. 135 (October 13, 2000).

34. *Al-Ayyam,* October 12, 2000, translated in MEMRI, no. 135 (October 13, 2000).

35. Salah Abdel Jawad, "The Intifada's Military Lessons," *Palestine Report,* October 25, 2000.

36. Deputy Commander of Force 17, Muhammad Dhamrah (Abu Awdh), interview with *al-Hayat,* August 17, 2001, translated in MEMRI, no. 260 (August 22, 2001).

37. Ibid.

38. Clyde Haberman, "City Israel Raided Is Oddly Jubilant," *New York Times,* August 15, 2001.

39. "Yassir Arafat," *Third World Quarterly* 8, no. 2 (April 1986), and also *South,* January 1986, 18; *al-Anwar* symposium of March 8, 1970, cited in Y. Harkabi, *The Palestinian Covenant and Its Meaning* (London: n.p., 1979), 12; Arafat, May 1969, *International Documents on Palestine, 1968* (Beirut, 1969), 400.

40. Arafat interview, January 22, 1968, in *International Documents on Palestine, 1968* (Beirut, 1969), 300; *Filastin al-Thawra,* January 1970, 8; Raphael Israeli, *PLO in Lebanon: Selected Documents* (London: n.p., 1983), 31.

41. Fahed al-Fanek in *al-Rai,* March 22, 2001, translated in MEMRI, no. 203 (April 5, 2001).

7

Jordan

Walking a Tightrope

YEHUDA LUKACS

The signing of the free trade agreement (FTA) between the United States and Jordan on October 24, 2000, was intended to herald a new era in Jordanian-American relations. The trade pact, ratified by the U.S. Senate on September 24, 2001, would remove all trade barriers between the two countries for ten years. Jordan is only the fourth country, after Canada, Mexico, and Israel, to have signed such an agreement with the United States. King Abdullah II had hoped that the agreement would provide evidence of tangible "peace dividends" to those who have opposed Jordan's peace with Israel. The agreement would demonstrate that Jordan was now en route to an economic recovery led by the country's integration into the global economy. With his ambitious liberalization plan the king aims to attract foreign direct investments, bolster exports, and create new jobs to address Jordan's chronic unemployment problem. The signing of the trade pact, however, took place under the shadow of the daily violent clashes between the Israeli military and Palestinian youth known as the al-Aqsa intifada that started in late September 2000. The killings of over 1,500 Palestinian youth by Israeli soldiers (as of April 2002) has led to a severe backlash inside Jordan in support of the Palestinians; several hundred demonstrations have taken place since the beginning of the uprising. The demonstrators vociferously denounced the trade pact with the United States, Israel's staunchest ally, demanded the expulsion of the Israeli ambassador from Amman, and called on the king to sever all ties with the Jewish state.

These demonstrations have underscored King Abdullah's predicament. Since he became monarch in February 1999 after the death of King Hussein, Abdullah's top priority has been to reform the stagnant Jordanian economy by launching an ambitious liberalization program. This plan was inextricably linked to upgrading Jordan's relations with the industrialized West—particularly the United States—from whom the king obtained cancellation of Jordanian debt, one billion dollars a year in foreign aid, and a free trade agreement. Relations with the United States, however, are also linked to sustaining the peace treaty with Israel—opposed by most Jordanians—and playing a mediating role in the faltering Israeli-Palestinian negotiations. At the same time, reforming the Jordanian economy also depends upon improved relations with Iraq, Jordan's largest trading partner prior to the Gulf War—a move supported by the majority of Jordanians, but opposed by the United States. The eruption of hostilities between Israel and the Palestinians in the occupied territories has threatened to destroy this very delicate and complex policy construct built by King Abdullah since his coronation.

Juggling multiple interests simultaneously without seriously undermining the legitimacy of the regime or alienating Jordan's Palestinian majority as well as the Islamist opposition, and preserving a modus vivendi with Jordan's powerful neighbors—Israel, Syria, Iraq, and Saudi Arabia—have been the hallmark of Jordanian domestic and foreign policy in the last several decades under the leadership of the late King Hussein. It is clear that King Abdullah is following in his father's footsteps, but it is too early to ascertain whether the new monarch will be as adroit and successful as his father was in navigating Jordanian politics and foreign policy problems, given the formidable challenges that lie ahead.

Since 1963, when he first met secretly with Ya'acov Herzog of the Israeli Foreign Ministry, King Hussein participated in dozens of clandestine gatherings with Israeli leaders. These encounters took place in London, on an Israeli missile boat in the Gulf of Aqaba, in a safe house near Tel Aviv, and in several other locations.[1] Most meetings focused on the question of the West Bank (in the post-1967 period) and on the possibility of reaching a formal understanding between the two countries regarding a contractual peace. The meetings also focused on issues of bilateral concern. One of the best examples attesting to Israeli-Jordanian convergence of interests took place in 1970, when Israel mobilized its military to deter the Syrian army from advancing toward Jordan's heartland and threatening the regime during the civil war between Hussein and the PLO. By doing so, Israel demonstrated its willingness to risk a war against Syria in order to protect its vital interests—the preservation of the Hashemite monarchy and opposition to the establishment of a Palestinian state on either bank of the Jordan River.

Other issues of mutual concern between Israel and Jordan included agriculture; the transfer of Israeli irrigation technology to Jordan; the sale of Israeli medical supplies to Jordan during the 1970 civil war; the sharing of the Yarmouk waters; banking in the West Bank; communication links between the Aqaba and Eilat airports to prevent accidents; joint energy projects in the Dead Sea; Jordanian financial and administrative involvement in the West Bank; and even joint efforts against insects and mosquitoes in the Gulf of Aqaba.

According to Aaron Klieman, the underlying interest galvanizing the interdependence between Israel and Jordan "has been the parallel quest for security through the exclusion and subordination of the Palestinian national movement."[2] The ascendance of the PLO after 1967 to center stage in regional and international politics has posed a challenge to both Israel and Jordan. Prior to King Hussein's 1988 administrative disengagement from the West Bank, the PLO and Jordan were engaged in an overt and covert battle over the question of who represented the Palestinians. The Arab world formally recognized the PLO as the "sole legitimate representative of the Palestinian people" in the 1974 Rabat resolution. Jordan, however, attempted to bypass the formal endorsement of the Palestine Liberation Organization by continuing its financial and administrative links to the West Bank and attempting to woo the Palestinians to accept Jordan as their representative. Israel, as part of its strategy in the territories, was very encouraging of these attempts to "Jordanize" the West Bank and minimize the influence of the PLO. These efforts were ultimately aimed at creating an Israeli-Jordanian condominium or joint rule in the West Bank. All these undertakings, however, came to an end as a result of the Palestinian uprising that began in December 1987 and led to King Hussein's July 1988 announcement of Jordan's administrative and legal disengagement from the West Bank.

Israeli-Jordanian Relations after 1967

Faced with Israel's refusal to withdraw from the territories occupied in the 1967 war, Jordan had no choice but to accept the reality imposed by Israel. King Hussein maintained that the Palestinians and the Jordanians were the same people who were part of the East Arab nationalist ideal, of which his great-grandfather was the first titular head. Nevertheless, he was often forced by circumstance to pursue a pragmatic approach designed to protect his dynastic power. In order to enter into an open, public dialogue with Israel (before the Madrid Conference), King Hussein needed Arab backing, Palestinian passivity, and, above all, Israeli willingness to return the entire West Bank and East Jerusalem. In the absence of such willingness, Hussein chose to pursue "functional cooperation" with Israel, a policy developed by Israel's defense minister, Moshe Dayan, who encouraged Jordan to maintain an administrative foothold in the West Bank after 1967 even though it had lost the territory to Israel. This cooperation coalesced around the Open Bridges policy and included joint Israeli-Jordanian collaboration in a wide range of activities.[3] King Hussein believed he had little to lose from endorsing this arrangement. He would try to maintain Jordanian influence in the West Bank and at the same time engage in a secret dialogue with Israel, hoping that eventually the diplomatic impasse would be broken and Jordan would regain its lost territory. The fact that neither Hussein's secret meetings with Israel's leaders nor Jordanian-Israeli cooperation in the territories was public knowledge allowed Hussein to accept the functionalist approach. Since the king could not get what he really wanted, he settled for second best. The formal state of war with Israel provided Hussein with a cover to deny any contacts with his formal enemy.

Jordan's policy toward Israel and the West Bank has been shaped by a number of factors. First, the historical links between the East and West Bank have been extremely important in shaping Jordanian policy following the 1967 war. The removal of Transjordan from the provisions of the British Mandate in 1922 was never fully accepted by Hussein's grandfather, Abdullah, who sought to establish the Kingdom of Greater Syria under his rule. Abdullah was also the first Arab leader who attempted to negotiate a peace agreement with Israel after the 1948 war. In addition, it was the Arab Legion under Abdullah's leadership that secured the Old City of Jerusalem during the 1948 war and prevented an Israeli takeover of the city. When King Abdullah was murdered in 1951 at the al-Aqsa mosque in Jerusalem, Hussein was standing by his grandfather's side. Hussein never accepted the loss of East Jerusalem in 1967, the city that his grandfather secured, and regarded the liberation of Jerusalem as a top priority. Even after Jordan's administrative and legal disengagement from the West Bank in July 1988, King Hussein remained as the protector of the Muslim holy places in Jerusalem. In its peace treaty with Israel, Jordan is granted a "special role in Muslim holy shrines in Jerusalem." Second, demographic factors have played a crucial role in shaping Jordanian foreign policy. During the 1948 war, 750,000 Palestinians became refugees by being forced out of or fleeing from Palestine to the East and West Banks. Following the Six Day War, over 200,000 Palestinian refugees crossed from the West to the East Bank, thus increasing the Palestinian population on the East Bank. The Palestinian population further grew following the Gulf War when approximately 300,000 refugees fled to Jordan. It is estimated that Jordan's 5 million population is composed of 50–60 percent Palestinians, including 1.57 million refugees.

While the Hashemites' power base rests on the Transjordanians who are most loyal to them, the Palestinians themselves have been integrated into the mainstream of Jordan's social, political, and economic life. Although Palestinians are not fully represented in key political positions such as the army and security services, they have nonetheless acquired a real stake in the continued stability and security of Jordan. As long as the final status of the territories has not been determined, few desire to jeopardize what has become a second home and risk returning to a precarious situation. The best testimony to the Palestinians' stake in the status quo was their relative noninvolvement in the Jordanian 1970 civil war when Hussein fought the PLO. While the Jordanian security services kept a close watch on the Palestinians during the war, most of them did not join the PLO in their struggle against the regime. Also, the king's support of Iraq during the Gulf crisis and war earned him high respect among the Palestinians living in Jordan, most of whom were ardent supporters of Iraq's president Saddam Hussein.

In the period 1967–88, Jordan pursued a dual-track approach in its dealings with Israel, reflecting the constraints on its freedom of action and the ambivalence that characterizes its relationship with the Palestinians. Jordan faced the dilemma of how to incorporate Palestinian national aspirations within a Jordanian framework without jeopardizing the delicate balance underlying Hashemite supremacy on the East Bank. Despite official adherence to the Arab consensus on the need to establish an independent Palestinian state on the West Bank, established in Rabat in 1974, Jordan was extremely uneasy about such a development. Hussein feared that an independent Palestinian state might inspire irredentist tendencies among East Bank Palestinians, who would then attempt to destabilize the regime as was the case during the 1970 uprising.

As part of the first track, between 1967 and 1988 Jordan attempted to check the influence of the PLO in the West Bank by utilizing the Open Bridges policy, which provided for a linkage between the two banks so Jordanian influence could be exerted on the West Bank. The Jordanians have had an additional motive in maintaining a modicum of involvement in the West Bank. By aiding the Palestinians in the West Bank, Jordan hoped to stem emigration from the West Bank since it feared that movement of Palestinians to Jordan would undermine the already precarious demographic balance in the East Bank. In July 1988, however, during the Palestinian intifada, King Hussein decided to sever all administrative and legal ties to the West Bank and abandoned any claim to represent the Palestinians in any future negotiations. He feared that maintaining Jordanian involvement in the West Bank could lead to an anti-Hashemite backlash on the East Bank and undermine the regime.

The second track entailed consistent involvement in the peace process, attempting to bridge the gaps between the Arab and Israeli positions so a formal peace could be signed. In this context, Hussein met secretly with Israeli leaders for hundreds of hours in search of an Israeli agreement to withdraw. Publicly, however, Jordan abided by all Arab League resolutions concerning peace with Israel, and King Hussein stood at the forefront of Arab political and diplomatic efforts to secure an Israeli withdrawal. This included an active encouragement of all international and particularly American efforts to resolve the conflict. Jordan participated in both the Geneva and Madrid international conferences held in 1973 and 1991 respectively. Its negotiations with Israel following the Madrid Conference culminated in a peace treaty signed in October 1994. The only major effort in which Jordan refused to participate was the Camp David peace process, although Jordan was mentioned in the agreement fifteen times.

When examining Israeli-Jordanian functional cooperation between the Six Day War in 1967 and Jordan's disengagement from the West Bank in 1988, it is argued here that the sub-rosa peace, rather than promoting a formal Israeli-Jordanian peace, in fact contributed to the status quo during that period. It effectively forestalled resolution of the Arab-Israeli conflict because it met the immediate needs of both countries without having to end the formal state of war. Sub-rosa interaction certainly contributed to a quiet border, reduced tensions, and helped foster habits of cooperation between the two formal enemies. However, de facto peace with its eastern neighbor was perceived by Israel's leaders as *yielding the benefits of peace without having to decide on the fate of the occupied territories* and thus resulting in the prolongation of the diplomatic status quo. Likewise, Jordan was unwilling to forfeit or expose its clandestine relationship with Israel and engage in a public diplomatic process that would endanger the regime and yield few benefits, given Israel's position vis-à-vis the territories. Neither Israel nor Jordan was willing to take a major risk in open-

160 | Yehuda Lukacs

ing a public dialogue in light of the lack of societal consensus in Israel over the question of withdrawal and Jordan's reluctance to openly break Arab ranks over recognition, negotiations, and peace with Israel.

The impact of Israeli-Jordanian cooperation on the Palestinians was also significant. The Open Bridges policy, for example, enabled Palestinians to continue to trade with Jordan and travel from the territories to destinations in the Arab world; it also maintained the dinar as the legal tender, and Jordan continued its administrative involvement in the educational, legal, and economic spheres of the West Bank. Above all, it was hoped that "Jordan would continue [after 1967] to exercise the sociopolitical influence it had wielded so effectively during the years of its rule. This entailed preserving the traditional leadership, reinforcing localism, and co-opting newcomers through traditional *hamula* [familial] channels—elements of political control that Israel, as a non-Arab occupier, could not control."[4] In other words, cooperation with Jordan became an instrument of managing the occupation of the territories in order to prevent a popular nationalist uprising, an interest shared by both Israel and the Hashemites. It took the Palestinians twenty years, from 1967 to 1987, to start such an uprising. The intifada had tremendous impact on the Palestinians, Israel, and Jordan and increased the outside world's sympathy toward the Palestinians. It is impossible to speculate what might have happened had Jordan refused to cooperate with Israel in the territories after it lost the West Bank in 1967, but it is safe to assume that the Palestinians would have attempted to rise up against the occupation much earlier than 1987.

The nature of the two countries' relations, however, was transformed in the wake of the Palestinian intifada and Jordan's July 1988 administrative and legal disengagement from the West Bank. Jordan was no longer the party with whom Israel was expected to negotiate over the Palestinian question. This was left to Israel and the PLO.

The Gulf War, the end of the Cold War, and the persistence of President George Bush and Secretary of State James Baker in starting an Arab-Israeli dialogue were largely responsible for the Madrid Conference and the ensuing bilateral and multilateral talks. The new regional and international climate, coupled with Jordan's need to rehabilitate its image as a result of the support it gave to Saddam Hussein during the Gulf War, propelled the kingdom into talks with Israel, initially as part of a joint Jordanian-Palestinian delegation. Israel started the negotiations with the joint team over West Bank autonomy, but it had no intention of making any significant concessions to the Palestinians. Former Prime Minister Shamir, for instance, admitted that he sought to prolong the negotiations for as long as ten years until the West Bank would be totally populated by Israeli set-tlers.[5] Consequently Jordan, unburdened by the weighty issue of the West Bank, began to pursue bilateral concerns such as water, refugees, and Is-raeli withdrawal from Jordanian territories occupied by Israel outside the West Bank, culminating in the October 1994 peace treaty.

Given the remarkable level of functional cooperation that took place under the shadow of formal war, it was expected that the formal peace between Israel and Jordan would inaugurate a new era in the two coun-tries' relationship. The Treaty of Peace, aimed at establishing full normal-ization, included specific clauses in the agreement that governed coopera-tion in, inter alia, trade, tourism, transportation, water, Dead Sea resource management, and joint policing efforts against drugs and crime. Yet con-trary to expectations, Jordanian-Israeli peace did not materialize in a "warm" peace, nor did it transform into a model of mutually beneficial Arab-Israeli agreement. Although the two countries have implemented several agreements, as stipulated in the Treaty of Peace, the overall tenor of the relationship has deteriorated considerably. By early 2001, it no longer reflected the optimism and triumphalism that existed when the agreement was signed. Instead, misguided policies, deceit, and lost oppor-tunities have marred the relationship, especially during Benjamin Netan-yahu's tenure as Israel's prime minister, and have subsequently resulted in disappointment and opposition to the process of normalization by the majority of Jordanians, many of whom are of Palestinian origin.

The election of Benjamin Netanyahu in May 1996, following the as-sassination of Yitzhak Rabin, had far-reaching negative implications for the Arab-Israeli-Palestinian peace process. Netanyahu was determined to slow down the Oslo negotiation process started by Rabin and to con-tinue building Jewish settlements in the occupied territories. As leader of the Likud Party, he adhered to his party's platform, which called for an end to the "territory for peace" formula championed by the Labor Party, re-fusal to establish a Palestinian state, and insistence on Israeli sovereignty over all of Jerusalem. Netanyahu's anti-Palestinian policies and lack of sensitivity to Jordan's precarious position vis-à-vis the Palestinian issue led to a significant deterioration in the relationship between the two countries.

What were the specific causes of the crisis in the relations between the two countries? There are at least four interrelated explanations for this situation: First, the stalemate in negotiations between Israel and the Pales-tinians had a direct negative impact on Jordanian-Israeli relations. Second, several actions taken by the Netanyahu government strongly back-fired, including opening of the "archaeological" tunnel near the Temple Mount in September 1996, as well as the attempt to assassinate Khalid Mishal, a leader of Hamas, in Amman in September 1997. Third, Jordan's need to export to the West Bank and Gaza was overridden by the persis-tence of powerful Israeli interests who wanted to maintain economic hege-mony over the Palestinian territories. Fourth, given Jordan's chronic water shortages, King Hussein had expected that Israel would be generous in establishing an equitable water-sharing regime between the two countries. In fact, water became a litmus test according to which Israel's real commit-ment to peace with Jordan would be measured. Yet, in spite of a May 1998 water agreement, Jordanians still feel that Israel has not lived up to the spirit of their accord.

Despite the fanfare that surrounded the signing of the Wye River Mem-orandum in October 1998—an agreement that called for further Israeli redeployment in the West Bank—its numerous provisions were not imple-mented in full by Israel. It should be noted that the negotiations leading to the signing of the Wye Memorandum were salvaged, in large part, by King Hussein's last-minute appearance and strong emotional appeal. Hussein, who flew to Maryland from the Mayo Clinic in Minnesota, where he was being treated for cancer, used his moral authority in making a last-ditch effort for peace. Yet the Netanyahu government refused to implement the agreement because of pressure from inside the Likud Party as well as from other right-wing members of the governing coalition who opposed any further Israeli redeployment. This crisis led to Netanyahu's downfall and the election of Ehud Barak in May 1999.

Opposition in Jordan to normalization of relations with Israel is wide-spread. It is not limited only to opposition Islamist groups; almost all professional associations, chambers of commerce, and ordinary Jordani-ans share this sentiment. Those who reject normalization cite Israel's con-tinued harsh practices against the Palestinians and only partial adherence to implementing the various agreements signed with Jordan and the Pales-tinians. According to Mustafah Hamarneh, former director of the Center for Strategic Studies in Amman, 80 percent of Jordanians expected con-crete economic results from the peace with Israel.[6] A poll conducted in August 1994 showed 66 percent support by Jordanians for the Washing-ton Declaration that ended the state of war between the two countries. However, in the last few years this support has evaporated. In 1998, a *Jordan Times* survey indicated that 80 percent of Jordanians viewed Israel as an enemy.[7] Jordanians point to unfulfilled promises made by the late King Hussein that peace would improve their daily lives.

As noted by Laurie Brand, King Hussein's response to the growing popular opposition to the peace with Israel was to reverse the process of political liberalization that began in Jordan in 1989. The king showed little tolerance for criticism of his relations with Israel. Brand cites the dismissal of Prime Minister Abd al-Karim Kabariti, who strongly objected to the king's visit to Israel in March 1997. After seven Israeli schoolgirls were killed by a Jordanian soldier while visiting a peace park along the Israeli-Jordanian border, King Hussein cut short a trip to Spain and Washington and came to express his personal condolences to the bereaved families. The king's gesture moved the entire Israeli nation. Yet, Kabariti argued against Hussein's visit, which he regarded as humiliating. The disagreement with the king cost the prime minister his job.[8] As an example of the anti-Israeli mood that has prevailed in Jordan in the past few years, many Jordanians now regard Ahmed Daqamseh, the 26-year-old soldier who murdered the Israeli children, as a hero.

When Benjamin Netanyahu was elected in May 1996, King Hussein was the only Arab leader who welcomed the newly elected Israeli leader, asserting that Netanyahu would support the peace process. Soon thereafter, however, Netanyahu's September 1996 decision to open a tunnel with archaeological significance near Haram al-Sharif (Temple Mount) led to large-scale Palestinian demonstrations and to fighting between the Israeli and Palestinian police. Hussein reacted with considerable anger, saying that he viewed the Israeli action as an attempt to undermine the status quo in Jerusalem, a disregard of Israel's pledge to safeguard the Muslim holy places in the city, and a violation of the Israeli-Jordanian treaty. After all, Jordan's historic role in Jerusalem was recognized both in the July 1994 Washington Declaration and in the peace treaty that was signed later, in October of that year. As an example of Israeli duplicity, Hussein pointed to the visit to Amman of Dore Gold, the Israeli premier's adviser, who met with Hussein just one day before the opening of the tunnel without providing the monarch with any notice of the Israeli plan.

During a hastily arranged summit in October 1996 convened by President Bill Clinton and attended by Yasser Arafat, Netanyahu, and Hussein, following the violent explosion in the territories resulting from the opening of the tunnel, the Jordanian monarch blasted the Israeli leader for his ill-conceived decision, growing intransigence, and lack of consideration of Jordanian interests. King Hussein felt that the actions of the Israeli government were jeopardizing the very delicate balance the Hashemites had maintained with the Palestinians, inside and outside the monarchy, and embarrassed Hussein, who had placed such blind faith in the relationship with the Israelis.

A year later, on September 25, 1997, Israeli Mossad agents bungled an assassination attempt against Khalid Mishal, leader of Hamas, the Palestinian Islamist organization responsible for numerous suicide attacks inside Israel. The attempt almost culminated in severance of diplomatic relations between Israel and Jordan. It was the worst crisis between the two countries since their treaty was signed. King Hussein felt personally betrayed and humiliated as a result of the Mossad's failed operation on Jordanian soil. Israel's attempt to inflict a blow against Hamas in fact backfired; not only did King Hussein force Israel to release Sheikh Ahmed Yassin, the spiritual leader of the Palestinian organization, from jail, but also the little credibility Israel enjoyed in Amman vanished as a result of this episode.

This event convinced even those Jordanians who were not actively engaged in opposing normalization that Israel was behaving as a foe rather than a friend. Popular anger swept throughout Jordan, and Hussein was deeply offended by what he considered to be Netanyahu's callous act. The Mossad operation made the Jordanian king vulnerable, especially given the already existing domestic opposition to relations with Israel. Jordanians began referring to the peace with Israel as the "King's peace." Indeed, the Mishal affair was a nadir in the relationship between the two countries that reinforced the perception that the Netanyahu government was trying to actively undermine the Jordanian government.

The third reason underlying the difficulties between the two countries is rooted in Israeli economic interests in the Palestinian territories. Very shortly after the capture of the West Bank in 1967, Israeli officials opted to turn the newly occupied territories into a satellite of the Israeli economy—a source of cheap manual labor and a captive market for Israeli goods. While the number of Palestinians who work in Israel has decreased to approximately 35,000 from over 150,000 in the mid-1980s, Israel still maintains an economic iron grip over the territories despite the redeployment of its troops from several areas in the West Bank and Gaza. Israeli economic interests have superseded any ideological division that has divided Israeli society over the fate of the occupied territories. Although Israel and the PLO have signed a number of agreements, including the May 1994 trade and economic protocol, Israel still controls imports and exports to and from the West Bank and Gaza. Thus, Israel's economic hegemony over the Palestinians has hurt not only the Palestinians but also Jordan, which has been keenly interested in exporting to the territories, especially in light of the UN embargo on Iraq, which is still Jordan's most important trading partner.

King Abdullah II inherited a country with a $6.8 billion foreign debt, a colossal public sector (one out of every seven Jordanians is employed by the government), and an unemployment rate of nearly 30 percent. While Jordan's economic malaise is attributed to regional developments and domestic economic policies, nonetheless, Jordanians expected that the peace treaty would yield some peace dividends. Jordanian officials point to Israel's refusal to allow Jordan to trade freely with the Palestinian territories as a clear example of Israeli protectionism intended to safeguard Israel's selfish economic interests at Jordan's expense. Indeed, the discrepancy between Israeli and Jordanian annual exports to the territories is glaring: In 1999 Israel exported $1.8 billion while Jordanian exports were merely $22 million, almost a hundred times less than Israel's trade with the territories. The West Bank and Gaza are the second largest market for Israeli goods after the United States. Even Stuart Eizenstat, Undersecretary of State for Economic, Business, and Agricultural Affairs and considered to have been one of Israel's staunchest supporters in the Clinton administration, called on Israel to act with a "sense of urgency" to address these "unacceptably low" Jordanian export levels.[9]

Another bone of contention has been the establishment of a water-sharing regime. Jordan expected that Israel would be generous in this regard. Despite several agreements signed, including the last one signed in May 1998 and negotiated by Ariel Sharon, Israel's then minister of agriculture, Jordan still feels that the question of water sharing is far from resolved.

The events surrounding the al-Aqsa intifada and the failure of the Palestinian-Israeli negotiations in July 2000 at Camp David, including President Clinton's unsuccessful last-minute efforts to reach a final-status agreement in December 2000, demonstrated that despite its 1988 disengagement from the West Bank, Jordan cannot disengage from the Palestinian issue. Jordan now has to face up to the reality that it is highly unlikely that an Israeli-Palestinian peace treaty will be signed in the foreseeable future. This new reality, coupled with a new Israeli government headed by Ariel Sharon, champion of the "Jordan is Palestine" idea, means that the peace treaty signed with Israel will not be supplanted either by the Jordanians, the Palestinians in the West Bank and Gaza, or the Arab world. Pressure will continue to mount on King Abdullah II to sever all ties with Israel, but breaking diplomatic relations with the Jewish state could adversely affect Jordanian regional interests and its vital relationship with Washington and its new free trade agreement, a linchpin of King Abdullah's economic reform policies. The king now faces serious tensions at home. These multiple challenges and his ability to deal with them are likely to impact the long-term survivability of the Hashemite dynasty.

The al-Aqsa intifada erupted on September 28, 2000, against the background of the failure of the Camp David negotiations to produce a final-status agreement and following a provocative visit of Ariel Sharon to Haram al-Sharif or the Temple Mount. The Palestinians regard Sharon, whose anti-Palestinian views are well known, as a war criminal for his role in the 1982 Sabra and Shatila massacre of hundreds of Palestinians by Lebanese Christian Phalangists during Israel's invasion of Lebanon. Sharon's visit was meant to underscore the position of the nationalist camp in Israel, which opposes relinquishing Israeli sovereignty over any part of Jerusalem, especially the Temple Mount, site of the ancient temple and Judaism's holiest site. The violent clashes between Palestinian youth and the Israeli military, resulting by April 2002 in over 1,500 Palestinians dead and thousands wounded, have led to a serious backlash inside Jordan.

In a speech to the Arab League summit held in Cairo on October 23, 2000, King Abdullah sent an unambiguous warning to Israel: "Israel's stand, marked by its barbaric reaction and its excessive use of unjustified military force, calls for condemnation. We warn [Israel] against pursuing further similar acts that can only lead to adverse political consequences in the entire region, including Israel itself."[10] Hundreds of anti-Israeli demonstrations took place in Jordan, culminating in several clashes between the demonstrators and Jordanian police. One of the demonstrations included a "March of Return" of over 10,000 legislators, political activists, and trade unionists representing Jordan's thirteen opposition parties, who attempted to cross the border linking Jordan with the West Bank and clashed with police in fighting that injured over 100 demonstrators. It was also reported that the twenty-two-mile road from Amman to the border was filled with Jordanian armored personnel carriers, and security forces kept many people from reaching the demonstration.[11] Moreover, a petition signed by twenty-three deputies from the lower house (House of Representatives) demanded the expulsion of the Israeli ambassador and the severing of all ties with Israel: "To hell with a peace treaty that is going off track and not fulfilling the needs of its people or implementing the agreements. . . . as deputies, we saw fit to act in accordance with the demands and pulse of the Jordanian public that has been demanding the closure of the Israeli embassy."[12]

As part of this highly charged atmosphere inside Jordan, the families and all nonessential employees of the Israeli embassy in Jordan were evacuated to Israel in early December 2000 after assassination attempts were carried out against two Israeli diplomats. Israel's ambassador to Jordan, David Dadon, became the most sought-after target and required extraordinary security protection.[13] In a signal to Israel, Jordan's government decided not to dispatch Abdullah al-Kurdi, its new ambassador to Tel Aviv.

Even those few individuals who were supportive of peace with Israel changed their minds. The propeace sentiment existed in isolated pockets of businesspeople, academics, artists, and a few journalists. These individuals were often stigmatized and even expelled from their professional associations and were branded as "normalizers," which carried the connotation of treachery. As a result of what was perceived as Israel's excessive violence against the Palestinians during the al-Aqsa intifada, those few propeace voices fell silent. Some even apologized in public for previously promoting peace with Israel. Amal Dabbas, for example, an actress well known for her roles in the Nabil and Hisham Theatre of Political Satire, issued a formal letter of apology to the Jordanian Artists Association for her travel to Israel alone and with her theater:

> The facts have revealed themselves. We are living an unfair and unjust peace and we are dealing with an elusive enemy that does not want to respect treaties or peace.... I am Muslim and I believe in the Quran and the sayings of the Prophet Mohammad.... the Quran said kill the Jews.... This is befitting for the enemy. Therefore, I express the total conviction of my deepest soul and my apologies for visiting Israel. It's not shameful to admit I was wrong. There is nothing wrong in apologizing to the people who were wiser than me and who can see all sides of the issue.[14]

Another challenge faced by the Jordanian government has been the Palestinians' "right to return," an issue that came to the fore as a consequence of the final-status negotiations between Israel and the Palestinian Authority. In his last-ditch proposal to salvage the Israeli-Palestinian negotiations before ending his term as president in January 2001, President Clinton in December 2000 offered a framework proposal calling upon both parties to make significant concessions. Israel was asked to cede sovereignty to the Palestinian Authority over Haram al-Sharif and the Arab neighborhoods of East Jerusalem. Concerning the 3.7 million refugees' right to return, Clinton offered five possible homes for them: the State of Palestine; areas transferred by Israel as part of a land swap (Israel handing over territory gained in 1967 in exchange for Israeli retention of land in the West Bank where most settlement blocs are located); relocation in countries where they are currently located, such as Jordan; resettlement in third countries; or admission to Israel. He stated that priority ought to be given to refugees currently living in Lebanon and proposed that an international commission be established to facilitate compensation, resettlement, and rehabilitation of refugees. Acceptance of this proposal would constitute, according to Clinton, full implementation of UN Resolution 194.[15]

The Jordanian public is adamantly opposed to absorbing any new refugees. This was clearly expressed by Jordan's prime minister, Ali Abul Ragheb, during a meeting with deputies of the Jordanian parliament in early January 2001.[16] Members of the parliament, representing a Transjordanian constituency, have demanded that Jordan not only reject any proposal to settle new refugees but also require compensation for the fifty years that Jordan has "hosted" Palestinian refugees on its soil. They even calculated a figure of $40 billion in compensation—$20,000 for each of the 2 million refugees.[17] Clearly, the Jordanian government refuses to endorse any solution that would increase the proportion of Palestinians living in Jordan. In this regard, Jordan, Lebanon, and Syria—hosts of the largest number of Palestinian refugees—all agree that a resolution of this problem should not be carried out at their expense, but, rather, should be consistent with UN Resolution 194, which calls for either a return or compensation. The Lebanese government, in particular, has expressed very clearly that once an agreement between Israel and the Palestinians is reached, the 365,000 Palestinian refugees in Lebanon will be forced to leave, and Jordan is very concerned that the refugees will end up on Jordanian territory.

The question of Palestinian refugees and their right to return is clearly a vital concern of the monarchy. This issue affects the fabric of Jordanian society and touches upon the very delicate relationship between the Transjordanians and the Palestinians. This situation could potentially destabilize the kingdom. Here again, King Abdullah must balance his desire for a resolution of the conflict with pragmatic considerations of maintaining demographic stability at home and with his reluctance to allocate already scarce resources to settle new refugees beyond those 1.57 million refugees who currently live in Jordan.

As with the question of refugees, although Jordan is not a direct party to the final-status negotiations between Israel and the Palestinians, its interests are clearly affected by the terms of settlement or unilateral actions taken by the parties. When a Palestinian state will finally be established—

either as part of a peace agreement or a unilateral declaration by the Palestinian leadership—the nature of the triangular relationship between Jordan, Palestine, and Israel will be of penultimate importance in determining the long-term viability of the Hashemite Kingdom of Jordan. If Israel implements a plan for unilateral withdrawal from the West Bank and separation from the Palestinians, and Jordan and Palestine establish a confederation, long-term demographic processes might lead to the end of the rule of the Hashemites. After all, the Palestinians constitute the majority of the population; over half of the deputies in the Jordanian parliament are Palestinians, several Palestinians hold cabinet posts, and they play a vital role in the Jordanian economy.

Moreover, Israeli prime minister Ariel Sharon is suspected by most Jordanians to hold the belief that "Jordan is Palestine and vice versa." Sharon was the first Israeli leader to support such a position as early as September 1970, when King Hussein battled the PLO during the civil war. Sharon, who wore a military uniform at that time, called on the Israeli government to remove its strategic support of the Hashemites and help establish a Palestinian state in Jordan instead of the West Bank. Sharon, however, has recently clarified his position vis-à-vis Jordan in an interview given to the Paris-based Arabic journal *Kulal Arabi*:

> Jordan, contrary to all other Arab countries, agreed to settle Palestinian refugees which are within it. Now the situation is different. [In 1970] I didn't think of a Palestinian state on both banks of river Jordan. When I spoke then, I meant a Palestinian state in the East of [the] Jordan. But now something took place and we are facing a Palestinian state which is being established [in the West Bank]. I want to again say that the Hashemite Kingdom of Jordan is a factor that is very supportive of stability in the Middle East. This factor is the most important one in the stability of the Middle East.[18]

Despite this clear pronouncement, many Jordanians are uncertain about Sharon's real intentions, especially if a serious crisis were to erupt in the future. Jordanians point to statements made by other Israeli officials indicating that a body of opinion—small as it may be—still would solve the Palestinian problem at Jordan's expense. For example, when King Abdullah II was crowned in February 1999, individuals in the Israeli intelligence community put forward an assessment that in all likelihood Abdullah would be the last Hashemite monarch.[19] Even Haim Ramon, one of the Labor Party's leaders and a member of Barak's cabinet, stated in 1997 that, although he had differed with Sharon in the past, he had changed his views and was fully convinced of the inevitability of Jordan being turned into a Palestinian state in the future.[20]

It is now clear that Jordan and Israel no longer enjoy the strong bonds that the two countries maintained for several decades, especially during the reign of King Hussein. A few Jordanian officials have voiced concern that Israel's support and protection of the Hashemites, continued for over three decades after 1967, cannot be guaranteed in the long term, given the vicissitudes of politics in the Middle East, especially if the conflict lingers on with no solution in sight.

In a similar vein, a few Israeli officials have speculated that even though the PLO formally and unequivocally supports the political integrity of the Hashemite kingdom, it is plausible to assume that when a new leadership emerges in the post-Arafat era, enlarging the borders of the Palestinian state eastward could become tempting, especially if Israel maintains its vehement opposition to the repatriation of refugees and Lebanon insists on the Palestinians leaving. Jordan, then, could become the only safe haven for the refugees, thus tilting the demographic balance inside Jordan even further in the Palestinians' favor. Therefore, given the long adversarial and problematic relationship between the Hashemites and the PLO, and between Transjordanians and the Palestinians inside Jordan, the longevity of the Hashemite dynasty cannot be taken for granted.

The al-Aqsa intifada has also had a negative impact on the already vulnerable and fragile Jordanian economy. Tourism, the kingdom's third-largest foreign currency earner, has declined considerably since the violence erupted in the territories in late September 2000. Moreover, in light of the measures taken by Israel against the Palestinians in the territories, including the temporary closure of the Allenby Bridge as a result of an attack by a Jordanian citizen on an Israeli bus, Jordanian companies have been unable to export to the West Bank and Israel.

Relations with the Arab World

Against the backdrop of these challenges emanating from the Palestinian issue, King Abdullah has concentrated on improving Jordan's ties to its Arab neighbors—especially Iraq, Syria, and the Gulf states—as well as launching a serious economic reform plan with the free trade agreement with the United States.

In an interview given to the London-based newspaper *al-Quds al-Arabi*, King Abdullah outlined his approach toward the Arab world: "With the new reign, we are opening a clean sheet with everyone based on mutual respect. Jordan is Arab first and last and cannot shed its skin . . . what concerns us in Jordan is to have a united and stable Iraq whose people are not suffering. . . . [Jordan] will not be a launching pad for any hostile actions against Iraq."[21] Abdullah is determined to avoid repeating a policy that cost Jordan political alienation and financial punishment following his father's support of Saddam Hussein during the 1991 Gulf War, yet Jordanian public opinion is firmly against the UN sanctions regime. Indeed, Jordan was the first Arab country to dispatch a plane with medicines to the people of Iraq in a direct challenge to the UN embargo. Before the Gulf War, Iraq was Jordan's main trading partner, and its exports to Iraq totaled $1 billion per year.[22] In appreciation for Jordan's gestures, Iraq now supplies Jordan with oil well below world market prices and remains its main trading partner.

The thorny issue of the embargo against Iraq was one of the two main items on the agenda of the summit of the heads of Arab states convened in Amman in March 2001. Despite the failure of the conference to reach an agreement on this question, King Abdullah played a leading role in attempting to bridge the gap between Kuwait and Iraq. Kuwait was demanding that Iraq apologize for its August 1990 invasion and return the 600 Kuwaiti prisoners believed by Kuwait to be languishing in Iraqi jails. Moreover, Kuwait expected that a mechanism would be put in place by the Arab leaders that would prevent another Iraqi invasion in the future. Iraq objected to the Kuwaiti conditions.[23] For Jordan, however, removing the embargo against Iraq goes beyond assisting an Arab neighbor. As noted by a Jordanian analyst: "We reached the conclusion that it is not possible to allow the Jordanian economy to continue to be a hostage to the insanity of the Palestinians and Israelis, and we need to find alternative sources. If we do not export we cannot survive. . . . Iraq is almost our lifeline."[24]

Jordan has also improved its relationship with Syria, the Arab Gulf states, and Libya, whose president visited Jordan in October 2000 to sign an agreement financing half of a $600 million water project inside Jordan.[25] The daily *Jordan Times* summarized the new Jordanian foreign policy toward the Arab world. It suggested that the fact that "a Jordanian prime minister [Ali Abul Ragheb] is able to travel to Iraq only days after signing a free trade agreement with Washington and a day after a Kuwaiti military official was decorated by His Majesty King Abdullah . . . is indicative of the political acumen of the Kingdom."[26]

This new multipolar orientation in Jordan's approach toward the Arab world is best reflected in the reinvigoration of its relations with Syria. For the past three decades, Jordanian-Syrian relations have oscillated between discord and cooperation. The April 1999 visit of King Abdullah to Syria marked a turning point in the bilateral ties, frosty since Jordan signed a peace treaty with Israel in October 1994. Today, the two countries enjoy a blossoming relationship marked by several joint economic projects, increased trade, and above all, a close rapport between Abdullah and the new Syrian president, Bashar al-Assad, both of whom are part of the new generation of young Arab leaders.[27]

In September 1970 a Syrian armored unit crossed its border with Jordan in an attempt to assist the Palestinian guerrillas who were fighting the Jordanian army. The Syrian unit was repulsed, partly as a result of Israel's signal to Syria that the integrity of the Hashemite kingdom constituted a vital Israeli interest. By 1975–77 the two countries were able to mend their differences and even explored ways in which they could integrate their economies, from linking their electrical grids to publishing textbooks for use in both Jordanian and Syrian schools.[28] However, internal unrest and the ensuing violent crackdown on supporters of the Muslim Brotherhood (Ikhwan) in Syria led to a significant deterioration in the relationship during the winter of 1979–80, and Damascus suspected and accused Jordan of aiding the Ikhwan inside Syria against the Assad regime.[29] Jordan denied Syria's accusations, but a cold war followed. The relationship further deteriorated on the eve of the Arab League's summit in Amman in November 1980. The summit was boycotted by Syria, whose support of Iran in its war against Iraq irritated most of the Arab world, especially Jordan, Iraq's closest ally. The boycott was accompanied by a propaganda campaign against the Jordanian regime, closure of the common border, and the massing of Syrian troops at Darʿa, the place from which the Syrians had invaded Jordan in September 1970.[30] Syria agreed to withdraw its troops from the border only after a Saudi diplomatic intervention, but the escalating tensions remained and both countries recalled their ambassadors. The hostility between the two countries affected several joint economic schemes, such as the al-Wahdah dam (until 1986 named the al-Maqarin dam) over the Yarmouk River, which Jordan abandoned in favor of an irrigation scheme in cooperation with Iraq. The Jordanian-Syrian cold war reflected the deep divisions in the Arab world in the wake of the Iran-Iraq war and over different approaches to the Arab-Israeli conflict. The support of opposition groups within each country—such as Syria's ties to the illegal Jordanian Baʾath Party and the Jordanian Communist Party, and Jordan's assistance to the Ikhwan—were also part of the confrontation between the two regimes. By mid-1985, the two countries began a process of narrowing their differences, partly because of the adverse impact of the Iran-Iraq war on both countries' economies. They were desperately "in need of whatever an economic boost in improvement in bilateral relations could secure."[31]

Jordan's support of Iraq, Syria's traditional nemesis, during the 1990–91 conflict in the Gulf, however, led to a considerable renewed strain between the two countries. Jordan's media promoted anti-Syrian broadcasts, and Syria imposed temporary restrictions on border crossings in retaliation. The rift deepened after Jordan signed a peace treaty with Israel in 1994. The Syrians regarded the Jordanian treaty as well as the 1993 Oslo Accords between Israel and the PLO as betrayals of pan-Arab solidarity, similar to the manner in which Syria viewed Egypt's separate peace with Israel. After all, Syria had also participated in the U.S.-sponsored international conference in Madrid, but unlike Jordan and the PLO, the Syrian-Israeli track did not yield any agreement. This left the Syrian president Hafiz al-Assad ever suspicious and frustrated by his inability to recover the Golan Heights from Israel. Assad strongly opposed both agreements, which he regarded as capitulations to Israel and the United States resulting from the inherent weakness of the Jordanian regime and the PLO leadership. As late as the fall of 1998, Syria's defense minister, Mustafa Tlass, characterized the Jordanian royal family as attempting to "Judaize" their country, implying that Jordan's existence was a quirk of British colonial fate.[32]

Another issue that has caused considerable anxiety in Damascus and in numerous Arab capitals has been the emergence of a possible American-Turkish-Israeli military axis in the eastern Mediterranean. In January 1998 a representative of the Royal Jordanian Navy was an observer at a Turkish-American-Israeli search-and-rescue exercise, "Reliant Mermaid," and this led to numerous charges by Syrian and Arab officials that Jordan was secretly forming a military alliance with Turkey and Israel.[33]

The first sign that Syrian hostility toward Jordan was beginning to ebb occurred when President Assad surprisingly attended King Hussein's funeral in February 1999. The April 1999 reciprocal visit by King Abdullah to Syria symbolized the opening of a new chapter in the history of the two countries' complex and unstable relationship. The appointment of Abdel Fatah Amura as the new Syrian ambassador to Jordan—the first ambassador since 1993—reflects the improvement of relations, especially since Bashar al-Assad became president in June 2000. On the practical level, numerous cooperative ventures were signed, including a Syrian transfer to Jordan of 3.5 million cubic meters of water in light of Jordan's severe water shortage, an agreement to proceed with the al-Wahdah dam on the Yarmouk, a free-trade-zone agreement, and a revival of the dormant Jordanian-Syrian Higher Committee that coordinates all cooperative ventures between the two parties.

Syria under Bashar is facing numerous internal challenges similar to those tackled by King Abdullah—economic growth, privatization, improvement of the infrastructure, foreign investment, and relations with the West—some of which are tied to the question of peace and normalization with Israel.

Conclusion

It is clear that the continuation of the Israeli-Palestinian conflict will affect Jordan's domestic and foreign policy agenda. The al-Aqsa intifada has revealed the vulnerability of the kingdom to domestic unrest and has pitted the government against those Jordanians who have demanded the closure of the Israeli embassy in Amman and the expulsion of the ambassador. The official ban on demonstrations has shown that the government is seriously concerned about the long-term impact of popular anger. But the ban is not a solution to the rage expressed by most Jordanians against Israel, nor did it prevent the shooting of two Israeli diplomats in Amman.

Jordan's strategic interest in maintaining its peace treaty with Israel will be seriously hampered if the government succumbs to public pressure to sever ties with the Jewish state. King Abdullah's attempts to reform the economy by attracting foreign direct investment, especially American, European, and Asian, will fail to materialize should Jordan reverse its peace agreement. Its relationship with the United States—with the new free trade agreement—could also deteriorate. However, if Israeli-Palestinian violence persists and the peace process is not reinvigorated, the young monarch will not be able to ignore popular opinion forever, especially if the long-term survival of the Hashemite regime is at stake. The late King Hussein ruled Jordan for thirty-six years and met numerous domestic, regional, and international challenges in an adroit manner. Whether the son will be able to follow in his father's footsteps and successfully tackle these formidable challenges in the future remains to be seen.

Notes

1. For an overview of Israeli-Jordanian relations, see Yehuda Lukacs, *Israel, Jordan, and the Peace Process* (Syracuse, N.Y.: Syracuse University Press, 1999);

Adnan Abu Odeh, *Jordanians, Palestinians, and the Hashemite Kingdom in the Middle East Peace Process* (Washington, D.C.: United States Institute of Peace, 1999); Adam Garfinkle, *Israel and Jordan under the Shadow of War* (New York: St. Martin's Press, 1992); and Mark Lynch, *State Interests and Public Spheres* (New York: Columbia University Press, 1999).

2. Aaron Klieman, *Statecraft in the Dark: Practice of Quiet Diplomacy* (Boulder: Westview Press, 1982), 95.

3. See Lukacs, *Israel, Jordan, and the Peace Process,* ch. 3.

4. Samuel Sandler and Hillel Frisch, *Israel, the Palestinians, and the West Bank* (Lexington, Mass.: Lexington Books, 1984), 59.

5. *New York Times,* June 27, 1992, 1.

6. Mustafah Hamarneh, "The Opposition and Its Role in the Peace Process: A Jordanian View," in *Palestine, Jordan, Israel: Building a Base for Common Scholarship and Understanding in the New Era of the Middle East,* Research Studies no. 105 (Jerusalem: PASSIA, 1997).

7. *Jordan Times,* January 7, 1998.

8. Laurie Brand, "The Effects of the Peace Process on Political Liberalization in Jordan," *Journal of Palestine Studies* 28, no. 2 (winter 1999): 2.

9. *Ha'aretz,* March 4, 1999.

10. *Jordan Times,* October 23, 2000.

11. Associated Press, October 24, 2000.

12. *Jordan Times,* October 9, 2000.

13. Snadar Peri, "Afraid of Arafat, Afraid of Israel," Weekend Supplement, *Yediot Ahronoth,* December 8, 2000.

14. Amy Henderson and Alia Shukri Hamzeh, "True Believers in Peace Disappointed," *Jordan Times,* October 26, 2000.

15. *http://www.brookings.org/dybdocroot/press/appendix/appen_z.htm.*

16. See *Jordan Times,* January 11, 2001.

17. Zvi Barel, "What Price Repatriation?" *Ha'aretz,* December 29, 2000.

18. *Kulal Arabi,* January 12, 2001.

19. Peri, *Yediot Ahronoth,* December 8, 2000.

20. Ibid.; *www.ArabicNews.com* (December 25, 1997).

21. Douglas Davis, Jewish Telegraphic Agency, "Jordanian King: Ties with Israel Take Back Seat to Arab Relations," April 13, 1999.

22. Roula Khalaf, "Survey—Jordan: It's Tough Going for Monarch," *Financial Times,* November 7, 2000.

23. Zvi Barel, "A Summit That Gave Abdullah Status," *Ha'aretz,* March 28, 2001.

24. Ibid.

25. *www.ArabicNews.com* (September 22, 2000).

26. "Political Tightrope," *Jordan Times,* November 3, 2000.

27. Michael Hudson, "Transition in Syria: Prospects for President Bashar," *http://www.ccasonline.org.publicaffairs/Hudson08302000.html* (August 30, 2000).

28. "Can Jordan-Syria Thaw Bring Stability?" *Christian Science Monitor,* April 23, 1999.

29. See Laurie Brand, *Jordan's Inter-Arab Relations* (New York: Columbia University Press, 1994), 166–72.

30. Avraham Sela, *The Decline of the Arab-Israeli Conflict: Middle East Politics and the Quest for Regional Order* (Albany, N.Y.: State University of New York Press, 1998), 227–28.

31. Brand, 178.

32. *Christian Science Monitor,* April 23, 1999.

33. "Jordan," *Jane's Sentinel Country Focus, http://www.janes.com/region_news/africa_middle_east/sentinel/country_focus/jords080.shtml* (April 1, 2001).

8

Flanks, Balances, and Withdrawals

Syrian Policy in the Middle East since the 1979
Egyptian-Israeli Treaty

DAVID W. LESCH

Egyptian president Anwar Sadat and Israeli prime minister Menachem
Begin signed the Egyptian-Israeli peace treaty, witnessed by U.S. president
Jimmy Carter, on March 29, 1979, at the White House. For Syria the
Middle East was suddenly a dramatically different place. For twenty-five
years Egypt had been the unquestioned (albeit sometimes reluctant) leader
of the Arab nationalist movement, which had as one of its few widely
accepted tenets the liquidation of Israel. The sine qua non for any Arab
war coalition that entertained even the slightest bit of hope of defeating
Israel or, after 1967, regaining lost territories was the active participation
of Egypt, the most populous and powerful of the Arab states. Furthermore, after the 1967 Arab-Israeli war, the Arab states had a goal at least
of the reacquisition of the occupied territories and a just settlement of the
Palestinian issue in accordance with UN Security Council Resolution 242.

As foreshadowed by Anwar Sadat's strategy and tactics in the 1973
Arab-Israeli war, Egypt had decided to go its own way. It had bled too
much in the past for the sake of the Arab cause with too little to show for
it in return except the loss of territory, revenues, and dignity. It was better
to regain the Sinai Peninsula, with its oil fields, reopen the Suez Canal,
with its tolls, and insert some stability into the region that would reignite
the flocks of tourists with their credit cards. Attachment to the West, specifically the United States, accompanied by tremendous amounts of eco-

nomic and military aid would more than compensate for the flaws of the peace treaty that essentially signaled the abandonment by Egypt of the Palestinian cause. Washington had expertly maneuvered a willing Cairo to sever its relationship with the Soviet Union and, in effect, the Arab world by signing what was in essence a separate treaty with the Jewish state; progress on Egyptian-Israeli bilateral issues was no longer bound to a comprehensive Arab-Israeli settlement. To Syria's President Hafiz al-Assad, Egypt was again leaving Syria out in the cold, just as, during the 1973 conflagration, Sadat had pursued his own battle plan based on a defensive posture for Egypt, thus allowing Israel to concentrate militarily on Syria. The multifront strategy of confronting Israel was no longer a serious option, and Syria felt itself alone against Israel.

Following the peace treaty, Damascus immediately scrambled about in an attempt to redress the perceived gross imbalance of power between the Arab states and Israel, reacting to a plethora of events in the Middle East that spanned the region and intertwined the Persian Gulf with the Arab-Israeli arenas. Syria desperately tried to prevent Israel, now freed up in the south, from outflanking it either through military intervention in Lebanon or diplomatic démarches through Jordan. Becoming more and more isolated in the Arab world throughout much of the 1980s, Syria felt compelled to achieve a strategic balance, or strategic parity, with Israel that would at least act as a deterrent against an Israeli attack. Finally, having prevented Lebanon from becoming an Israeli client-state and after having acquired a deterrent capability vis-à-vis Israel by the late 1980s, the regime of Hafiz al-Assad utilized (or adapted to) the new regional environment brought about by the end of the Cold War and the 1990–91 Gulf crisis and war. Highlighted by its participation in the Madrid peace process that eventually also peeled away Jordan and the PLO into agreements with Tel Aviv, Syria embarked upon its own foreign policy path that focused upon the complete withdrawal of Israel from the Golan Heights—a path that is still under construction and promises to be as long and winding in the future as it has been in the recent past. In all of these foreign policy endeavors, Syria has attempted to form alliances, unions, and alignments with other states and groups in the Middle East, and has usually tried to be the dominant player in each of these coalitions because of one simple fact: Syria's objectives exceed its capacity to achieve on its own.[1] Syria simply does not have the resources or population base to unilaterally attain its regional goals, so Hafiz al-Assad constantly manipulated shifting alliances and regional balances of power to construct defensive and offensive associations that would elevate Syria's status. He attempted to do this by making Syria indispensable in any diplomatic paradigm and by entering into Syrian-dominated alliances with other Arab entities that were leaning toward or had already adopted policies that countered his own, thus protecting his country against Israeli attack and enhancing his negotiating leverage. Practicality overcame ideology as a means to an end, and, as such, Syrian foreign policy discourse has largely revolved around the shifting exigencies of flanks, balances, and withdrawals.

The Correction

Hafiz al-Assad came to power in a 1970 intra-Ba'ath coup that cast out the radical wing of the party, which had been ideologically committed to the destruction of Israel. The dangerous policies of the radical wing were clearly displayed with its role in instigating the 1967 Arab-Israeli war that resulted in Syria's loss of the Golan Heights to Israel. Assad's assumption of power signaled the departure of an ideologically based foreign policy to a much more pragmatic one that was prepared to diplomatically resolve the Arab-Israeli conflict, albeit from a position of strength, and wholeheartedly committed to a full return of the Golan Heights.[2] Domestically, it also signaled a retreat from the radical socialist-based economic policies of the previous regime; indeed, Assad's political program upon his ascension to power in Syria is called the Corrective Movement *(al-Harakat al-tashishiyya)*, whose applications in some ways were applied in the foreign policy arena as well. Its primary intent was to bring Syria back within accepted parameters in the Arab world and open up the economy to the private sector. Politically it meant establishing a working relationship with Egypt and Saudi Arabia (the so-called Cairo-Damascus-Riyadh axis) in order to coordinate policy toward Israel. This cooperative arrangement came to fruition in the 1973 Arab-Israeli war, when Saudi Arabia promised its fellow Arab combatants that it would employ the oil weapon if necessary, which, of course, it did in the latter stages of the conflict, resulting in the almost fourfold increase in the price of oil (from $3.01 per barrel before the war to $11.65 per barrel by January 1974). The non-oil Arab states that bordered Israel, such as Syria and Egypt, benefited from the new economic realities in the Middle East, not only from direct aid from the Arab oil-producing countries seeking to build up their Arab credentials the only way they could, but also from remittances from its citizens who were arriving by the tens of thousands in the Arab Gulf states as laborers. The 1970s thus resulted in impressive growth in the Syrian economy. In fact, Assad's decision to open up the economy to allow more flexibility for the private sector was not as much a reaction to the inability of the public sector to accumulate capital (as would be the case in the 1980s) as it was an effort to find mechanisms to distribute the wealth suddenly entering the country. The growth, however, was not structurally stimulated but was due largely to transfers from the Arab countries and good seasonal rainfalls.

Sadat's penchant for dramatics as well as his inclination to pursue a separate path toward retrieving the Sinai became clear during and immediately after the 1973 conflict and after signing two disengagement agreements with Israel, the first in January 1974 and the second in August 1975. The dialectic in Assad's foreign policy approach was displayed during this interval. Syria also signed a disengagement agreement with Israel in May 1974; as with the others, it was mediated by U.S. secretary of state Henry Kissinger. Although taking advantage of the opportunity to push Israeli troops further away from their precariously close proximity to Damascus, this clearly indicated a different foreign policy track emanating from the Syrian capital than had been the case with prior regimes—that it was willing, under certain circumstances, to negotiate; indeed, while the text of the disengagement accord stated that it was not a peace agreement, it did assert that it was a step toward one. On the other hand, Syria could not continue along the path that Egypt seemed to be mapping out for itself, that is, further agreements under U.S. tutelage without any realistic probability of a comprehensive settlement in accordance with UN Resolutions 242 and 338.³ Syria had long considered itself the standard-bearer of Arab nationalism and the Palestinian cause—it absolutely could not pursue negotiations unless everything was on the table, and it could not allow for any other Arab state, least of all Egypt, to engage in separate agreements with Israel that would immeasurably weaken the bargaining power of the Arab side as a whole. To Syria, of course, it increasingly became apparent as Egypt moved closer and closer to its peace treaty with Israel (certainly after Sadat's historic trip to Israel in November 1977) that isolating Egypt from the inter-Arab system was an offensive strategy masterminded in Tel Aviv and Washington. From Assad's point of view, in light of what he perceived to be happening, it was important to acquire more leverage in the inter-Arab arena to either disrupt an Egyptian-led moderate Arab consensus from emerging or prepare for the worst in case Cairo successfully achieved its seemingly narrow aims. Assad believed that time was on his side, especially considering the enhanced wealth and power of the Arab oil producers due to the dramatic increases in the price of oil and the apparent (and related) economic progress throughout much of the

Arab world that would provide the fuel for overall modernization as well as military parity with Israel. Syria's involvement in the 1975–76 Lebanese civil war, which ended in the emplacement of over 40,000 Syrian troops in Lebanon, as well as its continuing tussles with Arafat's PLO, can be seen within this prism of potential shifting regional alliances to confront Israeli opportunism and prevent Syria's isolation.

Desperation and Opportunity amid Pressure and Change

The events of 1979 perforce dramatically altered Assad's conception of Syria's role in the Middle East. Faced with losing the leverage and threat of Egypt, Assad frantically searched for allies to confront an empowered Israel that could now focus its attention on the north. The Steadfastness Front, including Libya, Algeria, and the People's Democratic Republic of Yemen, formed in large measure to counter what was feared to be an emerging Egyptian-led consensus of moderate Arab states, diplomatically fortified fellow member Syria to a certain extent, but these countries were largely on the fringes of the Arab-Israeli conflict—the fact that this was the only front Damascus dominated in its attempts to forestall vulnerability suggests Assad was less than successful in establishing an effective regional counter to Israel. Assad even briefly flirted with an entente with his Ba'athist rival, Saddam Hussein of Iraq, in the aftermath of the Camp David process in order to shore up Syria's eastern front to contain Israel—it would be an association that inevitably floundered over continuing differences between the two countries, ranging from persistent Ba'athist elite quarrels and personal animus between Assad and Saddam Hussein to more practical matters such as water sharing of the Euphrates River and the question of who should be the dominant partner in any planned union. The answer to this question would, in effect, determine who should fill the vacuum of power in the Arab world created by Egypt's departure.

The Iranian revolution in February 1979 and subsequent Iraqi invasion of Iran in September 1980 obliterated whatever slim reed of hope existed for an Iraqi-Syrian rapprochement.[4] With the arrival of the Ayatollah Khomeini in Tehran, an implacable foe of Israel and the United States, Hafiz al-Assad saw a definite convergence of interests with Iran, taking steps even before the Iran-Iraq war to develop a relationship that still remains intact; indeed, from Assad's point of view, Iran provided some strategic depth now that the multifront approach against Israel was defunct. When Saddam Hussein invaded Iran in 1980, it made it that much easier for Damascus to openly side with the Islamic Republic. Not only did

Assad believe that Hussein's follies were an untimely and misdirected application of vital Arab resources and assets away from the Arab-Israeli
arena, but it also created an opportunity. Ever since the days of the Arab
cold war in the 1950s and 1960s, it had been something of an axiom that
the pecking order in the Arab world was as follows: Egypt, Iraq, then Syria
(and this was before the oil price hikes of the early 1970s, after which
many were compelled to include Saudi Arabia in this elite group—and
probably also ahead of Syria). Syria could play a leading role in the Arab
world only as long as Egypt and Iraq were otherwise occupied and/or had
somehow decided to abandon the Arab fold. Egypt had signed a peace
treaty with Israel and was ostracized and isolated, and now Iraq, partially
in an attempt to fill the Egyptian shoes, leapt into an unexpectedly pro-
tracted war with Iran, directing its attention (as well as that of most of the
Arab Gulf states, including Saudi Arabia) to matters eastward rather than
westward toward Israel.[5]

And therein lay Syria's dilemmas. At times Syria preferred to work with
Iraq, Egypt, and/or Saudi Arabia, as it did in the 1973 Arab-Israeli war;
without them, Syria had to move from being one of the leaders within the
Arab-Israeli arena to being the dominant leader in order to preserve the
possibility of achieving its regional objectives. Syria was left to form alliances with countries and groups that were (1) too small, weak, and/or
amorphous to effectively support Syria's position and, in fact, have often
been viewed as liabilities, such as Jordan, Lebanon, and the PLO; (2) too
diverse in interests and capabilities to allow Damascus to assume a leadership position in terms of policy coordination and implementation; and (3)
too vulnerable to influence and interference from Cairo, Baghdad, and/or
Riyadh, all of which are capable of steering these countries in directions
inimical to the interest of Syria.

Because of its support of non-Arab Iran against Arab Iraq in the Iran-
Iraq war, Syria became more isolated in the early 1980s in the Arab world.
The Gulf Arab states, on whom Syria depended so much for financial and
political support, were more consumed with matters concerning the Gulf
and less with the Arab-Israeli arena. While Syria's connection to Tehran
created some valuable leverage over the Gulf Arab shaykhdoms in terms
of being able to restrain Iran and keep the war from expanding beyond
Iraq, there was clearly more distance between the immediate interests of
Damascus and those of the capitals of the Gulf states. In addition, Syria
had never quite repaired the damage done to its relationship with the PLO
during the 1975–76 Lebanese civil war when, fearing Israeli intervention
if the PLO-Muslim contingent emerged victorious over the Israeli-sup-

ported Maronite side, Damascus suddenly switched its support in the war toward the Christian elements. Despite Syria's frequent efforts to mend its relations with the PLO, especially after Sadat engaged in the peace process with Israel, the PLO never totally cut off its line to Cairo, much to the consternation of Assad. From PLO chairman Yasser Arafat's point of view, Syria was trying to turn the PLO into something of a protectorate in order to strengthen its own bargaining power and indispensability so as not to be left out in the cold again by another Arab participant in the Arab-Israeli equation. Jordan also did not obediently follow Syria. Amman was typically caught between pressures from a variety of sources, including Syria, Iraq, Saudi Arabia, Egypt, and the United States, and of these, Damascus espoused the most radical program. With this array of pressure, Jordan naturally gravitated toward the more moderate front within the Arab world, in the process of which it established closer ties with Iraq and mended its own fences with the PLO. Iraq, now ensconced in war with Iran, toned down its rhetoric and began cooperating with the moderate Arab states so as to buffer its ability to withstand an Iran that had weathered the initial Iraqi attacks and by 1982 was clearly on the offensive.[6] This emerging moderate bloc in the Arab world, due to a significant degree to the repercussions of the Iran-Iraq war, also allowed Egypt to rehabilitate itself and quietly reenter the Arab fold.

By the end of 1980, Syria seemed as isolated as it had ever been in the Middle East. Clearly, Assad's diplomacy had failed. Egypt had signed a separate peace treaty with Israel and yet no serious coalition of Arab states would align their positions consistent with Damascus. Worse still the attention of most of the Arab states, indeed most of the world, was consumed with events in the Persian Gulf and South-Central Asia following the December 1979 Soviet invasion of Afghanistan, not the Arab-Israeli arena.

Syria had to make a tactical change if it was to contain what the Syrian regime perceived as Israeli pressure and carve out an indispensable role for itself in the Middle East. Israel's de facto annexation of the Golan Heights in 1981 reinforced Syria's assessment of its own weakened position in the region. Something had to be done, and it seemed from Assad's point of view that Syria would essentially have to go it alone in the region for the time being. Assad began to put forward the possibility of attaining strategic parity with Israel, not so much to defeat the Jewish state but to act as an effective deterrent against any enemy while at the same time strengthening Syria's bargaining leverage in any peace process that might develop. To do this, Syria needed massive amounts of military aid from the outside.

The Soviet Union and Syria began to build upon what had been a tenuous relationship, exemplified by the 1980 Treaty of Friendship and Cooperation signed between the two countries. Moscow had also had its nose bloodied in the Middle East, with Egypt embracing the United States and Iraq, against the wishes of the Kremlin, invading Iran. Baghdad had systematically distanced itself from the Soviet Union ever since its own Treaty of Friendship and Cooperation with Moscow was signed in 1972, and its more moderate stance following the Iranian revolution and the initiation of hostilities with Iran caused a good deal of consternation inside the Kremlin.[7] In a sense, if not for the virtual disabling of Iraq and Egypt, the Soviets would not have been tempted to invest so much in Syria. For his part, Assad felt he had little choice but to draw closer to Moscow. The search for indispensability and bargaining power led these two countries to similar ground. As such, as Hinnebusch stated, "Syrian policy in the 1980's manifested a tactical rejectionism that sought in the meantime to obstruct the U.S.-sponsored peace process."[8]

Syria's relative isolation in the Middle East was not its only problem in the early 1980s. Economically, the decade of the 1980s was as bad for Syria as the 1970s had been good. Not only were the structural defects and inefficiencies of Syria's state-dominated economy becoming obvious; the regional and international political and economic environments exacerbated already existing problems. Most damaging was the precipitous drop in oil prices by the mid-1980s due to the world oil glut. Not only did this adversely affect Syria's own not-insignificant oil revenues, but it also reduced remittances from abroad as well as financial aid from the oil-rich Arab states in the Persian Gulf, who were already displeased with the decision by Damascus to support Iran against Iraq. Concurrent with this development was an unfortunate decade-long drought that devastated an agricultural sector already suffering under the regime's policy of import substitution industrialization that favored industrial over agricultural enterprises. In addition, the general Third World debt of the early 1980s reduced capital inflow, and the recession in the industrialized countries had negative runoff effects on developing nations seeking outside investment. Finally, the winding down and end of the superpower Cold War and subsequent retrenchment of the Soviet bloc deprived Syria of the military and economic aid it had been receiving in such large amounts earlier in the decade. As a result, Syria developed in the 1980s a severe balance of payments and foreign exchange crisis. It had become clear that the state could no longer be the engine of capital accumulation; therefore, the regime decided that the private sector had to be given more leeway to fill the capital void, and the country as a whole had to create a more investor-friendly business environment to attract foreign investment. This second *infitah*, or economic "opening," was brought about by economic crisis and not economic largesse. With a series of decrees throughout the 1980s Assad attempted to ameliorate the situation, launching Syria on the road to what has been called selective liberalization—"selective" because if Assad liberalized the economy too much or too quickly he might undercut the public sector patronage system that maintained the regime in power. His subsequent zigzag approach to economic reform experienced some success, but on the whole, by the end of the decade it produced disappointing results.[9]

Also confronting the Assad regime in the early 1980s was a very serious internal threat from the Muslim Brethren (MB) in Syria, mirroring similar rising Islamist movements in other Middle East states by the late 1970s.[10] After enduring a number of attacks by Islamic militants against various representations of the regime, Assad ordered a full-scale attack against the center of Muslim Brethren activity in Syria. The result was the virtual sacking of the city of Hama, with anywhere from 20,000 to 40,000 deaths. Islamist opposition virtually ceased to exist after this crushing blow, but Syria's reputation regionally and internationally also suffered a measurable blow.

It was under these conditions that Syria encountered the next challenge to its position in the Middle East, the Israeli invasion of Lebanon in June 1982. As in most crises, there exists possible opportunity in the face of vulnerability, and Assad was determined to make the best out of a potentially catastrophic situation, but he would have to dig down deep into the resources available to him to weather another challenge to his position in the region.

From the Syrian perspective, the Israeli invasion of Lebanon was the expected repercussion of the Egyptian-Israeli peace treaty. It was thought that Israel, freed up on its southern flank, could now concentrate on securing its position to the north. To Assad the invasion was an attempt to outflank Syria, something Damascus had been wary of for years, a concern that, of course, precipitated its involvement in the 1975–76 Lebanese civil war. Syria seemed to be vulnerable, with its regional isolation and domestic problems; to Assad, the timing of the invasion, coming just on the heels of the return of the final portion of the Sinai Peninsula to Egypt, was anything but a surprise. One could almost sense that this was something of a last stand for Syria, or at least for Assad's policies, and, as such, Syria would fight tooth and nail to prevent an Israeli victory in Lebanon, one that would complete Syria's isolation—and potential impotence—in the region.

The story of the Israeli invasion of Lebanon has been told elsewhere. As is well known, what at first seemed like a repetition of the 1978 Israeli sweep of Palestinian positions in south Lebanon escalated into what has been described as Prime Minister Menachem Begin's and Defense Minister Ariel Sharon's hidden agenda, that is, the elimination of the PLO as a force in Lebanon and the placing in power in Beirut of a Maronite president (Bashir Gemayel) who would be willing to sign a peace treaty with Israel, thus, in effect, also eliminating Syria's position there. Assad's troops were compelled to fight the Israelis alongside the PLO, and they suffered severe losses on the battlefield and in the air despite determined resistance. As the full scope of the Israeli plan unfolded and as casualties mounted inside and outside of Beirut, the international community, led by the United States, attempted to bring the bloodletting to a close, just as the Israeli forces stopped on the outskirts of Beirut, hesitant to enter into a house-to-house expulsion of PLO and Syrian forces. With the United Nations hamstrung by an expected Soviet veto, the United States, Britain, and France led a multinational force (MNF) into Beirut in August 1982 with the defined objective of escorting the PLO forces out of Beirut. This was accomplished in short order, followed by the departure of the MNF.

Whether Syria was directly behind the next important episode is ultimately left to conjecture, for there were many factions in Lebanon that did not want an Israeli-Maronite triumph regardless of the position of Damascus, but it definitely benefited from the ensuing course of events: Bashir Gemayel was assassinated in September. Shortly thereafter, in an act of revenge, Christian Phalangist units, apparently with a green light from Israeli forces, attacked two Palestinian camps in south Beirut, Sabra and Shatila, massacring hundreds, mostly old men, women, and children. The MNF, still anchored offshore, felt obliged to return to Beirut with the nebulous and ill-defined task of restoring order to the chaotic situation.

The longer the U.S.-led MNF stayed in Lebanon the more it began to be seen, certainly from Syria's perspective, as a pro-Maronite, and thus Israeli, prop. The attempt by the Reagan administration to consummate an Israeli-Lebanese peace agreement negotiated in May 1983, without Syrian or Soviet participation, seemed to be a case of the United States trying to do diplomatically what the Israelis had tried to do militarily. This came on the heels of the Reagan peace plan put forward during the Israeli invasion in 1982. That plan attempted to take advantage of the PLO's and Syria's weakened positions (thus excluding the Soviet Union), in what some have called an alternative version of Camp David, this time pushing for Palestinian-Jordanian cooperation for more autonomy in the West Bank and Gaza Strip (or what came to be called toward the mid-1980s the Jordanian-Palestinian condominium option). Again, from the point of view of Damascus, this particular approach also seemed to be a flanking operation against Syria through diplomatic means, this time through Jordan. Wherever the direction of diplomacy brokered by Washington, Syria was left out, and if the supposed U.S.-Israeli plan were to succeed, its isolation would be complete, and its bargaining strength vis-à-vis a return of the Golan Heights would be virtually nonexistent.

From this seemingly desperate position, Syria lashed out against the pincer movement any way it could. Fortunately for Damascus, the MNF presence and extended Israeli stay in Lebanon were vehemently opposed by a variety of Lebanese factions, such as the Druze, Amal, and the emerging Iranian-backed Shiite force, Hizballah, thus producing a coincidence of interests that Syria would employ to its advantage. It is in this atmosphere that one can read the April 1983 bombing of the U.S. embassy and the October 1983 bombing of the U.S. marine barracks in Beirut—and countless other smaller attacks against what was perceived as a hostile MNF—leading to the withdrawal of the MNF by early 1984. The enhanced factionalization of Lebanon due to the breakdown of the state and the subsequent external interference by a multitude of powers made a chaotic situation worse, and the opposition to the Israeli occupation increased, forcing Israel in early 1985 to withdraw further southward to the security zone it would maintain along the Israeli-Lebanese border until May 2000.

Assad had won. Through his strategic use of various Lebanese factions, rearming by the Soviet Union (after Moscow was criticized for not supporting Syria and the PLO more during the first few months of the Israeli invasion), and the commitment born by being pressed against the wall, Syria reemerged as the dominant power in Lebanon, its western flank secure. And Syria's Arab credentials were somewhat restored for taking on Israel and the United States and not just surviving but emerging as the victor.

On the other hand, Assad's attempt to take advantage of Arafat's weakened condition following his expulsion from Lebanon paralleled the U.S.-Israeli push to do the same, albeit for different reasons. For Assad it would be to finally gain control of the PLO and push his longtime nemesis, Arafat, to the sidelines; for Washington and Tel Aviv, it would be to utilize Arafat's desperate situation to force him to adopt the path of least resistance, that is, the Jordanian option envisioned by the Reagan plan. While Assad won Lebanon, the United States and Israel, relatively speaking, would win the PLO. Syria fomented in 1983 an uprising in Lebanon against Arafat's Fatah faction, in the process of which it brought together traditional radical factions of the PLO (such as the DFLP and PFLP) to establish the Damascus-controlled Palestine National Salvation Front. In the end, however, Arafat's popularity, or maybe it would be more appropriate to say his institutionalization, within the PLO as a whole prevented Assad's own outflanking attempt from succeeding. And Syria's intervention against Arafat caused it to lose many of the points in the Arab world that it had gained in Lebanon—the self-professed standard-bearer of the Arab cause does not foment intra-Palestinian discord that weakens the movement as a whole. Even though the Jordanian option had fizzled out by 1986, by the end of the decade Arafat had clearly chosen a negotiated solution to the Palestinian problem and situated himself within the moderate Arab camp. The Palestinian intifada begun in December 1987 further led to Arafat's revival as a negotiating partner, resulting in late 1988 in the PLO's recognition of Israel, acceptance of UN Security Council Resolutions 242 and 338, and the renunciation of terrorism. Much to Syria's consternation, the PLO had been added to the growing list of Arab entities that seemed to be striking out on their own toward potential peace agreements with Israel.

By the end of the 1980s, Syria's position did not seem to be measurably better than when it began. Assad had prevented, for the time being, a Camp David consensus from emerging in the Arab world, yet because of the regional effects of the Iran-Iraq war and such episodes as the intifada, a moderate Arab consensus had developed, one that had rehabilitated Egypt, naturally resulting in the swinging of the power pendulum in the Arab interstate system toward Cairo and away from Damascus, bringing Jordan and the PLO along for the ride. Syria was successful in its attempts to avoid being outflanked either through Jordan or Lebanon, and it rose from the proverbial ashes in the latter to emerge as an indispensable power broker actively backed by the Soviet Union; however, even though victorious in Lebanon, some might consider this to have been more Pyrrhic than triumphant. Indeed, by 1989 Syria's position seemed to get even worse. Iraq had emerged victorious in the Iran-Iraq war after Tehran reluctantly accepted a UN-brokered cease-fire in August 1988—and it was an Iraq that wanted to reexert its influence in the Middle East. Saddam Hussein remembered Syrian support for its enemy and would make life as difficult as possible for pro-Syrian forces in Lebanon and would draw

Jordan deeper and deeper into Baghdad's orbit. Furthermore, the pillar of Soviet support that had braced the teetering policies of Assad for most of the decade virtually crumbled with the coming to power of Mikhail Gorbachev in 1985 and the Red Army exit from Afghanistan in 1989, both of which led to a dramatic reassessment of Soviet foreign policy that emphasized a drawing down of Soviet commitments abroad, more concentration on domestic restructuring, and improving ties with the United States. This did not bode well for Syria, as Moscow first urged and then backed the PLO's decision to pursue a negotiated solution, and the USSR also improved its relations with Israel. Gorbachev demonstrably made it clear to Assad upon the Syrian president's visit to Moscow in April 1987 that Syria's "reliance on military force in settling the Arab-Israeli conflict has completely lost its credibility," and he went on to suggest that Damascus abandon its doctrine of strategic parity and seek to establish a "balance of interests" toward a political settlement in the Middle East.[11]

In addition to these problems in the foreign policy arena, Syria's economy continued to deteriorate, due in large measure to the concentration of economic resources in the military in the attempt to achieve strategic parity with Israel.[12] Compounding the continuing burden of an overly dominant public sector were a number of problems inhibiting economic growth, including the lack of a private banking system or stock market to organize capital; an inadequate regulatory regime and insufficient transparency; a private sector too fragmented to lead the way toward capital accumulation; rampant corruption creating proscribed entrances into the Syrian economy in connivance with government officialdom; and finally, perhaps most damaging of all, a population growth rate of about 3.6 percent per annum, placing more pressure on a dilapidated economy to keep pace, the failure of which could lead to further socioeconomic disruption, with possible domestic political repercussions.[13]

Assad's isolation seemed complete. Emblematic of this was the creation of the Arab Cooperation Council in 1990, consisting of Egypt, Iraq, Jordan, and North Yemen, and pointedly excluding Syria.[14]

The Beginning of Another Decade and Another Opportunity

Because of his position at the end of the 1980s, Assad was forced to change his policy as dramatically as that which had occurred at the beginning of the decade—he took Gorbachev's advice. In December 1988, Assad "acknowledged the importance of Egypt in the Arab arena," the first time he had publicly praised Egypt since before the Egyptian-Israeli peace treaty, and by the end of 1989 Damascus had reestablished full diplomatic relations with Cairo.[15] With an eye toward isolating Iraq as well as building bridges to the United States, Syria also began to improve its relations with Saudi Arabia. While maintaining the link with Iran, partly to contain the Iraqi threat and continue its relationship with Shiite groups in Lebanon, and attempting to remain a credible military threat to Israel, Syria made a strategic choice to join the Arab-Israeli peace process, the ultimate objective of which was the return of the Golan Heights and a just and lasting comprehensive peace accord.[16]

To the rest of the world, the outward manifestation of this policy shift was Syria's participation in the U.S.-led coalition to expel Iraq from Kuwait in the 1990–91 Gulf crisis and war. Not only was it participating in an alliance whose objective was to weaken, if not destroy, the war-making capacity of its arch nemesis in the Arab arena, it was clearly situating itself in the Arab world's moderate camp and opening up the economic doors of investment and aid from the West and grateful Arab Gulf states. To the United States, Syria's attachment to the coalition, although mostly symbolic, was, in effect, the most important of all the Arab states. Since Syria had been at the vanguard of the "Steadfastness Front" of Arab states arrayed against Israel, its joining up made the coalition seem as if it consisted of the entire Arab world against Saddam Hussein rather than the usual pro-Western Arab suspects, which Baghdad could have utilized to its own propaganda advantage.[17] It also broke a number of taboos since, although Israel was purposely excluded from the Gulf War coalition, Syria and the other Arab states were, in essence, aligned with U.S. and Israeli objectives vis-à-vis Iraq. Syria's sponsorship of and participation in the Damascus Declaration security grouping shortly after the end of the Gulf War, consisting of the GCC states plus Syria and Egypt, demonstrated the regional thrust of its new policy. Ironically, just as Iraq's invasion of Iran compelled Syria to embark upon its own strategic path in the region, albeit with substantial Soviet assistance, Iraq's invasion of Kuwait accelerated Syria's backpedaling toward Egypt, Saudi Arabia, and the American-sponsored peace process, essentially rejoining the paradigmatic lineup of the mid-1970s. For Assad, establishing a stronger link with Washington was very important, and to do this he had to go through Israel; indeed, some Israelis have accused Assad of engaging in the peace process not so much to redefine Syria's relationship with Israel as to improve Syria's ties with the United States and the West. This would not only have economic benefits at a time when Syria desperately needed them, but Assad's engagement in a peace process brokered by the United States was his best defense against

Israeli pressure, as Washington, it was thought, would act to curtail Israeli pressure in order to maintain Syria's involvement in the process, one that could lead to an entirely new American-dominated Middle East system.

As such, Syria emerged as the key Arab player in the convening of the Madrid peace conference in October 1991, cosponsored by the United States and the Soviet Union and including a Lebanese delegation (clearly acting under the direction of Damascus) and a Jordanian delegation that also consisted of Palestinian representatives from the occupied territories. For the first time, Syrian officials publicly sat down with Israeli officials to discuss peace. As with the Gulf War coalition, Syria's participation was important, because without it any conference held (which would have been unlikely in any event) would include only pro-Western Arab states. Even though the exchanges among the participants in Madrid were more acrimonious than civil, a truly comprehensive peace process was under way, and the Arab parties continued to meet separately with Israel in Washington, paralleled by multilateral talks at various locales focusing upon such issues as arms control, trade, and water sharing.

By 1992–93, even though Israel's new prime minister, Yitzhak Rabin, and the Clinton administration preferred to concentrate on the Israeli-Syrian track over the Israeli-Palestinian track, primarily because of the inherently less complex nature of the former, progress with Syria was limited, and it would soon be overshadowed by the September 1993 Israeli-PLO Declaration of Principles, largely negotiated outside of the Madrid process, and then the 1994 Jordanian-Israeli peace treaty. Assad was furious with both Arafat and King Hussein for, in his view, doing something very similar to what Sadat had done. It had been an axiom of Syria foreign policy to maintain a united front in the Arab world vis-à-vis Israel in order to maximize Arab bargaining leverage. In essence, the failure of Assad to corral Jordan and the PLO within Syria's orbit in the 1980s had now become manifest. On the other hand, now that the PLO and Jordan had signed accords with Israel, no longer would Damascus feel completely obligated to subscribe to the Palestinian or Arab nationalist line, for the PLO itself had compromised its position. Though bereft of some of its bargaining power, Syria now felt free to pursue its own interests, that is, the return of the Golan Heights.

Amid constant delays in implementing the Israeli-PLO Declaration of Principles and Rabin's disposition toward settling the Syrian front first, progress on the Israeli-Syrian track was, indeed, made, particularly on security and demilitarization issues (and at least the notion of Israeli withdrawal from the Golan Heights, although negotiations tended to get bogged down over the extent and timetable for withdrawal).[18] After the assassination of Rabin in November 1995, the Israeli-Syrian track was accelerated by his successor, Shimon Peres, seeking to take advantage of the postmortem momentum to conclude an agreement with Damascus. The rapidity of the push by Peres, which was totally inconsistent with the incremental negotiating tactics that Assad preferred, made Syria feel somewhat uncomfortable, but any prospects for the conclusion of an agreement in the short term were derailed by a series of events in early 1996: enhanced Israeli-Turkish defense cooperation; the Hamas bombings in Israel in February and March, which Damascus chose not to condemn, and, indeed, Syrian radio attempted to justify; intensified Hizballah attacks in March and April against Israeli positions in southern Lebanon and northern Israel and the subsequent Israeli Grapes of Wrath operation in reaction; and finally, and due in large measure to the rising tension in the region because of the aforementioned events, the election of Likud Party leader Benjamin Netanyahu as Israeli prime minister in May, who immediately took a more hard-line stance with regard to Syria, stating what became the mantra of his tenure in power, that is, "peace with security," and no withdrawal from the Golan Heights. For the remainder of Netanyahu's tenure in power (until May 1999), both tracks tended to stall, and it was only through direct intervention by the White House that limited progress was made on the Palestinian-Israeli track, resulting in the Hebron Agreement of January 1997 and the Wye accords of October 1998.

During this whole process, it became clear to many that Assad's approach to peace with Israel was fraught with many of the same strategic concerns that were incorporated in his approach to war with Israel. He wanted to prevent Syria's isolation and not allow Israeli dominance in the region garnered through peace agreements and common markets any more than he wanted to see Israeli dominance through military pressure. As Assad himself noted on one occasion, "Our stance in the battle for peace will not be less courageous than our stances on the battlefield."[19] Shimon Peres observed that Assad "is conducting the peace process just as one conducts a military campaign—slowly, patiently, directed by strategic and tactical considerations."[20] This did not obviate the possibility of a peace agreement, but it certainly tended to complicate negotiations hampered by suspicious tactics—Syria was still focusing on flanks and balances of power.

Assad's utilization of Hizballah in south Lebanon was an example of his negotiating strategy. While the Israelis tended to see an increase in

Hizballah activity as an indication that Syria was less interested in peace and/or should match the scope of Hizballah attacks with their own tougher posture in negotiations with Damascus, Assad saw the Shiite group as one side of the same coin, that is, as a pressure valve that he could turn on and off in order to extract more concessions from Israel on the other side of the coin, the peace talks. To many, Hizballah's attacks that led to the Grapes of Wrath operation in 1996 were actually an attempt by Assad to counter what Syrians perceived to be a pincer move-ment concocted by Israel (if not also the United States) from its enhanced defense cooperation arrangements with Turkey, consummated by a wide-ranging defense agreement in February 1996—all meant, from the per-spective of Damascus, to pressure Syria into making concessions on the peace front. Syria had fought back attempts to outflank it through Leba-non and Jordan, but with less leverage vis-à-vis Turkey (indeed, with a deteriorating relationship with Ankara based on Kurdish and water-shar-ing issues), Assad lashed out with one of his few remaining assets to let Israel know that Syria could still inflict some pain. The results, however, severely hampered the peace process and contributed to Peres's defeat at the polls.[21]

The Syrian-Israeli track (as well as the Palestinian track) received a boost when Rabin's protégé in the Labor Party, Ehud Barak, convincingly won the election for prime minister in May 1999. He ran on a platform of carrying the peace process forward, and, like his mentor, he also preferred the relatively less complicated Syrian track over the Palestinian one. With the Clinton administration acting as facilitator and broker, the two sides again engaged in serious negotiations, highlighted by Barak's meeting with Syrian foreign minister Farouk al-Sharaa, interspersed with visits by President Clinton, in West Virginia in December 1999. Syria, under pres-sure from the United States and seeing the opportunity presented by the change of power in Israel, agreed to publicly reenter the peace process; in addition, the noticeable decline in Assad's health along with his desire to secure an agreement before his untested son, Bashar, might have to take over the reins of power were added inducements for the Syrian president to step forward. Again, however, by early 2000, the negotiations had un-raveled. An ill-timed leak in Israel of a draft agreement between Syria and Israel, outlining some significant concessions by Damascus and probably designed to drum up domestic support for Barak in the negotiations as well as the promised public referendum on any accord, had embarrassed, if not infuriated, Assad. It compelled him to lurch backward away from the negotiating table, which further placed in full view the incongruity of the perception of the other on both sides of the equation in terms of understanding what is necessary for the other to do in order to garner domestic support for its position. An attempt by President Clinton to heal the rift with a meeting with Assad in Geneva in March 2000 failed, as apparently the Syrian leader expected the United States to present a new proposal that included the sine qua non of Syrian acceptance, that is, an Israeli withdrawal from the Golan Heights to the June 4, 1967, border. It did not, and Syria suspended any further discussions.[22] Hafiz al-Assad's death in June 2000 obviously ended the prospects for any early resumption of negotiations with Israel. Typically shifting back and forth between the two remaining peace tracks as dictated by circumstances, Clinton and Barak began to concentrate on the Palestinians for the remainder of the year, convening what would turn out to be a less-than-successful meeting between Barak and Arafat at Camp David in July.

Again, it seemed, the policy track adopted by Syria at the beginning of the decade had paid less-than-expected dividends by its end. For Syrians this was particularly galling. They felt that they were the key to convening the Madrid process, and what did they have to show for it? The PLO had an accord with the Israelis, Jordan had a peace agreement with Israel, and Lebanon had finally seen the IDF withdrawal from the south, the latter removing one of Syria's primary bargaining chips vis-à-vis Israel regarding withdrawal from the Golan Heights. On top of this, the economy was in virtual shambles. The May 1991 Investment Law 10 was supposed to establish the standard for Syria's opening up to foreign investment. This law offers the same incentives to local and foreign investors, that is, companies that obtain licenses receive duty-free privileges for the import of capital goods and materials necessary for a particular project. At the time, this was hailed as an important step in the economic liberalization of Syria, and to a certain degree it was, but only if it were followed up with other necessary economic reforms, such as legitimate regulatory regimes, greater transparency, and real privatization. But between the promulgation of the investment law and the end of Assad's time in power, nothing much happened in terms of economic liberalization. The brief economic upturn in the early 1990s was due not so much to an intrinsically strong economy as to the economic windfall of financing and investment from the European Union and the Arab Gulf states, especially for infrastructural projects as compensation for Syria's participation in the Gulf War coalition. Economic growth has dropped precipitously since that time amid all of the other shortcomings of the Syrian economy.

Entering the Twenty-first Century

For Syria the 1970s started out with great promise. A new regime had come to power that implemented a corrective movement internally and embarked upon a more pragmatic foreign policy. The economic boom fueled by the dramatic increase in the price of oil along with a disengagement agreement with Israel that held out a reed of hope for regaining the Golan Heights through diplomacy seemed to bode well for a prosperous and secure Syrian future. By the end of the decade, however, Syria was isolated in the region amid clear signs of economic retrenchment and internal unrest. The most powerful country in the Arab world had just signed a peace treaty with Israel, leaving Damascus to grasp around for regional allies, even Ba'athist rival Iraq for a time, to prevent Israel from outflanking it either through Lebanon or Jordan. Syria's support for Iran in its war with Iraq further estranged Damascus from its erstwhile Arab friends. Prospects for the future of Syria, certainly at least the Assad regime, seemed bleak.

A change of tactics at the beginning of the 1980s—to achieve strategic parity with Israel—propelled Syria in quite a different direction in its attempt to contain Israel and reassert itself in the regional area. As it virtually stood alone in the Arab world, Damascus, perforce, moved closer to the Soviet Union. The results were not entirely bad. By the middle of the decade, Syria had beaten back Israel and the West from Lebanon, it had seen any enlargement of the Camp David model frittered away, and the regime had eliminated significant opposition domestically. Against considerable odds, Syria seemed to be back in (or near) the center of the fray despite a flurry of attempts to marginalize it. By the end of the decade, however, Syria was as isolated as it had been at the end of the previous one. Egypt had rehabilitated itself in the Arab world, and it naturally displaced Syria in the regional balance of power. Jordan and the PLO had discarded the Syrian model and had chosen a negotiated solution to the Arab-Israeli conflict. Iraq had claimed victory in its war with Iran and seemed as menacing as ever on Syria's eastern border. Perhaps most disturbingly, the Soviet prop dissipated with Gorbachev's new foreign policy approach, the end of the Cold War, and the beginning of the end of the Soviet Union itself. And finally, the economy was experiencing severe problems, with little hope of improvement on its own.

At the dawn of a new decade, circumstances intervened again to provide the regime of Hafiz al-Assad another chance; the seesaw of pragmatism continued. By joining the Gulf War coalition and then attending the

Madrid Conference, Syria had made, as Assad often called it, a strategic choice for peace. And in the early 1990s, Syria seemed to have chosen correctly. Syria's international image improved immensely. At the same time, Damascus seemed to finally receive a commitment from Israeli leaders regarding withdrawal from the Golan Heights. The economic dividends of joining the Gulf War coalition combined with more regular seasonal rains and an increase in its own oil production to fuel a period of economic growth. Delegations from the West, even the United States, were frequently seen in Damascus preparing the ground to take advantage of Syria's untapped economic potential once the expected peace treaty with Israel was signed. But peace did not come. Instead, Assad saw his rivals Hussein and Arafat sign accords with Israel, beating Syria to the punch. Syrian and Israeli officials, despite some progress, in the end wrangled over the extent of the withdrawal from the Golan Heights, with Assad doggedly insisting that the redrawn border be the June 4, 1967, line.[23] Despite brief flirtations with success, by early 2000 Syrian-Israeli negotiations had been suspended. And one of Syria's major bargaining chips in negotiations with Israel, that is, Syrian control over Hizballah vis-à-vis Israel's security zone in south Lebanon, had disappeared due to the Barak government's decision to unilaterally evacuate the IDF from Lebanon in May 2000 (with the concurrent disbanding of Israel's ally, the South Lebanese Army). In addition, the stultifying effects of Syria's politico-economic structure, beating down the hints of economic liberalization and growth that emerged in the early 1990s, led to economic stagnation by the end of the decade.[24]

Again, Syria seemed to be at a turning point, only this time it would be without its venerable leader. Hafiz al-Assad died in June 2000 and was succeeded by his young and relatively untested son, Bashar.[25] As a result, questions abounded as they never had before in the preceding thirty years over whether or not Syria could recover this time around and which course the new regime would chart in its attempts to do so.

At this early stage in Bashar's tenure in power, it is too soon to properly assess the direction of his presidency on the domestic front or in the foreign policy arena. There do, however, exist some possible clues. In his inaugural address in July, Bashar made reform of the economy a clear priority; indeed, the frankness of his criticism of the prior system is unprecedented.[26] The new president declared that the state bureaucracy had become a "major obstacle" to development, and he admitted that economic progress had been uneven due in large measure to the state-dominated economy: "Don't depend on the state. There is no magic wand. The process of change requires elements that are not the preserve of one person. . . . Authority without responsibility is the cause of chaos." He went on to say that "[W]e must rid ourselves of those old ideas that have become obstacles. In order to succeed we need modern thinking."[27] Bashar has also apparently shied away from the personality cult that enveloped his father, ordering the removal of his pictures from all nongovernmental buildings.[28] In addition, he has shaken up the state media, replacing several directors of major state-run news organizations in Syria as well as bringing in new people to the Ministry of Information.

On the economic front, the new regime has announced some steps toward reform, such as enhancing the 1991 Investment Law 10, and it has talked about such measures as allowing private banking (albeit in free trade zones) and a stock exchange.[29] Talking about economic reform and successfully implementing it, however, are two entirely different things.[30] Entrenched interests in Syria, the combination of private business tied into the state apparatus, could, and probably will, continue to act as a brake on any type of economic reform that threatens their position.[31] While bringing new blood into the ruling inner circle, Bashar, perforce, has also had to rely on several members of the old guard at least during this transition phase, such as Defense Minister Mustafa Tlass and Foreign Minister Farouk al-Sharaa.[32] The anticorruption campaign carried out in Bashar's name for about a year prior to his father's death was very popular among most Syrians, and it associated Bashar with a popular cause—anticorruption has become a mantra of the new regime and, along with calls for technological progress, was delineated as such at the Ba'ath Party congress held in July. But it was also a tool to eliminate actual and potential opponents to Bashar in order to prepare the ground for succession. In what almost seemed a race against the deteriorating health of Hafiz al-Assad, apparently enough reshuffling was accomplished in order to assure Bashar's accession, at least in the short term. As one senior Arab official stated, "[Hafiz al-]Assad took power thirty years ago by putting his rivals in jail and getting the party to back him as leader. Bashar used modern concepts of democracy and anti-corruption to reach the same goal."[33] In other words, is it politics as usual in Syria, but just operating underneath a different, albeit a more modern and possibly less overtly abrasive, veneer?[34]

On relations with Israel, it seems that as of this writing Bashar plans to continue in his father's footsteps, that is, still maintaining peace as a strategic choice while insisting on a return of the Golan Heights to the June 4, 1967, line. In his inaugural address, Bashar stated, "Peace is our choice.

The liberation of the Golan is a primary goal for us. It is just as important to us as peace. If these few meters [along the Sea of Galilee] are not an obstacle, why do they [the Israelis] not return them?"[35] All things remaining relatively constant (a tall order in the Middle East by any measure), it is the consensus of opinion among Syria watchers that Bashar will be occupied with consolidating his own power base in Syria for a while, for at least a year from his accession to the presidency, before he is prepared to reenter the peace process with Israel.

In the meantime, building on what his father had begun in recent years, Bashar has made a concerted attempt to improve relations with a number of states in the region, including Turkey and Iraq (which seem to run in an inverse proportional manner to Syria's relations with Israel). With the failure of the Camp David summit between Barak and Arafat in July 2000 and the heightened tensions in the region resulting from the al-Aqsa intifada launched in September, Syria is playing a game of wait-and-see, and the Syrian president has been in close contact with his Egyptian and Saudi counterparts. Bashar has carefully positioned Syria so that it can reenter the peace process if necessary as well as play a significant Arab leadership role if the Arab-Israeli conflict heats up again; Syria is one of the few countries in the Arab world that has this type of flexibility. At the emergency Arab League summit meeting held in Cairo in October 2000 to discuss the Israeli-Palestinian miniwar, Bashar delivered what has been described as an impressive and impassioned speech that called for "Arab solidarity" in the face of Israeli "aggression" and on Arab states to sever their relations with Israel and reimpose the Arab economic boycott.[36] While reiterating Syria's strategic choice for peace, he was definitely situating himself between the hard-liners, such as Iraq and Libya, who called for a declaration of war against Israel, and the moderate pro-West countries such as Egypt, Jordan, and Saudi Arabia. As with many of the other Arab leaders in this difficult situation, Bashar has to listen to the Arab "street," that is, the vehement outburst of pro-Palestinian demonstrations exacerbated by the information and communications technology revolution that has spread both picture and word across the region in a more unabated fashion than ever before; therefore, he has to give at least an outward appearance of taking an active stance, and this is especially important for a country that, as stated previously, has been the self-anointed standard-bearer of Arabism.

There still remain a number of questions surrounding Bashar's regime. A number of observers suspect his reign is not yet totally secure; a tall hurdle will be crossed when he survives his first mistake, not when the spotlight of the international community is on Syria amid the outpouring of support that convulsively erupted following his father's death. Can he tame the military-security apparatus, which is dominated by Alawites, whose first priority is to maintain the structure of power that benefits them so enormously? Can economic and even political reform truly be implemented under such conditions, especially if by doing so power naturally becomes more dispersed, particularly toward the Sunni Arab community?[37] Will Bashar continue the "Bonapartist" tradition, that is, make survival of his regime the ultimate priority and institute economic and diplomatic policies only as a means to that end, thereby damning Syria to its typical snail's pace of change? Or will he be able to break away and establish new traditions in order to enter the march of globalization with a new elite class of reformers willing to take the risk of trying? Will a Bashar who is securely in power resume negotiations with Israel? Or will his inability to rule as well as reign inhibit his flexibility in a reactivated peace process? Will those ten meters between the 1923 and June 4, 1967, lines become another Haram al-Sharif/Temple Mount type of controversy? And will Syrian policy in the region itself find a new foundational basis with new alliances, or will it still be guided by the parameters that defined Hafiz al-Assad's pragmatic approach: flanks, balances, and withdrawals?

Notes

1. See Moshe Ma'oz, "Changes in Syria's Regional Strategic Position vis-à-vis Israel," in *Modern Syria: From Ottoman Rule to Pivotal Role in the Middle East,* ed. Moshe Ma'oz, Joseph Ginat, and Onn Winckler (Brighton: Sussex Academic Press, 1998), 257–71, and Raymond A. Hinnebusch, "Revisionist Dreams, Realist Strategies: The Foreign Policy of Syria," in *The Foreign Policies of Arab States: The Challenge of Change,* ed. Bahgat Korany and Ali E. Hillal Dessouki (Boulder: Westview Press, 1991), 374–409.

2. Assad was minister of defense in the Syrian government at the time of the 1967 war, so he felt a personal responsibility to regain in its entirety the land lost to Israel.

3. As Hinnebusch states regarding the disengagement agreements and the increasingly negative Syrian view of the emerging peace process, "The agreement facilitated the U.S. effort to defuse the wartime crisis as a substitute for an overall settlement and legitimized step-by-step diplomacy, an approach that weakened the Arabs' hand and especially those, Syria and the PLO, to whom the Israelis were least likely to make concessions" (Hinnebusch, "Revisionist Dreams, Realist Strategies," 395).

4. Also, Saddam Hussein, long the strongman in Iraq, officially became president in July 1979. He immediately convened a Ba'ath Party regional congress meeting, at which scores of high-level Iraqis were openly accused of plotting against the regime. They were removed from office and many were executed. The Iraqis quietly accused Syria of backing the plotters, although a majority of the accused were Shiite, long suspected by the Sunni Arab ruling clique as something of a fifth column within the country. The incident contributed to the souring of Iraqi-Syrian relations, thus making any real possibility of union even more remote than it already was.

5. Iraq, primarily, saw the new Shiite Islamic Republic of Iran as a threat, as the ayatollah openly espoused the exportation of the revolution to surrounding states, first among them Iraq with its majority Shiite population ruled by a Sunni Arab minority. With the apparent disarray in Iran after the revolution, especially within the military, and clearly now bereft of American military assistance following the hostage crisis begun in November 1979, Saddam Hussein thought the best defense was an offense. At the same time, he thought he could establish a hegemonic position in the Persian Gulf and assume the leadership role in the Arab world as well, as exemplified by his "protection" of Arab lands from Persian expansionism.

6. Even before the war broke out, in response to the threat of the Iranian revolution, Iraq started improving relations with Jordan and the Gulf Arab states. Saddam Hussein paid a visit to Jordan in June 1979, the first by at least the de facto Iraqi head of state since the overthrow of the Iraqi monarchy in 1958. A wide variety of military, economic, and political agreements were signed, thus drawing Amman closer to Baghdad and away from Damascus. Interestingly, this burgeoning relationship between Iraq and Jordan would severely damage Jordan's credibility in the Gulf and with the United States when the 1990–91 Gulf crisis and war occurred, as Amman was reluctant to condemn the Iraqi invasion of Kuwait or sever its ties to Baghdad.

7. Indeed, Moscow withheld arms deliveries to Iraq for eighteen months following the beginning of the conflict due in large part to its anger over Iraqi actions—it was also a period when the Soviets were exploring the opportunity to build up a relationship with Iran, which, of course, had severed its ties with the United States. See Robert O. Freedman, *Moscow and the Middle East: Soviet Policy since the Invasion of Afghanistan* (Cambridge: Cambridge University Press, 1991).

8. Hinnebusch, "Revisionist Dreams," 402.

9. Steven Heydemann, "The Political Logic of Economic Rationality: Selective Stabilization in Syria," in *The Politics of Economic Reform in the Middle East,* ed. Henri Barkey (New York: St. Martin's Press, 1992), 11–39. On Syria's political economy, see Volker Perthes, *The Political Economy of Syria under Assad* (London: I. B. Tauris, 1995), or, for a briefer treatment, see David W. Lesch, "Is Syria Ready for Peace? Obstacles to Integration in the Global Economy," *Middle East Policy* 6, no. 3 (February 1999): 93–111.

10. Causes for the rise of the Sunni Muslim Brethren in Syria as a serious threat were (1) the avowedly secular nature of the Ba'athist regime, especially one led by a minority schismatic Shiite sect, the Alawites, who most Muslims do not even consider to be true Muslims; (2) the economic difficulties and disparities that had become increasingly apparent by 1980; and (3) the inspirational example of the Iranian revolution, which, although led by Shiites, still set an example of an Islamist movement successfully overthrowing what it considered to be a tyrannical and non-Islamic regime. No doubt the Muslim Brethren in Syria were also galvanized by the assassination of Anwar Sadat by Islamic Jihad elements in October 1981, which, of course, only made Assad more wary of his own predicament.

11. Quoted in Ma'oz, "Changes," 266. Also see Freedman, *Moscow and the Middle East*; and Helena Cobban, "The Nature of the Soviet-Syrian Link under Assad and Gorbachev," in *Syria: Society, Culture, and Polity,* ed. Richard T. Antoun and Donald Quataert (Albany: State University of New York Press, 1991), 116. As a sign of discontent, Assad withdrew the Syrian ambassador to Moscow shortly after his return (ibid.).

12. It is also fair to say, however, that a significant portion of this effort was funded by outside sources, primarily the Soviet bloc, and that if it were not for Syria's strategic value, it would have received very little military or economic aid from the Soviet Union or the Gulf Arab states. Various estimates place the range of the Syrian debt to the USSR/Russia in the neighborhood of $10–12 billion (some say it is as high as $20 billion). Russia obviously wants some or all of this amount eventually paid back; however, Hafiz al-Assad firmly believed that the debt was erased when the Soviet Union ceased to exist, and in his view Moscow had already received an in-kind return on its money: the political and diplomatic influence it was seeking in the Middle East due in large part through Damascus. Moscow and Damascus today are still negotiating a satisfactory outcome to this situation, especially as Syria is still dependent on Russian weaponry and as Russia still seeks to maintain some influence in the region as well as markets for its arms. It is also worth noting that there are a good many economists who debate the supposed debilitating effects of an overly large military. It depends on the specific situation, but a large military can provide a measure of economic relief for the regime by employing thousands of young men who would otherwise be unemployed and a possible source of unrest. See Patrick Clawson, *Unaffordable Ambitions: Syria's Military Buildup and Economic Crisis* (Washington, D.C.: Washington Institute for Near East Policy, 1989).

13. Lesch, "Is Syria Ready for Peace," 100–101.

14. Hinnebusch, "Revisionist Dreams," 403.

15. Quoted in Ma'oz, "Changes," 267.

16. Even as early as 1987, Syria's deputy foreign minister was exclaiming that "our economic links in the region are with the West. We are not allies of the East" (quoted in Cobban, "The Nature of the Soviet-Syrian Link," 121).

17. In return, Syria received tacit recognition within the Arab world and by the

United States of its dominant role in Lebanon. Iraq's preoccupations also allowed Syria to push out Iraqi-backed factions in Lebanon that had been resisting Syrian control. Syria's position was cemented with its Friendship and Cooperation agreement with the regime in Beirut in May 1991.

18. For details on the Israeli-Syrian negotiations through 1995–96, see Itamar Rabinovich, *The Brink of Peace: The Israeli-Syrian Negotiations* (Princeton, N.J.: Princeton University Press, 1998), and Uri Savir, *The Process: 1,100 Days that Changed the Middle East* (New York: Random House, 1998). Both Rabinovich and Savir were lead negotiators for the Israelis on the Syrian track. Also see Helena Cobban, *The Israeli-Syrian Peace Talks, 1991–1996 and Beyond* (Washington, D.C.: United States Institute of Peace Press, 1999).

19. Quoted in Patrick Seale and Linda Butler, "Assad's Regional Strategy and the Challenge from Netanyahu," *Journal of Palestine Studies* 26, no. 1 (autumn 1996): 36–37.

20. Quoted in Raymond Hinnebusch, "Does Syria Want Peace: Syrian Policy in the Syrian-Israeli Negotiations," *Journal of Palestine Studies* 26, no. 1 (autumn 1996): 44–45. Assad was quoted in *al-Ahram* (Egypt) in December 1995 as saying that Shimon Peres's vision of a Middle East common market was ultimately an attempt to "eliminate the concept of Arabism, and by extension the Arabs . . . our inner feeling of being a nation, and our national and social identity" (quoted in Seale and Butler, "Assad's Regional Strategy," 36).

21. It is interesting that, even in the aftermath of the Israeli withdrawal from Lebanon in May 2000, Hafiz al-Assad's son and successor, Bashar, seems to be using Hizballah in much the same fashion in relation to the deteriorating situation on the Israeli-Palestinian front following the failure of the July 2000 Camp David summit and the subsequent Palestinian al-Aqsa intifada initiated in September. Syria is shoring up its bargaining leverage vis-à-vis Israel and padding its anti-Israeli credentials in the Arab world by supporting an increase in Hizballah activity against Israel on the border. At the same time it is providing a rationale for the continuation of Syrian troops in Lebanon amid more vocal calls by various Lebanese factions (mostly Christian but also including Druze leader Walid Jumblat) for a Syrian withdrawal from Lebanese territory. Increased tension between Israel and Lebanon, on the wane since Israel ended its occupation in the south, diverts the Lebanese from focusing on Syria and, Syria hopes, causes Syria to be seen as protector rather than occupier.

22. In the aftermath of the failed summit with Clinton, it was reported that Assad increased Syria's defense budget and purchased up to $2 billion worth of Russian weaponry (*Middle East Newsline*, May 18, 2000). Syria has also increased its military ties with North Korea and China, particularly in terms of missile technology. Syria reportedly successfully tested SCUD D missiles in September 2000, with a range of 600–700 kilometers (it already has SCUD C missiles provided by North Korea with a range of 550 kilometers), which gives Syria the capability to strike at any part of Israel as well as its other neighbors and allows Syria to deploy them in areas that are more difficult for the Israelis to reach. Along

with this, Syria is also said to have improved its chemical weapons capability and is building a biological weapons capability, with the potential of loading chemical and biological warheads onto the SCUD C or D missiles. This, however, does not detract from the general consensus that Syria's weaponry generally is in a dilapidated state, with very little offensive capability. Its procurement of missile technology from sources such as North Korea and China is most likely aimed at enhancing the Syrian deterrent. In September 2000, it was reported that Russian officials have stated that military and economic cooperation with Syria might include a nuclear reactor and the most advanced aircraft, tanks, and antiaircraft systems. Some officials have asserted that this is part of a concerted effort to raise Russia's profile in the Arab-Israeli peace talks. Interestingly, one Russian official reportedly stated that "[R]ight now, the Syrians love to look at what we have and take what they want. Then, when it comes time to pay, you don't hear from them anymore." *Middle East Newsline,* September 20, 2000.

23. The June 4, 1967, line would bring Syria to the Sea of Galilee (called Lake Tiberius by Syrians), giving it, at least in theory, water and fishing rights. Israel wants to withdraw to the 1923 international border demarcated between then French-mandated Syria and British-mandated Palestine. The 1923 border is about ten meters from the Sea of Galilee. The June 4 line represents Syrian advances during the Arab-Israeli war of 1947–49. It is popularly suspected that Assad insisted on the June 4 line so that Syria would appear to have more territory returned, that is, beyond the 1923 international border, than what Sadat received in the Egyptian-Israeli treaty.

24. With unemployment ranging, by most estimates, between 20 and 25 percent and per capita GDP at less than $3,000, Syria was a lower-middle-income country on the road to what one economist termed a "second-rate modernization." In other words, Syria may have embarked on an economic plan that actually retards economic growth and income distribution by replacing traditional crafts and occupations that provide value added with menial production-line jobs that produce inferior products. If this is true, Syria's economy will perpetually be at a comparative disadvantage with the West. See Rodney Wilson, *Economic Development in the Middle East* (London: Routledge, 1995), 49. Having said this, some economists point to the possibility that emerging-market countries that are in a preindustrial or early industrial stage might leapfrog over the development of a manufacturing base and enter into the service-oriented economic stage that has become increasingly characteristic of economies in the West. This could happen with Syria, which has potential in the heavily service-oriented tourism industry. It becomes a definite possibility once a serious economic reform program is enacted and an Israeli-Syrian peace agreement is concluded. The Syrian government newspaper *Tishrin* acknowledged the severe unemployment problem in a cartoon depicting an apparently wealthy man leisurely eyeing a want-ad entitled "just one work opportunity," while thousands of people huddled around the newspaper (reported in *Middle East Newsline,* May 10, 2000, *www.menewsline.com*).

25. As is well known, Bashar was brought home from London, where he had

been studying ophthalmology, in 1994 when his elder brother, Basil, who was being groomed to succeed his father, died in a car accident. Bashar was slowly elevated in the military and in the country propaganda over the course of the decade. His only official position had been president of the Syrian Computer Society, but in 1999 he was given the very important Lebanese portfolio, that is, he was put in charge of Syria's dominant, yet delicate, position in Lebanon. Having met him on a couple of occasions, I can confirm the popular perception of him as someone who is in the mild-mannered intellectual mold. Syrians have often wondered whether or not he is simply too compassionate and nice to be the president of Syria. He is definitely a modernizer, having lived in and being culturally sympathetic to the West.

26. Soon after his father's death, Bashar was quickly elevated from a colonel to lieutenant-general, commander of the armed forces, and secretary-general of the ruling Ba'ath Party. In addition, Syria's National Assembly almost immediately passed an amendment to the Syrian constitution lowering the minimum age one could become president from forty to thirty-four years old, the latter being Bashar's age.

27. *Financial Times,* July 18, 2000, 10.

28. In his inaugural address, Bashar stated that "the approach of the great leader, Hafiz al-Assad, was a very special and unique approach and therefore it is not easy to emulate, especially as we remember that we are required not just to maintain it but to develop it as well" (text of speech in Syrian Arab News Agency, *www.sana-syria.com*).

29. Prime Minister Mustafa Miro, Bashar's ally appointed to the position a few months before Hafiz al-Assad died, has suggested that banks from Lebanon would soon be allowed to operate in Syria. A Saudi consortium, Arab Investment Holding Company, announced soon after Bashar's accession to the presidency that it would invest $100 million in Syria, targeted especially toward the tourism and telecommunications industries. The general manager of AIHC is Saad Hariri, a son of the newly elected billionaire prime minister of Lebanon, Rafiq Hariri. *Middle East Intelligence Bulletin* reports that $40 million of the initial investment is being directed toward the construction of a five-star hotel along the Mediterranean coast near Latakia, stating that "it is being built in a predominantly Alawite area—the laborers who are hired to build it will be predominantly Alawite, the appreciation in real estate prices will benefit Alawite landowners, and revenue generated from increased tourism in the area will mainly enrich Alawite businessmen." As such, it is suggested, with some legitimacy, that "just as the state-centered economy of the late president Assad was geared to benefit the Alawite community in general and a select strata of commercial elites in particular, the benefits of Bashar's limited drive toward economic liberalization are likely to accrue disproportionately to the same constituents" (*MEIB* 2, no. 7 [August 5, 2000]). On AIHC's venture, see also *Middle East Newsline,* July 16, 2000. Investment Law 10 was "enhanced" by, for example, permitting investors to own land and transfer profits from Syria abroad and exempting investors from taxes for seven years.

30. In the economic sphere, Bashar is facing a great many problems. The Milken Institute, an independent think tank in Santa Monica, California, compared a host of Middle Eastern countries in terms of the degree to which their capital markets foster entrepreneurial capitalism. The countries examined were Morocco, Tunisia, Egypt, Israel, Lebanon, Jordan, Syria, and Turkey. Syria ranked last (Israel, Lebanon, and Tunisia were at the top), the only one without a stock exchange and having the lowest per capita income in the group. This also suggests an economic and business rationale for why Lebanon is so important to Damascus. Forbes Global, *www.forbes.com/forbesglobal/00/1002/03119084a.htm* (September 22, 2000). Syrian industrialists and economists estimate that Syria needs at least $50 billion to repair the nation's infrastructure.

31. Bashar's father's regime created too many clientele networks to implement change in anything but an incremental fashion.

> Despite some macroeconomic policy changes that have trimmed the public sector base to a certain extent, more effort has actually been exerted by the regime to co-opt important elements of the private sector, i.e., the potential avenues of opposition, into the idea of regime maintenance. As a result, the private sector is still largely fragmented and too dependent upon the state to become a significant pressure group. Syria's selective liberalization has been as much directed by a desire to broaden the regime's support base during a time of change as by the need to improve its economic situation in general. Significant elements of the bourgeoisie have, therefore, been brought (some would say forced) into a coalition of sorts with the state. (Lesch, "Is Syria Ready," 102)

See also Perthes, *The Political Economy of Syria under Assad*, 254.

32. In his inaugural speech, Bashar stated that "some people may believe that creative minds are linked to age and that they can frequently be found with the youth, but this is not quite accurate. Some young people have strong minds that are still lively and creative" (text of speech from Syrian Arab News Agency, *www.sana-syria.com*).

33. Quoted in *Financial Times,* July 8/9, 2000. In a televised public address on July 17, Bashar stated that it would be "impossible" for Syria to become a Western-style democracy and called for "democracy specific to Syria, that takes its roots from its history, and respects its society." He added,

> We cannot apply the democracy of others on ourselves. Western democracy, for example, is the outcome of a long history that resulted in customs and traditions that distinguish the current culture of Western societies. In order to apply what they have, we have to live their history with all of its social significance. As this is, obviously, impossible, we have to have our democratic experience that is special to us, that stems from our history, culture, and civilization, and that is a response to the needs of our society and the requirements of our reality. (text of speech in Syrian Arab News Agency, *www.sana-syria.com*)

Most took this to mean that Syria's authoritarian type of government constructed under his father would remain largely intact. See also *Middle East Intelligence Bulletin* 2, no. 7 (August 5, 2000). The *MEIB* is published online by the U.S. Committee for a Free Lebanon. While it is certainly anti-Syrian in its opinions, particularly concerning Syrian withdrawal from Lebanon, I have found its factual reporting to be accurate.

34. Some would say that this could also apply to Bashar's policy toward Lebanon. While many, including the United States, hailed Lebanon's parliamentary elections in September 2000 as the most open and free in recent memory, recognizing the number of opposition candidates who won seats as well as Rafiq Hariri's return as prime minister over Syria's apparent choice, others claim that Syria still is solidly entrenched in Lebanon and that Bashar astutely allowed the impression of a reduction of Syria's iron grip while in effect maintaining firm control there. Syria depends too heavily on its current relationship with Lebanon to let go in any significant fashion, especially in economic terms—there are over 1.2 million Syrian laborers in Lebanon. Bashar has made it one of his early policy priorities to invest money in Syria in order to alleviate the growing unemployment problem.

35. Quoted in *Financial Times,* July 18, 2000.

36. Excerpts from Arab League speech can be found in Syrian Arab News Agency, *www.sana-syria.com.*

37. The fiasco surrounding former military chief of staff (and a leading Sunni Arab) General Hikmat al-Shihabi's exile followed by his return soon after Hafiz al-Assad's death suggests that Syrian intelligence was wary of an expansion of Sunni influence in the immediate aftermath of Assad's passing. Reports are that Bashar did not know about this. Apparently, rumors of Shihabi's arrest, which compelled him to leave Lebanon (where he was at the time) and go to the United States, were initiated independently by elements in Syrian intelligence. This suggests possibly one of two things: that this type of confusion was to be expected in the often chaotic process that takes place during a transfer of power; or that Bashar does not have as much control of the military-security apparatus as his father did, and that this type of cross-purpose behavior may not be atypical in the near future—all of which means that Bashar may have to watch his steps very closely, especially if he actually tries to implement the level of reform he has thus far indicated. Another indication of some wariness about the Sunni leadership, even before Assad's death, was the marginalization of Vice President Abd al-Halim Khaddam, including an investigation into his activities upon the ascent of the new regime—apparently, he is back in the good graces of the government at the urging of some other members of the old guard (see *Middle East Newsline,* July 3, 2000).

9

Lebanon since 1979

Syria, Hizballah, and the War against Peace in the Middle East

MARIUS DEEB

Lebanon in its heyday (1943–75) was a model of what Arend Lijphart called a consociational democracy and, as such, was in the company of advanced European countries such as Switzerland and Austria.[1] Lebanon then was the envy of the countries of the Middle East and North Africa because of its standard of living, its high literacy rate, and its political environment characterized by freedom, tolerance, and pluralism.

Many Lebanese intellectuals believed that Lebanon was Mediterranean in its culture, at once part of the West and of the Middle Eastern region. The basis of this unique society was a symbiosis of its mountain dwellers, who sought refuge from religious persecution and intolerance elsewhere in the Middle East, and its seafaring coastal inhabitants, who believed in free trade rooted in their Phoenician past.

Lebanon as Syria's Battlefield against the Peace Process

The year 1979 witnessed the completion of the Egyptian-Israeli negotiations, with active U.S. mediation, culminating in the signing of the Egyptian-Israeli peace treaty on March 29, 1979. There were two reactions to President Anwar Sadat's peace initiative. The first reaction was a positive one, from those who wanted to emulate Sadat and to end the conflict with Israel. The most enthusiastic were the Lebanese Christians who had watched how Lebanon had become the only arena where the PLO was engaged in armed struggle against Israel, to the detriment of Lebanese sovereignty and at a very high cost for the Lebanese population of Jabal 'Amil (southern Lebanon). Imam Musa al-Sadr, the religious leader of the Shia of Lebanon, became openly critical of the war in southern Lebanon, especially in the wake of the Israeli Litani operation of March–June 1978. Al-Sadr was very much concerned about the welfare of his community in Jabal 'Amil, and that was the most likely reason for his disappearance in late August 1978 in Libya, as both Syria and the PLO viewed him as an obstacle for the continued struggle against Israel via southern Lebanon.[2]

Lebanon had avoided participation in any of the Arab-Israeli wars except for that of 1948–49, and the Lebanese-Israeli border did not witness any significant incidents during the period from 1949 until 1967.[3] After the June 1967 war the situation changed when the Palestinians and their leftist allies began attacking Israel from the Lebanese border and their attacks led to Israeli retaliation.

There is a great irony in what happened to Lebanon after 1967. Until then Lebanon was a peaceful and democratic polity, never constituting a danger to either Israel or Syria. The irony is that Lebanon, which consciously sought to avoid being involved in the major Arab-Israeli wars, was compelled by the PLO to become, after June 1967, a battlefield of the Arab-Israeli conflict. There was no doubt about the fact that, by the late 1970s, the PLO constituted a state within a state in Lebanon.[4]

The Lebanese Christians were particularly upset about the role of the PLO because when Lebanon became an independent country in 1943, the founding fathers, Bisharah al-Khuri and Riyad al-Sulh, reached a compromise known as the National Pact (al-Mithaq al-watani). It stipulated that the Lebanese Christians would give up France as their protector, in exchange for renunciation by the Lebanese Muslims of unity with the Arab hinterland. The creation by the PLO of a state within a state in Lebanon violated the National Pact, by surrendering parts of Lebanon to a quasi-state of the Arab hinterland. The National Pact had created a partnership of Christians and Muslims in ruling Lebanon. By having the PLO in Lebanon, the balance would tilt in favor of the Muslims at the expense of the Christians. After all, the very raison d'être of Lebanon was the presence of a large Christian community.

What also irritated those who wanted to follow in the footsteps of Sadat in Lebanon, primarily but not exclusively the Christians, was the fact that all the other Arab countries had closed their borders to guerrilla operations against Israel, while supporting the PLO's military activities across the Lebanese-Israeli border. Another irony is the fact that Lebanon is the only country bordering Israel that has never had any territorial disputes with Israel, but its border with Israel has been the only border after 1967 in which war was fought, with the exception of the 1973 Arab-Israeli war. Jordan had not permitted any guerrilla operation from its borders with Israel in the aftermath of its expulsions of the PLO in September 1970 and July 1971, long before the Jordanian-Israeli peace treaty was signed in October 1994. Egypt did the same as early as the first Egyptian-Israeli disengagement agreement of January 1974. The greatest irony of all is that Syria, which sealed off its border with Israel to guerrilla operations following the Golan Heights agreement of May 31, 1974, at the same time has waged a war against the peace process, through proxies engaged in guerrilla operations and terrorism primarily from or via the Lebanese territories.

The second reaction to Sadat's peace initiative that resulted in the Egyptian-Israeli peace treaty was to fight the peace process through a continuing war spearheaded by Syria. Lebanon became, more than ever, the arena where Syria's proxies, both Palestinian and Lebanese, conducted war. In 1979 the Islamic revolution in Iran provided Syria with additional support against the peaceful resolution of the Arab-Israeli conflict.

Revolutionary Iran: Strategic Ally of Assad's Syria

The late Syrian president Hafiz al-Assad realized from the onset that when the Islamic revolution against the Shah triumphed in Iran in February 1979, it would have tremendous potential to help him. First, it was Shia in character and would be a natural ally to an Alawi-dominated regime in Syria. The Alawis regarded themselves as Shia and managed through Imam Musa al-Sadr, the president of the Higher Shia Council in Lebanon, to get a religious edict or *fatwa*, in 1973, declaring that the Alawis do belong to the mainstream Twelvers (Ithna Ashari) Shia denomination like those of Iran and southern Iraq. Second, the Iranian Shiism of the new revolutionary regime would be a counterbalance to the Arab Sunnism, exemplified by Saudi Arabia, Iraq, Jordan, and Egypt, and which, in the innermost recesses of his Alawi psyche, Assad feared. Third, allying himself to an Islamic Iran would be helpful in Assad's fight against the Sunni Muslim fundamentalists who were seriously challenging his regime. Fourth, by 1979 Assad needed more than ever to mobilize and utilize the Shia in Lebanon, and his alliance with Iran would make his task easier. Assad's erstwhile allies, the Christians of Lebanon, had become hostile to Syria because Assad had reneged on his promises to force the PLO to abide by its agreements with the Lebanese government. The Sunnis of Lebanon had by then become increasingly unreliable, as Assad was crushing their Syrian coreligionists.

Finally, the Islamic revolution in Iran was strongly opposed to Israel and to the peaceful resolution of the Arab-Israeli conflict. As Assad had been waging a war against the peace process, as is documented in my forthcoming book, *Syria's Terrorist War on Lebanon and the Peace Process: 1974–2002,* Islamic Iran became the ideal ally for Syria.

Those who regard the Syrian-Iranian alliance from 1979 onward as tactical in nature, because Syria is Ba'athist in ideology and therefore secular while Iran is a theocracy, are deceived by appearances. The Assad regime is sectarian in nature, because all the major military and intelligence officers who wield real power are Alawis. Ba'athism is simply a convenient secular ideology needed to justify and legitimize the Assad regime domestically and regionally. In reality the alliance between Syria and Iran is strategic and of a permanent nature as long as the Alawis are in power in Syria and the Shia clergymen are in power in Iran. Syria is the closest and, in a way, the *only* ally of theocratic Iran in the world.

The PLO exploited the existence of the Palestinians camps in Lebanon to use Lebanese territories to launch its attacks against Israel. When the mainstream PLO was obliged to evacuate West Beirut in August–September 1982, in the wake of Israel's Operation Peace for Galilee, Syria substituted dissident PLO factions and, more significantly, Hizballah, for Arafat's PLO. Consequently the Lebanese-Israeli border has not been pacified because it has been part and parcel of Syria's strategy to keep it in ferment whether under the late Hafiz al-Assad or his son, the present president of Syria, Bashar al-Assad.[5]

Hizballah, borrowing a concept from the Islamic revolutionaries of Iran, when the latter wanted to continue the war against Iraq even after Saddam Hussein was willing to stop it by the summer of 1982, has regarded its war against Israel in southern Lebanon as an imposed war *(harb mafrudah).* The truth is just the opposite of that. In fact Hisballah itself has imposed the war on Israel. Hisballah has fought and is still fighting in southern Lebanon because its very raison d'être is war. The very basis of Hisballah is what it calls war society *(Mujtama' Harb).* The present secretary-general of Hisballah, Hasan Nasrallah, stated as early as January 1987 that, "when there will be in Lebanon 2 million hungry people, our mission will not be to provide bread for them, but to enable them to wage war (al-halat al-jihadiya)."[6]

Assad's War on the Lebanese Polity

One of the myths propagated by the latter-day post-Orientalist scholars on the Middle East, and which is a complete figment of their imagination, is that Assad was able to dominate Lebanon because he had considerable support among the Muslim communities. The facts on the ground show just the opposite of this contention. Since 1980 and despite earlier Christian-Muslim differences, a Christian-Muslim consensus was forged that wanted to end the war within Lebanon and the war across the Lebanese-Israeli border. A year later, in the summer of 1981, the Christian-Muslim consensus called for the withdrawal of Syrian troops from Lebanon by August 1, 1982. This consensus continued to exist and manifested itself again and again in 1982, 1983, 1984, 1987, and 1989.

The truth of the matter is that both the PLO and Syria prior to 1982, and after 1982 Syria alone (with some input from Iran), have prevented, by force or by the threat of force, reconciliation among the Lebanese and putting an end to the conflict within Lebanon and the war across the Lebanese-Israeli border. It took the late president Hafiz al-Assad almost a decade, until 1991, to complete his domination of Lebanon. Assad did that by coercing the Muslim communities and segments of the Christian communities through the systematic use of violence against civilians by means of car bombs, bombardment by artillery, and the assassination of major political and religious leaders. Assad's Lebanese proxies were well-armed militias that he utilized to bomb embassies, take foreign nationals as hostages, and engage in terrorism against Israel and the West.

Let me make some illustrations. There was an attempt by President Sarkis to form a cabinet of national reconciliation headed by the patrician politician Taqi al-Din al-Sulh, in August 1980 that was accepted by the vast majority of political leaders but was nipped in the bud when Syria vetoed the formation of such a cabinet. Another attempt for ending the conflict in Lebanon was made by August of 1981 when President Sarkis and Prime Minister Wazzan, representing Christian-Muslim consensus, agreed on a Working Document *(Warqat 'amal)* that would have put an end to the PLO's operations against Israel from Lebanon. This working document also had a specific date, August 1, 1982, for the withdrawal of Syrian troops from Lebanon. Syria, however, did not budge and the PLO augmented its arsenal of arms in Lebanon and continued to engage in terrorist operations against Israel, despite the cease-fire declared in July 1981. Consequently the Israeli Operation Peace for Galilee was launched in June 1982. It forced the PLO and Syrian troops out of the southern half of Lebanon as well as from West Beirut.[7]

Bashir Gemayel, commander of the Christian Lebanese Forces, was elected president on August 23, 1982; he managed to capture the hearts and minds of the Lebanese during the few weeks after his election. Bashir could have ended the Syrian occupation of Lebanon and returned Lebanon to the status quo ante bellum but was assassinated on September 14, 1982, by a Syrian agent. Assad again aborted an attempt to end the conflict in Lebanon.

Another attempt to end the conflict was the American- sponsored Israeli-Lebanese negotiations that resulted in the May 17, 1983, accord. This accord involved security arrangements in southern Lebanon to end the conflict there and the withdrawal of Syrian troops from Lebanon.[8] Assad refused to let the Lebanese leaders put an end to the conflict and rejected the U.S.-sponsored Lebanese-Israeli agreement. Instead, he mounted an offensive against the Lebanese government using as proxies Walid Jumblat's Druze militia and Nabih Birri's Amal militia. The newly formed Hisballah was utilized to launch terrorist attacks against the U.S. embassy in Beirut in April 1983 and against both the U.S. Marines, and the French Foreign Legion of the peacekeeping multinational force in October 1983. By means of terrorism perpetrated by his Lebanese proxies, Assad forced the withdrawal of the multinational force in February 1984 and the abrogation of the Israeli-Lebanese accord by the Lebanese government. This period came to an end with the unsuccessful attempt by Syria to impose a tripartite agreement that involved the redeployment of Syrian forces in Lebanon. It was signed by pro-Syrian militia leaders in December 1985 but was rejected by President Amin Gemayel and the new commander of the Christian Lebanese Forces, Samir Ja'Ja'.[9]

Assad increased his terrorism to undermine the peace process and to dominate Lebanon. Followers of the radical Palestinian leader Abu Nidal were sent from Damascus in December 1985 to attack the counters of El Al Airlines in Vienna and in Rome, resulting in the killing of scores of Americans and Israelis. In April 1986, a Syrian agent in London was caught red-handed trying to blow up an El Al plane bound for Israel. American and French nationals became the target of hostage takers such as the Syrian proxy Hisballah starting from March 1984.[10] President Gemayel tried to negotiate an agreement with Syria in early 1987, but instead the Syrian troops returned in February 1987 to West Beirut in full force.

The sharp decline in the value of the previously powerful Lebanese currency impoverished the country, and in April 1987, Prime Minister Rashid Karami called for the reconvening of the Lebanese cabinet for the first time since January 1986. Due to Syrian intransigence about the Lebanese cabinet, Prime Minister Karami resigned in May and made statements to the effect that the differences among the Lebanese were no longer significant. Karami's views were identical to those of the Christian Lebanese Front headed by former president Camille Chamoun. This worried the Syrians, and Karami was assassinated on June 1, 1987.

All attempts supported by active U.S. mediation to end the conflict and to reach an agreement on a successor to President Gemayel when his term ended in September 1988 failed because of Syrian intransigence. The Syrians refused to allow the Lebanese Chamber of Deputies to elect a president from a list of five candidates approved by them.[11]

The appointment of the commander of the Lebanese army, General Michel 'Awn, as interim prime minister on September 23, 1988, was a constitutionally correct act, following the precedent set by President Bisharah al-Khouri when he resigned in September 1952 and appointed the commander of the Lebanese army, General Fu'ad Chehab (a Maronite Christian) as prime minister until presidential elections were to be held.

Although 'Awn was constitutionally appointed as prime minister, Assad refused to deal with him and instead insisted on dealing with the outgoing pro-Syrian acting prime minister, Salim al-Huss. In its continued appeasement of Assad, the United States decided to deal with both prime ministers. 'Awn, as commander of the Lebanese army, tried to close down illegal ports run by pro-Syrian militias, and the inevitable confrontation with Syrian troops in Lebanon took place. Prime Minister 'Awn called it "the war of liberation," which lasted from March until September 1989. During the conflict 'Awn sought to negotiate with Syria to withdraw its troops from Lebanon but failed. The religious head of the Sunni community, Mufti Hasan Khalid, who had been critical of Syria, was assassinated in May 1989.[12]

With sheer Syrian military force and Saudi Arabian mediation, sixty-two Lebanese parliamentarians met in the Saudi city of Ta'if and approved a constitutional document that virtually made Lebanon a satellite of Syria. The document made the president of the Republic, a position allotted to the Maronite Christian community, almost a figurehead. According to the Ta'if Agreement, the president could preside over the cabinet meetings but could not vote. The president could no longer choose his prime minister, nor command the Lebanese army. The Ta'if Agreement destroyed the very foundations of the National Pact of 1943, which had provided for an equal partnership between the Maronite Christian president and the Sunni Muslim prime minister. The stripping of the prerogatives of the president was done purposely by Assad, because the president had hitherto been the main obstacle to Syrian domination of Lebanon. Furthermore, there was no stipulation in the Ta'if Agreement about an eventual withdrawal of Syrian troops. It was not surprising that Prime Minister 'Awn rejected the Ta'if Agreement.[13]

When the United States needed Syria to join the coalition against Iraq in 1990 to liberate Kuwait, Assad took advantage of the situation and mounted an air and ground attack against General 'Awn in the presidential palace in Ba'abda on October 13, 1990. Hundreds of Lebanese army troops were massacred after they surrendered, and Syria took over all the archives of the Lebanese presidency and the Ministry of Defense. General 'Awn then sought and obtained political asylum in France.

When the Syrians, under force majeure, agreed to participate in the Madrid peace conference in October 1991, they simultaneously increased the weaponry provided to Hisballah, which it used to escalate attacks on the security zone and northern Israel. Hisballah had managed to provoke Israel into major retaliations, especially with Operation Accountability in August 1993 and Operation Grapes of Wrath in April 1996. Lebanon remained a hostage in Assad's hands and was not allowed to make peace with Israel, even though there are no outstanding issues between the two countries. The senseless war in southern Lebanon, waged by Hisballah as Assad's instrument after the Madrid peace conference convened, was clear evidence for those who believed that Assad was interested in making peace with Israel, to start questioning their assumptions. In fact, the Israeli cabinet officially accepted, on August 1, 1998, UN Resolution 425 of March 18, 1988, which called for the unilateral withdrawal of Israeli forces from southern Lebanon. The Lebanese government was prevented by Syria from reacting positively to this Israeli initiative. When Ehud Barak won the elections of May 1999, he lived up to his promise that he would withdraw the Israeli army from the security zone in southern Lebanon, doing so on May 24, 2000.

The proof that Israel and Lebanon never had a territorial dispute of significance was the demarcation by the United Nations of the blue line between Lebanon and Israel within two months of Israel's withdrawal and the dismantling of its security zone on May 24, 2000. This was done without any assistance from the Lebanese government because Syria had precluded it from being of any help to the United Nations.[14]

Thus the war waged by Hisballah prior to May 24, 2000, was a contrived and artificial war with the objective of keeping Israel in the security zone rather than what it had claimed about "liberating" southern Lebanon. Syria was very upset about the Israeli withdrawal because it could have led to the pacification of the Lebanese-Israeli border. Before President Hafiz al-Assad died on June 10, 2000, he managed to find a pretext for the Lebanese government, which he controlled, and his proxy Hisballah to claim that the Israeli withdrawal had not been completed. He argued that a piece of land called Mazariʿ Shibʿa, which is part of the Golan Heights, belonged to Lebanon, and unless Israel withdrew from it, then Hisballah's military operations against Israel should continue. Therefore, the senseless war waged by Hisballah as a direct instrument of the Assad regime in Damascus against Israel is back in full swing.

Syria has neither allowed the Lebanese-Israeli border to be pacified (while the Golan Heights lines that separate Syrian and Israeli troops are pacified) nor permitted Lebanon to negotiate separately with Israel, although Syria had done precisely that during the cabinets of Yitzhak Rabin and Shimon Peres from August 1992 until March 1996, and again during Ehud Barak's government from December 1999 until March 2000. The reasons are clear. Lebanon could easily sign a peace treaty with Israel and it could be negotiated with less effort than either the Egyptian-Israeli peace treaty or the Jordanian-Israeli peace treaty. If Lebanon were to be left alone to make peace with Israel, then it would be, unlike the cold peace between Egypt and Israel and the lukewarm peace between Jordan and Israel, a real, genuine peace.

Lebanese Attitudes toward Israel

The vast majority of the Christians want peace with Israel and feel no hostility whatsoever toward the Israelis. On the contrary, they feel some affinity to another non-Muslim community that is Western in outlook.

The patriarch of the Maronite Catholic community, Cardinal Sfair, has publicly declared his position on southern Lebanon, a stand that represents not only the Maronite community but all the Christian communities of Lebanon. He demanded "the spread of the Lebanese state's authority in the south."[15] This could only mean that southern Lebanon should not be left to Hisballah to dominate and to use it to launch operations against Israel. Sfair called for the withdrawal of Syrian troops from Lebanon in accordance with UN Resolution 520 of 1982. Because of Syrian domina-

216 | Marius Deeb

tion, Lebanon is neither independent nor sovereign. Syria not only nominates the politicians of Lebanon but also its civil servants and even members of the judiciary.[16]

The Greek Orthodox journalist Jubran Tueni, who is the present publisher of the most prestigious and influential newspaper in Lebanon, *al-Nahar,* concurred with the declaration issued by Sfair and stated that the issues raised by Sfair have frequently been raised by the vast majority of the Lebanese themselves.[17] Tueni strongly objected to allowing Hisballah to hold armed rallies even in Beirut itself with "sectarian slogans."[18] He also called for the return of the legitimate authorities to southern Lebanon so that the villagers would feel protected by the Lebanese government, thus encouraging them to return to their families and properties.[19] Tueni has a profound understanding of the history of the conflict in southern Lebanon. In an article written on August 10, 2000, he praised the officers and rank and file of the Lebanese army in Marji'yun who refused to join the renegade officer Ahmad al-Khatib. Al-Khatib had established, in 1976, the breakaway so-called Lebanon's Arab Army (LAA),[20] which was "under the control of the Palestinians and was financed by the Iraqi Ba'th."[21] Tueni wrote, "We all remember [in 1979] when the Lebanese state asked permission from Arafat and his allies to let the Lebanese army be sent to southern Lebanon, and how they refused. They wanted to keep southern Lebanon aflame to serve the Palestinian cause!"[22] After the Israeli withdrawal from the security zone in May 2000, Tueni argued that there should be no authority in southern Lebanon except that of the Lebanese state with all its institutions. Hisballah should be allowed neither to have barricades to stop travelers on the roads nor to raid villages and arrest people in their homes. Otherwise, southern Lebanon would revert to the days of the armed Palestinian presence that "constituted a state within a state."[23] The Lebanese authorities should close down the "Fatima Gate" that is used by "whoever wants to harm Lebanon by means of undertaking actions against Israel." Tueni invited "the heroes of throwing stones and Molotov cocktails to proceed to another Arab-Israeli border. Let them go to the Golan Heights, but I doubt whether the Syrian state would allow the rekindling of the conflict at its borders."[24]

Jubran Tueni defends those who served in the South Lebanon Army and condemns the fact that they have been singled out and imprisoned for no reason whatsoever. He quotes a letter sent by a former member of the South Lebanon Army who is incarcerated in the Roumieh prison and who was going to spend Christmas alone without his wife and children, in which he states that he was indicted because he loved his homeland and was attached to his land. Tueni points out that all those who carried arms from other regions of Lebanon were given a general amnesty except those of southern Lebanon.[25]

The Sunni community has been dispelled of its illusions after its support of the PLO in the late 1960s to the early 1980s brought disaster to Lebanon. Prime Minister Rafiq Hariri was displeased with Hisballah's operations against Mazari' Shib'a. Hisballah mounted an operation that killed an Israeli soldier and wounded two others on February 16, 2001, the ninth anniversary of the assassination by Israel of Hisballah leader 'Abbas al-Musawi.[26] Prime Minister Hariri issued a statement critical of Hisballah's action, but he had to recant on February 18, 2001, after meeting Hisballah officials and endorsing their operation, because Hisballah operates in accordance with Syrian instructions.[27]

Even the majority of the Shia community who have not been enticed or entranced by Khomeini's ideology know very well that the operations by Hisballah have brought nothing but death and destruction to southern Lebanon. The proof is in the continuous demand by people in southern Lebanon for the return of the legitimate authorities represented by the Lebanese army to keep law and order and for its deployment at the Lebanese-Israeli border.

An analysis of the social and economic situation in the security zone region of southern Lebanon eight months after the Israeli withdrawal shows that the people complain about the absence of legitimate governmental authority that could provide security and law and order in the region.[28] Syria has vetoed the deployment of the Lebanese army (500 soldiers and another 500 members of the gendarmerie were sent to southern Lebanon on August 9, 2000, but they were confined to the army barracks in Marji'yun and Bint Jubail) in order to keep the region in turmoil and under its proxy Hisballah.[29] The whole former security zone, irrespective of whether the villages are Shia or Christian, became the exclusive domain of Hisballah, which is "energetically creating new realities on the ground which would make it difficult to alter them in the future."[30] The villagers of southern Lebanon are not taken in by Hisballah's propaganda that claims that sending the Lebanese army to southern Lebanon is an "American-Israeli demand" and is "for the security of Israel and not for the security of Lebanon."[31]

Lebanese-Syrian Relations

The very basis of Lebanon as envisaged in the National Pact of 1943 is that the Lebanese polity will enjoy all the basic freedoms of the press, speech, and religion as well as free elections. The Christians of Lebanon are sui generis, unlike the Christians in other countries of the Middle East, because they revere their freedom and absolutely refuse to live as *dhim-miyyun,* that is, subservient to their Muslim compatriots.[32] Jubran Tueni, in an open letter addressed to Bashar al-Assad in March 2000, called for the withdrawal of Syrian troops from Lebanon, For this he was attacked and belittled by the Syrian foreign minister, Farouk al-Sharaa. The latter claimed that Syria will withdraw its troops only if the request comes "from the Lebanese government [which Syria controls] or from the representatives of the Lebanese people [who have been chosen by Syria] . . . and not from a person [Jubran Tueni] who writes in a Lebanese newspaper *[al-Nahar]."*[33] Jubran Tueni took al-Sharaa to task by pointing out that it is not surprising that al-Shara' has no understanding of how a journalist could represent Lebanese public opinion because

the press in Syria, as it is in all political systems of the same ilk, does not represent public opinion but the opinion of the regime in power . . . perhaps with the passage of time, and through al-Sharaa's travels abroad . . . he would discover the importance of free press and the importance of public opinion which are bases of democratic systems. While waiting for Minister al-Sharaa to comprehend this aspect of the problem . . . we shall continue writing our opinions and transmit the points of view of the Lebanese, because we are convinced that Lebanon is the model to emulate. To adjust to the new civilized world, others [Syria] have to follow in the footsteps of Lebanon and not vice-versa![34]

The primacy of freedom is not confined to the Christians; other religious communities cherish it as well. 'Alaya' al-Sulh, the eldest daughter of the founding father of the National Pact of 1943, Riyad al-Sulh, wrote an article in *al-Nahar* on November 21, 2000, in which she reminded the readers that Lebanon got its independence in 1943, before Syria. The prime ministers of the two countries—in the case of Lebanon it was her father and in the case of Syria it was her maternal uncle—congratulated each other officially and in a civilized manner. *Mutatis mutandis,* Lebanon does not need to wait for Syria to get its Golan Heights back to have peace in southern Lebanon. The two tracks, the Lebanese and the Syrian, are different. The very bases of the Lebanese polity are freedom and pluralism. Lebanon was the bulwark of freedom of thought and a refuge for those in the Arab world who suffered from subjugation and oppression. Now there is an attempt to impose on Lebanon a monolithic ideology. Syria should deal with Lebanon on equal footing and should stop interfering in its domestic affairs. Al-Sulh maintained that it is easier for the Syrian troops to leave Lebanon now than it was for them to enter Lebanon in 1976.[35]

The Shia leader of Jabal ʿAmil, Kamil al-Asʿad, president of the Chamber of Deputies prior to 1984, openly attacked, in a TV interview on January 14, 2001, the present dominant leaders of the Shia and other communities as instruments of the Syrian Intelligence Services.[36] He claimed that the last three parliamentary elections, in 1992, 1996, and 2000, were rigged. By contrast, the elections held in 1972 were free. Prior to the elections of 2000, al-Asʿad predicted that the elections would be rigged.[37] On July 30, 2000, al-Asʿad returned to his hometown of al-Taybay in the Marjiʿyun district and gave an eloquent defense of democracy as the rule of the people through their representatives who are fully accountable to their electorate, bemoaning the present condition of the people of the south who are oppressed and downtrodden and suffering from deprivation and poverty because they are robbed of the Lebanese government funds allocated to their villages and towns by those who "indulge in corruption . . . [and] impose their hegemony" (that is, the militias of Hisballah and Amal) over the region of southern Lebanon.[38] Al-Asʿad's public call for the return of democracy and free elections was shared by thousands attending the rally at the ruins of his family residence.[39]

The Druze leader Walid Jumblat, who has been a major ally of the Syrians, called publicly in October 2000 for the redeployment of Syrian troops in Lebanon in accordance with the Taʾif Agreement of 1989, which Syria itself had imposed on Lebanon.[40] He was immediately taken to task by Syrian proxies. ʿAsim Qansu, the vice president of the pro-Syrian Baʾath Party in Lebanon, accused Jumblat of ingratitude because "the late Syrian president Hafiz Assad gave Jumblat whatever he wanted."[41] This was a reference to the arms, logistics, and manpower (dissident Palestinians and other leftist militias) given by Syria to Jumblat's Druze militia in its battles against the Christian Lebanese Forces and the national Lebanese army from 1983 until 1990. The president of the Chamber of Deputies, Amal's leader Nabih Birri, who is also a Syrian proxy, declared publicly that Jumblat became a persona non grata in Syria and would not be permitted to visit Damascus where he has kept an office for the last two decades. On November 6, 2000, ʿAsim Qansu raised the ante by accusing Walid Jumblat of being "an agent of Israel."[42] This was an allusion to the special relationship the Druze have always enjoyed with Israel, as their coreligionists have regularly served in the Israel Defense Forces. Under the pressure of threats from Syrian proxies, Jumblat was forced to recant his demand for the redeployment of Syrian troops in Lebanon and was forgiven by the Syrians.

The Role of Hisballah

The role of Hisballah, as envisaged by the Assad regime in Syria is, inter alia, to create artificially, through the conflict, a hostility between Lebanon and Israel that in reality does not exist. Hisballah was the major instrument of the late Syrian president, Hafiz al-Assad, in confronting Israel in southern Lebanon. The prevalent view that Hisballah represents Iran only is erroneous. Hisballah is the embodiment of the strategic alliance between Iran and Syria. But it is the latter that controls it and sets its agenda. The evidence comes directly from the horse's mouth, that is, from the leader of Hisballah himself, Hasan Nasrallah. On the fortieth day following the death of Hafiz al-Assad, Hasan Nasrallah gave a speech eulogizing Assad and called him "the great leader *(al-Oaʾid al-ʿazim)*."[43] Nasrallah added that the leaders of Hisballah felt joyful when they were informed that Assad was elated and very proud of Hisballah's victory over Israel [the Israeli withdrawal on May 24, 2000]. Nasrallah addressed the late Assad by stating, "Victory was the work of your hands; the fruits of your thought, and [a product] of your school of struggle and waging war."[44] Nasrallah showered praise on the new Syrian president, Bashar al-Assad, whose support is needed for the continuation of Hisballah's role in Lebanon and the region.[45] Conversely, for Bashar al-Assad, Hisballah is absolutely indispensable for Syria's continued war on the Lebanese polity and the peace process. Hasan Nasrallah was invited to speak to a Syrian Youth Congress, held in Damascus, celebrating the taking of power by the Ba'ath Party. He told his audience that the liberation of southern Lebanon was done with Syrian help. "Syria has changed the equation and proved that Israel is not invincible."[46]

When the Israeli withdrawal from the security zone took place on May 24, 2000, the late president Hafiz al-Assad, as noted above, contrived a pretext for Syria's proxy, Hisballah, to continue to be heavily armed and to wage war against Israel by claiming that Mazariʿ Shibʿa, which is part of the Golan Heights, is occupied Lebanese territory. On October 11, 2000, the new Syrian president Bashar al-Assad himself stated that "Mazariʿ Shibʿa is a Lebanese territory occupied by Israel, and it is the right of the resistance (al-Muqawamah) to struggle against the occupier."[47]

On October 7, 2000, Hisballah matched its threats with deeds by launching its first guerrilla operation since the withdrawal of the Israeli forces from Lebanese territories on May 24, 2000, against Mazari' Shib'a. The operation resulted in the capture of three Israeli soldiers.[48] Earlier on the same day, and most probably coordinated with Hisballah as a diversion, about 1,000 Palestinians, who traveled from their camps in Beirut, demonstrated in support of their Palestinian compatriots at the Marwahin Gate, throwing stones and Molotov cocktails at an Israeli post on the other side of the border. The Israelis retaliated by firing at the Palestinians, killing two persons and wounding twenty others.[49]

The popular Lebanese deputy Albert Mukhayber, whom no one dared to challenge in the August 2000 parliamentary elections for the Greek Orthodox seat in northern Matn,[50] took the Lebanese government to task for allowing Hisballah to launch its operation against the Israelis on October 7, 2000. Mukhayber, expressing the views of the vast majority of the Lebanese, pointed out that he "has been repeatedly warning the Lebanese authorities of militias (Hisballah) which have been making numerous attempts to open a new military front on Lebanese territory to serve the interests of others [Syria]."[51] Mukhayber added that "[I]f the Arabs fear these wars on their lands, we are telling them loud and clear: Lebanon has paid the head tax *(jizya)* of the Arab-Israeli struggle for too long, so enough is enough."[52]

The leader of Hisballah, Hasan Nasrallah, tried to justify the operation of October 7, but he sounded on the defensive by claiming that the Lebanese would endorse it. Nasrallah gave three reasons for the operation against the Israelis. First, he claimed that the three Israeli soldiers were abducted to exchange them for the Hisballah prisoners held by Israel. Second, he claimed that the operation's objective was the liberation of Mazari' Shib'a. Finally, although the operation was planned before September 28, he said that it was in support of the Palestinian intifada.[53] On October 15, 2000 Nasrallah publicly announced that an Israeli businessman, Elhanan Tennenbaum, was in captivity in Lebanon after he was lured by Hisballah operatives from Europe.[54] This shows that Hisballah operates independently from the Lebanese authorities, as an abducted Israeli was brought to Lebanon without the latter's knowledge.

The role of the Palestinians in Lebanon has become greater since the intifada. On October 21, 2000, two armed guerrilla fighters were killed trying to attack the Mazari' Shib'a region. On January 26, 2001, two Palestinian members of Ahmad Jabril's PFLP-GC were killed and their guerrilla operation was foiled by the Israelis. A ship carrying weapons and ammunition to be smuggled to the Palestinian territories by Jabril's organization was intercepted by the Israelis, and Jabril publicly boasted that he was behind the operation.[55] Ahmad Jabril, in a public speech delivered in Lebanon on November 23, 2000, criticized those who were demanding the withdrawal of Syrian troops and described the military presence of the Syrians and the Palestinians in Lebanon as a "Pan-Arab right (Haq Qawmi)."[56] Nasrallah has urged the Palestinians to continue their intifada by what he called "low-technology" operations like that of the Palestinian bus driver who killed eight Israelis on February 14, 2001.[57]

Commemorating the assassination of the Hisballah leader 'Abbas al-Musawi by Israeli helicopters in 1992, Hisballah attacked an Israeli army convoy on February 16, 2001, killing one soldier and wounding two others. Nasrallah boasted in a rally held in memory of 'Abbas al-Musawi that Hisballah's operation scored "a direct hit."[58]

There is no doubt whatsoever that Syria utilizes Hisballah to continue its war on Lebanon and the peace process. Hisballah's role is a destructive one to keep the situation in Lebanon in turmoil. As has been pointed out by the noted Lebanese sociologist and writer Waddah Shararah, Hisballah has contributed to the continued Lebanese economic crisis by preventing the Lebanese state from extending its authority and regaining its power to collect revenues; without these revenues, no economic recovery is possible.[59]

In a meeting of the Lebanese cabinet in early February 2001, Cabinet Minister Pierre Helou asked whether Lebanon will be "a Hanoi or a Hong Kong."[60] Will Lebanon be "open to military confrontation or open to large foreign investments?"[61] It seems that Syria under Assad (whether the late father or the present son) has decided that the answer is Hanoi. Hisballah is fulfilling this mission. It is not surprising that Hisballah supports strongly the Syrian military occupation of Lebanon because without it, it would not survive. Nasrallah maintains that Syria is needed in Lebanon to prevent sectarianism from reemerging. Hisballah is the epitome of sectarianism, and it is the ultimate irony that Syria imposed Hisballah on the Lebanese as the so-called liberator of southern Lebanon. Israel wanted to leave Lebanon as early as June 1983, and Hisballah's attacks on the Israelis were meant to create artificially a hostility that had not existed between Israel and Lebanon since 1949. The Shia clergymen who are close to Syria, such as Muhammad Husain Fadlallah and the mufti al-Ja'fari 'Abd al-Amir Qabalan, had to reaffirm in their Friday khutbahs (sermons) that the Lebanese should fear Israel and not Syria,[62] knowing very well that the Lebanese public holds the opposite view.

If Lebanon were left alone to make peace with Israel, then it would be a real peace for two basic reasons. First, the topographies of southern Lebanon and northern Israel are similar, with villages and towns close to each other. Lebanon's borders with Israel are different from Egypt's, where the Sinai Desert separates Egypt from Israel, and even different from Jordan's borders, where the Jordan River valley, as well as uninhabited arid regions, separates Jordan from Israel. No geographical barrier exists between Lebanon and Israel; on the contrary, many of the tributaries and springs of the Jordan River, like the Hasbani, the Wazzani, and the Derdarah, originate in southern Lebanon.

Second, the Lebanese, the descendants of the Phoenicians, are by nature traders, entrepreneurs, and adventurers who have traversed the globe for economic opportunities and therefore would be elated with open borders with Israel for the exchange of goods and services.

There is a very strong feeling among the Lebanese and especially among Lebanese Christians that they have been forced to pay a heavy price for the "war of others" *(harb al-akharin)* on their territory. Many have realized the hollowness of the so-called "war of liberation" *(harb al-tahrir)* that has been fought by Hisballah against Israel in southern Lebanon. As Albert Mukhayber, the Lebanese deputy, pointed out after Israel destroyed a Syrian radar station in Dahr al-Baydar in central Lebanon, on April 19, 2001, the only solution is for Syrian president Assad to withdraw his troops from Lebanon because the Lebanese have had enough of wars and they are against a new war precipitated by Syria's actions in Lebanon.[63]

Notes

1. Arend Lijphart, *Democracy in Plural Societies: A Comparative Exploration* (New Haven: Yale University Press, 1977).

2. See, for instance, Peter Theroux, *The Strange Disappearance of Imam Moussa Sadr* (London: Weidenfeld and Nicolson, 1987), 124–27.

3. I personally spent many summers with my family during the 1950s and early 1960s in the Marji'yun region, and I can recall clearly the peaceful and serene conditions at the Lebanese-Israeli border.

4. When Arafat was asked in September 1993 whether he had any experience in governing a territory, he answered in the affirmative, citing his experience in ruling Lebanon.

5. Marius Deeb, *How Terrorism Works: Syria's Terrorist War on Lebanon and the Peace Process, 1974–2002* (New York: Palgrave, 2003), chaps. 3, 6, and 7.

6. *Al-Nahar,* January 27, 1987.

7. See Ariel Sharon and David Chanoff, *Warrior: An Autobiography* (New York: Simon and Schuster, 1989), 422–92.

8. For the negotiations of the May 17, 1983, Israeli-Lebanese accord, see the memoirs of the Lebanese foreign minister Elie Salem, *Violence and Diplomacy in Lebanon: The Troubled Years, 1982–1988* (London: I. B. Tauris, 1995).

9. See Marius Deeb, "Lebanon in the Aftermath of the Abrogation of the Israeli-Lebanese Accord," in *The Middle East from the Iran-Contra Affair to the Intifada,* ed. Robert O. Freedman (Syracuse, N.Y.: Syracuse University Press, 1991), 323–40.

10. For hostage taking by Hisballah to serve the interests of Syria and Iran, see Marius K. Deeb, "More Than Meets the Eye," *The World and I* 5, no. 7 (July 1990): 60–67.

11. Elie Salem, *Violence and Diplomacy in Lebanon,* 259–70.

12. For the ʿAwn era, see William Harris, *Faces of Lebanon* (Princeton, N.J.: Marcus Wiener Publishers, 1997), 243–78.

13. For the Taʾif Accord, see Mary-Jane Deeb and Marius Deeb, "Internal Negotiations in a Centralist Conflict: Lebanon," in *Elusive Peace: Negotiating an End to Civil Wars,* ed. I. William Zartman (Washington, D.C.: Brookings Institution, 1995), 132–46.

14. See John Kifner, "U.N. Criticizes Lack of Help by Lebanon," *New York Times,* August 13, 2000.

15. *Al-Nahar,* September 21, 2000.

16. See the interview with Patriarch Sfair by Chantal Rayes in *Liberation,* November 30, 2000.

17. *Al-Nahar,* September 21, 2000.

18. Ibid.

19. Ibid.

20. For the emergence of the LAA, see Marius Deeb, *The Lebanese Civil War* (New York: Praeger, 1980), 88–90.

21. *Al-Nahar,* August 10, 2000.

22. Ibid.

23. Ibid.

24. Ibid.

25. Ibid., December 30, 2000.

26. *Washington Post,* February 17, 2001.

27. *Al-Nahar,* February 19, 2001.

28. Ibid., January 19, 2001.

29. *New York Times,* August 10, 2000.

30. *Al-Nahar,* January 19, 2001.

31. Ibid., August 14, 2000.

32. This characteristic of the Lebanese Christians has been missed by the latter-day post-Orientalist Western scholars on the Middle East, as well as pundits and policymakers, because they lack an understanding of Middle Eastern realities.

33. Ibid., June 7, 2000.

34. Ibid., June 8, 2000.

35. Ibid., November 21, 2000.

36. Ibid., January 15, 2000.

37. Ibid., July 31, 2000.

38. Ibid. Kamil al-As'ad did not name Hisballah and Amal as such but referred to them as "the roller or the bulldozer *(al- mihdala aw al-jarrafa)."*

39. Ibid.

40. Ibid., October 11, 2000.

41. Ibid., October 13, 2000.

42. Ibid., November 7, 2000.

43. *Al-Ba'th,* July 21, 2000.

44. Ibid.

45. Ibid.

46. *L'Orient-Le Jour,* March 1, 2001.

47. *Al-Safir,* October 12, 2000.

48. *Al-Nahar,* October 8, 2000.

49. Ibid.

50. The Chamber of Deputies in Lebanon is divided in such a manner as to represent all the major Christian and Muslim communities. A seat allotted to the Greek Orthodox community can be contested only by members of that community; however, the voters can be of any religious affiliation depending on the composition of the population of that particular constituency.

51. *Al-Nahar,* October 10, 2000.

52. Ibid. Albert Mukhayber uses the word *jizya* (the head tax on non-Muslims under Muslim rule) instead of the word *daribah,* which simply means tax, to imply that Lebanon has been singled out because of its large number of Christians.

53. *Al-Nahar*, October 8, 2000.

54. Ibid., October 16, 2000.

55. Ibid., May 10, 2001.

56. Ibid., November 24, 2000.

57. *Washington Post,* February 17, 2001, A24.

58. Ibid.

59. Waddah Shararah, *Dawlat Hizballah: Mujtam'an Islamiyan* (Beirut: Dar al-Nahar Publishers, 1996), 363.

60. *Al-Nahar,* February 19, 2001.

61. Ibid.

62. Ibid., November 11, 2000.

63. Ibid., April 20, 2001.

Part III

Egypt and North Africa

10

Egypt

Moribund between Past and Future

LOUIS CANTORI

Egypt is the most important country.

Napoleon

Napoleon's statement was true in 1798 when he is said to have made it, and it remains true today. Whether in terms of geopolitics, regional international politics and issues of stability and conflict, or size of population and culture, Egypt is the most important of the Arab states. It also shares with Iran, Israel, and Turkey, for many of the same reasons, the characterization of being one of the four most important countries in the entire Middle East including North Africa. Geopolitically, Egypt is located in the northeast corner of the African continent astride north and south, sea (Suez Canal) and air lines of communications linking the Mediterranean to Africa, and east and west the same communications between Europe and Asia. Egypt until 1991 was the key hegemonic state in the international relations of the Middle East and now shares this status with Iran, Turkey, and Israel. It is the self-identified chief peacemaker and, on occasion, chief war maker in the region. It was Egypt, for example, who crafted the unprecedented Arab alliance against Iraq in 1991. It is also militarily powerful in terms of size (300,000) and quality of armed forces as well as the size of its population, which at about 60 million contains practically one-half of all Arabs. In the aftermath of the Islamic revolution in Iran, Egypt is the most important country from the point of view of American foreign policy. These factors by themselves are sufficient reason for making the effort to understand its politics.[1]

Egypt may be the most important country, but it is also a very troubled country. In the first half of the 1990s, the macro indicators of the Egyptian economy suggested dynamism and momentum. At the present time, however, the economy is in recession with an expected growth rate of less than 5 percent and a banking system whose speculative real estate loans are overextended while overall credit is tightening.[2]

Despite this negative analysis, overall, Egypt gives a contrary impression. For example, it has had only three rulers in the forty-nine years since its revolution in 1952. This correctly suggests an extraordinary political stability. The Egyptian state is thus politically strong. In addition, it is also militarily strong not only in terms of size of forces but also in battlefield performance. At the same time, however, this state is weak in terms of its difficulties in extracting taxation revenues, in terms of law enforcement, and, most of all, in not being able to develop economically.

This question of "strong" versus "weak" is an important theoretical problem, but it also has two important practical implications for foreign policy. As a strong, stable state dominated by a secure patrimonial leader with the support of the political class, Egypt until recently has been able to make authoritative foreign policy, given Egypt's role as a regionally hegemonic state. With the greater effect of globalization in the 1990s and the emergence of regional rivals, however, Egypt in new regional political economic terms has declined in relative power terms. In the words of Usama al-Baz, foreign policy adviser to President Mubarak, the fear of violent reactions to the second Palestinian intifada has resulted in apprehension regarding possible domestic instability. In the present circumstances, Egypt is engaged in an effort to limit potential conflict and not engage in domestic and foreign policy risk taking.[3]

The Conceptual Challenge

The seeming paradox of a state that exudes all the evidences of strength on the one hand yet is girded by weakness on the other begins as a conceptual challenge.[4] This conceptual analysis will assist in understanding not only Egypt but also other Middle Eastern countries. One of the striking features common to most scholars attempting to understand the politics of the Middle East is the importance attached to the state. The state is virtually ignored in American political science because of the domination of that discipline by concepts drawn from the American political experience. But even if the importance of the state is granted in Middle Eastern scholarship, there is a vigorous debate as to its relative strength.

Thus the Middle Eastern state is referred to as being "fierce," "strong," or a security or a *mukhabarat* (secret police) state. One thing that all scholars agree upon is that it is an authoritarian state. But the meaning of authoritarian differs from state to state. There is, for example, the severely repressive case of Iraq, the greater degree of openness of the monarchies of Jordan, Kuwait, and Morocco, and the highly controlled politics of Egypt. One of the anomalies of the scholarship on these states is that there is little doubt of their repressive capabilities—a single ruler is self-evidently in charge. Not only is this true, but such leaders experience long periods of relatively unchallenged rule. In Egypt, for example, in the forty-nine years since the revolution of 1952, there have been only three rulers; the most recent is Hosni Mubarak, who has been in office for nineteen years.

On the other hand, it is also common to speak of the Middle Eastern state as "weak." On the face of it, in view of the foregoing points, this seems like a curious characterization. But as was noted briefly in the case of Egypt, it is true that there is some basis for this labeling. While Egypt, for example, is able to maintain order and to impose political obedience, it is neither able to impose or collect direct taxes nor is it able to impose the rule of law.[5] Instead, Egypt collects its revenues indirectly, and customary law is the way in which grievances at the local level are addressed. This perspective on the "weak" state thus has merit. The argument of weak or strong goes beyond the issues of stability and control to address the question of state capabilities. Consider the further extension of this argument, namely, that the Middle Eastern state is also weak because it does not develop. In the case of Egypt, while it has been sustaining respectable growth rates of 5 percent or more, these rates have neither raised economic productivity nor have they benefited the population as a whole in terms of improved health, education, or quality of life. Therefore, is Egypt a strong or a weak state? As can be seen, this question that started out as a seemingly paradoxical assertion that an authoritarian state can be weak actually lays bare some important issues. These will be addressed again by way of conclusion.

Beyond this issue of the state there is one even more important for the present concerns regarding Egypt. This is the question of the choice of an appropriate analytical framework. Most scholars when studying politics adopt one of three frameworks or paradigms.[6] Two of these are less appropriate for application to the Middle East. There is first the liberal pluralist paradigm, which denies the importance of the state and assumes the existence of egalitarian values and envisions political structures competing on a level playing field on which power is dispersed. It is fair to say these conditions do not prevail in the Middle East. Second, there is the Marxist radical paradigm, which focuses upon the ownership of the means of production and the inevitability of class conflict. Like liberalism, these conditions by and large also do not exist in the Middle East. These two approaches can apply sometimes in limited cases, but their greater importance is as critical theories that address respectively human rights and gender questions and questions of economic injustice.

The point of view adopted in the present chapter is that of a third paradigm, conservative corporatism. The preceding paradigms are direct formulations of Enlightenment postulates. The kind of conservatism referred to here is derived from Burke, de Toqueville, and especially Hegel as critics of the Enlightenment.[7] Hegel posited the past and tradition (in Arabic, *asala*) as the guide to a progressive future, the importance of the community *(umma)* as opposed to the individual, and the notion that the basic goal of government is to strengthen and foster ethical and moral behavior (*Quran*: "Prohibit that which is evil and promote that which is good"). As the Arabic terms imply, these features of conservatism are remarkably the same as the Islamic formulation. Corporatism (*takafuliya*: a neologism signifying taking care of or responsibility for) is a structural concept that centers on the state. The state is seen as organic, characterized by patrimonial (father-like) leadership, a ruling class *(ayyan)*, and a licensing relationship *(mithaq)* of groups reflecting the division of labor in society (trade unions, bar associations, etc.). The leaders of these groups tend also to be members of the ruling class. Corporatism tends to be populistic. As such, it seems to apply to an earlier Arab nationalism as well as the contemporary Islamic revival.

Ideological Change in Egypt

Egypt has had two ideological phases since the 1952 revolution. The first is that of the Arab nationalism or Arabism of Gamal Nasser from 1952 until the military defeat of 1967. This ideology has the appearance of being radical in the manner in which it challenged the political and social status quo, but as a nationalist ideology it arguably also shared some of the features of conservatism noted above in application to Islamism after 1967. The ideology of Nasser emphasized the state and the need for individual sacrifice for the community, it emphasized the glories of the Arab past even while it sought an improved future, and it emphasized that the future was to be a disciplined one of social justice. In its radicalism it utilized the foregoing qualities to express an anticolonialism directed against the presence of the British in Egypt. Nasser's nationalism was radical in its effort to change both the international status quo via foreign policy and the domestic status quo via new leadership and efforts to reorganize society and mobilize its population. Egypt became a strong state in terms of its ability to mobilize its population, redistribute wealth via land reform, and increase social benefits. It was weaker, however, in developmental terms because its redistributive efforts were carried out from seized foreign and upper-class assets rather than from its ability to produce an economic surplus. The state's massive industrial infrastructure construction had successes in the maintenance of the nationalized Suez Canal and the construction of the Aswan Dam, but such construction in other areas failed to develop its economy.[8]

Some of the conservative features of nationalism mentioned in the foregoing provided a kind of preconditioning for the conservative Islamism that has followed upon its heels. Islamism can be characterized as a conservative ideology. It is conservative in three senses. First, it sets as its purpose the achievement of a moral society. This objective is stated in the *Quran* as "[c]ommanding that which is good and preventing that which is evil." Second, the group or community *(umma)* comes before the individual. Third, the achievements of the past are held to be the standard to judge performance. For example, the *rashidun* or the "divinely guided ones" of the first four caliphs of early Islam represent the standard by which to judge a progressivist future. These conservative principles stand in stark contrast to principles of liberalism such as materialism, individualism, and a utopian future of freedom.[9]

In the case of Egypt, Arab nationalism and Islamism as two expressions of conservatism not only can be used insightfully to understand Egyptian politics, but they also assist us in understanding change in Egypt because they exist in a dialectical relationship to one another. Nasser led a revolution in 1952 that was guided by the principles of a combination of Egyptian and Arab nationalism. In the years following, he became the leader of the Arab world in the struggle against European imperialism and Israel. In the 1960s, this Arabism was expressed as a top-down socialism that once again was populistically conservative in its effort to benefit society.

The Egyptian defeat in the 1967 war against the Israelis signaled the beginning of the end of Arabism and the advent of an Islamic revival. Nasser's successor in 1970, Anwar Sadat, sought to establish a political base in this revival, and in the process he began to dialectically challenge Arabism. Sadat, unlike Nasser with Arabism, was unable to capture the leadership of this Islamist revival, and in fact some members of an Islamic group were to assassinate him in 1981. The Islamist revival before 1981 possessed a radical program in challenging Sadat's authority and attempting to seize the state.

Hosni Mubarak succeeded Sadat just as the Islamist challenge to Arabism became the synthesis of Islamic nationalism, that is, Islamism with a political program of Arab and Egyptian nationalism. In this synthesis, the Islamists themselves want to take part in a more democratic Egypt, but Mubarak is unwilling to distinguish between them and a numerically small, violent Islamist minority. He stubbornly holds onto the secularism of Arabism even as his society has by now become overwhelmingly Islamized.

The foregoing can be cast as a theory of political change that can be drawn from the theoretical literature on corporatism.[10] Political change can be presented as culture and values progressing in a determinative dialectical manner. In terms of Egypt, for example, this means that Arab socialism and Nasserism came to be challenged by the Islamic revival in the 1970s and 1980s. Therefore, what is presently occurring is a synthesis that can be termed Islamic nationalism, but progress toward this synthesis is impeded by a state still determined to hold to the older principles of Nasserism, secularism, and even Arabism or Arab cultural identity. Egypt is thus not making progress dialectically toward the Islamic nationalism ("Islamism in one country") present elsewhere in the region. Egypt is presently stuck in place in terms of these factors as well as other factors and therefore the regime's Islamized mass base does not accord it political legitimacy. Its earlier Arabism resonated as Nasserism in the Middle East and strengthened Egyptian foreign policy. Due to the fact that Egypt is stuck between Arabism and Islamism, that is, between its past and its future, it no longer has a regional ideological ascendancy.

The Corporatist Structure of Egyptian Politics and the Patrimonial Leader: Nasser, Sadat, and Mubarak

Gamal Abd al-Nasser (1952–70), Anwar al-Sadat (1970–81), and Hosni Mubarak (1981–present) can all be characterized as patrimonial leaders both in terms of how they presented themselves and how they were perceived.[11] The principle of legitimacy of the patrimonial leader is an ascribed one, that is, it is a characteristic of the leadership role and is attributed to the leader by his followers. This principle, while strengthening the authority of the leader, also is not sufficient in itself. Each of these leaders was also operating as the leader of a regime that was legitimized by the dominant idea of his time. For all three this has been Arabism, although from Sadat onward, this was dialectically challenged by the political Islamism of the Islamic religious revival. In the case of patrimonialism, all three leaders when addressing the Egyptian people often used the vocabulary of the family. This was especially evident when Sadat began a radio address in 1978, while negotiating the Camp David peace agreement with Israel, by saying, "My brothers and sisters, my sons and daughters, I have terrible news to relate to you tonight. Today our sons prevented their fathers from going to work [i.e., students on university campuses were engaging in a campus boycott by way of protest]." It was Nasser among the three leaders who was able to go beyond the inherited patrimonialism of the leadership role and connect himself with the ideological principle of Arabism. In so doing he exceeded patrimonialism, and by a combination of personality and ideology, his leadership became charismatic and even exceeded the bounds of Egypt.

Nasser's anticolonialism forced the British military to withdraw from the Suez Canal zone in 1954 and turned him into a leader of Third World international stature. In 1955 he joined the positive neutralism of the Bandung Conference. In 1956 he engaged in a dispute with the United States and the West over funding for the construction of the high dam at Aswan and nationalized the Suez Canal, still owned by British and French capital. Although militarily defeated by a British, French, and Israeli invasion force, he was to emerge as the political victor upon their evacuation and his ability to remain in power. It was the prestige of these accomplishments that led him to another blow for Arabism when he engineered the union not only of Egypt and Syria but also briefly Yemen into the United Arab Republic (1958–61). This union did not last, however, and was followed by a military intervention in Yemen on the side of revolutionaries that was to drag on until 1967. Earlier in that year, still within the framework of Arabism, as the preeminent Arab leader, Nasser was to rhetorically test Israel only to have the latter inflict a devastating defeat upon him in the 1967 war.[12]

In November 1970 he succumbed to diabetes and heart failure and was succeeded by his vice president, Anwar Sadat. Sadat was the last of the officers in power who had engineered the revolution of 1952. He was able to survive due to his near political invisibility. Until his ascension to power he was known in Egypt as Nasser's lap dog or alternatively as "Sayyid Na'am Na'am [Mr. Yes Yes]." Unlike the revolutionary Arab leader Nasser, he had no ideological principle of legitimacy attached to himself. In any case, the 1967 defeat was the death knell of Arabism. In a remarkable fashion, Sadat quickly sensed that the next ideological stage in

Egypt's political development was to be Islam. The 1967 war had triggered the beginning of the Islamic revival. Sadat moved to gain its support by beginning to free from prison the thousands of Islamic radicals placed there by Nasser. In addition, he became a conspicuous "consumer" of Islam by ostentatiously acquiring the dark callus on the forehead called a *zabiba* that results from repeated contact with the prayer rug. This permitted him not only to play the role of father but also of a father-like *imam* or leader of prayer.

Sadat had to address the humiliation of the Israeli military occupation of the huge expanse of the Sinai peninsula as a consequence of the 1967 war. This occupation not only was humiliating but was costing Egypt hundreds of millions of dollars annually in revenues from the closure of the Suez Canal and lost revenues from seized oil fields. He began to boldly plot the military expulsion of the Israelis. Nasser had after 1967 invited 15,000 Soviet military advisors into the country in order to reform his military. By July 1972 they were ordered out of the country. They had completed their mission, and their arrogance and the fact that they restricted the military planning of Egypt meant they had to go. Sadat shrewdly planned the limited war of October 1973. The Egyptian surprise assault caught the Israelis off guard, and in the first two weeks the Egyptians accomplished a limited territorial gain in Sinai sufficient to bring about serious diplomatic negotiations. On the other hand, in the last two weeks of the war, the Israelis surrounded an Egyptian army, and in effect this restored lost dignity to the Israelis. Sadat initiated the diplomacy that was eventually to lead to the complete withdrawal of the Israelis by 1982, but his nation was economically impoverished. He therefore began a program of political and economic liberalization (called *infitah* or "opening" after the military success in Sinai) designed to appeal to the Americans. The combination of this policy plus his willingness to break ranks with the other Arab states and negotiate with America's ally Israel was to result in at first small and then later greater economic assistance. The result ultimately was, after two preliminary agreements, the peace treaty of 1979 in which Israel agreed to evacuate the Sinai and Egypt established diplomatic relations with Israel.[13]

The Political Class

The political class provides the patrimonial leader with the support necessary to make him authoritative politically. The relationship is one of political support on the one hand and economic benefits on the other. This represents the strategic weakness of the state in performance terms. The developmental potential of the state is traded off for enduring political loyalty and stability.[14] The definition of ruling class *(ayyan/khassa)* in Egypt is that it consists of the top 20 percent of the population who receive 48 percent of the income of the country. Accompanying this concentration of wealth is also the ability through government and, increasingly, private-sector leadership to dominate the corporatist group structures of the society. It is this symbiotic relationship that accounts for how, in the pre-1991 period of more singular geopolitical Egyptian regional hegemonic leadership, domestic stability strengthened the leaders' foreign policy hand. On the other hand, in the post-1991 geoeconomic period this relationship becomes one of a dysfunctional inability to develop, thus weakening Egypt's ability to compete economically.

Informal Corporatist Groups

The corporatist group structure reflects the division of labor necessary for the maintenance of society. These groups consist of two categories. First, there are informal groups of family, peer group, and "old boy" networks, which provide the basic procreational and support functions of society.[15] Second, there are the formal groups that carry out the labor of society, for example, trade unions, bar associations, and so on. The Egyptian family *(aila)* is classically Middle Eastern sedentary in character. It is patriarchical, extended, endogamous, and patrilocal. It is both the model of political authority as reflected in the concept of patrimonialism and the basic unit of allegiance in Egyptian society. Family loyalties and the authority of the father are primary. The extension of loyalty to a network of grandparents, aunts, uncles, cousins, and so on makes the range of the family extensive. The practice of arranged marriages and first-cousin marriages increases its solidarity. The tendency to live concentrated in a single geographical area further reinforces its solidarity. At the age of puberty, the boy leaves the house of his close-knit family and forms a play and membership peer group called a *shilla*. The *shilla* is a lifetime membership group that has responsibilities for the security of the neighborhood and on occasion, such as the 1977 bread riots in Cairo in protest over the raising of the price of bread, they can become politically activated.

Those who graduate from high school, university, or military academy have alumni status as a *duffaa* known by the year of graduation. For example, it was the *duffaa* of 1938 from the Royal Military Academy that carried out the revolution of 1952. This solidarity grouping provides a further potentially political membership group.

Formal Corporatist Groups

Corporatist groups are formal for at least two major reasons. The first is that by law they cannot exist at all except with the permission of the state. It is the need to formally apply for such approval that makes them corporatist groups and not civil society groups. The second reason is that in fact, once given approval to operate, they then have a familiar identity as trade unions, medical associations, engineering societies, and so on.[16] With the granting of approval, an informal compact *(mithaq)* is entered into whereby the organization agrees that it will not engage in political activities and will support the state in exchange for a grant of a monopoly of its sector. It will have the primary responsibility for its internal affairs, including the ability to benefit itself economically. The internal affairs of such groups are characterized by the presence of informal corporatist groups such as family, peer groups, and old boy networks in elections to the presidencies and executive committees of the trade unions, bar association, and so on. The informal groups have acted as political parties/factions. More recently, Islamic groups, notably the moderate Muslim Brotherhood, have supplanted informal groups. This has prompted government interference in these elections and even their cancellation.[17]

The Dualism of Egyptian Society

The existence of a political class of great wealth and privilege suggests the possibility that Egyptian society might be interpreted in terms of class structure, for example, bourgeois, proletarian, and peasant classes. It is a further expression of the politically strong and capability weak state that this is not the case. The ability of a strong executive and a cooperative political class to maintain themselves in power does not mean that they can organize the society for productive purposes or coerce or mobilize the masses of the population for greater levels of production. In other words the quietism of the politically strong state distances the political class from the masses, and the weakness of the economic state creates a gap and space. As a result, there is political and economic distance between the political and economic capabilities of the state on the one hand and the masses of the other. It is estimated that 80 percent of small businesses are in the informal sector, free from the payment of taxes, and constitute 30 percent of the gross domestic product.[18] This gap is reinforced by the 54 percent illiteracy that creates dialectical and regional differences. A further gap is in law enforcement where sometimes the most serious of criminal acts are dealt with informally by means of customary law.

The Parliamentary Elections of October and November 2000

The parliamentary elections in October and November 2000 were illustrative of these themes of the strong and the weak state. The elections were evidence of the relative strength of the state in that in the final analysis the results showed the ability of the state to continue to manufacture a desired political outcome. The government's National Democratic Party (NDP) was finally able to cobble together a majority of 388 seats (87 percent) out of a total of 444 contested seats (10 can be appointed by the president). This percentage compared with 97 percent in 1995. But these figures do not show the degree of the government's declining ability to authoritatively dictate the desired outcome by the forced mobilization of the voting population. In fact, in actual voting success the NDP won only about 265 seats outright and had to pressure/bargain with 123 "independents" to persuade them to switch to the government party.

The genuine electoral contest was not with the official opposition parties but rather with independent candidates who in fact were identified as the illegal, politically moderate Muslim Brotherhood (MB). They ended up with a remarkable 17 seats, gained despite beatings, intimidation, and occasional killings. What is further remarkable is that the perpetrators of the violence were not the usual state security forces but rather male and female toughs hired by NDP candidates intent upon gaining their due. In other words, even the classic exercise of coercion had slipped from the hands of the state into the hands of the state's underlings. The relative success of the Muslim Brotherhood was further evidence of the degree of the Islamization of the Egyptian state.[19]

Egyptian Foreign Policy

The Strong State, the Weak State, and Foreign Policy

Egyptian foreign policy expresses the characteristics of the state in its strong and weak dimensions. The foreign policy process is strengthened by the centralization of authority in a patrimonial executive supported by an acquiescent political class, characteristics of a strong state. On the other hand, foreign policy is constrained by those features that make it a weak state.

As a weak state, judged by its economic incapabilities, Egypt has had to pursue a foreign policy of rent collection, that is, continuously seeking infusions of foreign capital as "development and security assistance."[20] Egypt is a rent-seeking nation and not a developing nation. It has had to do the same thing to gain military assistance in order to protect its security.[21] It has been very successful in these objectives. During the Cold War prior to the 1970s, Egypt played one superpower against the other in furtherance of its objectives. During this period, alternately either the Americans or the Soviets were ready to pick up the tab. Egypt was indeed seeking rents, but at the same time the tensions of the Middle East were such that these rents could be used for building military strength, which in turn made Egypt a strong state in foreign policy terms.

Economic Rents and the Weak State

Beginning in the 1970s, Sadat began a policy of cultivating very large American economic and military assistance. Essentially, he pursued a policy of force and diplomacy with Israel that began with a surprise attack upon the Israeli defensive positions along the Suez Canal in 1973 and ended with a bilateral peace treaty with Israel in 1979. Since that time, in exchange for that peace, Egypt has been receiving the second largest economic assistance given by the United States worldwide, next to Israel itself. This assistance has strengthened the weak infrastructure of Egypt without requiring Egypt to achieve developmental capability and economic independence. It has increased the potential for development without achieving its goal.[22] The effect is to allow the strong and weak characteristics of the Egyptian state to coexist and continue. The nonproductive Egyptian state has taken on the coloration of market economics and reform.[23] But the showcase quality of this has weakened the state in foreign policy terms, so much so that it cannot even attract foreign investment, never mind exert foreign policy influence. The collection of other rents—remittances from Egyptian workers in the oil-rich states, Egypt's own oil revenues, and Suez canal revenues—has reinforced Egypt's economic weakness since rents operate to keep the state afloat while maintaining the political status quo.[24]

In the era of globalization and the appearance of the peaceful settlement of disputes in the 1990s, Egypt was a weakened player. The Oslo Accords of 1993 created seven years of a peace process on the Palestinian issue while Iraq was contained by U.S. policy. In the absence of foreign policy crises, which might have allowed Egypt to exert its influence and exercise regional hegemony, Egypt was the foreign policy wallflower of the region. During this period of presumed movement toward peace in the 1990s, economic globalization became the theme of regional conferences in the Gulf and in Morocco at which Israel was a prominent attendee. The rent-seeking Egypt of weak economic capabilities was not a meaningful player in the search for foreign investment and technology. This does not mean that Egypt was not useful to American policy when from time to time it was able to play an intermediary role in Palestinian-Israeli negotiations. It does mean, however, that it was Israel itself that emerged as a potential economic power and Turkey and Iran that exercised hegemonic influence.

The Second Palestinian Intifada and Egyptian Foreign Policy

The road to the second Palestinian intifada was the result of the shortcomings of the American foreign policy of the Clinton administration. This American policy began in a hapless fashion by the exclusion of the Americans from the Oslo meetings. These secret meetings also excluded the internal Palestinian leadership whose leadership of the first intifada had created the political pressure to make the diplomacy behind the Oslo Accords possible. Thus the signatories to the accords had narrower concerns than the achievement of peace. Arafat was desperate to abandon the diaspora and gain the appearance of sovereignty in Palestine, while Israel wanted to do the Americans' bidding and give the Arabs a reward for having stood as allies against Saddam Hussein in the second Gulf War. The major issues of Jerusalem, the settlements, the right of return for the Palestinians, and even the final boundaries of Israel and the new Palestinian state were to be put off until last, and secondary, procedural, largely confidence-building issues were discussed over the next seven years. At the same time, in contradiction to the alleged goal of land for peace, the Israeli settlers who were theoretically slated to be removed from the occupied area or at least reduced in numbers were in fact increased by one-third.[25]

In July 2000 at Camp David unresolved issues came to a boiling point. There was the appearance of concessions by the Israelis, for example, a vaguely worded formula for a Palestinian presence in Jerusalem but no maps. In the absence of maps, it became clear to the Palestinians that what appeared to be additional territorial concessions to themselves were in fact crisscrossing corridors of continued Israeli control of a nonterritorially contiguous Palestine.[26] Even an Arafat who was inclined to go along with most compromises could not accept this without risking his own overthrow. Palestine was now seething with resentment when General Sharon proved that he could visit the Temple Mount as any Israeli could and was entitled to do so. The hundreds of police who accompanied him in this exercise saved his life from the violent protest that erupted.[27]

The second intifada has put Mubarak and Egypt into a reactive and defensive stance. The first intifada, from 1987 to 1992, occurred in a regional context in which Islamism had not as yet firmly established itself politically in Egypt or elsewhere, with the important exception of Iran. The trend was evident but the political arrival had not yet been achieved. Mubarak had been fighting a secularist war to contain Islamism domestically. In a very complicated way his very effort to achieve the limitation of Islam actually fostered its growth. In an important study of this process, an author has termed this "Islamization by stealth."[28] Mubarak has successfully repressed a violent minority Islamic opposition group, but in the process he now has to carefully pay attention to nearly universal Islamic sympathy for the Palestinians. Partly for this reason and partly in order to carve out a negotiator role for itself, Egypt withdrew its ambassador from Israel.[29]

The domestic pressures building upon Mubarak necessitated the withdrawal of its ambassador. From the beginning of the second intifada Egypt has attempted to accommodate American pressure to act as an intermediary between Arafat and the Palestinians and the Israelis. U.S. efforts under Clinton took the form of committing the American Central Intelligence Agency to efforts aimed at arriving at a common formula for the cessation of violence and mutual security arrangements. This also involved feverish peace efforts in the final weeks of the Clinton administration. With the election of President Bush, an American hands-off policy was initiated.

In the face of this, Egypt, in company with Jordan, attempted to propose a peace program of their own involving a cessation of settlement activity in return for a reduction in violence. Then, at the Arab summit meeting on May 19, 2001, Egypt played an Arab leadership role in rallying support for the Palestinians.[30] This was facilitated by the fact that former Egyptian Foreign Minister Amr Mousa had become secretary-general of the Arab League. In that position, he was able to get the Arab states to take a position of recommending cutting off contacts with Israel.

In sum, the second, or al-Aqsa intifada has presented Egyptian foreign policy with a major challenge. This challenge goes even deeper than the politically strong and the economically weak state distinctions developed in this chapter. The strong state after all has had important foreign policy advantages for Egypt. What is beginning to happen, as observed in the weakening of the capabilities of the National Democratic Party in the recent parliamentary elections, is that the popular and Islamic support for the Palestinians is now so great that it threatens the very stability of the regime itself.

Conclusions

(1) Egypt as a politically strong authoritarian state is able to use political repression to maintain political stability, including the suppression of militant and moderate Islamic opposition groups.

(2) Egypt has also been able to divert wealth to the political class, including a new grouping of young businessmen. It has accomplished this through undertaking structural economic reform and directing the benefits of privatization of a segment of state enterprises to the same class. As a result, the macro figures of the economy appear positive whereas, in fact, the economic capabilities of the economy have improved only slightly.

(3) As a result of its political repression and diversion of wealth to the political class, Egypt is in other respects a weak state. It is a state that does not develop and consequently fails to benefit the masses of the population.

(4) In the era of globalization, Egypt is not a player. It can neither attract significant foreign investment nor play a dynamic role in seeking foreign markets. It is a state that sits on the international economic sidelines.

(5) Even as a politically strong state with an important military capability, Egypt cannot assert itself in foreign affairs. The reason is that as a rentier state it must cater to the interests of the sources of its rent-producing neighbors and allies.

(6) Egypt's decisions to exercise leadership in regional affairs, as in its support of the Palestinians, are due as much to reasons of regime survival as they are to the advancement of the Egyptian national interest. A declining Arabism and an ascending Islamism in Egypt also contribute to the policy.

(7) For the economic, political, and cultural reasons indicated in this analysis, until fundamental political change occurs, Egypt is a country that is moribund between its past and its future.

Notes

1. For a recent useful summary volume of Egyptian politics and foreign policy, see Phebe Marr, ed., *Egypt at the Crossroads* (Washington, D.C.: National Defense University, 1999). For suggestive analyses of Egyptian foreign policy, see especially Abdul Moneim Sa'id Ali, "From Geopolitics to Geoeconomics," in Marr, ibid., 153–70; and Ali Hillal Dessouki, "Managing Ambivalence: Egypt's Changing Regional Environment," in Marr, ibid., 193–201. See also my "Egypt at the Crossroads: Domestic, Economic, and Political Stagnation and Foreign Policy

Constraints," in *The Middle East and the Peace Process,* ed. Robert O. Freedman (Gainesville: University Press of Florida, 1998), 154–68.

2. For a comprehensive 16-page analysis of present-day Egypt, see the *Financial Times* (London), May 9, 2001.

3. See ibid., the article by Rouhala Khalaf, "Egypt and the Arab World," quoting al-Baz.

4. An important book on the general issue of strong and weak states is Joel Migdal, *Strong Societies and Weak States* (Princeton, N.J.: Princeton University Press, 1988). See Nazih N. Ayubi, *Overstating the Arab State* (London: I. B. Tauris, 1999) for a critical treatment of the issue, including extensive references to Egypt.

5. For the ineptness and failures of the Egyptian bureaucracy, see Jamil E. Jreisat, *Politics without Process: Administering Development in the Arab World* (Boulder, Colo.: Lynne Rienner, 1997), 93–112. On local law, see Louis J. Cantori and Peter Benedict, "Local Leadership in Urban Egypt: Leader, Family, and Community Perceptions," in *Local Politics and Development in the Middle East,* ed. L. Cantori and Peter Benedict (Boulder, Colo.: Westview Press, 1984), 46–59.

6. For a discussion of these three paradigms, see Louis J. Cantori and Andrew Ziegler, eds., *Comparative Politics in the Post-behavioral Era* (Boulder, Colo.: Lynne Rienner, 1988).

7. Corporatism in present-day political science had its origins in the study of Latin American politics where it emphasized the relationship of the state to organized political groups. See Howard Wiarda, *Corporatism and Development* (Amherst: University of Massachusetts Press, 1977), for a summary of this literature. In this formulation, the state licensed such groups. In a classic article, the concept then became generalized as a form of interest group mediation and came to be applied in Western Europe as "neo-corporatism." See Phillippe C. Schmitter, "Still the Century of Corporatism?" in *The New Corporatism: Social-Political Structures in the Iberian World,* ed. Frederick B. Pike and Thomas Strich (Notre Dame, Ind.: Notre Dame University Press, 1974).

Beginning with Robert Bianchi, *Unruly Corporatism: Associational Life in Twentieth-Century Egypt* (New York: Oxford University Press, 1989), and John Waterbury, *The Egypt of Nasser and Sadat: The Political Economy of Two Regimes* (Princeton, N.J.: Princeton University Press, 1983), the concept began to be applied to Egypt and the Middle East with increasing attention to the role of the state in relationship to groups. The most recent application of the concept to Egypt is in Marsha Pripstein Posusney, *Labor and the State in Egypt* (New York: Columbia University Press, 1997).

The present usage of this concept differs from others in that it traces the origins of the concept back through Durkheim and others to Hegel, *The Philosophy of Right* (1822) as a current of conservative thought that arose in criticism of the Enlightenment. As such, it bears a striking similarity to the assumptions of Islam. See Cantori and Ziegler, *Comparative Politics,* as well as Louis J. Cantori, "Corporatism, Conservatism, and Political Development in the Middle East," paper presented to the American Political Science Association conference, Washington, D.C., August 14, 1986.

8. For this appraisal of Egypt, see Waterbury, *The Egypt of Nasser and Sadat,* and Alan Richards and John Waterbury, *A Political Economy of the Middle East,* 2d ed. (Boulder, Colo.: Westview Press, 1996).

9. Cantori and Ziegler, *Comparative Politics.*

10. This concept of dialectic is what Hegel is noted for. It is found most succinctly presented in his *Philosophy of History,* trans. J. Sibree (New York: Dover, 1956), 63–79.

11. The concept of patrimonialism is derived from Max Weber. James Bill and Robert Springborg, *Politics in the Middle East* (New York: Longman, 2000), 101–31, developed the concept in application to the Middle East.

12. For an authoritative account of Nasser, see Waterbury, *The Egypt of Nasser and Sadat.*

13. See Raymond Hinnebusch, *Egyptian Politics under Sadat* (New York: Cambridge University Press, 1985).

14. On the Egyptian political elite, see Leonard Binder, *In a Moment of Enthusiasm: Political Power and the Second Stratum in Egypt* (Chicago: University of Chicago Press, 1978).

15. See Bill, *Politics in the Middle East,* 63–130, for a comprehensive treatment of Middle Eastern informal groups.

16. See Bianchi for an earlier comprehensive treatment of the state and such groups, as well as Waterbury, *The Egypt of Nasser and Sadat,* and Ayubi, *Overstating the Arab State,* passim, for extensive discussion and bibliography of this relationship, and, more recently, Posusney, *Labor and the State in Egypt.*

17. Mark Huban, "The Informal Sector," in the *Financial Times,* special section on Egypt, May 9, 2001.

18. Ibid.

19. For coverage of the elections and results, see *http://www.cnn.com/world. middle_east* (October 18–November 14, 2000).

20. For a succinct and telling account of the various kinds of rents, including "security" rents, collected by Egypt and their undercutting of economic productivity, see Alan Richards, "Dilatory Reform vs. Making a Break for the Market" in Marr, *Egypt at the Crossroads,* 65–92.

21. See Stephen H. Gotowicki, "The Military in Egyptian Society," in Marr, *Egypt at the Crossroads,* 105–28.

22. For a comprehensive factual and historical but uncritical review of U.S. assistance, see Hadia Mostafa, "Closing the Aid Gap," *Egypt Today, www. egypttoday.com* (January 20, 2001); for a similar but more critical view, see Howard Schneider, "U.S. Aid Remakes Egypt," at the same web site.

23. For a critical account of the development asymmetries of the Egyptian economy suggested above in reference to dualism, see David Hirst, "A Middle East

Indonesia in the Making: Egypt Stands on Feet of Clay," *Le Monde Diplomatique,* October 1999. This criticism is largely one noting that while Egypt has made advances in macroindicators such as foreign currency reserves, debt reduction, and so forth, it has done less well in terms of statistics of sectoral growth, especially in agriculture and industry. Even at the macro level, there have developed recent problems in liquidity and in the stalling of privatization. For an annual U.S. Embassy Commercial Section report that continues a tradition of objective reporting and supports these points, see "Economic Trends: Report for the Arab Republic of Egypt," *http://usembassy.egnet.net/etr.htm* (July 2000).

24. The figures for these particular rents are tourism ($2.2 b., 99/00), Suez Canal ($1.7 b., 98/99), oil ($1.3 b., 98), labor ($6.1 b., 92), and foreign aid ($2.25 b., 99). From U.S. Embassy Commercial Section Report, cited in the preceding note, and Alan Richards and John Waterbury, *A Political Economy of the Middle East,* 2d ed. (Boulder, Colo.: Westview Press, 1996), 379, for the figure on labor remittances. The figure on foreign aid is from the CIA *World Fact Book* (*www.cia.gov/cia/publications/factbook*). At $2.25 billion, Egypt among developing nations is second only to India ($2.9 b.) in size of aid.

25. For a scathing and well-documented interpretation along the foregoing lines, see Edward Said, *The End of the Peace Process: Oslo and After* (New York: Pantheon, 2000). His further point is that the Israelis and Americans engaged in a peace process that was not one of negotiations but rather of carefully calculated concessions by the two states in order for Israel to obtain its objectives.

26. For a succinct account of the negotiating points of the Camp David meeting, see the BBC analysis, "What Did Camp David Achieve?" July 26, 2000, *BBC World: Middle East* (*news.bbc.co.uk/hi/english/world/middle east*).

27. For a carefully documented account of the violence that followed and the events of the next days that were to become the second intifada, see the detailed report of the Israeli human rights organization B'Tselem, *Events on the Temple Mount 29 September 2000* (Jerusalem, October 2000).

28. Geneive Abdo, *No God But God: Egypt and the Triumph of Islam* (New York: Oxford University Press, 2000).

29. In making this decision, Egypt, the rent-seeking state, was walking the knife's edge between possibly offending the Americans and being compelled to respond to mounting popular anger domestically. Asked about a possible American and Israeli reaction, Foreign Minister Amr Mousa, always outspoken regarding Israel, said that this was an Egyptian decision and that "we do not deal with reactions" Cairo, Middle East News Agency, FBIS (November 22, 2000).

30. *New York Times,* May 20, 2001.

11

Militant Islam and the State in North Africa

MARY-JANE DEEB

The single most important development in the Maghreb in the last two decades has been the emergence of radical Islamist movements as a major political force. The advent of the Ayatollah Ruhallah Khomeini and the Islamic revolution in Iran radicalized Islamist groups throughout the Muslim world and more particularly in the Arab world. It created a model of an Islamic theocratic state, an ideal never realized before, despite claims to the contrary. It also demonstrated the means that could be used to achieve that state, namely, organizing a movement starting at the grassroots level and empowering it to overthrow a regime in power, using any means including armed violence to do so. And finally, it provided the justification to rebel: the right in Islam to challenge an unjust ruler and to establish a "just society."

Islamist organizations that had existed quiescently for decades in the Maghreb were awakened in the early 1980s to the opportunities that this new revolutionary Islamic paradigm held for them. One by one each of the four countries of North Africa saw the emergence of radical Islamic groups challenging the existing regimes and demanding their overthrow and the reconfiguration of the state. The irony is that those very governments had all, at different times, given the Islamist movements a helping hand in order to create a counterbalance to the radical leftist groups that they perceived as a threat to the state.

Algeria

Although Islam played a mobilizing role during the war of independence against the French, *shari'a* (Islamic law) was never made an integral part of the legal system of the state at independence. Muslim jurists were not allowed to play an autonomous role in legislative matters at the national level. Religious affairs were put firmly in the hands of the state, and a ministry of religious affairs attended to the appointment or dismissal of *imams* or Muslim clergymen, the building of mosques, the review of Friday sermons, the administration of religious endowments, and the setting up of Islamic institutions of higher learning.

Islamic opposition to this state of affairs emerged from the start. In 1964, an Islamic movement calling itself al-Qiyam (Values), linked to the Muslim Brotherhood movement, surfaced in Algeria. It was led by Muhammad Khider, a hero of the war of independence. The movement that would become a precursor to the Islamist movement of the 1980s and 1990s was banned by the government of Boumédienne, and Khider was assassinated in 1967.

A decade later, another Islamic movement, Ahl al-Da'wa (People of the Call), with links to the original al-Qiyam movement, began to voice the growing dissatisfaction of many Algerians with state policies and to call for the application of *shari'a*.

In the 1980s supporters of Ahl al-Da'wa became more assertive, building new mosques without government consent and taking over existing mosques. When government forces attempted to stop them, as happened in Laghouat, for instance, in 1981, they fought back and bloody clashes erupted. In November 1982, clashes between Islamists and left-wing students on university campuses culminated in the death of a student on the Ben Aknoun campus of the University of Algiers. This led the government of President Chadhli Benjedid to finally clamp down on Ahl al-Da'wa and arrest its leaders.

In 1982 al-Harakat al-Islamiyah al-Jaza'iriyah, the Algerian Islamic Movement, was created by Mustafa Bouyali, an independence war veteran and a militant Islamist whose brother had been killed by the police. He opposed government policies and wanted to set up an Islamic state in Algeria. He believed in using violence to achieve his goals and would be the first to initiate attacks on government forces and buildings in Algeria. Unlike the other more urban movements, his operated in the countryside and in the mountains south of Algiers. In 1987 he was captured and killed by security forces, while his followers were given long prison sentences, and four were condemned to death.[1]

Partly as the result of Islamic pressure and partly due to the free fall of the price of oil in the mid-1980s, Chadhli Benjedid, then president of Algeria, started a process of political and economic liberalization. In

1987 he allowed the Algerian League of Human Rights to be formed and various independent political organizations, critical of the government, to operate freely. Despite these reforms, major strikes and riots broke out in October 1988, leading to a confrontation with the military and hundreds of casualties. Benjedid then introduced a new constitution in February 1989, one that no longer proclaimed that Algeria was socialist or a one-party state.

Political parties were subsequently legalized by new legislation, and over fifty parties were formed in the following two years. Al-Jabhah al-Islamiyah lil-Inqadh or the Islamic Salvation Front (FIS), an umbrella organization, was formed in early 1989, on the eve of the referendum on the new constitution. It included at one time or another a range of militant groups that had emerged in the wake of the collapse of the Bouyali group.

The FIS leaders, however, did not include some of those who helped build up their organization. Mahfoudh Nahnah, for example, who had expected a top position in the FIS, was kept on the sideline. He left the FIS and went on to form his own party, Harakat al-Mujtama' al-Islami or Hamas, the Movement of Islamic Society, a moderate Islamist party. Also not included in the leadership of the FIS was 'Abdallah Djaballah, who had helped build the FIS organization in Constantine. He ended up creating his own party, al-Nahda, or the Renaissance Party.[2]

In June 1990, the first free and fair local elections in Algeria's post-independence period took place. The FIS got the lion's share of the vote, spelling the demise of the state party, the Front de Libération National (FLN).[3] National elections followed in December 1991. The FIS was again the clear winner in the first round. It was apparent that the FIS would win again in the second round and by more than the two-thirds majority needed to transfer parliamentary powers from the Benjedid regime to the Islamist opposition. The military, headed by the minister of defense, Major General Khalid Nizar, fearing this outcome, called for the suspension of the second round of elections and asked for the resignation of the president.

The country fell into a state of civil war as Islamists began a campaign of assassinations and violence first against government forces, then against civilian targets. The government responded with ruthless military force, killing countless suspected Islamists.

In 1993 some of the more radical members of the FIS split and took to the hills. They tried to emulate guerrilla groups that operated during the war of independence. The main Islamic militarized group called itself al-Harakat al-Islamiyah al-Musallah, the Armed Islamic Movement. It seemed to work in tandem with the FIS. Al-Jaysh al-Islami lil-Inqadh, the

Islamic Salvation Army, also evolved from the FIS, becoming a kind of military wing to the more political FIS. It would reach an agreement on a unilateral cease-fire with the Algerian government in 1997.

Al-Jama'ati al-Islamiyah al-Musallahah, the Armed Islamic Groups better known by their acronym the GIA, also appeared at the time. They seem to have originally been part of the FIS and then became offshoots of the Armed Islamic Movement, eventually evolving into small groups of people quite autonomous from either. They were led by their own *emirs*, semireligious chieftains who issued religious *fatwas* or edicts that were often at odds with those of the more traditional *'ulama* and were obeyed by their followers. These groups became the most violent of all the Islamists and have been accused over the years of the most barbaric atrocities perpetrated against civilians. Other radical groups include al-Takfir wa al-Hijra (Apostasy and Migration), al-Jihad (the Struggle), and the veterans of the war in Afghanistan.[4]

It is estimated that between 1992 and 2001 there were more than 100,000 war casualties. Despite numerous attempts at reconciliation and inclusion of the more moderate groups such as Hamas and Nahda into the parliamentary system, and more recently, under Bouteflika, an amnesty for the fighters of the GIA and the Islamic Salvation Army who surrendered and gave up their weapons, violence still continues in the north-central part of the country.

Morocco

In Morocco, as in the rest of North Africa, Islamist groups are old and rooted in maraboutic orders such as Tijaniyah, the Sanusiyah, the Kattaniyah, the Butshishiyah, and the Qadiriyah. Morocco, however, is unique in that its monarch is also *amir al- mu'minin*, or Commander of the Faithful. The king and his descendants are believed to be direct descendants of the prophet Muhammad. As such, therefore, they have greater legitimacy to rule, in the eyes of their own people, than the rulers of the other Maghrebi states.

Nevertheless, in Morocco as in the other three North African states, modern radical Islamist groups did emerge at about the same time as they did in the rest of the region. The earliest of the Islamists who were critical of the government and, indirectly, the king, was al-Faqih al-Zamzami. He lived and preached in Tangier and had a small following there. He was more a puritanical revivalist than a political activist, but he did address the social problems of poverty, corruption, and exploitation. His most important political statement was made in a political tract published, interestingly enough, at the time of the Iranian revolution, 1979, and immediately banned in Morocco. It was titled *Mawqif al-Islam min al-Aghniya wal-fuqara* (The position of Islam on the rich and the poor).[5] He died in 1989.

More radical and more of an activist is ʿAbd al-Salam Yassin. He was influenced by different schools of thought. "From the Sufis and Al-Tabligh, Yassin emphasizes the issue of socialization, moral education, and spiritual preparation. From the Muslim Brotherhood's experience, he stresses the importance of organization, activism, and the sociopolitical dimension of change."[6] He was also influenced by the Pakistani thinker Abu al aʿla al-Mawdudi and the Egyptian Muslim Brothers Hasan al-Banna and Sayyid Qutb.

Because of his more direct attacks on the monarchy, the Moroccan government, and the West, accusing them of corruption and materialism, Yassin spent a number of years in prison or under house arrest. He has also called for the creation of an Islamic polity and a just society, a return to Islamic values, the elimination of poverty, and the banning of political parties and Western ideologies. His movement is called al-ʿAdl wa al-Ihsan (Justice and Benevolence) and is the most popular, especially among students in Morocco. In 1991 students were the backbone of the largest demonstration in the Arab world against the Gulf War.

The most radical group has been Harakat al-Shabibah al-Islamiyah (the Islamic Youth Movement), founded in 1969 by ʿAbd al-Karim Mutiʿ, a civil servant in the Ministry of Education.[7] Harakat al-Shabibah al-Islamiyah is divided into five major groups and is openly opposed to the monarchy in Morocco, seeing it as corrupt and subservient to the West. It is also strongly anti-Semitic, referring in some of its publications to "Jews who impoverish and starve its [Morocco's] inhabitants."[8] In January 1984 it was accused of causing some of the major riots in Morocco, and seventy-one militants from that organization were jailed. In 1987, four of its members were arrested for allegedly fomenting unrest to overthrow the monarchy. It has not been active in the nineties.[9]

Dissidents from Harakat al-Shabibah formed in 1981 another movement called al-Jamaʿa al-Islamiyah (the Islamic Group). Its founders included ʿAbd al-Ilah Binkiran, ʿAbdallah Baha, Muhammad Yatim, and Saʿad al-Din al-ʿUthmani. Its agenda was proselytizing and promoting the *shariʿa*. It firmly rejected the use of force or violence. In 1985 it decided to change its name to Harakat al-Islam wa al-Tajdid (Movement for Reform and Renewal). It has now stopped criticizing the institution of the monarchy and is pushing for reforms within the existing institutions.[10]

In 1994, a new Islamic movement was created in Rabat, Rabitat al-Mustaqbil al-Islami (League of the Muslim Future). Its founder was Ahmad al-Risuni. He brought together three autonomous branches of al-Jama'a al-Islamiyah under this Islamist umbrella organization. They included Jama'a al-Da'wa (the Proselytizing Group) in Fez founded in 1976, al-Jami'yat al Islamiyah (the Muslim Association) in the city of Qasr al-Kabir, also created in 1976, and Jami'yat al-Shuruq al-Islamiyah (the Association of the Islamic Dawn), an offshoot of al-Shabibah al-Islamiyah, founded in 1985. This new organization professed to be a cultural, educational, and proselytizing organization that rejected violence. It attempted to be recognized as a political party under the name of Hizb al-Wihdah wa al-Tanmiyah (the Party of Unity and Development), but the government rejected its appeal. Its support came primarily from students and graduates of Mohammed V University, and its leaders were academics. The group was quite moderate and emphasized education and reforms.[11]

In October 1995 another Islamist movement was formed in the city of Fez, under the name of Harakat al-Badil al-Hadari (the Movement of the Civilizational Alternative). It is headed by al-Amin al-Rikalat, whose platform emphasizes the importance of a cultural dialogue between the various power elites in Morocco. It is important to note that some of the leading members of this group originally belonged to al-Shabibah al-Islamiyah.[12]

A year later, in 1996, a major merger took place between various Islamic groups: Rabitat al-Mustaqbil al-Islami joined Harakat al-Islam wa al-Tajdid, to form a new group calling itself Harakat al-Tawhid wa al-Islah (the Movement for Unity and Reform). This movement focused squarely on political reform. It became a legal political party and participated in the 1997 Moroccan legislative elections. It now holds ten Senate seats and one seat in the second House of Representatives.

Finally, in 1998, al-Harakat min Ajl al-Umma (the Movement for the Sake of the Moslem Community) was formed in Rabat, headed by Muhammad Marwani. The movement called for political and constitutional reform and for inclusion of groups marginalized by the state. The movement was also critical of calls for democratization and human rights in an environment they perceived as corrupt.[13]

Tunisia

The Islamist movement in Tunisia has its roots in the Quranic Preservation Society founded in 1970. The Tunisian government encouraged its development to counterbalance the leftist movement on university campuses. In the late 1970s a loose coalition of Islamists, many of whom had links to the Quranic Preservation Society, emerged as an important opposition movement on the Tunisian political scene. This coalition, which became known as al-Ittijah al-Islami (the Islamic Tendency Movement or MTI) voiced the social, economic, and political grievances of many Tunisians and was perceived as a threat to the Tunisian regime of Habib Bourguiba.[14]

Starting in 1979, the Tunisian government began cracking down on the coalition's members and by 1981 had arrested a significant number of its leaders. Throughout the 1980s, as the political system opened up and political parties were legalized, the MTI tried to accede to the status of a political party within the constitutional framework of Tunisia. Its application, however, was rejected by the authorities.

In 1979, al-Jama'a al-Islamiyah was founded. It became part of a larger coalition of Islamist organizations called Harakat al-Tajdid al-Islami (the Movement for Islamic Renewal). It was supportive of the Iranian revolution and began developing a political agenda and publishing journals such as *al-Ma'rifa* and *al-Mujtama'*. Those were quickly suppressed by the government as it began cracking down on Islamist organizations.[15]

In the mid-1980s a more militant Islamist movement emerged in Tunisia, which rejected any compromise with the state and advocated violence. Al-Jihad al-Islami (Islamic Jihad) began to bomb tourist hotels. The leaders were arrested, as were members of the MTI who were accused of being in collusion with the Iranian government and planning to overthrow the government. All were brought to trial in 1987, provoking large antigovernment demonstrations.

When the State Security Court began handing down death sentences for some of the leaders of the MTI, the government feared that the reaction in the country would be destabilizing. Consequently, in November 1987 Bourguiba, who allegedly was planning to reopen the trials and extend the death penalty to other Islamists, was ousted from power. His successor, Zayn al-'Abdin Bin 'Ali, decided to pursue a policy of reconciliation rather than confrontation with the Islamists. In December 1987, he granted amnesty to 2,487 prisoners, including 608 MTI members. He pardoned one of the main MTI leaders, Rashid Ghannushi, and commuted the death sentences of another, 'Ali Laaridh, to twenty years imprisonment. In 1988, Abdin 'Ali allowed the secretary-general of the MTI, 'Abd al-Fattah Muru, to return to Tunisia after a two-year exile.[16]

In the spring of 1989, when Tunisians went to the polls to elect their president and members of parliament, Islamists running as independents under the banner of the Nahda (Renaissance) Party, which was not recognized as a legal party by the state, won 14.6 percent of the vote at the national level and an estimated 30 percent of the votes in Tunis.[17] Because of the type of electoral system in Tunisia, these votes did not translate into parliamentary seats, but the message to the government was clear: the Islamists had become the single most important opposition force in Tunisia.

After the elections it appears that the Nahda became more radical. It openly criticized the government and allegedly began setting up a secret apparatus or underground organization to infiltrate the army, the gendarmerie, and the national security forces. The ultimate goal was to overthrow the regime and create an Islamic state. This secret apparatus was headed by Muhammad Shammam.

The combined threat of the electoral results and the potential danger of those planning to take over power by other means if necessary convinced the government that it was time to crack down on the Islamists. Many were arrested and put on trial in 1992. The trials were public.

Since the mid-1990s the Islamist movement has declined in Tunisia. The government crackdown is certainly one of the reasons, but there are other reasons as well. The first may be the bloody civil war that broke out in Algeria between the Islamist organizations and the military, and the impact that it has had on the stability and development of the country. Tunisians have been very worried that conflict would spill over into their own country and have therefore withdrawn or given only lukewarm support to radical Islamist movements. And finally, the government has addressed the problem of poverty in Tunisia, which was at least in part at the root of Islamist protests. According to the U.S. Department of State Human Rights reports, the Tunisian government "devotes 60 percent of the [national] budget to social and development goals."[18]

Libya

Islam and politics have been intertwined throughout Libya's modern history. Like the other Maghrebi countries the relation has its roots in a maraboutic order, the Sanusiyah brotherhood. It first emerged as an Islamist reformist movement in the Hijaz, in Saudi Arabia, in the nineteenth century, and then moved to North Africa, where it eventually found a welcoming environment in Cyrenaica. The Grand Sanusi, leader of the movement, set up his headquarters in Libya, from where he and his followers would proselytize throughout North Africa and as far as Senegal, Chad, Mali, and Niger. In the twentieth century, resistance to the Italian colonial power was primarily spearheaded by Sanusi leaders such as the famed 'Umar al-Mukhtar. Libya's first head of state, who negotiated Libya's independence in 1951, was the leader of the Sanusi order, King Idris I.

Today, however, the Qadhdhafi regime, like those of Libya's neighbors, is perceived by militant Islamists as a regime that is secular and anti-Islamic. An Islamist opposition has called for the overthrow of the regime and its replacement by an Islamist government. This opposition is made up of a large number of groups with somewhat different agendas. The more established ones are rooted in al-Ikhwan al-Muslimin (the Muslim Brothers) movement that was founded in the 1950s as a result of the impact of the Muslim Brothers of Egypt on Libya. Their ideas were spread throughout the schools and universities in the first decade of independence, when many Egyptians came to Libya as teachers and university professors.[19]

The Hizb al-Tahrir al-Islami (the Islamic Liberation Party) is an offshoot of the Muslim Brothers and has been linked to similar Islamist organizations in the Maghreb, Egypt, and Jordan, where the party was originally founded in the 1950s. It is essentially an urban movement whose popularity has spread to university campuses and military barracks. It has called for the restoration of Islamic ethics and values in Libyan society, accused the government of corruption, and approved the use of violence to achieve its objectives.[20]

The most outspoken and best organized of the Libyan opposition organizations has been al-Jabhah al-Wataniyah li-Inqadh Libya (the National Front for the Salvation of Libya, or NFSL).[21] It was formed in 1981 in Khartoum by Yusif al-Maqaryaf. Many of its members are Islamists, although by no means all, as it is an umbrella organization that subsumes a number of minor groupings. Some of its members were high-level government officials who defected and sought a safe haven abroad in Egypt, the United Kingdom, and the United States. Others remained in Libya and coordinated their activities with fellow members outside Libya. In 1984, it carried out a major attack on the Bab al-'Aziziya military barracks in an attempt to overthrow the regime. The attack failed, and the movement was battered in Libya but survived abroad.[22]

That same year two well-known religious leaders, Shaykh Muhammad al-Khalifi and Shaykh Hamida al-Hami, were accused of being members of the Ikhwan al-Muslimin and were arrested and sent to jail without trial.

Also in 1984, two students accused of belonging to an obscure organization called the Jabhat al-Tahrir al-Islami (the Islamic Liberation Front) were hanged by the security forces on the campus of al-Fatih University in Tripoli.[23]

The Jihad al-Islami (the Islamic Struggle) was formed in the early 1970s, again modeled after its Egyptian counterpart. It became very active in the mid-1980s when twenty-six of its members were arrested and accused of two assassinations and various acts of sabotage. In 1987 nine members of that organization were hanged and their execution televised.[24]

Another well-established Islamist group is al-Jama 'a al-Islamiya 'Libya' (the Islamic Group–Libya), founded in 1979. It has added Libya to its name to differentiate itself from al-Jama 'a in Egypt, although the addition could also mean that it is the same organization but simply the Libyan branch of that movement.[25] Like a number of its counterparts, it publishes a magazine, *al-Muslim,* and a newspaper, *al-Ra'id.*

Al-Haraka al-Islamiya 'Libya' (the Islamic Movement–Libya), which was founded in 1980 and publishes *al-Shuruq,* is an opposition movement with links to other Islamist groups outside Libya, as indicated by the addition of Libya to its name.

There are also other more shadowy groups that appeared in the late 1980s and early 1990s, such as al-Takfir wa al-Hijra (Apostasy and Migration) that seem to be a counterpart to the Egyptian organization of the same name and al-Tabligh (the Warning). Some of the earliest references to these groups in Libya were made by Qadhdhafi himself in a speech on July 19, 1988, when he threatened with extermination all the members of those groups.[26]

Other obscure Islamist groups include Harakat al-Shuhada' al-Islamiyah (the Martyrs' Islamic Movement). It claimed its members attacked some security posts in Benghazi in February 1997, killing a number of security officers and losing eight of their own when they were apprehended by the Libyan authorities.[27] Al-Jama'a al-Islamiyah al-Muqatila (the Fighting Islamic Group) is another such group. Founded in 1991, it publishes a magazine called *al-Fajr* (the Dawn).[28] The group has claimed a number of terrorist operations inside Libya since 1995, the most recent being in May 1997, when the group attacked a military post and reportedly seized 100 machine guns.[29]

These groups have been active in the past decade, not only in launching terrorist attacks against the Libyan government and the military, but also in publishing in Libya and abroad materials discrediting the Libyan government. There is, however, no accurate record of the activities of Islamist groups in Libya. The government blames all disturbances on these groups, and the Islamist opposition may in turn exaggerate its role in order to enhance its own credibility.[30]

Throughout the nineties these groups were active in Libya and abroad, but Qadhdhafi has cracked down severely on this Islamist opposition and may have succeeded, at least for now, in repressing it. In fact, in comments to *al-Hayat* newspaper, in August 1999, Qadhdhafi acknowledged (something he apparently had never done before) that there had been an Islamist opposition in Libya. He described it as a movement of young people who had been trained and paid by Americans to fight the Russians in Afghanistan and who, on their return to Libya, had resumed their destructive habits. But he added "this group was finished easily and quickly."[31]

The Economist reported in October 1999 that Libyan security forces had checkpoints every twenty kilometers along the main road of Jabal al-Akhdar in Cyrenaica and the city of Benghazi. Scorched hills around Benghazi are a testimony to the fierce fighting that had taken place between government forces and Islamist guerrillas since 1996. Opponents of the regime admitted that armed resistance had "dwindled to the odd shoot-out between policemen and diehard insurgents hiding in the hills."[32]

Human rights organizations and State Department reports decry the repressive measures used to put down insurrections and muzzle opposition. Those include "extrajudicial, arbitrary or summary executions,"[33] arrests, and long detentions without trial, and systematic torture and inhumane treatment of prisoners, as well as the abduction or elimination of political dissidents.

Libya has also passed a whole set of very broad laws that increase the rights of the state over individuals, groups, and communities in Libya. Such laws include the 1994 Purge Law to fight corruption, allowing the state to crack down on private businesses and confiscate private assets; a 1996 law that applies the death penalty to those who speculate in foreign currency, food, or clothing; a March 1997 collective-punishment law that allows for the punishment of any group, large or small, that supports, harbors, or helps in any way "criminals," meaning virtually anyone the state disapproves of.

Implications of the Rise of Radical Islamist Movements

Although unable to take power in any of the four countries, Islamist movements have had an indelible impact on the polity and society in the Maghreb.

In an article written almost a decade ago,[34] I discussed the socioeconomic and political conditions under which Islamic movements grew and thrived. Those included political stagnation, economic decline, deteriorating security conditions, perceived Western cultural invasion, and political attempts at secularization of the society. The radical Islamist movements in the Maghreb highlighted those problems, mobilized their foot soldiers around those concerns, and promised that if they came to power they would be able to remedy these issues. Furthermore, the Islamists linked economic problems to the corruption of the political elites and the pervasive influence of the West. As they had never been in power, their claims could not be tested.

Unquestionably, pressure from the Islamists had a significant impact on the governments of the region. Although they had resisted pressure from the West, the World Bank, and other international financial organizations to introduce significant economic reforms, the North African governments gave in to pressure from the "street." In other words, they realized that they had to address the problems of poverty and unemployment in more than perfunctory ways or their days were numbered. Islamists could mobilize enough support to overthrow those governments, as they had done in Iran.

Structural-adjustment reforms were introduced in Morocco, Tunisia, and Algeria in the 1980s, which included among other measures privatization and trade liberalization. Even Libya allowed some privatization and loosened its tight grip on the economy.

Tunisia was the most successful, spending almost 60 percent of its national budget on social and development projects.[35] Real GDP growth in Tunisia grew to 5.4 percent in 1997, 5.0 percent in 1998, and 6.2 percent in 1999. Per capita GDP rose to $5,500,[36] and the unemployment rate fell below 16 percent.[37] It is interesting to note that the Islamist opposition is weakest today in Tunisia, a fact that could be attributed, in part at least, to the economic improvements.

Morocco came next, but because its economy is largely based on agriculture, its economic growth is at the mercy of the weather, rainfall being critical. "While good rainfall during 1996 resulted in . . . GDP growth of 11 percent, erratic rainfall resulted in GDP growth in 1997 of negative 2 percent. According to government statistics, GDP grew 6.7 percent in 1998."[38] Although the unemployment rate fell significantly from the 30–35 percent of the 1980s, it was still high at an estimated 21.5 percent in 1999.[39]

Algeria is in third place. Its economy has been buffeted by the civil conflict going on since 1992 and by the fall of the oil and gas prices in the mid-to-late 1990s. However, it pursued a structural-adjustment policy privatizing or liquidating 1,000 state enterprises since 1996.[40] Although this increased unemployment in the short term, estimated at 28 percent in 1999, it is having a positive impact overall on the economy. With the significant increase in the price of gas and oil in 2000 and 2001, the estimated annual GDP growth rate is 5 percent for 2000–2003.[41]

Libya's economy had its ups and downs in the 1990s. Despite the fact that its GDP per capita was the highest of the four Maghrebi countries at $5,869 in the mid-1990s[42] and its external debt was the lowest, at under $4 billion, the economy was state controlled, and people's savings could not be invested. The seesaw of oil prices in the 1990s affected the Libyan economy negatively, as did the UN sanctions on Libya in the aftermath of the Lockerbie bombing. The Libyan leader allowed for limited privatization of retail trade, and authorities closed their eyes to a thriving black market with Tunisia. The lifting of international sanctions and the rise of the price of oil and natural gas since 1999 will do much to improve the economic situation in Libya and raise the standard of living.

Politically, the Maghrebi governments have had to address the issue of political participation that Islamists were raising. The political systems of Algeria, Morocco, and Tunisia all went through a process of political liberalization in the 1990s, becoming more inclusive and more transparent. Thus, although none of the governments allow religion to be used to define a political party's platform, Algeria and Morocco have allowed moderate Islamist groups to run for office and be represented in their national legislatures. For instance, in the elections of 1997 Morocco allowed independent Islamists to run for office and approved one Islamist party, Hizb al-'Adl wa al-Dimuqratiyah (the Party for Justice and Democracy), to represent candidates. It now has officially nine seats in Parliament. Algeria also included a number of Islamist political parties in its 1997 legislative elections, such as the Movement for a Peaceful Society (also known as Hamas) and Nahda (the Renaissance Party). Hamas won 69 seats and Nahda 34 seats in the Lower House of Parliament out of a total of 380 seats. The Algerian and Moroccan cabinets also have Islamists.

Regionally, the Islamists also linked together the four states of the Maghreb more closely. There are underground links among all the Islamist groups in North Africa. They offer safe haven to each other; members exchange their literature and publications. Sometimes they even share the same names and philosophy with others in different regions, as, for example, Islamic Jihad, Jama'at Islamiyah, and al-Takfir wal-Hijrah.

The governments of North Africa (including Egypt) have also been sharing intelligence on the activities of those movements through their interior ministries and their security services. Muammar Qadhdhafi has been included as an equal partner with the other regional leaders and has cooperated in sharing intelligence and in arresting Islamists fleeing from neighboring countries to Libya.[43]

Regionally and internationally Islamists have had an important influence on the policies of their governments and on the relations between the West and the Maghreb. Recognizing the danger of terrorism many European governments have worked more closely with their North African counterparts to identify, trace, and dismantle networks of Islamists in Europe. Those governments have invested heavily in the South Mediterranean countries of North Africa to create jobs that would diffuse some of the pent-up frustrations of supporters of radical Islamist groups. European governments have also attempted to put pressure on Maghrebi governments to respect human rights and behave humanely toward Islamists. The Western press and human rights organizations have criticized those governments and have achieved some measure of success in improving the human rights records in Morocco, Tunisia, and Algeria.

Islamists have also been able indirectly to affect the policy of Mahgrebi states with respect to Israel. Because the issue of the Israeli-Palestinian conflict is not merely one of national identity but has a powerful religious component to it as well, Islamists have often invoked issues such as that of Jerusalem to mobilize support for their cause. Morocco, for instance, had tried since the 1970s to discreetly broker a rapprochement between Israel and the Arab states and established low-level diplomatic relations with Israel after the Oslo agreements in 1994. Tunisia was also very supportive of the peace process, tried to play a catalytic role between Palestinians and Israelis, invited French Jews of Tunisian descent to visit Tunisia on a regular basis, and established low-level diplomatic relations with Israel. However, when the peace negotiations between Palestinians and Israelis collapsed in September 2000 and Palestinians began a new intifada in the territories, both Tunisia and Morocco broke off their ties to Israel, on October 22 and 23, 2000, respectively.

Morocco's official news agency stated that "Because of the failure of the peace process due to Israeli violence against Palestinian civilians for several weeks, Morocco decided to shut down the Israeli liaison bureau in Rabat and its diplomatic representation in Tel Aviv."[44] Although that was the official reason given, governments throughout the region feared an Islamist reaction and decided to preempt it by severing their ties with

Israel. Protests and marches throughout the Arab world convinced them that that was the best policy given the tense situation.

In 1991 a similar regional crisis arose. This was the Gulf War against Iraq's invasion of Kuwait. A multinational military force led by the United States and including a number of Arab battalions attacked the Iraqi army and drove it out of Kuwait. Islamists throughout the region condemned the attack and criticized Arab governments for participating in the force and for supporting a Western attack on "Muslims." Although Morocco, under pressure from the West and Saudi Arabia, did send a token force, it allowed one of the largest street protests to take place in Rabat and all over the country against the war on Iraq. Tunisia, fearing the domestic repercussions primarily from its own radical Islamist movement, refused to send troops and lost U.S. aid for taking this position. Both Algeria and Libya condemned the attack and sent no forces to the Gulf.

Conclusion

Islamist organizations have become an intrinsic part of the political landscape in North Africa, as they have in other parts of the Arab and Muslim world. They have influenced the domestic, regional, and international policies of Maghrebi governments. Some of the changes that those governments had to make have proven beneficial to their countries, including greater inclusiveness and accountability of legislatures and an active policy to combat poverty. On the other hand, they have had a less-than-progressive influence on domestic issues such as personal status laws and the role of women in North African societies. They have also had a constraining impact on the relations between the Maghreb, Israel, and, to a lesser extent, the West. It is clear that Islamist movements are here to stay and that their power and resilience cannot be underestimated.

Notes

1. Mary-Jane Deeb, "Militant Islam and the Politics of Redemption," *ANNALS, AAPSS,* no. 524 (November 1992): 55–58.

2. William B. Quandt, *Between Ballots and Bullets: Algeria's Transition from Authoritarianism* (Washington, D.C.: Brookings Institution Press, 1998), 50.

3. For a discussion of those elections, see Robert Mortimer, "Islam and Multiparty Politics in Algeria," *Middle East Journal* 45, no. 4 (autumn 1991): 583–86.

4. Graham E. Fuller, *Algeria: The Next Fundamentalist State?* (Santa Monica, Calif.: Arroyo Center, Rand Corporation, 1996), 37–42.

5. Henry Munson, Jr., *Religion and Power in Morocco* (New Haven: Yale University Press, 1993), 155.

6. Emad Eldin Shahin, "Secularism and Nationalism: The Political Discourse of 'Abd al-Salam Yassin," in *Islamism and Secularism in North Africa,* ed. John Ruedy (New York: St. Martin's Press, 1994), 169.

7. See 'Abd al-'Ali Hami al-Din, "Al-Harakat al-Islamiyah bi al-Maghrib," in the special issue on Islamic movements in Morocco in the Moroccan periodical *Wajha,* no. 4 (summer 1999): 6.

8. Munson, *Religion and Power in Morocco,* 160.

9. For an excellent discussion of Islamic movements in Morocco, see Muhammad Darif, *al-Islamiyyun al-Magharibah* (The Moroccan Islamists) (Casablanca: Journal of Political Sociology, 1999).

10. Hami al-Din, "Al-Haraket," 6–7.

11. Ibid., 8.

12. Ibid., 9.

13. Ibid.

14. Mary-Jane Deeb, "Tunisia," in *Religion in Politics,* ed. Stuart Mews (Essex, U.K.: Longman Group UK Limited, 1989), 268–69.

15. See Michael Collins Dunn, "The Al-Nahda Movement in Tunisia: From Renaissance to Revolution," in *Islamism and Secularism in North Africa,* ed. John Ruedy, 151.

16. Ibid.

17. Ibid., 157.

18. U.S. Department of State, "1999 Country Reports on Human Rights Practices: Tunisia" (Washington, D.C., February 2000).

19. See Marius K. Deeb, "Libya," in *Political Parties of the Middle East and North Africa,* ed. Frank Tachau (Westport, Conn.: Greenwood Press, 1994), 376.

20. See Mary-Jane Deeb, "Militant Islam and the Politics of Redemption," 60.

21. For a discussion of the NFSL, see Marius K. Deeb, "Militant Islam and Its Critics: The Case of Libya," in *Islamism and Secularism in North Africa,* ed. John Ruedy, 192–96.

22. See George Joffe, "Islamic Opposition in Libya," *Third World Quarterly* 10, no. 2 (1988): 628.

23. Mary-Jane Deeb, "Libya," in *Religion in Politics,* ed. Stuart Mews, 170–71.

24. Ibid., 171.

25. Many Islamist organizations, such as Hizballah, that are to be found in various parts of the Muslim world have a regional addendum to their name, for example, Hizballah-Gulf.

26. *Libya under Gaddafi, the NFSL Challenge: An Anthology of the NFSL News Reports, 1989–92* (Chicago: NFSL, 1992), 213.

27. "Libya: News and Views," March 9, 1997, from *al-Hayat* report on the Internet.

28. Information on this group appeared on the Internet and could have been put there by the group itself.

29. "Libyan Chronology," for the month of May 1997, on the Internet.

30. See Mary-Jane Deeb, "Political and Economic Developments in Libya," in *North Africa in Transition,* ed. Yahia H. Zoubir (Gainesville: University Press of Florida, 1999), 78–79.

31. Quoted in the Associated Press report from Cairo, August 28, 1999.

32. *The Economist,* October 30, 1999.

33. UN Report of the Human Rights Committee, concluding observations at its 1,720th meeting, November 2, 1998.

34. Mary-Jane Deeb, "Militant Islam and the Politics of Redemption."

35. U.S. State Department, "1999 Country Reports on Human Rights Practices" (Washington, D.C., February 25, 2000), 1.

36. CIA, *The World Fact Book 2000: Tunisia* (CIA Publications on the Internet), 6.

37. U.S. Department of State, "1999 Country Report: Tunisia," 1.

38. U.S. Department of State, "Morocco Country Report on Human Rights Practices for 1998" (Washington, D.C., February 26, 1999), 1.

39. U.S. Department of State, Bureau of Economic and Business Affairs, "1999 Country Report on Economic Policy and Trade Practices: Morocco" (Washington, D.C., March 2000), 1.

40. U.S. Department of State, Bureau of Economic and Business Affairs, "1999 Country Report on Economic Policy and Trade Practices: Algeria" (Washington, D.C., March 2000), 3.

41. Ibid.

42. United Nations Development Program, *Human Development Report, 1997* (New York: Oxford University Press, 1997).

43. Reuters reported in May 1997 that the Algerian Brotherhood in France had complained officially that 500 FIS members had been arrested and jailed in Libya in late 1996 and were still being held there against their will.

44. *Jerusalem Post,* October 24, 2000.

Part IV

The Outside Powers

12

U.S. Policy toward the Middle East

DON PERETZ

Long before the establishment of Israel, Palestine was present in American consciousness. The Old Testament aroused strong sympathy for the Jewish people among early political leaders. John Adams wrote, "I will insist that the Hebrews have done more to civilize men than any other nation."[1] Decades before Israel existed, U.S. government officials proclaimed their backing for a Jewish state in Palestine, perceiving the country as an empty wasteland waiting for the return of the Jews. Following World War I, President Wilson assured American Zionists of his support, promising that "in Palestine shall be laid the foundation of a Jewish Commonwealth."[2] This cultural affinity with the Old Testament and the "Hebrew people" has been a leading element in formation of American policy toward Israel. "As members of a biblically-based religion, Christians appreciate that Israel was promised—and given—to Jews as the physical center of the covenant between them and God. Many Christians support the State of Israel for reasons far more profound than mere politics."[3] The antithesis of this perspective has been American ignorance of Palestine's role in Arab and Islamic consciousness, resulting in policies that overlooked their claims in the Holy Land.[4]

Other important elements in forming American policy toward Israel in the late twentieth century include Western reaction to the Holocaust, the Cold War between the United States and the Soviet Union, the rise of Jewish influence in American politics, and emergence of a strong pro-Israel lobby that include a variety of interest groups such as Christian fundamentalists, both liberal and right-wing political factions, and labor unions.

Although the United States voted for the 1947 UN partition resolution creating Israel and was the first country to grant de facto recognition to the new Jewish state, initial relations between the two were strained because of policy differences over several issues including the Arab refugee problem, the status of Jerusalem, borders of the new state, and illegal arms shipments from the United States. The new state did not automatically become a strategic ally. Israel's initial policy of nonidentification with either the United States or the USSR prior to the Korean War and the pro-Soviet orientation of the second largest political party, Mapam, aroused suspicions among many American officials. Initial economic assistance was in the form of small loans from the Export-Import Bank rather than the huge interest-free grants that came later.[5] Although American politicians profusely praised Israel and promised it support, policymakers were apprehensive about detrimental influences the new state might have on broader regional interests. The oil produced by America's Arab friends, a critical element in the Marshall Plan for European reconstruction, seemed to many in government more important than close ties with the Jewish state. Some doubted its ability to remain viable as a pariah in such a hostile environment. Until the 1960s some U.S. policymakers proposed Israel's return to the original UN partition plan, large-scale return of the refugees, and division of Jerusalem between Israel and Jordan. Israel's victory in the 1967 war convinced many that it would be a permanent fixture in the Middle East.

The 1967 victory strengthened Israel's diplomatic standing and led to the beginning of a new relationship with the United States. Although no military pact was signed, the two developed an intimate strategic relationship, and Israel eventually became the largest recipient of American economic and military assistance. Today there are few U.S. government agencies that do not have contacts with Israel. For all practical purposes Israel has become America's closest ally. Each supports the other in most UN votes. On several occasions Israel and the United States voted, with one or two small nations such as Micronesia, against a large UN majority. Since the 1960s there have been close economic ties with Israel. Many American businesses have invested there, and the United States has become a major importer of Israeli exports. Scores of Israeli high-tech companies have been registered in the United States, and hundreds of Israeli engineers are employed by American firms.

Despite this intimacy there are still asperities in the relationship. Over the years these have included Israel's attack on the U.S.S. *Liberty* during the 1967 war, dispute over U.S. financing of the Israeli Lavi aircraft, the recent disagreement over Israel's contract to supply China with the Phalcon surveillance system, Israel's development of nuclear weapons, the Pollard spy case, the status of Jerusalem, and Israeli settlements in the West Bank and Gaza. The quasi-alliance between Israel and the United States remains a complicating factor in American relations with the surrounding Arab and Islamic nations even though they regard Washington as an essential intermediary in the Middle East peace process and, in the case of Kuwait and Saudi Arabia, as protection against Iraq and Iran. Oil exported by these countries is still crucial in the economies of America's NATO partners.

The Peace Process

Since the beginning of the struggle between Israel and the Arab states, the United States has been a principal intermediary striving to resolve the disputed issues—the refugee problem, borders, Jerusalem, equitable distribution of scarce water resources, and Israel's security concerns. Every American president or secretary of state since 1948 has offered his own peace plan based on compromise over these items. Each president has sent his own emissary to devise proposals for ending the conflict. Proposals have included President Eisenhower's Johnston scheme for regional economic development, Kennedy's plan for resolving the Arab refugee problem, Secretary of State Henry Kissinger's disengagement agreements during the Nixon and Ford administrations, Carter's mediation leading to the peace treaty between Egypt and Israel, Reagan's attempt to end the Lebanon imbroglio, Bush's inauguration of the Madrid Middle East peace conference, and Clinton's various proposals and interventions between Israel, the PLO, and Syria.

American policy in the peace process resulted from Washington's reaction to a variety of interests. Before Israel was perceived as a regional ally, Washington frequently pressured it to concede on issues such as permitting return of Arab refugees or surrendering territory beyond the partition borders. As Israel gained military power, ironically through large-scale U.S. assistance, pressures diminished and Washington became far less demanding. U.S. policy on Jerusalem characterized the transition, often reflecting general American policy and efforts to resolve the conflict.

Contrary to the claims of each president that his Jerusalem policy represented continuation of his predecessor's policy, there have been major changes from one administration to the next. In 1947–48 the United States backed the UN partition plan designating Jerusalem as an international city, removing it from the claims of both Arabs and Jews. With division of the city between Israel and Jordan as a result of the 1948 war, the United States abandoned support for territorial internationalization in favor of functional internationalization; that is, administrative jurisdiction of the city would be left to Israel and Jordan, with holy sites controlled by the respective faiths. Although Israel moved its capital to Jerusalem in 1949, Washington rejected suggestions to follow suit by transferring the U.S. embassy from Tel Aviv to Jerusalem. Until 1967 the status of Jerusalem was considered sui generis and the American consul general there still reports directly to Washington rather than to the embassy in Tel Aviv.

Following Israel's capture of Arab East Jerusalem in the June 1967 war, questions about the city's status rose again. The issue of whether the city was part of Israel had been left in abeyance. The Johnson administration took the position that "a just settlement of the status of Jerusalem is inseparably connected with other aspects of the [Arab-Israeli] problems which still defy solution." The United States "does not believe that the problem of Jerusalem can be realistically solved apart from other aspects of the situation in the Middle East. . . . all aspects of the Middle East problem, including Jerusalem, must be achieved by an agreed and accepted peaceful settlement."[6] This formulation has remained the basis of American policy since Israel's conquest of East Jerusalem in 1967.

With Nixon's assumption of office in 1969, for the first time the United States declared East Jerusalem subject to the 1949 Geneva Convention on Occupied Territory, which proscribed changes by an occupying power. Nevertheless, no strenuous objections were raised by Washington to the extensive construction of new Jewish neighborhoods in East Jerusalem or to Israel's extension of the city's borders well into the West Bank.

In December 1969 Nixon's secretary of state, William P. Rogers, proposed return to the "approximate" borders existing before the 1967 war but recommended that Israel and Jordan settle the problem of Jerusalem "recognizing that the city should be unified, with both countries sharing the civic and economic responsibilities of city government."[7]

Although President Carter opposed establishment of Jewish settlements in the occupied territories, he generally avoided including Jerusalem in his objections. Carter explained that the single instance when the United States supported a Security Council resolution bracketing Jerusalem with the territories was a mistake. "Jerusalem and the territories were not the same, and U.S. condemnation of settlements applied exclusively to the territories."[8] The Jerusalem issue was bypassed in the Camp David negotiations between Egypt and Israel. In a letter from Carter to Sadat at the conclusion of negotiations, Carter simply declared that U.S. policy conformed with that enunciated above at the UN by former U.S. ambassadors Goldberg and Yost.[9]

President Reagan revised Carter's policy by rejecting the view that settlements in the occupied territories were illegal and that East Jerusalem was occupied territory. Although the Reagan administration believed that Jewish settlements in the territories, including Jerusalem, "did not help the peace process," it refrained from labeling them illegal or calling East Jerusalem "occupied territory." No steps were taken to oppose the right of Jews "to settle in any part of the Land of Israel."[10]

President George Bush introduced a dramatic change in American policy. He was the first president to endorse UN resolutions declaring East Jerusalem "occupied *Palestinian* territory." His condemnation of Jewish construction in East Jerusalem conformed with the declaration of Israel's West Bank settlement as illegal.[11] This stance inevitably led to confrontation with Prime Minister Yitzhak Shamir and his nationalist Likud government.

President Clinton again reversed American policy, introducing substantive changes. Although the new administration still designated East Jerusalem as occupied territory, it refrained from condemning Israel's construction projects there. Like Carter, Clinton tolerated but did not welcome Israel's construction program in East Jerusalem.[12] To prevent any question about U.S. recognition of Israel's annexation of East Jerusalem, Clinton refused to allow Mayor Ehud Olmert to accompany him on a tour of the Old City. The State Department also refused to permit attendance by the U.S. ambassador at opening night of celebrations commemorating the 3,000th anniversary of the city's founding, according to Israel's version of history.

In negotiations between Israel and the Palestinians, questions about the future of Jerusalem were deferred from the Oslo agreement in 1993 until the final-status summit at Camp David in July 2000. Although tentative agreement was reached under President Clinton's supervision on most other issues, Jerusalem was the stumbling block causing collapse of negotiations and postponement of further summit meetings. Prime Minister Barak and Palestine Authority President Arafat reached what each considered the limits of compromise acceptable to their respective constituencies. Clinton and his staff offered a variety of "bridging" proposals that would have given the Palestinians authority in the Temple Mount, known to them as Haram al-Sharif, an area also considered sacred to Jews as the site of their ancient temples. According to the Clinton plan, the area within the walls of the Old City would be divided between Israel and the Palestinians but sovereignty would remain Israeli.[13] Although the U.S. "bridging" proposals required Israel to relinquish more than any Israeli government since 1967 had considered viable, Arafat felt that he could not abandon his claim to East Jerusalem as the capital of a Palestinian state. The enthusiastic reception he received upon his return from the failed Camp David negotiations indicated the extent to which his constituency and the larger Arab/Islamic world considered Arab sovereignty over East Jerusalem as nonnegotiable.[14]

President Clinton's advisers claimed that the Camp David parleys were a major success despite failure to reach a final accord. "Before Camp David, there was a huge iceberg," said National Security Adviser Sandy Berger. "We sent an icebreaker through it, and we cracked it open 100 different ways—refugees, Jerusalem, security, borders. The good news is that this is no longer an iceberg. It's 100 pieces of ice. Can this be reassembled into something like a bridge? I don't know."[15]

Shortly after the Camp David meetings violent altercations erupted between Israelis and Palestinians sparked by a visit to the Temple Mount/ Haram al-Sharif by Likud leader Ariel Sharon. His stated purpose was to demonstrate Jewish rights in the area. However, the visit was particularly provocative because Sharon was accompanied by a retinue of fellow Likud leaders and hundreds of Israeli armed police. Furthermore, Sharon was perceived by most Palestinians as one of the Israeli leaders most hostile to their aspirations. The violence quickly spread throughout the country and was labeled the Haram al-Sharif or al-Aqsa intifada, totally disrupting the peace negotiations.

The conflict soon became an issue in American politics. Hours after Clinton called on Palestine Authority President Arafat to reduce the level of violence, the U.S. House of Representatives passed a resolution of support for Israel and condemning Palestinian leaders for the violence. The measure was passed by a vote of 365 to 30. The conflict also became an issue in the New York election campaign when the Republican Senate candidate announced his opposition to a Palestinian state and denounced Democratic candidate Hillary Rodham Clinton for her pro-Palestinian sympathies.

Transfer of the U.S. embassy from Tel Aviv to Jerusalem has been considered emblematic of American policy toward Israel since the 1960s. Although some Israeli supporters demanded transfer as early as 1950, momentum for the move gathered after Israel's conquest of East Jerusalem in 1967. Prior to their election each president either supported or was ambivalent about the move. However, after assuming office they were more cautious, supporting the move "in principle" but deferring action until an "appropriate" time. Caution was advised because the move might "disrupt the peace process" or alienate other U.S. friends such as Jordan or Saudi Arabia.

Nevertheless, transfer of the embassy has acquired domestic political significance. Republican and Democratic candidates for office—both local and national—frequently compete to determine who is the more ardent Israeli supporter, the criterion being who most favors transfer of the U.S. embassy to Jerusalem. The 2000 Republican Middle East platform stated that the United States "has a moral and legal obligation to maintain its ambassador in Jerusalem. Immediately upon taking office, the next Republican president will begin the process of moving the U.S. embassy from Tel-Aviv to Israel's capital, Jerusalem."[16]

The embassy transfer became an issue in the race for New York's U.S. Senate seat between Hillary Rodham Clinton and Rick A. Lazio during the 2000 election. When Clinton called for the move "before the end of the year," Republican candidate Lazio accused her of flip-flopping and demanded that the move be made "immediately."[17]

In 1995 the U.S. Senate and House of Representatives passed the Jerusalem Embassy Relocation Act recognizing a united Jerusalem as the capital of Israel and demanding removal of the embassy to Jerusalem no later than May 31, 1999. The law called for money to construct embassy facilities there and threatened punishment of the State Department by withholding funds for "Acquisition and Maintenance of Buildings Abroad" should the secretary of state be unable to report that the new Jerusalem embassy "has officially opened." However, the law included a waiver authorizing the president to suspend implementation "to protect national security interests of the United States."[18]

When President Clinton used the waiver to defer implementation because moving the embassy might "undermine the peace process," the issue was raised in both houses of Congress. Several prominent senators, including Robert Dole (soon to be a presidential candidate) and Joseph Lieberman (later to become a candidate for vice president) attacked the State Department for U.S. abstention on a UN General Assembly resolution declaring Israel's 1967 reunification of Jerusalem null and void and calling for removal of foreign embassies from the city. The senators declared that the United States should have voted against the resolution because "it stands in direct contradiction to the Jerusalem Embassy Relocation Act of 1995."[19]

Following collapse of the July 2000 Camp David negotiations, President Clinton again raised the issue, asserting that he "always wanted to move our embassy to West Jerusalem" but postponed action because "I didn't want to . . . undermine our ability to help broker a secure and lasting peace." However, "in light of what happened, I've taken that decision under review and I'll make a decision" before the end of the year.[20] Republican presidential candidate George W. Bush responded by stating his commitment to move the embassy, although not immediately "because many details have to be worked out."[21]

Not all Israelis were enthusiastic about Clinton's threat to "reassess" the U.S. position. Akiva Eldar, writing in *Ha'aretz*, observed that a promise to reconsider the move was "music to the ears of the anti-peaceniks among both the Palestinians and the Israelis." The Arab demand for restoration of the status quo existing in Jerusalem before June 4, 1967, would be no less legitimate than an Israeli demand to annex 10 percent of the West Bank, Eldar observed. "Any Israeli Prime Minister genuinely interested in advancing the peace process should never have taken the unfortunate step of asking America, the honest broker, to play with fire by tossing the 'embassy in Jerusalem' idea into the air. Clinton should have flatly refused the request at the time instead of threatening the Palestinians with a review of American relations," Eldar cautioned.[22]

Fluctuations in U.S. policy toward Jerusalem have paralleled policy changes on other critical items. As ties became more intimate following the 1967 war, U.S. criticism of Israel at the United Nations lessened. Since 1967 the United States has used its Security Council veto or abstained in voting on most of the more than forty resolutions condemning Israeli occupation of territory seized in the Six Day War.[23] Jewish settlements in the West Bank that were called "illegal" by President Carter became "an obstacle to peace" under Reagan and Bush, while Clinton declared them "unhelpful."

On the other hand, the United States voted for several Security Council resolutions declaring annexation of the Golan Heights null and void, deploring "Israel's violation of human rights in the occupied [Golan] territories, and destruction of the Syrian [Golan] city of Quneitra."[24] From year to year Israel has been cited in the Department of State *Country Reports on Human Rights Practices* for actions contrary to the "1949 Fourth Geneva Convention Relative to the Protection of Civilian Persons in Time of War." The citations included deportation of civilians from the occupied territories, including journalists and labor leaders, transfer of detainees from the territories to Israeli prisons, punishments such as demolition of civilian homes, and lengthy administrative detention without trial. In its 2000 annual report, the State Department's Democracy, Human Rights, and Labor Division criticized Israel for unfair treatment of Arabs, vandalism and discrimination against Christian groups and non-Orthodox Jewish factions, and sanctions against Muslim citizens desiring to make the pilgrimage to Mecca.[25]

In policy statements and UN discussions on the peace process, the United States has deemphasized UN General Assembly Resolution 194 calling for return of the Palestine refugees. Instead, Security Council Resolutions 242 and 338 became the basis for American policy. As Resolution 242 was deliberately ambiguous, calling for Israeli withdrawal "from territories" rather than "the" territories occupied in 1967, American negotiators believed this wording provided room for maneuver in seeking an exchange of "land for peace." State Department officials argued that their position at the United Nations was required to win Israel's confidence and reassure its supporters that the United States had not abandoned the Jewish state and would remain its loyal ally.

A major change in policy was the U.S. decision to open negotiations with the PLO in 1988. Until the 1970s the Palestinian problem was perceived as a refugee rather than a political/national issue. The PLO was regarded as a terrorist organization and an agent of the Soviet Union. Although Secretary Kissinger began to pay attention to the Palestine issue after the 1973 war, his approach was similar to Israel's, that is, denial of Palestinian national identity. In 1975 Israel won a commitment from Kissinger not to "recognize or negotiate" with the PLO unless it recognized Israel's right to exist and accepted UN Resolution 242, a restriction that was codified in U.S. law in 1985.[26]

The Carter administration was the first to accept the idea of a Palestinian homeland and to contact the PLO despite Israel's vehement opposition. At the 1978 Camp David summit, Carter persuaded Israel's Prime Minister Begin to include establishment of a Palestinian "self-governing authority" in the final accords. For the first time "Palestinian homeland" and "Palestinian rights" were accepted as legitimate concepts by the U.S. government.

Although Reagan's secretary of state, George Shultz, accepted the need to include Palestinians in the peace process, he regarded the PLO as a terrorist organization and refused to deal with it. The intifada in 1988 stimulated new thinking about the Palestinians in both the United States and Israel and within the PLO itself. By the end of the year the PLO revised its political platform by recognizing a two-state solution (Israel and a Palestinian state), recognized Israel's right to exist, accepted UN Resolution 242, and renounced terrorism. This led to Shultz's reevaluation and to the Bush administration's recognition and direct negotiations with the PLO. President Clinton became directly involved in negotiations with Israel and the PLO after he hosted the first meeting between an Israeli prime minister (Rabin) and PLO leader Arafat.

Despite Clinton's role as "honest broker," too close an association with Arafat remained anathema in American politics. In the previously mentioned 2000 New York Senate race, Republican and Democratic candidates castigated each other for either shaking hands with Arafat, kissing his wife, or calling for establishment of a Palestinian state.[27]

After Oslo, the United States became the principal intermediary in the series of negotiations between Israel and the Palestinians from 1993 until the 2000 Camp David summit. Despite Arab skepticism about the American role of honest broker, Egypt, Syria, Jordan, and the Palestinians all considered the United States the most viable intermediary. They believed that only the United States, by virtue of its economic, military, and political ties, could persuade Israel to make even minimal concessions. In addition, because of the Israeli lobby's perceived influence in U.S. politics, other states frequently approach it to act as intermediary with the U.S. government. When Poland sought U.S. approval for joining NATO, for example, its emissaries sought assistance from American organizations affiliated with the Israeli lobby.

The Strategic Relationship

The strategic relationship between Israel and the United States developed over time as a result of the Cold War, the decline of Western influence in the Arab world, the emergence of militant anti-Western nationalist movements in the Middle East, and Israel's increasing influence among diverse U.S. constituencies.

After the Korean War Prime Minister Ben-Gurion concluded that Israel's future depended on close ties with a strong Western power.[28] Israel increasingly cast its UN votes with the West against the Soviet Union and the Third World bloc. While Israel drew closer to the United States, nationalist revolutions in Egypt, Syria, and Iraq and growing hostility to the West in Lebanon, Jordan, and Iran resulted in closure of British bases and the rise of anticolonial movements. American policy based on containment of the Soviet Union through treaties like the Baghdad Pact collapsed; instead, Moscow succeeded in establishing quasi-alliances with Arab states surrounding Israel. Anti-Western fervor in the region corresponded with deep hostility to Israel pervading the Islamic world and the Arab states in particular. Throughout much of the Third World Israel was perceived as a Western intrusion, a last bastion of colonialism and imperialism in the Middle East. The result in the United States was a growing perception that only Israel could be relied on to defend American interests in the region. Anti-Communist organizations, including labor unions, both liberal and conservative political factions, and Protestant fundamentalist groups regarded Israel as an "outpost of democracy" in a region of the world hostile to the United States. Both Republican and Democratic politicians vied with each other in assertions of support for the Jewish state. Numerous pro-Israeli political action committees (PACs) raised funds for senators and congressmen who supported recommendations of one of Washington's most powerful lobbies, the American Israel Public Affairs Committee (AIPAC).[29] While public opinion strongly favored Israel and Congress generally supported AIPAC recommendations, diplomats concerned about wider U.S. interests in the Middle East and the importance of the region as a whole in the scheme of American policy urged caution or restraint in Washington's dealings with Israel.

Following the 1967 war, Israel demonstrated its potential as a strategic ally by shipping quantities of Soviet-made weapons to the United States for close analysis. During the 1969–70 War of Attrition, Soviet-made artillery, antitank and antiaircraft guns and missiles were also provided to American intelligence. Israel's potential as an ally was enhanced following Syria's invasion of northern Jordan in 1970. In response to appeals from President Nixon and National Security Adviser Kissinger, Israeli forces were put on alert and moved toward Jordan's border, resulting in Syria's withdrawal. Washington responded with a promise to deter any Soviet retaliation.[30]

The first formal strategic pact was the United States–Israel Memorandum of Agreement on defense cooperation signed in 1979 between Defense Secretary Harold Brown and Defense Minister Ezer Weizman. It provided for cooperative research and development and authorized Israeli military exports to the United States. The Carter administration also designated Israel as a non-NATO country eligible for U.S. technology transfers.[31]

A closer and more formal agreement was signed during the Reagan years. In 1980 the Republican Party platform underscored Israel's deterrent role in the Middle East and the value of its armed forces in the East-West military equation. At the convention candidate Reagan declared Israel "an important ally of the United States as well as a major strategic asset." Reagan's secretary of state, Alexander Haig, concocted a new scheme for regional security through a "strategic consensus" based on an alliance of anti-Communist nations in the Middle East. Because of Arab hostility, it was decided to formulate a separate memorandum of understanding (MOU) with Israel. The pact signed in November 1981 called for cooperation to "deter all threats from the Soviet Union to the region" and for "consultation and cooperation to enhance their national security by deterring such threats to the whole region." The pact provided for joint military exercises and working groups to develop cooperation in research and development and in defense trade.[32]

Israel's Labor opposition feared that the MOU imposed obligations far beyond Israel's own defense requirements while exempting the United States from assisting it in the event of Arab aggression. Three weeks after signing the MOU, Reagan suspended implementation because Israel imposed its legal jurisdiction on the Golan Heights, a measure regarded tantamount to annexation. Relations were further strained during the next two years because of U.S. AWACS aircraft sales to Saudi Arabia and concerns about the violence in Israel's 1982 invasion of Lebanon.

Strategic cooperation was revived in 1983 with establishment of a Joint Political and Military Group (JPMG) of high-level defense officials from both countries. A new MOU was signed in 1984 to facilitate joint military planning and exercises and to preposition arms and ammunition in Israel for use by American forces. The agreement included joint exercises in antisubmarine warfare, U.S. leasing of Israeli-made Kfir aircraft, and training of U.S. forces in the Negev.

In 1987 Congress formally designated Israel a "Major Non-NATO Ally." As a result terms of the original 1979 agreement were expanded into a detailed Memorandum of Understanding between the Government of Israel and the Government of the United States of America concerning the Principles Governing Mutual Cooperation in Research and Development, Scientist and Engineer Exchange, Procurement and Logistic Support of Defense Equipment. In addition to the JPMG, a Joint Security Assistance Planning Group (JSAPG) and a Joint Economic Development Group (JEDG) were formed resulting in even closer cooperation between military and naval forces. The agreement greatly facilitated technology transfer and U.S. assistance in development of diverse Israeli weapons systems. Israeli and American defense industries began joint competition for U.S. and international weapons contracts.[33]

Under the 1983 MOU Israel asked the United States to finance development of a new fighter jet, the Lavi, a controversial project that strained relations between the two countries. After investing half a billion dollars in development, it was discovered that the project would cost far more than anticipated and deliver much less than promised. Pressure from the U.S. Defense Department and sharp disagreement among Israeli officials finally led to cancellation, but not without bitter regrets among both Americans and Israelis who had supported the Lavi.[34]

Israel's plans for development of nuclear weapons affected the strategic relationship. Despite American efforts to curb the expansion of nuclear powers, Israel was considered a special case, a country that could be trusted to handle its nuclear potential responsibly. Although Washington sought universal adherence to the Nuclear Nonproliferation Treaty (NPT) and requested Israel to sign it, the United States was reluctant to use pressure until a comprehensive Middle East peace could be attained. U.S. tolerance of Israel's nuclear development was conditioned by a tacit agreement that Israel would refrain from taking an overt nuclear posture, openly conducting tests, or transferring nuclear technology to a third party. When Israel took unilateral action to undermine Iraq's nuclear capacity by bombing its Osiraq reactor in 1981, Secretary of State Haig seemed quite pleased. During the 2000 U.S. presidential campaign, Republican vice presidential candidate Richard Cheney thanked Israel "for the outstanding job you did on the Iraqi nuclear program in 1981, which made our job much easier in Desert Storm!"[35]

U.S.-Israeli strategic agreements received little if any publicity until 1989 lest the publicity further alienate American's Arab friends in the region. However, in September of that year, the agreements were publicized to increase the deterrent effect; then Defense Minister Rabin revealed that some twenty-seven joint military exercises with the United States had been conducted in recent years.

During the 1990–91 Gulf crisis, direct contact was established between the Israeli defense minister and the American defense secretary through a communication system code-named "Hammer Rock." An American major general was seconded to Israeli military headquarters, facilitating communications and liaison between the two armies. During Operation Desert Storm the United States airlifted Patriot surface-to-air (SAM) missiles to Israel accompanied by American military personnel. This marked only the second time foreign forces played an active role in Israel's defense. (The first time was during the 1956 Suez War when French air squadrons were sent to Israel.)

Strategic cooperation also involved joint development of military industries and export of Israeli weapons systems to the United States. As sophistication and production costs rose, Israel had to expand overseas markets to pay for weapons required by its own forces, resulting in frequent competition for customers with American military contractors. By the 1990s Israel was the fifth largest arms exporter; Israel Aircraft Industries was the country's major exporter based on its military sales.

After the Cold War world arms markets shrank. This resulted in greater international competition and a crisis in relations with the United States during 1999–2000. Israel contracted with China to supply the Phalcon, a $250 million early-warning radar and communications system mounted on refurbished Ilyushin aircraft. Washington objected to the sale, claiming that it could be used against Taiwan, an American protégé in the Pacific. The projected sale greatly angered several influential members of Congress who threatened to punish Israel by cutting its military aid. Under pressure by the U.S. Defense Department and President Clinton, Prime Minister Barak canceled the sale in July 2000. Following the Phalcon incident and other military sales to China totaling several billion dollars, the State Department requested formal consultations prior to future Israeli weapons sales. The United States presented a list of twenty-seven "countries of concern," including several of Israel's important arms clients, where consultation was considered vital.[36]

The United States promised to reward Israel with a new strategic agreement, upgrading its status to "strategic ally" as compensation for giving up the Phalcon contract. The accord would supersede the 1988 memorandum of agreement and would provide Israel with additional military assistance, including compensation for withdrawal from Lebanon in May 2000. However, to prevent another Phalcon incident, Israel would be required to consult the United States on military deals with four "states of concern"—India, Pakistan, China, and Russia.[37] Mention was also made of the 1998 plan finalized by Congress with the previous Netanyahu government to reduce economic aid by $120 million a year, transferring half that amount, or $60 million a year, to military assistance, which would thus be increased to $2.4 billion a year within a decade.

Israel's former defense minister, Moshe Arens, criticized Israel's overdependence on American military assistance and questioned the value of the strategic alliance. He argued that an agreement giving the United States veto rights over Israel's exports would be "disastrous" to its defense industries and "severely damage Israel's defense capability." Additional aid to purchase American weapons, he said, "is likely to further throttle Israel's defense industry." The new plan "by any Israeli measure . . . is a substantial downgrading of this relationship."[38] Ze'ev Schiff, Israel's leading military correspondent, observed that some high-ranking Israeli officers complained that if "the upgrading ['strategic relationship'] also entails threats to down-scale foreign aid or humiliating forms of punishment, perhaps the whole idea of upgrading can be dispensed with. . . . The Sino-Israeli spy plane deal has reminded many that the American-Israeli partnership is asymmetrical. One partner is a superpower while the other is a small country, one the giver, the other the taker. . . . This partnership," he cautioned, "had led to the situation where the taker, Israel, has, in recent years gotten into the habit of utilizing every opportunity, even when there is no need to do so, to ask for additional cash or additional compensation for various things. . . . Israel's position as the side that always takes can undermine its own sense of integrity and could weaken its backbone. Israel must do a lot of soul-searching as to how it can gradually reduce its dependence on American financial aid."[39]

Economic Aid

As political support for Israel increased, economic and military assistance were linked and grew geometrically. From 1948 until 1967 economic and military assistance to Israel compared to aid received by other countries was relatively small. However, following its 1967 victory when Israel demonstrated military superiority, aid increased by 450 percent. During Nixon's administration aid greatly increased because Israel was regarded as a key element in containing the Soviet Union. According to Kissinger, when confronted with the realities of power in the Middle East, Nixon decided to pursue a strategy "to reduce Soviet influence, weaken the position of the Arab radicals, encourage Arab moderates, and assure Israel's security." When Israel was confronted with the danger of defeat in the 1973 war, Nixon ordered all-out military assistance with the largest U.S. airlift in history and an 800 percent increase in military assistance totaling over $2 billion.[40]

The 1973 Yom Kippur or Ramadan war polarized the Soviet and American positions in the Middle East more than ever. By the end of the war Israel was a firmly accredited Cold War ally of the United States and was rewarded with increasingly generous economic packages. U.S. aid grew from $93.6 million in fiscal 1970 to $2,646.3 million in 1974. Substantial increases in economic and military assistance to Egypt and Israel were integral components in the peace agreements engineered by President Carter in 1978–79. By the 1980s Israel was receiving an annual allocation of $3 billion, all of it in grants that would not have to be repaid. By now Israel had become the largest single recipient of American aid; in per capita terms it also received more than any other beneficiary. In addition to the more-or-less-fixed annual allocation of some $3 billion, several other programs totaling tens of millions of dollars included items such as participation in financing schools and hospitals, joint research and development of the Arrow antimissile project, establishment of a major petroleum reserve available for emergencies by Israel, and improvement of Haifa port for U.S. military use. Unlike other recipients of military assistance, Israel was permitted to use a portion it received to purchase local Israeli rather than American manufactured items. In most other instances the United States closely monitored distribution of economic and military assistance; Israel, however, was not required to line-item funds it received. In 1992 Democratic senator Robert V. Byrd of West Virginia observed that "we have poured foreign aid into Israel for decades at rates and terms given to no other nation on earth. . . . Beyond the massive economic and military aid, however, in our so-called strategic relations with Israel, we have served as a protector almost in the same sense as the government of the United States would protect one of our 50 states."[41]

There has been little controversy about maintaining the level of economic aid to Israel in Congress despite recent cuts in overall foreign assistance. Congress usually accepts executive branch proposals for funds to Israel although it frequently slashes allocations proposed for other countries. A rule of thumb is that Israel should receive funding sufficient to maintain a military force equal or superior to the combined forces of the surrounding Arab states. When seventy-eight senators demanded that President Carter continue existing levels of aid to Israel in 1978, they justified amounts requested to balance the massive arms procurement by Arab states, 80 percent of which were of U.S. origin.[42]

Since 1974 a substantial portion of funds Israel receives from the United States has been used to finance interest and principal owed American banks. A large part of the $1 billion received in Economic Support Funds covered repayment on previous loans to finance arms purchased in the United States. Much of the more than $1 billion in military assistance is a credit line to American arms suppliers to Israel.[43]

In 1985 when Israel was in the throes of a major economic recession, the United States assisted with a free trade agreement (FTA) eliminating American tariffs on most of its imports; today Israel is only one of four countries with a U.S. FTA (the others are Canada, Jordan, and Mexico) as well as being the recipient of a special $1.5 billion grant. By 2000 the

United States was Israel's largest trade partner, importing more than a third of its exports while the United States provided the lion's share of Israeli imports, about 23 percent.[44] Because of attractive tax policies, between 85 and 90 percent of Israeli high-tech companies have been registered in the United States. In 1999–2000, 60 to 70 percent of Israeli high-tech firms were registered in the state of Delaware.

If and when peace treaties are signed between Israel, Syria, and the Palestinians, the United States is expected to cover the costs of items such as redeployment of Israeli forces and refugee resettlement and/or compensation, amounts totaling tens of billions of dollars.

What of the Future?

In the half century since Israel was established, it has acquired a most favored place in American foreign policy for the reasons cited above. Will the factors that established this position remain as significant in the future as the past? Will memories of the Holocaust continue to arouse the same sympathy among Americans? As increasing numbers of American Jews intermarry, now estimated at 50 percent, will Jewish attachment to Israel and its role in American politics be so influential? As Israel's Middle Eastern neighbors modernize or secularize, will they continue to perceive Israel as a hostile Western outpost? If peace is established with its neighbors, will Israel have to depend on its strategic relationship with the United States to feel secure? As Israel's economy expands will U.S. economic assistance be necessary? As the number of Jewish immigrants from the Soviet Union decreases, will the need for aid from the U.S. government and American Jewry be so urgent? Finally, in the twenty-first century will Israel continue to regard its relationship with the United States as crucial for existence and will the United States continue to regard Israel as an indispensable ally in a turbulent Middle East?

U.S. Policy in the Gulf

Israel's security and well-being as well as a just and lasting peace between Israel and its Arab neighbors are primary objectives of American Middle East policy. Nevertheless, a security framework in the Gulf that assures access to U.S. energy supplies is no less significant. A major dilemma facing policymakers has been how to reconcile these goals. Some have argued that the strategic alliance with Israel, the largess extended to the Jewish state, and its close diplomatic affinity with Washington subvert relations between the United States and the Gulf states even though, next to Israel, they are America's closest Middle East allies.

Saudi oil exports, by far the largest in the region, remain vital for the economies of American NATO allies as well as for the rest of Western Europe's economic well-being. During the latter half of the twentieth century, Washington established close military ties with the Saudis, who carry great weight with other Islamic nations because of the kingdom's site of Islam's two most holy cities, Mecca and Medina, and because of Saudi oil wealth, which has been used to subsidize military, political, and economic projects of neighboring states.

Import of Saudi oil is no less vital for the American economy. Until recently the kingdom provided the second largest amount of American imported oil, which now accounts for approximately half of the petroleum used in the United States. With the world's largest reserves it appears that Saudi Arabia will continue to dominate the world's oil trade throughout the twenty-first century.

Recently when OPEC raised its prices, resulting in a nearly threefold increase per barrel within the past several months, the United States prevailed on Saudi Arabia to use its influence to moderate the price increase. Despite Saudi concern about the disruption of the peace process and anger at Israel's policies vis-à-vis the Palestinians, Saudi authorities released a significant amount of oil on world markets to arrest further price escalations.

Ties with Saudi Arabia, which include prepositioning of U.S. military equipment and inconspicuous stationing of troops in the kingdom, serve a mutual need. Since the 1991 Gulf War or Desert Storm, this quasi-alliance has served as a deterrent to Iraq's ambitions in the region. In the early 1990s Iraq was perceived as a threat, not only to Kuwait, but to other Gulf states as well, and to Saudi Arabia in particular.

Since Desert Storm the United States has maintained a strict embargo on imports of nonhumanitarian items to Iraq; along with Great Britain the United States has flown air surveillance missions over no-fly zones established by allies after the war and has urged the UN to enforce monitoring of nonconventional (nuclear, biological, and chemical) weapons manufactured in Iraq. However, the alliance forged by the United States against Iraq during the Gulf War has gradually unraveled. Russia, France, and Turkey and several Arab and other countries have recently taken measures to weaken the UN sanctions regime. The original UN mission established to monitor weapons production was banished by Iraq, and a new UN agency to replace it has been unable to carry out its mission. A number of international organizations and other agencies, including the American Council of Roman Catholic Bishops, have urged cancellation of sanctions, maintaining that their severity has resulted in a sharp decline of health and the deaths of thousands of Iraqi children. One reaction to the recent Palestinian al-Aqsa intifada has been renewal of Arab ties with Iraq and overt steps to break the blockade.

Both Iraq and Iran were targets of the U.S. dual-containment policy initiated after the 1991 Gulf War. Previous administrations had chosen one country or the other to promote and protect American interests in the Gulf, first, Iran, under the shah, then, after he was overthrown by groups hostile to the United States, Saddam Hussein's Iraq. In terms of what followed, both approaches were later considered failures. Dual containment aimed to achieve a regional balance of power favorable to the United States and its friends without depending on either Iraq or Iran. Until Desert Storm Iraq was perceived as an important element in containing Iran's ambitions in the Gulf. During the first Gulf war between Iran and Iraq, the United States backed Arab support for Iraq. However, after Iraq's invasion of Kuwait and defeat, Saddam Hussein was no longer considered a likely partner to maintain a favorable power balance. The two Gulf wars, the anti-Iraq alliance, the end of the Cold War, and diminishing Soviet influence in the region seemed to call for new security arrangements to replace dual containment.

Dual containment also involved U.S. support for the Gulf Cooperation Council and positioning of American military equipment and/or troops in Saudi Arabia, Kuwait, Qatar, and Bahrain as well as economic measures to contain Iraqi and Iranian influence. By the late 1990s, when dual-containment policies had lost their credibility, the embargo against Iraq dissipated, and changing political conditions in Iran indicated possibilities of renewed relations with the United States, ending the embargo and boycott of Iranian goods, and restoration of its ties with several Arab and other countries.

A major component of U.S. Middle East policy is a heavy emphasis on military ties with Saudi Arabia and the Gulf states. They have been encouraged to purchase billions of dollars worth of spy planes, missiles, and other sophisticated American equipment, and thousands of U.S. servicemen have been stationed there. This emphasis on military dimensions of achieving regional security contradicts statements calling for an end of the Middle East arms race. However, by the end of the 1970s the region had become the world's largest importer of weapons. The Iran-Iraq war and the Gulf crisis in 1990–91 stimulated an even greater level of arms transfer agreements with Saudi Arabia and the Gulf states. Attempts during the early 1990s by the UN to limit arms sales have failed. During this period the U.S. Congress even approved substantial increases in arms sales to the region.

Whether or not the United States achieves its objectives in the region will depend less on its foreign policy than on the course of internal economic and social developments there. The United States can influence the pattern of these developments by discouraging large weapons expenditures, by deciding either to support or censure undemocratic regimes, and by withholding or extending economic assistance to creative development programs.

Notes

1. *New York Times,* October 4, 2000, op-ed article by Michael Novak.

2. Lawrence Davidson, "Historical Ignorance and Popular Perception," *Middle East Policy,* November 2, 1994, 145.

3. *New York Times,* September 10, 2000.

4. See Kathleen Christison, "Perceptions of Palestine: Their Influence on U.S. Middle East Policy," *U.S. Policy in the Gulf* (Berkeley: University of California Press, 1999).

5. U.S. economic assistance began shortly after Israel was established with $135 million in loans from the Export-Import Bank and $1.2 million under Public Law 480 in 1949, extended in 1950. Between 1950 and 1961, U.S. aid reached $831.09 million. Between 1978 and 1981, total aid reached over $11 billion, a large part in military assistance related to the Camp David agreements.

6. *U.S. Official Statements: U.N. Security Council Resolution 242* (Washington, D.C.: Institute for Palestine Studies, 1992), 182; Shlomo Slonim, *Jerusalem in America's Foreign Policy, 1847–1997* (The Hague: Kluwer Law International 1998), 362.

7. Slonim, 364.

8. William Quandt, *Peace Process* (Washington: Brookings, 1993), 455.

9. Slonim, 364.

10. Ibid., 365.

11. Ibid., 366.

12. Ibid., 368.

13. *Ha'aretz* (Israel), August 18, 2000.

14. Hilal Khashan, "Arab Attitudes toward Israel and Peace," *The Washington Institute Policy Focus* (WINEP) Research Memorandum no. 40, August 2000 (Washington, D.C.: WINEP), 2000.

15. *New York Times,* September 8, 2000.

16. Jewish Telegraphic Agency, August 11, 2000.

17. *New York Times,* July 30, 2000.

18. Slonim, *Jerusalem,* 377.

19. Cited in *Washington Jewish Week,* April 11, 1996.

20. *New York Times,* July 29, 2000.

21. *Ha'aretz,* July 15, 2000.

22. Ibid., August 2, 2000.

23. *Honest Broker? U.S. Policy and the Middle East Peace Process* (Washington, D.C.: Center for Policy Analysis on Palestine, April 1997), 12.

24. *U.S. Official Statements: Israeli Settlement—The Fourth Geneva Convention* (Washington, D.C.: Institute for Palestine Studies, 1992), 132–33.

25. Ibid.

26. K. Christison, "U.S. Policy toward the Palestinians," *Encyclopedia of the Palestinians,* ed. Philip Mattar, 415–21.

27. *New York Times,* September 11, 2000.

28. See Zach Levey, *Israel and the Western Powers, 1952–1960* (Chapel Hill: University of North Carolina Press, 1997).

29. See Shai Feldman, *The Future of U.S.-Israeli Strategic Cooperation* (Washington, D.C.: Washington Institute for Near East Policy, 1996).

30. Ibid.

31. Ibid., 10.

32. Ibid., 65–66; Stephen Zunes, "The Strategic Functions of U.S. Aid to Israel," *Middle East Policy* 4, no. 4 (October 1996): 92–93.

33. Ibid.

34. See Dov S. Zakheim, *Flight of the Lavi: Inside a U.S.-Israeli Crisis* (Washington, D.C.: Brassey's, 1996).

35. *New York Times,* September 18, 2000.

36. Ibid., June 15, 28, July 12, 2000.

37. *Ha'aretz,* August 31, 2000.

38. Ibid., September 5, 2000.

39. Ibid., August 11, 2000.

40. Zunes, "Strategic Functions," 96.

41. Donald Neff, *Fallen Pillars: U.S. Policy toward Palestine and Israel since 1945* (Washington, D.C.: Institute for Palestine Studies, 1995), 179.

42. Zunes, "Strategic Functions," 97.

43. *Ha'aretz,* July 17, 2000.

44. Ibid., September 6, 2000.

13

Russian Policy in the Middle East under Yeltsin and Putin

ROBERT O. FREEDMAN

Introduction

It has now been eleven years since the Soviet Union collapsed and two years since Vladimir Putin replaced Boris Yeltsin as president of the Soviet Union's most important successor state, the Russian Federation. Given this time span, it is appropriate to evaluate Russian policy toward the Middle East over the last decade. This chapter will analyze the main thrust of Russian policy toward the Middle East under Yeltsin and will also examine the degree to which it has begun to change under Putin, who, after becoming prime minister in August 1999, became acting president in January 2000 and then was elected president two months later.

When the Soviet Union collapsed in December 1991, its chief successor state, Russia, faced a far different strategic situation than had the Soviet Union. With a host of new states on Russia's southern borders, six of them Muslim, the Russian leadership faced a series of new challenges in its dealings with the Middle East, and this was to affect its Middle East priorities. In addition, there was a change from ideologically driven policy to policy created as a pragmatic response to events. At least until 1988, the midpoint of Mikhail Gorbachev's term as Communist Party leader, Soviet policy was ideologically driven to some degree. Under Yeltsin, Middle East policy was far more pragmatic, if also far more disjointed, than that of his Soviet predecessors, as a number of often conflicting interest groups sought to openly influence Russian policy in the Middle East. Putin, for his part, has brought some of these groups back under control. Third, to a far greater degree than in the Soviet period, Russian policy making in the Middle East became an issue in Russia's domestic politics as Yeltsin, in responding to an increasingly right-wing Russian parliament (Duma), sought to tailor Russian policy toward the region at least to some degree to satisfy his critics in Parliament. Putin, working (so far) with a much more supportive Duma, has not had to face this problem, although his nationalist policies are in tune with the majority of the Duma. After exploring these major changes along with the economic and military weaknesses that greatly hamper Russia's foreign policy, this chapter will briefly analyze Russia's four most important regional relationships: (1) Iran (Russia's key regional ally); (2) Iraq (which has seen the greatest changes in Russian policy during the Yeltsin-Putin period); (3) Turkey (with which Russia has had a very mixed relationship); and (4) Israel (with which Russia has developed a very close relationship—quite the reverse of the situation in the Soviet era). This chapter will conclude with an evaluation of the main Middle Eastern challenges facing Vladimir Putin, Yeltsin's chosen successor as Russia's president.

New Regional Priorities

When the Soviet Union collapsed in December 1991, Russia suddenly found itself with fourteen new neighbors, six of them (Armenia, Georgia, and Azerbaizhan in Transcaucasia and Turkmenstan, Uzbekistan, and Tajikistan in Central Asia) directly bordering the Middle East. Since four of these states (Azerbaizhan, Turkmenstan, Uzbekistan, and Tajikistan) and two other states bordering or close to Russia on its southern border (Kazakhstan and Kyrgyzstan) were dealing with the revival of Islam, which had long been suppressed under Communism, concerns about Islamic radicalism were added to the geopolitical concern in Moscow about the future direction of these countries' foreign and domestic policies.[1] Russia also had concerns about drug and arms smuggling, as well as creating a new defense perimeter along Russia's southern frontier (most Soviet defense installations in the south now lie in the newly independent states). Consequently, what happened in these new countries became of paramount importance for Moscow. While regaining at least a modicum of control over these countries became a primary objective of Russian policy during the 1990s, the Russian leadership soon found itself in an influence competition with the United States and its NATO ally Turkey, and it was initially concerned that Iran's radical Islamic regime would seek to spread its influence in Central Asia and Transcaucasia. Consequently, Russia's primary foreign policy foci in the Middle East became Iran and Turkey as Moscow found itself dealing with them not only in such bi-lateral areas as trade and arms sales but also in the geopolitics of Trans-caucasia and Central Asia. These were regions that became increasingly challenging to Moscow given the two wars in Chechnya, the civil war in Tajikistan, the rise of the Islamic radical Taliban regime in Afghanistan, an Islamic insurgency in Central Asia, and the Russian-American energy competition over the oil and gas resources of the Caspian Sea.

If Turkey and Iran were Moscow's first priority in the Middle East, given their propinquity to Transcaucasia and Central Asia, the second main Russian priority was the Persian Gulf. Moscow sought, albeit without a great deal of success, to balance its policies toward Iran, Iraq, and the Gulf Cooperation Council, countries that, through much of the Yeltsin era, were often at odds with each other. Russia's situation was complicated during this period by the increasingly severe conflicts between Iraq and the United States.

The third and by far the least important priority for Moscow was the Arab-Israeli zone composed of Israel, Syria, Lebanon, Egypt, and Jordan and the Palestinians. During most of the post–World War II Soviet period this region was of primary importance to Moscow as the Soviet leaders sought to construct an "antiimperialist" Arab unity based on Arab hostil-ity to what the USSR called the linchpin of Western imperialism, Israel. In one of the major transformations of its policy, Moscow now sees Israel as its closest collaborator among this group of states. Not only is Israel Russia's leading trade partner in the Arab-Israeli zone, it is also home to a million Russian-speaking former residents of the USSR who have kept close cultural ties with their former homeland, and Russia and Israel, de-spite serious differences over Russia's supply of atomic energy and missile technology to Iran, have developed a close collaboration in developing military equipment such as AWACS aircraft for sale to Third World coun-tries.

In sum, Russia's regional priorities have shifted dramatically since the collapse of the Soviet Union, with Moscow's primary focus on Central Asia and Transcaucasia significantly affecting Russian policy toward the Middle East.

The Impact of Domestic Politics

Following the shock of the collapse of the Soviet Union, and in response to the highly pro-American policy of Yeltsin in the Middle East and else-where during his first year as president of an independent Russia (1992), opposition to his policies began to grow in Russia's Duma, which served as the most important sounding board for elite opponents of Yeltsin's foreign policy. As successive Duma elections in December 1993 and December 1995 produced increasingly hard-line nationalist and anti-Yeltsin majorities, Yeltsin, who had dissolved the Duma by force in October 1993, chose increasingly to tailor his policies to meet Duma criticism.[2] Indeed, following the 1995 Duma elections Yeltsin fired his pro-Western foreign minister Andrei Kozyrev and replaced him with the far more hard-line Yevgeny Primakov, a former KGB and FSB operative, highly respected in the Duma, and with extensive experience in the Middle East. Indeed, until he became prime minister following the August 1998 economic crisis, Primakov could be seen as Yeltsin's ambassador to the Duma.

Within the Duma during Yeltsin's era there were three major groups. On one end of the spectrum were the "Atlanticists," who placed primary emphasis on good ties with the United States and wanted Russia to be part of Western civilization. On the issue of Russian policy toward the "Near Abroad," the newly independent countries of the former Soviet Union, the Atlanticists stressed normal diplomatic relations, without Russia seeking to impose its will from a dominant position. In the area of economics, the Atlanticists advocated rapid economic reform and privatization.

In the center of the Russian political spectrum were the "Eurasianists." They advocated a balanced foreign policy approach for Russia, with equal emphasis on Europe, the Middle East, and the Far East. On the issue of relations with the Near Abroad, they advocated an assertive policy so that Russia would be clearly the dominant outside power. Finally, they advocated slower economic reform and privatization than the Atlanticists.

The group on the far end of the Russian political spectrum in the Duma was the odd combination of ultranationalists and unrepentant Communists. This grouping was outspokenly anti-American (and anti-Israel), called for the reestablishment of Russian hegemony in the Near Abroad, and, while divided on the issue of privatization, agreed that Russia should be a strong centralized state. In the period from 1993 to 1999, as the Duma moved steadily to the right, Yeltsin took an increasingly hard line in Russian foreign policy, especially toward the Near Abroad and the Middle East. While there were brief interludes of moderation in Russian policy, such as when Sergei Kiriyenko became prime minister in April 1998 and other reformers held positions of power, his replacement by Primakov in August 1998 returned Russia to a hard-line policy. While the Duma has, at least initially, been far more supportive of Putin, himself a strong Russian nationalist with an often confrontational policy toward the United States (until the terrorist attacks on the United States on September 11, 2001), especially in the Middle East, it remains to be seen whether Putin will be able to maintain the Duma's support given the huge economic, political, and foreign policy challenges facing Russia.

Quasi-Independent Centers of Foreign Policy Making under Yeltsin

As the Duma moved noisily to the right in its foreign policy pronouncements, something Yeltsin had to keep in mind despite the Duma's relatively limited powers, the organizations actually carrying out Russian foreign policy remained badly divided and often came into conflict with one another. While Yeltsin and his presidential staff, in theory at least, had the last word in Russian foreign policy, the Russian president, especially in the 1996–99 period was both ill and preoccupied with domestic politics. Consequently, there was almost a battle royal among a number of groups and institutions seeking to project their views on Russian foreign policy. The most important of the institutions, at least in theory, was the Russian Foreign Ministry. Yet, Kozyrev proved particularly ineffectual, not only in leading but also in coordinating Russian foreign policy, and this was one of the reasons he was replaced. Among the most influential of the groups making foreign policy on a quasi-independent basis was the oil and gas group made up of Lukoil, Gasprom, and Transneft, closely linked to former Russian prime minister Viktor Chernomyrdin. This group successfully stood up to the Foreign Ministry on a number of issues, including the development of the oil resources of the Azeri section of the Caspian Sea. Putin has moved to curb their power, and it remains to be seen how much influence they retain over policy making.

Another highly influential group in Russian foreign policy making consisted of reformers such as Boris Nemtzov and Anatoly Chubais, who were appointed deputy prime ministers in March 1997. Once in power, they were very influential in watering down the union between Russia and Belarus, and they also encouraged the 1997 agreement between Russia and Ukraine to divide the Black Sea fleet. The causes of both domestic reform and a more moderate foreign policy suffered when they became involved in a clash with some of the oligarchs during the summer of 1997 over the privatization of major Russian industries; nonetheless, as a result of the April 1998 government shake-up by Yeltsin, they retained very important positions. Boris Nemtzov became *primus inter pares* among the three Russian deputy prime ministers (he sat in for Kiriyenko when the then Russian prime minister was away from Moscow), and Anatoly Chubais became the head of Unified Energy Systems, a very important energy conglomerate. Finally, Chernomyrdin's successor as Russian prime minister, Sergei Kiriyenko, was himself numbered among the reformers who were foreign policy moderates. Indeed, when he was energy minister, he publicly stated that Russia was not opposed to the controversial oil pipeline route from Azerbaizhan through Georgia to the Turkish port of Ceyhan in the Mediterranean.[3] Yet the collapse of the Kiriyenko government in August 1998, before it had the opportunity to pursue serious domestic reforms, also meant an end to the moderation in Russian foreign policy. Putin has sidelined most of the reformers, although he did appoint Kiriyenko as one of his regional plenipotentiaries (see below).

Another very important group involved in the making of foreign policy under Yeltsin were the banking and media magnates known as oligarchs who have been in and out of government positions. Perhaps the most important of these was Boris Berezovsky who, as deputy secretary of the Russian Security Council (October 1996–November 1997) helped to finalize the agreement to end the first war in Chechnya. Vladimir Potanin, who served as deputy prime minister from July 1996 to March 1997, was allied to Berezovsky in 1996 in the effort to help reelect Yeltsin. He broke with Berezovsky during the summer of 1997 over the purchase of Rosneft, a major Russian oil company. Despite their divisions, the magnates had a similar philosophy that could be termed "make money, not war" and generally were supportive of a moderate foreign policy in which the pursuit of economic gain rather than geopolitical advantage was the main strategy. One of the main changes under Putin has been a crackdown on such oligarchs as Berezovsky and Vladimir Gusinsky, and he has greatly weakened their influence on policy making.

In addition to these influential nongovernmental groups, there are major government ministries in addition to the Foreign Ministry that have been active in making foreign policy. Included among these is the Russian Defense Ministry that played an important role in Russian policy toward both Tajikistan and the Armenian-Azeri conflict as well as in Russia's two wars with Chechnya. While the rapid turnover of defense ministers from 1995 to 1997 (Pavel Grachev to Igor Rodionov to Igor Sergeev) temporarily weakened the influence of the Defense Ministry, the second war in Chechnya, as well as the U.S.-Russian conflict over Kosovo, helped it regain influence—often at the expense of the Foreign Ministry. In December 1996, there was a major public disagreement between the Russian defense and foreign ministers over Iran. While Primakov was visiting Iran in an effort to bolster Russian-Iranian relations, then Russian defense minister Igor Rodionov was warning that Iran could be a military threat to Russia.[4] In addition, the movement of Russian forces into the Pristina airport in Kosovo also apparently caught the Foreign Ministry by surprise.

Yet the Russian military itself is badly divided over strategies to reform the armed forces, especially over the allocation of funds to the army versus to the strategic rocket forces, and this weakens their overall influence in Russian policy making under Putin.[5]

Another major actor under Yeltsin was the Russian arms sales agency, Rosvooruzheniye, which appeared to be willing to sell arms to any country in the world to make money, regardless of the political consequences, as in the case of the proposed SAM-300 sale to Cyprus that had the potential of precipitating a war between Russia and Turkey. Still, there were clear disagreements about Russian arms sale policy within the Russian establishment, as the then secretary of Russia's security council, Andrei Kokoshin, stated in 1998: "One of the main principles of the export of weapons should be the interest of our national security, our defense security, rather than commercial interests."[6] Putin has moved to bring arms sales under his direct control by combining Rosvooruzheniye with Promexport to form a new arms sales agency, Rosboronoexport.

Another important foreign policy force is the Ministry of Atomic Energy. It has been pushing the sale of Russian nuclear reactors throughout the world, and its efforts to sell nuclear technology to Iran have provoked a major clash between Russia and the United States.

Finally, in recent years, Russian regions and autonomous republics, such as Astrakhan and Tatarstan, have become increasingly important in Russian foreign policy, sometimes taking positions at variance with that of the Russian Foreign Ministry as in the case of the Muslim republics that backed the Turkish position on Cyprus.[7] To deal with this problem (among others), Putin has asserted control over the regions through the appointment of seven plenipotentiaries, five of whom have military or KGB backgrounds.

In sum, the Russian foreign-policy-making apparatus under Yeltsin was badly divided, something Russian observers were quick to note. Indeed, in commenting rather caustically on the multiple divisions in Russian foreign policy making, the Russian daily newspaper *Kommersant* stated: "It is impossible to pursue an integrated foreign and foreign economic policy today (in part) because Russia's political and economic elite, including its ruling elite, not only is not consolidated, but has split into competing, hostile factions, groups and groupings that are openly battling each other. It would be simply foolish for our foreign partners not to take advantage of this circumstance at any talks with Moscow."[8] Yeltsin's successor, Vladimir Putin, has sought to put an end to these divisions and thereby strengthen Russia's foreign policy stance. His success in this endeavor, however, remains to be seen, although he has made important strides in his first two years in office.

The Impact of Russia's Military and Economic Weakness

Traditionally, countries operating in the foreign policy arena have had two major instruments with which to pursue their foreign policy goals. First and foremost has been the threat or actual use of military force. Second, and increasingly important in the post–Cold War international environment has been the economic instrument, usually in the form of the granting of economic assistance or the denial of trade. A country's diplomacy ideally maximizes the utility of both foreign policy instruments. The problem that Moscow faces at the beginning of the twenty-first century is that both its military and economic instruments of foreign policy are very weak and there are very few resources to back Russian diplomacy, in the Middle East or elsewhere.

In the area of military power, despite still possessing an extensive—albeit deteriorating—array of nuclear weapons that are of limited utility in post–Cold War war crises, Russia has very little in the way of capability. The disastrous performance of the Russian army in the first Chechen war and its highly problematic performance in the second have shown just how weak the Russian armed forces have become. Indeed in mid-December 2000 Russia had to totally reorganize its military operations in Chechnya after suffering a number of stinging attacks by the Chechen rebels.[9] Despite efforts by Defense Minister Igor Sergeyev to reform the army, little progress was made. Under Yeltsin graft and corruption were endemic and there were numerous cases of soldiers and sailors not being paid for months at a time. Other problems limiting the Russian military's conventional capability to fight a war were its air force pilots' limited training in the air and the deterioration of much of the Russian army and navy's military equipment. Compounding the problem was a drop in spending on the Russian military under Yeltsin, estimated in 1999 by the Stockholm International Peace Research Institute (SIPRI) to have dropped by 30 percent per year since 1992.[10] While the dash of Russian paratroops to the Pristina airport in Kosovo at the start of the NATO peacekeeping effort there and Russian bomber forays to test U.S. defenses in Iceland and near the West Coast of the United States captured the headlines, they served primarily as a smokescreen for the decline of Russian military power under Yeltsin.

Putin has begun to shore up the Russian military in a number of ways. First he has decided to cut the number of civilian and military staff in the army by 600,000 people over the five-year period 2001–6. These numbers include 365,000 soldiers and sailors, 130,000 civilians, and 105,000 troops in other quasi-military forces such as Ministry of Interior troops,[11] border guards, and railway troops. Putin also appears to have begun to crack down on graft and corruption in the Russian military by indicting Col. General Georgi Olernik on suspicion of embezzling $450 million.[12] Perhaps most important of all Putin has moved to increase spending on the Russian military-industrial complex by 50 percent, hoping thereby to strengthen both Russia's military and its economy. Whether or not this proves successful remains an open question. Indeed, Putin appears still to be plagued by many of the same problems that beset Yeltsin. Thus the sinking of the Russian submarine *Kursk* may well have been caused by the lack of training of its crew, and Putin's mishandling of the crisis was widely criticized. Similarly, the Russian "buzzing" of the U.S. armada in the Sea of Japan on October 17, 2000, seemed to be another attempt to cover up Russian weakness by a showy maneuver.[13] More to the point, Putin's decision to cancel a major naval exercise in the Mediterranean following the *Kursk* incident demonstrated the real weakness of the Russian military.

If Russia has serious problems militarily, its economic strength is even more problematic. Even before the collapse of the ruble in August 1998, the Russian economy had been in sharp decline. In 1997, before the crisis, the Russian gross domestic product was only 58 percent of the 1989 figure, and economists of the European Bank of Reconstruction and Development have estimated that it declined another 3.5 percent in 1998.[14] While Russia continues to be the recipient of IMF loans—another sign of its economic weakness—it has yet to create a climate that fosters domestic investment, let alone one that would attract substantial foreign investment, because of fuzzy tax laws, local "partners" (some of whom are Mafia) who do not respect partnership agreements, and numerous other problems, including product counterfeiting and differences between the provincial and federal governments on taxation, regulation, and the protection of foreign investments.[15] Russia also suffers from a chronic problem of capital flight, with an estimated $100 billion having left Russia during Yeltsin's era. As if all these problems, along with deteriorating infrastructure and a continuing inability to collect taxes, were not enough, the Asian crisis of 1998 also struck a major blow at Moscow as some of Russia's Asian arms clients had to defer their purchases of Russian arms. Indeed arms sales, which along with oil are Russia's main exports, fell from a high of $5.3 billion in 1995 to only $2.3 billion in 1998, although with the Asian recovery arms sales rose to $4.1 billion in 1999.[16] Perhaps the only bright spots in the Russian economy—something that has greatly helped Putin—have been the rapid rise in oil prices in 1999 and 2000, giving Moscow a bit more breathing room, and the fact that the drop in the value of the ruble made many imports prohibitively costly, thus invigorating some Russian industries. Nonetheless, without serious structural reform, a problem Putin has only begun to work on, the Russian economy will remain in deep trouble, and Russia, dependent on aid from the United States, Western Europe, and Japan, may well remain a recipient of economic assistance, rather than a donor, as it was in the days of the USSR. This greatly restrains the ability of Moscow to have a serious influence on events in the Middle East, as well as elsewhere in the world. President Putin's plan to invest more heavily in Russia's military-industrial complex, while helpful to him politically, may not bode well for the health of the Russian economy as a whole.[17] Boris Yeltsin, in an interview with *Rossiskaya Gazeta* on May 13, 1998, acknowledged Russia's economic weakness, noting "Today's global centers of attraction stand because of their economic rather than military might." He went on to say that Russia had not inherited a solid economic foundation from the Soviet Union and that "redressing this abnormality is both a domestic and foreign political task."[18] The implications of Russian economic weakness were made clear in a February 14, 1998, *Izvestia* commentary on Moscow's inability to get the newly independent states of Central Asia and Transcaucasia to follow Moscow's lead on Caspian Sea oil policy: "Pressure can be used effectively only by those who have strength, economic, political and military strength. And, what is far more important, intellectual strength. Judging from the fact that the leaders of the Transcaucasus and Central Asia are more and more persistently bypassing Russia as they pave the way to the West for their countries and their resources, our country doesn't have that combination of strength. Trying to exert pressure without having strength makes one look ridiculous. An individual can afford to do this. But a state, never."[19]

Putin also recognized Russia's economic weakness. In a "State of the Federation" speech on July 8, 2000, calling for major economic reforms, he noted that despite "favorable external economic conditions" (high oil prices), Russia's economy was still weak and its growth was precarious.[20] The IMF was more blunt in its criticism, noting that Russia's progress in implementing structural reform has been disappointing despite improvements in its macroeconomic situation.[21] While Putin has pushed a tax code through the Duma, whether the tax laws can be enforced and other necessary legislation implemented remains an open question.

In the face of the divisions within the Russian foreign-policy-making establishment under Yeltsin, and Russia's severe military and economic weaknesses, Kozyrev, Primakov, and Primakov's successor as foreign minister, Alexander Ivanov, adopted two overall strategies. First, in order to achieve a modicum of cohesion in Russian foreign policy, it has been necessary for successive Russian foreign ministers to line up as many as possible of the quasi-independent actors, as well as the Duma, in favor of a particular policy. In the case of Russian policy toward both Iran and Iraq, they were able to build a consensus; in the case of Russian policy toward Turkey, however, the contradictions that existed during Kozyrev's era were exacerbated under Primakov. With a centralizing Putin as president, who gives every indication of preventing any challenges to his power, Ivanov may now find it easier to control Russian foreign policy.

A second strategy employed by Primakov and Ivanov in the face of Russia's economic and military weaknesses has been to seek allies with similar interests, such as France, so that Russia does not have to operate alone and can create, in the words of both Primakov and Putin, a multipolar world, not a unipolar world dominated by the United States. In some cases, as in Russian policy toward Iran, this strategy has met with success; in others, such as the Iraqi crisis of February 1998, it took the intervention of the UN secretary-general to save Russia from a possible diplomatic fiasco, a fate Russia was, however, to suffer ten months later, in December 1998, when it could not prevent a U.S.-British attack on Iraq. This chapter will now illustrate the dynamics of Russian policy toward the Middle East by examining four case studies.

Case Studies

Russia and Iran

The Yeltsin Era

Russian-Iranian relations began their rapid development in the late Gorbachev era. After supporting first Iran and then Iraq during the 1980–88 Iran-Iraq war, Gorbachev by July 1987 had clearly tilted to Iran. The relationship was solidified in June 1989 when the speaker of the Iranian parliament, Ali-Akbar Hashemi-Rafsanjani, visited Moscow and signed a number of major agreements, including one on military cooperation that permitted Iran to purchase highly sophisticated military aircraft from Moscow, including MIG-29s and SU-24s.[22] This Soviet equipment was very much needed at a time when the Iranian air force had been badly eroded by the Iran-Iraq war and by the refusal of the U.S. government to supply spare parts, let alone new planes, to replace losses to the aircraft it had sold the shah's regime.

The 1990–91 Gulf War increased Tehran's military dependence on Moscow. The war not only turned the United States, Iran's primary enemy after Iraq, into the leading military power in the Persian Gulf but also induced Saudi Arabia, then Iran's most important Islamic challenger and a Gulf rival, to acquire massive amounts of U.S. weaponry. In response, the pragmatic Rafsanjani, who had become president of Iran, was careful not to alienate Moscow. He ensured that Iran kept a low profile in both the Transcaucasus and Central Asia after the Russian republics in the two regions became independent in 1991, and promoted cultural and economic rather than Islamic relations in those regions. The Russian leadership appreciated Iran's restraint, which encouraged Moscow to continue supplying Iran with modern weaponry—including submarines—and to disregard strong protests about these arms sales from the United States.[23]

Relations between Iran and Moscow flourished in both the Kozyrev and Primakov periods, although they were not without their problems. Under Kozyrev, Russia went beyond selling arms to selling nuclear reactors, although in 1995 Yeltsin pulled back from selling Iran a gas centrifuge for its nuclear weapons development. The Russian leader also promised to end arms sales to Iran in 1999 when the 1989 contracts ran out.

Russian interests in Iran, however, went beyond the sale of arms and nuclear reactors. Yeltsin used the close relations with Tehran to demonstrate his independence of the United States to Russian nationalists in the Duma. In addition, Iran was seen as a major market for Russian oil and natural gas equipment. Despite U.S. protests, Gasprom, along with the French oil company Total and the Malaysian company Petromas, signed a major agreement with Iran in 1997 to develop the South Pars natural gas field.

From a diplomatic perspective, the close Russian-Iranian relationship helped both countries. Russian diplomatic support helped Iran against the dual-containment policy instituted by the United States against Iran (and Iraq) in 1993. For its part, Russia found Iran a very useful ally in a host of political hotspots near its southern borders during the Yeltsin era. During the first Chechen war, from 1994 to 1996, Iran kept a very low profile, despite the use by Chechen rebels of Islamic themes in their conflict with Moscow. In Tajikistan, Iran helped Russia bring an end to the 1992–97 civil war, although the peace settlement there remains shaky. In Afghanistan following the rise of the Taliban in 1996, both Iran and Moscow worked to prevent the Taliban's seizure of control over the whole country. Both Iran and Moscow have also worked to curb Azerbaizhan, which neither Iran (with a sizable Azeri population) nor Russia wishes to see become a powerful state in the Transcaucasus, and consequently both have opposed the Baku-Ceyhan oil pipeline. In addition, as NATO expands eastward and NATO member Turkey seeks to extend its influence in both the Transcaucasus and Central Asia, many in Russia see a close tie with Iran as a counterbalance.

Despite all of these factors promoting good relations, there were a number of problems in the Russian-Iranian relationship during the Yeltsin era, and some of those problems, along with several new ones, are confronting Putin. First, the Iranian economy has been very weak and Tehran has been hard put to repay Moscow for its economic and military exports. Indeed, by 1999, Iran's negative trade balance with Moscow had reached an estimated $2.5 billion.[24] Second, the two countries differ over the legal status of the Caspian Sea. Russia, which found significant oil in its sector of the Caspian, appears increasingly willing to divide the sea into national zones of economic exploitation and signed an agreement with Kazakhstan to partially divide the sea in 1998. For its part Iran, which has not yet found oil or natural gas in its sector of the sea, has called for an equal sharing of the sea's resources.[25]

A third problem is that Iran, since the mid-1990s, has increasingly pushed itself forward as the primary export route for Azeri and Central Asian oil and natural gas, thereby coming into direct conflict with an increasingly assertive Moscow, which has sought to control the oil and gas exports of Azerbaizhan, Kazakhstan, Uzbekistan, and Turkmenistan. While Iran has tried to defuse this problem by seeking to organize tripartite projects with Russia and the Central Asian states, the availability of an alternate Iranian export route remains a major problem for Moscow. If a rapprochement between Iran and the United States takes place, ending U.S. efforts to prevent foreign investment in Iran's oil and natural gas sector and in Iranian pipelines, this would create serious problems for Moscow because the least expensive and most secure route for Caspian Sea oil and natural gas to flow to foreign markets is through Iran.

It initially appeared that such a rapprochement would occur following the election of Mohammad Khatami as Iran's president in May 1997. Although Khatami began the process of rapprochement with the United States at the end of 1997, it was short-circuited by Iranian hard-liners during the summer of 1998. Moscow, however, fearing the rapprochement would continue, moved to solidify its ties with Iran. Yevgeny Adamov, head of Russia's Atomic Energy Ministry, visited Tehran in October 1998 and, to spur the lagging Bushehr nuclear reactor construction project, signed an agreement that transformed Bushehr into a "turnkey" project in which Russian technicians, rather than Iranian technicians, would build the project, with a target date for completion set for May 2003.[26]

The Putin Period

In the initial stages of the Putin period, relations between Iran and Russia appeared to be heading for difficulty because of Putin's role in the second Chechen war. The war erupted in September 1999, and Putin pursued it vigorously as the centerpiece of his administration, first as prime minister and then as Russia's president. Unlike the situation during the first Chechen war (1994–96), Iran was now the head of the Islamic Conference (OIC) and purported to seek the welfare of Muslims everywhere. During the Kosovo fighting, while Iran and Russia backed different sides, the issue never seriously strained Russian-Iranian relations. Chechnya, however, was to prove to be a different situation, particularly as stories of Russian soldiers massacring Chechen civilians began to leak out. The Iranian leadership, itself divided between reformists and conservatives, was on the horns of a dilemma. On the one hand it had important state-to-state interests in Russia, from the construction of the Bushehr nuclear reactor complex to the acquisition of sophisticated Russian military equipment. On the other hand, as the self-proclaimed defender of Muslims throughout the world and as the head of the Islamic Conference, Iran could not sit idly by while Russian troops slaughtered the Chechens, who were overwhelmingly Muslim. Consequently, while emphasizing that Chechnya was an internal affair of Russia, Iran gradually increased its criticism of Moscow's behavior. For its part, Moscow became increasingly critical of Iran, but just as Iran sought to play down the conflict, so too did Moscow, and the issue did not seriously harm Russian-Iranian relations.[27] This did not escape the attention of others in the Muslim world: The Saudi-owned London daily *al-Sharq al-Ansat* stated in an editorial on January 27, 2000, that Iran was guilty of "stabbing the Chechen Republic in the back" by continuing to emphasize that the Chechen war was an internal Russian affair.[28]

The overwhelming victory of moderate forces in the Majlis elections of February 2000 also had to be of concern to Moscow because for many of the reformers who were elected, an improvement in U.S.-Iranian relations (and the subsequent hoped-for improvement of the Iranian economy that would result once the United States removed economic sanctions) was an important policy goal.[29] Yet the moderate Parliament found itself checkmated by the conservative forces in the government and by the Iranian

supreme religious authority, Ayatollah Khameini, who opposed their reform efforts, and Iran's President Khatami has not yet been able to overcome them. Indeed, in a press conference at the United Nations in September 2000, Khatami urged the reformers in his country not to be impatient.
The Iranian president, evidently under pressure from Iranian conservatives, also attacked the United States for not "confessing" its involvement
in the coup that overthrew the Mossadegh regime in 1953, for its economic sanctions against Iran, and for U.S. opposition to the building of
pipelines through Iran from the Caspian. He also berated the United States
for its condemnation of Iran for the arrest and conviction of a group of ten
Iranian Jews as spies—a development that strained U.S.-Iranian relations.[30] The Iranian president, who had met Russian president Putin the
previous day, also stated that he hoped to forge a closer relationship with
Russia: "We share a lot of interests with Russia. We both live in one of the
most sensitive areas of the world. I believe the two countries can engage in
a viable and strong relationship. Russia needs a powerful and stable Iran.
A stronger relationship would allow both countries to marginalize external powers that are seeking destructive ends and which do not belong in
the region."[31]

The Khatami statement seemed to put aside, at least in the short run,
the possibility of a U.S.-Iranian rapprochement, although there was an
informal meeting of U.S. and Iranian parliamentarians during the UN
summit, and U.S. secretary of state Madeleine Albright and Iranian foreign minister Kamal Kharazzi participated in a UN meeting that sought to
end the civil war in Afghanistan.[32] Still, in a clear effort to reinforce Russia's relations with Iran, Moscow announced that Russia would build a
second reactor at the Bushehr complex[33] and that Russia would withdraw
from the 1995 agreement with the United States to cease selling arms to
Iran.[34] Russian defense minister Sergeev, perhaps in an attempt to pacify
the United States (the U.S. Congress was already furious with Russia for
the sale of missile technology to Iran), during a meeting of the Russian and
U.S. defense ministers in Brussels assured the United States that only "defensive" arms would be sold to Tehran.[35]

Nonetheless, despite Russian efforts to reinforce ties with Iran, if the
power of the conservative clergy in Iran weakens—and rising public discontent in Iran with the Islamic establishment seems to indicate such a
possibility—then a rapprochement with the United States may again become a strong possibility. Whether Putin can manage this situation without a serious erosion in Russian influence in Iran will be a test of his
diplomatic skills.

Russia and Iraq

The Yeltsin Period

During the Soviet years, Iraq was one of Moscow's primary allies, and the two states had signed a Treaty of Friendship and Cooperation in 1972. However, the Iraqi invasion of Iran, leading to the eight-year Iran-Iraq war, seriously disrupted Russian policy in the Middle East. This caused a chilling of relations, which cooled further when Russia tilted to Iran during the war.[36] Relations deteriorated further due to Gorbachev's support of the sanctions policy against Iraq following its invasion of Kuwait in August 1990, and although the Soviet leader sought to intercede on Iraq's behalf once the U.S.-led allied attack began on January 15, 1991, serious damage had been done to the Soviet-Iraqi relationship. Once the war ended at the end of February, the United States emerged as the dominant power in the Persian Gulf, much to the unhappiness of nationalists in the Soviet Union like Yevgeny Primakov, who saw their country's position in the Middle East erode badly.[37]

In the immediate aftermath of the Soviet Union's collapse, Yeltsin strengthened the anti-Iraqi policy of Gorbachev, not only voicing support for the sanctions against Iraq but also dispatching two warships to help enforce the anti-Iraqi embargo in the Persian Gulf. Although this pro-GCC, anti-Iraqi policy was followed by Yeltsin through 1992, the Russian leader soon ran into strong criticism. On the far right of the Russian political spectrum was Vladimir Zhirinovsky, who attacked Yeltsin for selling out Iraq, a Russian ally, and called for the unilateral lifting of sanctions on Iraq. More moderate, centrist Russians also questioned the wisdom of Russia's close cooperation with the United States on the embargo, given Iraq's $7 billion debt to Russia and its potential as a future market.

By January 1993 political pressure from the center and right of the Russian political spectrum began to have its effect on Yeltsin, a politician who always tacked with the political wind. At that time, Yeltsin began to attack the renewed U.S. bombing of Iraq (although the Russian Foreign Ministry, under the leadership of the then very pro-U.S. Andrei Kozyrev, initially supported the bombing). In addition, Yeltsin began to authorize visits to Iraq by Russian government ministers, and Iraqi ministers began to visit Moscow.

In October 1994, however, Russian policy toward Iraq suffered a major embarrassment. At that time, Saddam Hussein again moved his army toward Kuwait, an action that precipitated a massive U.S. reaction. President Clinton moved U.S. troops to Kuwait and warned Saddam not to invade. Yeltsin sought to exploit the situation by sending Kozyrev to Baghdad, where he claimed to have gotten Saddam Hussein's promise to pull back his troops and recognize Kuwait's border and sovereignty, in return for a gradual lifting of the sanctions. Not only was this deal rebuffed by the United States and Britain, it became a moot point because Iraq's parliament did not meet to recognize Kuwait and the Iraqi-Kuwait border. The end result of the crisis was a further strengthening of relations between the United States and the GCC states and a major embarrassment for Russia. The situation was not alleviated to any major degree when Kozyrev returned to Iraq in November and belatedly extracted the desired promises from the Iraqi parliament.

Despite this embarrassment, Moscow continued to pursue its policy of improving relations with Iraq. At the end of January 1995, an Iraqi parliamentary delegation visited Russia and was received by Prime Minister Chernomyrdin. Deputy Foreign Minister Posuvaliuk warned in February that unless the UN Security Council responded to Iraq's positive steps, the situation in the region would further deteriorate.[38] In August 1995 the Russian deputy foreign minister, who was also the country's highest-ranking Middle East specialist, also asserted that Russia was "doing more work than others to normalize Kuwait's relations with Iraq." (Kozyrev visited Kuwait on August 2, the fifth anniversary of the Iraqi invasion, to offer Kuwait reassurance.) He also noted that Iraq's "disarmament file is close to being closed and work on the biological file is proceeding in the same direction."[39]

Much to Russia's discomfort, however, the temporary defection of Saddam Hussein's son-in-law, Hussein Kamil, to Jordan led to Iraq's disclosure of hidden-weapons information. Perhaps seeking to make the best of the situation, a Russian Foreign Ministry spokesman said, "It is unimportant what considerations Iraq took into consideration in deciding to lift the previous veil of secrecy on military programs. In the end, not motives but the result plays a more important role." The spokesman went on to say that Moscow hoped that the reaction of Washington and of other Russian partners in the UN Security Council "will be adequate to Baghdad's new demonstration of readiness to fulfill the U.N. resolutions."[40] Neither the United States nor the GCC were persuaded by the Russian logic, however, and the sanctions remained in effect.

When Yevgeny Primakov, an old friend of Saddam Hussein, became Russia's foreign minister in January 1996, he stated that Russia would continue to observe the sanctions against Iraq and would not lift them unilaterally. Still, the advent of Primakov may have convinced Saddam

Hussein to begin to bargain in earnest with the United Nations for an oil-for-food agreement, an action he took one week after Primakov's appointment.[41] And, in order to help entice Russia into even more strongly backing the Iraqi position during the Security Council debates, Iraq made a multibillion dollar agreement with Moscow in mid-February 1996 for oil development and the training of Iraqi oil specialists.[42]

By the time Primakov became Russia's foreign minister, it was clear that Yeltsin had three major interests in developing Russia's relationship with Iraq. First, through international diplomatic activity, he wanted to demonstrate both to the world and to a hostile Duma that Russia was still an important factor in the world, despite its weakened condition, and was both willing and able to oppose the United States. The second interest Yeltsin's Russia had in Iraq was regaining the $7 billion Iraq owed to Russia, something that could not be achieved until sanctions against Iraq were lifted. The third interest in Iraq was in acquiring contracts for Russian factories and oil and gas companies, although the actual activities of these companies cannot begin until sanctions are lifted.

To spur the Russians to greater efforts to lift the sanctions, Saddam Hussein has cleverly dangled major contracts before influential Russian companies, such as Lukoil, that were part of a multibillion dollar agreement to develop the West Kurna oil field. The deal, reminiscent of the oil concessions when Iraq was a mandate of Britain, enabled Lukoil to keep 75 percent of the profit and also freed the company from paying Iraqi taxes.[43] Given the nature of this sweetheart deal, Lukoil has become a major factor in the Iraqi lobby in Moscow, pushing for the lifting of sanctions.

Primakov's behavior in both the October–November 1997 and January–February 1998 Iraqi crises clearly reflects Russian interests in Iraq. When U.S. weapons inspectors were expelled from Iraq and other UNSCOM inspectors left, the United States threatened to attack Iraq. Primakov, with dramatic flair, called U.S. Secretary of State Albright back from her visit to India, and met with her and other members of the UN Security Council at 2 A.M. in Geneva, Switzerland, on November 20, 1997. With the help of France, which also has major economic interests in Iraq and also opposed the U.S. use of force, he got their agreement to a deal whereby all the weapons inspectors, including the Americans, were allowed to return to Iraq in return for a vague promise to work for the lifting of sanctions. For the moment at least Primakov and Yeltsin could bask in international acclaim for averting a U.S. attack on Iraq. As Aleksei Pushkov, a correspondent for *Nezavisimaya Gazeta,* noted, "The denouement—perhaps a temporary one—of the latest crisis involving Iraq that was achieved by Primakov demonstrated the ability that Russia still has in world affairs, even in its current very weakened state."[44] Moscow's efforts to defuse the crisis indeed did prove short-lived; in January 1998 Saddam began backtracking on the agreement reached with Primakov by prohibiting inspections of his "palaces" and other sites where chemical and bacteriological weapons activities were suspected. As the United States and Britain massed military forces in the Persian Gulf and an attack on Iraq appeared imminent, Primakov again scurried to defuse the crisis, although this time the Russian diplomatic effort was far more disjointed than it had been in November 1997. First, with Deputy Foreign Minister Viktor Posuvaliuk in Baghdad, the Russian Foreign Ministry claimed it had reached a satisfactory agreement on inspection of the palaces, only to have that agreement immediately repudiated by Baghdad. Then, perhaps to regain the initiative for Moscow, Yeltsin himself seemed to take over leadership of the Russian diplomatic effort, threatening a world war if the United States bombed Iraq and pledging that Russia would not allow such an attack under any circumstances. Then he asserted that UN secretary-general Kofi Annan would go to Iraq, before Annan agreed to do so. While Annan was ultimately to go to Baghdad and negotiate an agreement satisfactory to both the United States and Iraq, it is clear that, unlike the November 1997 crisis, Russia had ceded the diplomatic initiative to the UN secretary-general. To be sure, Moscow benefited by the fact that Yeltsin's bluff was not called and by the Security Council's decision to allow Iraq to sell more oil, a decision that may enable Russia to get an early start in refurbishing Iraq's oil fields. Nonetheless, with all its diplomatic activity, Russia was very far from getting the sanctions lifted, and in the late fall of 1998, even its diplomatic efforts proved unable to prevent a U.S.-British attack on Iraq (at that point Yeltsin's bluff *was* called) when Saddam once again interfered with the weapons inspection process. Indeed, Russia could only stand by, fulminating, while the United States and Britain carried out air strikes against Iraq in late December.

The U.S.-British attack came at a bad time for Moscow. The August 1998 economic crisis had been a major blow to Moscow, which not only devalued the ruble but also had to default on a number of loans. Meanwhile Iraq was still pressuring Russia to take a more active role in pushing for the lifting of sanctions, and in July 1999 Iraq issued a warning to Lukoil that it could lose its contract to develop the Qurna-2 oil field unless it began work there.[45] This was the situation that greeted Vladimir Putin when he took over as Russia's prime minister in August 1998.

Putin, Iraq, and UNMOVIC

Putin's strategy was to work through the United Nations for a new Security Council resolution on Iraq, one that would make it easier to lift the sanctions but at the same time not alienate the United States, which remained strongly opposed to changing the sanctions regime. Consequently, after extensive haggling with the United States and despite the visit to Moscow of Iraqi deputy prime minister Tariq Aziz, who called on Moscow to veto the resolution then under discussion, Russia chose not to exercise its veto on the new Security Council resolution. The resolution, 1284, on which Russia, along with France, China, and Malaysia abstained, set up a new UN inspection agency, the United Nations Monitoring, Verification, and Inspection Commission (UNMOVIC) to replace UNSCOM. The resolution required that Iraq provide "unrestricted access and provision of information," and allow UNMOVIC teams "immediate, unconditional, and unrestricted access to any and all areas, facilities, equipment records and means of transport they wish to inspect." The resolution also reiterated Iraq's obligation to repatriate all Kuwaiti and third-country nationals whom it held and requested the UN secretary-general to report to the council every four months on Iraq's compliance with this part of the resolution. The resolution also held out some potential benefits for Iraq, including permission for *Hajj* pilgrimage flights; removal of the ceiling on the amount of oil Iraq could sell; possible increases in the amounts of oil, spare parts, and equipment to be imported (also of benefit to Russian oil companies), following an evaluation of Iraq's existing petroleum production and export capacity; and, more important, following reports from the executive chairman of UNMOVIC and the director general of the International Atomic Energy Agency (IAEA) that Iraq had cooperated in all respects with UNMOVIC and the IAEA, suspension of sanctions on the importing of civilian goods to Iraq for a 120-day period that would be renewable.[46]

Despite the efforts of Iraqi diplomacy, the sanctions resolution passed and Iraq continued to find itself isolated in world affairs. Possibly for this reason, only a few days after the passing of the resolution, Iraq agreed to go ahead with a $419 million deal with the Russian firm Technoprom Export to resume construction of a large power station that had been interrupted by the invasion of Kuwait and the sanctions regime.[47] In making this move Baghdad may have hoped that the somewhat looser regulations of UN Security Council Resolution 1284 and its emphasis on the humanitarian needs of the Iraqi people might enable Iraq to import the previously banned equipment. Indeed, despite the Iraqi rejection of

UNMOVIC, much depended on whom the UN would select for its chairman. Russia vehemently opposed Rolf Ekeus (who was supported by the United States), the first UNSCOM chairman who had been nominated by UN secretary-general Kofi Annan. The United States ultimately acquiesced in the second nominee, Hans Blix, the former head of the International Atomic Energy Agency.[48] Blix had been severely criticized for not discovering Iraq's efforts to develop nuclear weapons before 1990, and it remained to be seen if he would prove a more vigorous inspector as head of UNMOVIC. The selection of Blix may be seen as a small victory for Russia—and Iraq. Additionally, Blix's comment that his inspection teams would not force their way into suspected weapons sites in Iraq but would defer to UN headquarters to resolve any confrontations must have been good news for both Russia and Iraq, since such a procedure would weaken the inspection process.[49] Moscow won another small victory when its former ambassador to the UN, Yuli Vorontsov, was chosen as UN undersecretary-general with responsibility for solving the problem of the 600 missing Kuwaiti prisoners from the Gulf War, although, depending on how aggressively Vorontsov, a diplomat with extensive Middle East experience, pursued his mandate, a degree of friction with Iraq was a possible outcome of the appointment. Nonetheless, Iraq's unwillingness to accept UNMOVIC inspectors or even allow Vorontsov into Iraq to check on the missing prisoners, coupled with the U.S. unwillingness to push UNMOVIC when Blix said his inspectors were ready,[50] made the UN operation by September 2000 appear to be a dead letter. In these circumstances Russia began to whittle around the edges of the sanctions by supporting humanitarian flights to Baghdad and suggesting that Iraq might be more amenable to the lifting of sanctions if the United States and Britain stopped their flights to police their self-proclaimed no-fly zones in Iraq.[51]

Nonetheless, Russia's basic dilemma with Iraq continued, one that now faces Putin, as it had Yeltsin. A unilateral move to lift sanctions would cause a very serious crisis in U.S.-Russian relations, relations already badly strained by the war in Chechnya and the NATO intervention in Kosovo. Russia has to both convince the United States to moderate its position on Iraq and convince Iraq to agree to Security Council Resolution 1284 linking the suspension of sanctions to renewed international inspection of suspected Iraqi weapons of mass destruction sites. Perhaps an even worse result of a unilateral lifting of sanctions, from Putin's perspective, would be a grave weakening of the United Nations at a time when Moscow has sought to use the international organization to curb U.S. power.[52] It is questionable whether Moscow would be willing to absorb these costs to satisfy a problematic ally like Iraq, particularly in the post–September 11 period, when Putin has sought to improve Russia's ties to the United States.

Russia and Turkey

The Kozyrev Era

Unlike Russian-Iranian or even Russian-Iraqi relations, where the majority of key Russian foreign policy actors support close relations, thus making first Kozyrev's and then Primakov's and then Ivanov's stewardship of the relationship a relatively easy task, in the case of Turkey, there were sharp disagreements that until 1999 seriously hampered the Foreign Ministry's efforts to manage a coherent policy. On the one hand, Russia has numerous interests in pursuing a good relationship with Turkey. First, until the 1998 economic collapse, trade (including the so-called "suitcase trade") between the two countries was in the range of $10–$12 billion a year, making Turkey Russia's main trading partner in the Middle East. Not only are Turkish construction companies active throughout Russia, even acquiring the contract for repair of the Duma, damaged by the fighting in 1993, but there is also a large flow of Russian tourists to Turkey, especially to Istanbul and Antalya, and Turkish merchants donated $5 million to Yeltsin's reelection campaign in 1996.[53] Second, Turkey is a major purchaser of natural gas from Russia, thus giving Gasprom a strong incentive to promote Russian-Turkish relations. Third, Turkey purchases military equipment from Russia, including helicopters that had been embargoed by some NATO countries (including, until recently, the United States) because of concern that they would be used in Turkey's ongoing conflict with its Kurdish minority.

On the other hand, there are serious problems in the relationship. First, Turkey is competing for influence with Russia in the Near Abroad, especially in Transcaucasia and Central Asia. Second, Turkey, supported by the United States, is pushing an oil export route for Azeri oil that would go through Georgia and Turkey to its Mediterranean port of Ceyhan rather than to the Russian port of Novorossisk via Chechnya. In addition, concerned about the ecological dangers of supertankers going through the Bosporus and Dardanelles, Turkey has sought to limit such traffic, thereby leading Russia to threaten to build an alternate pipeline route from the Black Sea through Bulgaria and Greece, until 1999 a major enemy of Turkey. Third, Russia has complained that the Turks were active in aiding the Chechen rebellions and thereby threatened Moscow's control of the

North Caucasus, while for its part, Turkey condemned Russian support for the terrorist PKK. Underlying the tension in the Russian-Turkish relationship are memories of centuries of confrontation as the expanding Russian empire came into conflict with an Ottoman empire on the decline.[54] Turkey is also uneasy about the growing Russian military presence in Armenia, near Turkey's northeastern border.

When the Soviet Union collapsed, Turkish president Turgut Ozal and some of the Turkish elite saw an opportunity to expand Turkish influence into Azerbaizhan and throughout Central Asia. This would enhance Turkey's post–Cold War relationship with the United States as Turkey could serve as a bulwark against Iranian-inspired Islamic radicalism. Ozal's initial optimism led him to pledge more than $1 billion in credits for the newly independent Central Asian states in such areas as banking, education, and transportation. In addition, Turkey established direct air communications with the region;[55] Turkish television beamed programs to the Turkic-speaking countries of the former Soviet Union; and Turkish businessmen established numerous joint ventures in the new countries.

In February 1992, two months after the collapse of the Soviet Union, James Baker, secretary of state of the United States, Turkey's main ally, paid a visit to Central Asia. *Pravda* complained that Baker was doing more there than the entire Russian Foreign Ministry. It warned that the United States was drawing the Islamic states of the former Soviet Union both into the orbit of U.S. policy and into the U.S. view of the world—away from Russia, "their closest neighbor and natural ally."[56] The U.S. actions were linked by the Russian right to America's NATO ally, Turkey. Because of its Turkic culture and linguistic ties to Azerbaizhan, Uzbekistan, Turkmenistan, Kyrgyzstan, and Kazakhstan, Turkey was seen as seeking to create a Turkic alliance on the southern periphery of Russia by using such devices as the Black Sea Economic Cooperation Zone, which it created.[57] This Russian concern, despite the signing of a Treaty of Friendship with Turkey in May 1992,[58] was not baseless; the late Turkish president Turgut Ozal had noted in March 1993: "Whatever the shape of things to come, we will be the real elements and most important pieces of the status quo and new order to be established in the region from the Balkans to Central Asia. In this region, there cannot be a status quo or political order that will exclude us."[59]

While some in Moscow feared Turkish political expansion, others saw the secular Islamic model of Turkey as a useful counterweight to Iranian Islamic radicalism.[60] They were initially concerned by the threat of fundamentalist Islam emanating from Iran, which could infect not only the

Muslim states of the former Soviet Union but also the Muslims who live in Russia.

By 1993 the Russian leadership was taking a calmer view of both the threat of Islamic radicalism in Central Asia (the rise of the Taliban in Afghanistan and the second Chechen war were later to reawaken that concern) and the danger of Turkish competition in the region. While Turkish assistance was welcomed by the leaders of Central Asia and Azerbaizhan, it did not lead to the rapid expansion of Turkish influence. In the first place, having just rid themselves of one "big brother," the Central Asians had no desire for another, and they sought to maximize their ties with a number of states in order to avoid dependence on any one.[61] The economic problems of these states (with the partial exception of Turkmenistan) were great: rapid inflation, overpopulation, underemployment, water shortages, severe ecological damage, and more. Turkey simply did not have the economic capacity to meet their needs, especially as its own economy was reeling from a 70 percent annual inflation rate. Another factor was the resurgence of the Kurdish uprising, which diverted Turkish attention from Central Asia and the Armenian-Azerbaizhani war to more pressing needs at home. Similar concerns of Turkish policymakers were the fighting in the former Yugoslavia, pitting Bosnian Muslims, diplomatically supported by Turkey, against Serbs (supported by Russia) and, initially, Croats; and the continuing conflict with Greece over Cyprus.[62] The death of President Ozal, ironically just after he had completed a tour of Central Asia in March 1993, also seemed to weaken Turkish efforts to gain influence in the region, and Turkish leaders had to be disappointed that the Central Asian Muslim leaders did not back the Turkish position on such issues as Cyprus.

During the 1992–95 period, while the two states were competing in Transcaucasia and Central Asia, their bilateral relations were mixed. On the positive side both countries now shared a desire to lift sanctions against Iraq.[63] In addition, the Russians, long interested in gaining markets for their weaponry, signed arms sale agreements with Turkey. Russia provided helicopters and combat vehicles in partial repayment of the debt of the former Soviet Union to Turkey, which Moscow inherited.[64] Ironically, at a time when Turkey was under fire from its NATO allies for its repressive acts against the Kurds, Russia had thus become an important, if only partial, substitute arms supplier. Moscow, however, was not above using the Kurdish issue to pressure Turkey. For instance, in February 1994, as the Kurdish rebellion was heating up, Russia hosted The History of Kurdistan conference, which was cosponsored by an organization affiliated with the PKK—an action protested by the Turkish Foreign Ministry.[65] For its part Russia was unhappy about what it saw as Turkish aid to the Chechen rebels in the first Chechen war.[66] Yet another area of conflict between Ankara and Moscow was the Russian effort to increase the number of heavy weapons it could station in the Northern Caucasus under the CFE (Conventional Forces in Europe) treaty by claiming instability in Georgia, Armenia, and Azerbaizhan, something Turkey strongly opposed.[67]

On the other hand, trade, including the suitcase trade, rose to an estimated $10 billion by 1995. Turkish construction companies became active throughout Russia and, as noted above, even secured the contract to repair the Duma building, damaged in the conflict between Yeltsin and Parliament, and Turkey became a favorite vacation spot for Russian tourists.[68] Thus when Primakov became Russia's foreign minister in January 1996, he faced a decidedly mixed bag as he sought to forge Russia's policy toward Turkey. Unfortunately for Primakov, until January 1999, several months before he was to step down as prime minister (having been given that post by Yeltsin in September 1998 as Russia's economic crisis intensified), Russia's policy appeared to become even more confused than it had been in the 1992–95 period.

The Primakov Era

In looking at Russian-Turkish relations in the 1996–98 period, it often appeared that Russia's right hand did not know, or worse, perhaps did not care what its left hand was doing. Thus, in January 1997, the Russian arms firm Rosvooruzheniye, involved in selling helicopters to Turkey to help suppress its Kurdish rebellion even as the Russian foreign minister had been flirting with Kurdish nationalists by allowing formal Kurdish conferences in Moscow, agreed to sell a sophisticated surface-to-air missile system, the SAM-300-PMU-1, to the Greek Cypriot government on the divided island of Cyprus. While the Greek Cypriots claimed that the missiles would be there only to defend their section of the island against the Turks who occupy the northern section, the 100-mile range of the missiles reached into southern Turkey and if deployed would seriously complicate Turkish air maneuverability. Turkey took the threat of these missiles so seriously that it inspected, on various pretexts, ships going through the Bosporus and Dardanelles and warned that it would not allow the missiles to be deployed.

While tensions were rising between Turkey and Russia in the political-military arena, they were improving on the economic front. Gasprom chief Rem Vekhirev told Itar-Tass on November 3, 1997, that Gasprom would build a natural gas pipeline under the Black Sea from Russia to Turkey (the "Blue Stream" project) and would increase the supply of gas to Turkey from 3 billion cubic meters per year in the year 2000 to 16 billion cubic meters per year in the year 2010, thus providing Turkey with about half of its expected natural gas needs.[69] Viktor Chernomyrdin, then still prime minister, came to Turkey in mid-December 1997 to finalize the pipeline deal and also signed a series of other agreements. In an important political agreement, the two countries agreed to abstain from actions likely to harm the economic interests of either of them or threaten their territorial integrity.[70] If taken literally, that would mean Russia would not interfere with the construction of the Baku-Ceyhan pipeline, if that route is selected as the main oil export route from Azerbaizhan, and there were rumors that Turkey would hire Russian companies to help build the pipeline to Ceyhan. Nonetheless, despite the good feelings engendered by the natural gas agreement and the Chernomyrdin visit, there was no movement by the Turks to lift the limits on tanker traffic through the straits and, despite rumors to the contrary, no promise by Russia to drop the missile sale to Cyprus. Indeed, at the end of January 1998, Primakov stated that Russia intended to honor the deal in the absence of an agreement on the demilitarization of Cyprus—something the Turks were very unlikely to agree to.[71] Clearly, if the missile deal were to have proceeded and the Turks made good on their threats to destroy the missiles—possibly killing a number of Russian technicians in the process—a serious blow would have been dealt to Russian-Turkish relations. Fortunately for the future of the relationship and for overall stability in the Middle East, the Russian economic crisis intervened and in 1999 Moscow chose cooperation over confrontation with Turkey even as Russian trade with Turkey dropped precipitously because of the Russian economic crisis. On the question of deploying the SAM-300, Greece, under heavy U.S. pressure, chose to deploy the missiles in Crete rather than in the Greek area of Cyprus to which Greece was allied in an air defense agreement.[72] As noted above, Moscow, through statements by Primakov, had gone out on a limb in advocating the deployment of the missiles on Cyprus, together with Russian technical and air defense personnel, as a Cold War type of geopolitical move against the United States in the Mediterranean. However, a weakened Moscow did not have the political clout to reverse the Greek decision and acquiesced in the deployment of the missiles on Crete. While Turkey was not pleased by the Crete deployment, it was far less objectionable to Ankara than a deployment on the volatile island of Cyprus would have been.

Moscow was to suffer another blow in 1999 in what appeared to be its efforts to create a geopolitical bloc on its southern border that would have been pitted against Turkey. During the period Primakov was foreign minister, it appeared as if Russia was seeking to put together an alignment, if not an alliance, of itself, Iran, Armenia, Syria, and Greece—all of whom were to a greater or lesser degree in conflict with Turkey—that would be opposed not only to Turkey but also to its ally Israel in what was emerging as a de facto alignment of the United States, Turkey, Israel, Azerbaizhan, and Georgia. Russia suffered a major blow to its hoped-for alignment when Greece and Turkey began to improve relations. After being embarrassed by its involvement in protecting Kurdish terrorist leader Abdullah Öcalan, Greece moved to improve ties with Turkey and took the opportunity to help Turkey in the aftermath of the very severe earthquake that hit Turkey in August 1999.[73] When an earthquake hit Greece three weeks later, a Turkish rescue team reciprocated the Greek gesture by coming to Greece's aid. As relations warmed, Greece in early September made a major step toward improving relations with Turkey by removing its objection to Turkey's entry into the European Union.[74] The Greek gesture, coupled with some movement by the Turks to improve the treatment of their Kurdish minority, helped lead to an EU invitation to Turkey to apply for membership. Meanwhile, Greek-Turkish relations continued to improve rapidly and, during a visit by Greek foreign minister George Papandreou (who had replaced the anti-Turkish Theodoros Pangolos) to Turkey, the two states signed a series of agreements including cooperating in fighting organized crime, preventing illegal immigration, promoting tourism, protecting the Aegean environment, and protecting investments. The two countries also agreed to begin direct talks on reducing military tension in the Aegean. Turkish foreign minister Ismail Cem even raised the possibility of joint maneuvers in the Aegean, and an influential Turkish retired admiral, Guven Erkaya, recommended the disbanding of Turkey's 100,000-man Aegean army facing Greece.[75] The two countries, under U.S. prodding, also began discussions on the very difficult problem of Cyprus, and, as the rapprochement continued, observers began to recall the period of warm détente in the 1930s between Atatürk and Venizelos.[76]

As these events proceeded and as its diplomatic position in the Middle East weakened and its economy further deteriorated, Russia moved to improve ties with Turkey and moved from a confrontational to a cooperative posture. When the PKK leader Abdullah Öcalan was smuggled into Russia after his expulsion from Syria in 1998, the then hard-line Russian Duma voted 298 to nothing to grant him asylum.[77] Primakov, however, was not willing at this point to anger Turkey, and the PKK leader was forced to leave Russia, a departure praised by the Turkish ambassador.[78] The two countries also moved closer to solving their dispute over CFE limits on Russian forces near the Turkish border and even somewhat moderated their hostility over Turkey's policy in the straits.[79] The centerpiece of the improved relations, however, was the Blue Stream natural gas project as Russia sought to preempt competing natural gas pipeline agreements between Turkmenistan and Turkey that involved either a controversial pipeline across the Caspian or the routing of Turkmen natural gas to Turkey via Iran, or both. In 1999 Moscow also suddenly found a new natural gas competitor, Azerbaizhan, where a major gas field was discovered.

Putin and Turkey

Faced by a very difficult economic situation and pursuing an increasingly difficult war against the Chechens, Putin not only continued Primakov's policies of cooperation with Turkey, but carried them further. First, in the face of international competition Putin stepped up Russian support for the Blue Stream project. Thus in early December 1999 he got the Russian parliament to approve $1.5 billion in tax breaks for the construction of Blue Stream (although financing still remained a problem), and Gasprom and ENI signed a contract for the construction of the underwater section of the pipeline.[80] This led Turkish minister of energy Cumhur Ersumer to note that Russia had pulled ahead in the race to supply natural gas to Turkey.[81] Cooperation intensified in late October 2000 when Russian prime minister Mikhail Kasyanov journeyed to Turkey where he signed a number of agreements. Kasyanov made clearer than ever before Russia's policy change toward Turkey with his statement, "Our main mutual conclusion is that Russia and Turkey are not rivals but partners and our governments will from now on proceed from this understanding."[82] Kasyanov also pledged that Blue Stream gas would flow to Turkey by the fall of 2001 and also promised to increase natural gas supplies to Turkey through other routes during the late fall and early winter of 2000–2001.[83] Moscow, in an effort to get a major military contract from Turkey, also cut the price it was charging for the new Russian-Israeli KA-50 combat helicopter to come in well below the U.S. Bell King Cobra helicopter that Turkey was considering purchasing from the United States.[84] The two countries also promised to step up cooperation of their law enforcement and secret police forces in the war against terrorism and stated it was their goal to increase trade to the $10 billion per year level it had attained before the Russian economic collapse of August 1998.[85]

Despite this marked effort by Russia to improve relations with Turkey, a number of important problems complicated the rapprochement. First, the increasingly close military ties between Russia and Armenia, although primarily directed against Azerbaizhan, were also worrying to Turkey. Nonetheless, Ankara had to take satisfaction over the agreement reached with Moscow at the meeting of the Organization of Security and Cooperation (OSCE) in Istanbul in November 1999 under which Russia agreed to pull all of its 2,600 troops out of Moldova by 2002 and to dismantle two of its four bases in Georgia by 2001. That agreement also stipulated that a state cannot deploy forces in another state without the host country's consent, a provision aimed at protecting such countries as Azerbaizhan.[86] Still, Russia had more offensive military equipment on its southern flank than the CFE permitted—something that greatly concerned Turkey—so Turkey and the United States stated they would not present the revised CFE pact to their legislatures for ratification until Moscow came into compliance with the treaty.[87] Second, the Baku-Ceyhan project was also moving ahead. The rise in the price of oil and Turkey's increased willingness to financially support construction of the project made the pipeline a more desirable undertaking for the oil companies extracting petroleum from the Caspian Sea.[88] Should this project be completed—it received a strong endorsement at the OSCE meeting in Istanbul in mid-November 1999 and a feasibility study was approved in October 2000—it would reinforce Turkey's relations with Azerbaizhan and Georgia and further weaken the Russian position in the Southern Caucasus, as well as in Kazakhstan from which part of the oil for the Baku-Ceyhan pipeline would have to come, unless oil as well as gas was found in Azerbaizhan's new natural gas field.

Turkey also stepped up its activity in Central Asia in the fall of 2000, as its new president, Ahmet Necdet Sezer, not only visited Uzbekistan, Kyrgyzstan, Kazakhstan, and Turkmenistan but also sent two planeloads of arms and ammunition to Uzbekistan to help it combat Islamic insurgents.[89] This came into direct conflict with Russia's efforts to use the threat of Islamic fundamentalism in the region reflected by the emergence of the Islamic Movement of Uzbekistan, which was reportedly aided by the Taliban, to bring the Central Asian states more under its control. In addition, although Russia and Turkey had come somewhat closer on the issue of the straits, Turkey continued to warn about overcrowding of the straits by oil tankers and other vessels, and accidents reinforced the Turkish argument that the Baku-Ceyhan pipeline was the safest way to transport Caspian Sea oil.[90] Finally, Turkey was uneasy about the Russian military build-up in the North Caucasus as a result of the Chechen war and had embarked on its own military building-up.

In sum, despite these continuing challenges from Turkey, for the time being both Yeltsin and Putin, realizing Russia's economic weakness, have chosen the path of economic cooperation rather than geopolitical confrontation with Turkey.

Russia and Israel

The Yeltsin Period

The Russian-Israeli relationship, like the Russian-Turkish relationship, reflects a conflict between Russian economic interests seeking a good relationship with Israel and Russian hard-liners and geopoliticians who seek benefits for Russia out of the Arab-Israeli conflict. Unlike the case of Russian-Turkish relations, however, the geopolitical advocates did not come to the fore until Primakov, an advocate of close Russian-Arab relations, became foreign minister, and they receded somewhat when Putin became Russia's president. Russia has a number of interests in Israel. First, on the economic front, there is extensive trade, crossing the $500 million mark in 1995 (although it would later dip because of Russia's 1998 economic crisis), making Israel Russia's second leading trade partner in the Middle East after Turkey. Second, on the diplomatic front, a close relationship with Israel enables Russia to play, or appear to play, a major role in the Arab-Israeli peace process. Third, with almost a million Russian-speaking Jews now living in Israel, Israel has the largest Russian-speaking diaspora outside the former Soviet Union, and this has led to very significant ties in the areas of cultural exchange and tourism. The fourth major interest is a military-technical one as the Russian military-industrial complex has expressed increasing interest in coproducing military aircraft with Israel. This is of special interest because many of the workers in Israel's aircraft industry are former citizens of the Soviet Union with experience in the Soviet military-industrial complex.

From the Israeli point of view, there are four central interests in relations with Russia. The first is to maintain the steady flow of immigration, which has provided Israel with a large number of scientists and engineers. The second interest is to prevent the export of nuclear weapons or nuclear materials to Israel's Middle East enemies, including Libya, Iran, and Iraq. The third goal is to develop trade relations with Russia, which supplies Israel with such products as uncut diamonds, metals, and timber. Russia is also the site of numerous joint enterprises begun by Israelis who had emigrated from the former Soviet Union. Finally, Israel hopes for at least an even-handed Russian diplomatic position in the Middle East and, if possible, Russian influence on its erstwhile ally, Syria, to be more flexible in reaching a peace agreement with Israel.

During Kozyrev's period as Russia's foreign minister, there were relatively few diplomatic-political disputes, although Israel expressed displeasure at Russian arms sales to Iran, which Israel considers an enemy. When disputes between Israel and its Arab neighbors took place, as over Lebanon, Russia under Kozyrev took a very even-handed approach and was a strong supporter of the Oslo I and Oslo II accords and the peace treaty between Israel and Jordan in 1994. However, after Primakov took over as foreign minister, Russia became far more critical of Israeli activities, whether in Lebanon when Shimon Peres was prime minister or toward the Palestinians after Netanyahu took control of the Israeli government. As the Israeli-Palestinian peace process floundered under Netanyahu, Primakov thrust Russia forward both as a mediator—to gain world recognition for Russia's increased diplomatic role, just as he did during the Iraqi crises—and to reduce Arab dependence on the United States, which was perceived by many Arabs as siding too closely with Israel. The result was a chilling of Russian-Israeli political relations.[91]

Initially, when Benjamin Netanyahu became Israel's prime minister after defeating Shimon Peres in the May 1996 Israeli elections, there was hope for an improvement in Russian-Israeli relations. In 1997 both Netanyahu and Yisrael B'Aliyah leader Natan Sharansky, a former refusenik (a Soviet Jew denied permission to emigrate), made successful visits to Moscow with Netanyahu giving Russia a $50 million agricultural credit and discussing the purchase of Russian natural gas. There were also agreements in the military sphere as Russian and Israeli firms signed an agreement to coproduce an AWACS aircraft; in addition, there was a joint proposal to provide advanced helicopters to Turkey.[92] The Israeli food manufacturer TNUVA also filmed a "milk in space" commercial aboard the Russian space station Mir,[93] and there were frequent visits back and forth of security officials (including Vladimir Putin) as the two countries stepped up their cooperation against crime and terrorism.

But by the end of 1997 and throughout 1998 relations again soured. Netanyahu canceled further discussion of the natural gas deal because of the Russian supply of missile technology to Iran; Russia expressed (as did the United States) its unhappiness with Netanyahu's policy toward the Palestinians; the economic collapse of August 1998 in Russia damaged Russian-Israeli trade; and the rise in Russian anti-Semitism that coincided with Primakov's elevation to the post of prime minister in September 1998 also hurt relations.

The situation was to change once more at the beginning of 1999. With an Israeli election campaign under way, Netanyahu suddenly changed his position on Russia. Acting on the (mistaken) supposition that if Israel improved its relations with Russia, he would win the votes of Russian immigrants in a hotly contested election, Netanyahu not only supported Russia's quest for additional IMF aid, but through his foreign minister Ariel Sharon actually questioned, as had the Russians, the NATO intervention in Kosovo.[94] Primakov (who was soon to be deposed by Yeltsin) responded to the Israeli initiative by letting it be known that he was hoping for a Netanyahu victory;[95] subsequently, Russian foreign minister Igor Ivanov advised Arafat against proclaiming a Palestinian state on May 4, 1999, a major concern of Israel at the time.[96] The ploy by Netanyahu failed, however, as the Russian immigrant voters voted their local concerns—particularly concerns about their religious status in Israel—and supported Netanyahu's opponent, Ehud Barak.[97]

The Putin Period

Several months after Barak's election Putin became Russia's prime minister and quickly became deeply involved in the war against Chechnya—a development that was to positively affect Russian-Israeli relations. Barak met Putin in Oslo and raised with him, as he had with Yeltsin on a trip to Moscow in early August, the dual Israeli concerns about the sale of Russian military technology to Iran and the rise in anti-Semitism in Russia. While Putin was not to be responsive on the issue of arms to Iran, he was far more forthcoming in denouncing anti-Semitism than Yeltsin was (although he did not go as far as some Russian Jewish leaders wanted).[98] Nonetheless, his conflict with Vladimir Gusinsky, an oligarch who was also a leader of the Russian Jewish community, became an issue not only for Russian Jews but also for Russian-Israeli relations.[99]

In the period before the outbreak of the al-Aqsa intifada at the end of September 2000, there was a series of ups and downs in Russian-Israeli relations. Israel, despite its displeasure with Russian arms sales to Iran, asked Moscow to intervene in the case of the imprisoned Iranian Jews, and Moscow did so, although the effectiveness of the Russian intervention is not clear.[100] On the other hand, to please the United States on the eve of the Camp David II summit with the Palestinians, Israel unilaterally canceled the sale of the joint Israeli-Russian AWACS plane to China, something Moscow did not like.[101] But the issue of greatest importance to the relationship, at least from the Russian point of view, was Israeli support for Russian actions in Chechnya, with one Russian official stating that "Israel helps us break the Western information blockade of Russia over Chechnya."[102] Israel also helped Russia by sending medical supplies to the victims of the Moscow apartment house bombings claimed by Putin to have been perpetrated by the Chechens and also gave medical treatment to wounded Russian soldiers. Israeli help to Moscow over Chechnya was to pay diplomatic dividends when the al-Aqsa intifada broke out in late September 2000, when Putin took a very different position than did Primakov during similar crises in the 1996–99 period. Unlike the Russian position under Primakov, Putin's Russia was not only evenhanded, but he seemed to tilt to Israel as the crisis developed. Thus the secretary of the Russian Security Council, Sergei Ivanov, linked the violence on the West Bank and Gaza to the Taliban's increased activities in Afghanistan and Central Asia and to extremist activity in Chechnya, a position also espoused by Putin's adviser Sergei Yastrzhembsky. The Russian Duma, unlike its anti-Israel and anti-Semitic predecessor that went out of office in December 1999, took a very evenhanded position, voting 275 to 1 to blame not Israel but "extremist forces" for the escalation of the conflict,[103] and Putin himself called on both Barak and Arafat to take "decisive measures" to put an end to the violence, normalize the situation, and restore a direct dialogue.[104] When Arafat journeyed to Moscow in late November 2000, he may have been seeking to shift Moscow to the anti-Israeli position of the Primakov period. If so, he was to be sorely disappointed. The expected three-day visit lasted only a few hours, and Putin, who had been excluded from the U.S.-sponsored Sharm el-Sheikh summit and who used Arafat's visit to show that Moscow was still a factor in world affairs, reiterated his evenhanded position urging both Arafat and Barak to resume their dialogue and even arranged a three-way telephone conversation to get Barak and Arafat talking again, albeit this lasted only for a brief period.[105] Moscow also abstained in the Security Council vote of December 19 (which went down to defeat) on a Palestinian demand to deploy a UN observer force in the West Bank and Gaza Strip.[106]

Despite Putin's shift to an evenhanded position on the Palestinian-Israeli conflict and Russia's important diplomatic economic and military ties with Israel,[107] there are countervailing pressures in Moscow preventing too close a Russian-Israeli alignment. These include:

(1) Pro-Arab elements in Russia's Foreign Ministry and in the increasingly influential secret police who hope to restore the close ties Moscow had in the Arab world in Soviet times.

(2) Anti-Semitic forces who are also anti-Israel. They are primarily found in Russia's Communist Party and among Russia's ultranationalist politicians.

(3) Russia's arms sales agency, Rosoboronoexport. The new arms sales agency has been given a high priority in Putin's efforts to revitalize the Russian economy. Indeed, Russia's prime minister, Mikhail Kasyanov, has stated that the proceeds from the arms sales are to be invested in the development of new technologies for the economy. What makes this problematic for Israel is that Russian arms sales to Iran, an enemy of Israel, are already a matter of major concern. Should these be followed by arms sales to Syria (assuming Saudi Arabia is willing to pay for the arms—a possibility if the intifada escalates and draws in Syrian forces), a deterioration in Russian-Israeli relations could well result. The situation would worsen even more if the UN sanctions on Iraq were lifted—or if Russia decided to break them unilaterally (both unlikely prospects at the current time), because in the past Moscow has been a major weapons supplier to Baghdad.

(4) Russia's Muslim community. Approximately 20 percent of the Russian population, they are still quiescent politically. Nonetheless, the Russian leadership must take their views into consideration, given the dangers of radical Islam not only in Chechnya and elsewhere in the North Caucasus and the Russian Federation but also in Central Asia.

Because of the conflicting pressures on Putin, the Russian leader has chosen to take an evenhanded position on the Arab-Israeli conflict. He may be expected to seize on such events as Arafat's trip to Moscow to demonstrate that Russia is still an important player in world politics and thereby satisfy right-wing elements in Russia. However, until he succeeds in revitalizing Russia's economy and military power, Russia will be at best a marginal influence on the Arab-Israeli conflict.

Conclusions

In looking at the pattern of Russian policy toward the Middle East under Boris Yeltsin and his successor, Vladimir Putin, several conclusions can be drawn. First, Russia, during a period of growing economic and military weakness, has basically been on the defensive in the region. Its priority has been to try to reestablish Russian control over Transcaucasia and Central Asia while also putting down successive rebellions in Chechnya, in the

Northern Caucasus. This geostrategic situation has strongly influenced its policies toward Iran and Turkey, countries that are deeply involved in the politics of both Transcaucasia and Central Asia. In the case of Iran, which, during the Yeltsin era, basically cooperated with Russia in a series of regional conflicts from the civil war in Tajikistan, to resisting Taliban control in Afghanistan, to supporting Armenia against Azerbaizhan, very strong political ties developed that, at least until the time of writing (December 20, 2000), have withstood the second Russian military intervention in Chechnya. Iran has become a major trading partner of Russia (although the exports are primarily on the Russian side), as well as a major customer for Russian military equipment and nuclear technology. In the multipolar world that Russian leaders have hoped to see develop, Iran is a primary ally. There are, however, two issues on the horizon that have to concern Putin. First is the possibility of a rapprochement between the United States and Iran if, following the overwhelming victory of moderates in the February 2000 Majlis elections, Iranian president Mohammad Khatami, who desires such a rapprochement, manages to defeat the conservative opposition that has launched an attack against him. A second concern and one related to the first is whether, as the result of a U.S.-Iranian rapprochement, the United States will remove its opposition to investment in pipelines carrying Caspian oil and natural gas through Iranian territory to the Persian Gulf. Russia would face problems should such pipelines materialize as this would reduce the dependency of these states on Russia both as a market and as a transit route for their energy exports.

In the case of Turkey, which, unlike Iran, has had a more confrontational relationship with Russia, Moscow, perhaps out of necessity, seems to have settled on a policy of economic cooperation rather than one of geopolitical confrontation. After clashing with Turkey over Chechnya, the Kurds, and a projected SAM missile deployment on the Greek section of Cyprus, as well as over the proposed Baku-Ceyhan oil and Transcaspian natural gas pipelines, by 1999 the centerpiece of Russian-Turkish relations had become the Blue Stream natural gas pipeline connecting Russia and Turkey across the bottom of the Black Sea. Assuming the project is successfully completed, Blue Stream will make Turkey, already Russia's leading trading partner in the Middle East, into one of Russia's leading economic partners in the world, and this in turn should mitigate other areas of Russian-Turkish friction. However, Putin still has to contend with the fact that an increasingly prosperous Turkey, with improving ties to Greece and an invitation for EU membership, might also be an increasingly attractive economic partner for Azerbaizhan, Georgia, the states of

Central Asia, and, possibly, even Armenia if the Nagorno-Karabakh conflict is settled. How Putin balances Russia's growing economic ties with Turkey with Turkey's continuing geopolitical challenge to Russia in Transcaucasia and Central Asia will be an interesting test of his diplomatic and political skills.

A second conclusion about Russian policy toward the Middle East that can be drawn from this study is that Russian policy under Yeltsin was hurt by multiple and often conflicting actors. Elements that have influenced Russian policy in a major way include the energy companies, especially Lukoil and Gasprom, the oligarchs, the defense and atomic energy ministries, the arms sale companies, and, to a lesser degree, the Russian Duma and Russia's regions. Unlike Yeltsin, Putin, so far at least, seems intent on cutting down on the freedom of action of a number of these actors. He has already moved to limit the power of regional governors and is in the process of cracking down on the oligarchs, curbing the energy companies (some of which are linked to the oligarchs), and bringing Russia's arms sale agency under tighter control. With a far more supportive Duma than Yeltsin enjoyed, Putin may succeed in this endeavor, adding a degree of cohesion to Russian foreign policy that has been lacking over the last ten years.

A third conclusion that can be drawn from this study is that, as it was in Soviet times, the Middle East has become an area of conflict between Russia and the United States. Conflict has been the case in the U.S. quarrel with Russia over its supplies of missile technology and nuclear reactors to Iran, as well as its sale of conventional weapons to the Islamic Republic. Yet, for reasons mentioned above, Iran has become so important to Russian regional policy that Russia has been willing to incur the ire of the United States to maintain its alliance with Iran. Conflict has also characterized U.S.-Russian relations over Iraq, although Moscow has not yet been willing to unilaterally abrogate the sanctions regime.

Finally, unlike most of the post–World War II Soviet era, there has also been a modicum of cooperation between Russia and the United States in the Middle East. This has particularly been the case in the Arab-Israeli peace process. Russia strongly endorsed the U.S.-sponsored Oslo I and Oslo II interim agreements between Israel and the Palestinians as well as the Jordanian-Israeli peace treaty of 1994. While Primakov sought a more independent role for Russia in Middle East diplomacy, especially the diplomacy surrounding the conflict in Lebanon in April 1996, and unsuccessfully resisted the U.S. efforts to solve the conflict without Russian participation, the economic crisis of 1998 lowered Russia's profile in the

Arab-Israeli conflict, only a tertiary area of interest to Russia in any case. Putin, burdened by the Chechen war, has switched back to a more even-handed position on the conflict, while at the same time maintaining Russia's close economic, cultural, and even military ties with Israel. Such a strategy, in an area of less-than-vital interest to Russia, enables Putin not only to project Russia as a great power as cosponsor of the Arab-Israeli peace talks but also to maintain an area of cooperation with the United States at a time when U.S.-Russian relations are strained in a large number of other areas.

In sum, the Middle East legacy that Putin inherits as the leader of a weakened Russia is a rather modest one, befitting a country that has fallen from its position as a superpower. Whether Putin will be able to revitalize Russia so that it can play a more important role in the region is a very open question.

Notes

1. In November 2000, Russian defense minister Igor Sergeev said the greatest danger for Russia's security was posed by threats originating from the North Caucasian and Central Asian directions. *Rossiskaya Gazeta,* November 25, 2000, cited in FBIS-NES-2000–1124 (November 25, 2000).

2. For studies of politics in the Duma, see Lilia Shevtsova, *Yeltsin's Russia: Myth and Reality* (Washington, D.C.: Carnegie Endowment for International Peace, 1999), and Stephen White, *Russia's New Politics* (Cambridge: Cambridge University Press, 2000).

3. Cited in Gligori@aol.com, March 28, 1998. (This is an on-line service specializing in Central Asian and Transcaucasian affairs.)

4. See Robert O. Freedman, "Russian-Iranian Relations under Yeltsin," *Soviet and Post-Soviet Review* 25, no. 3 (1999): 268.

5. For an analysis of the influence of the Russian military on policy, see Vicken Cheterian, "Russia's Disarmed Response," *Le Monde Diplomatique,* September 2000, 3.

6. Cited in Steven Liesman, "Moscow Finally Seems Serious about Reorganizing the Military," *Wall Street Journal,* March 11, 1998.

7. Cited in Stephen DeSpiegeleire, WEU Institute for Security Studies, "Gulliver's Threads: Russia's Regions and the Rest of the World," paper presented at the Slavic Research Center International Symposium, Sapporo, Japan, July 22–25, 1998.

8. *Kommersant Daily,* August 23, 1995; translated in *Current Digest of the Post-Soviet Press* (hereafter *CDSP*) 47, no. 34 (1995): 25.

9. Andrei Shukshin, "Exasperated Russia Changes Tactics in Chechnya," Reuters (Moscow), December 15, 2000; cited in Johnson's Russia List 4690, Decem-

ber 15, 2000. (David Johnson@Erols.com is an on-line service specializing in Russian affairs.)

10. Agence France Presse, "Global Arms Spending Continues to Decline," *Washington Times,* June 21, 1999.

11. Arkady Ostrovsky, "Russia to Cut Military by 600,000 People," *Financial Times,* November 10, 2000.

12. Cited in Reuters report, *Washington Post,* December 14, 2000, and RFE/RL (Radio Free Europe/Radio Liberty Research Report), Newsline 4, no. 241, part 1 (December 14, 2000).

13. Bill Gertz, "Russians Fly Near Ship in Cold War Manner," *Washington Times,* December 1, 2000.

14. Stefan Wagstyl, "Russian Crisis: EBRD Sees Effect More Serious Than Expected as It Highlights Output Decline," *Financial Times,* April 16, 1999. See also Arkady Ostrovsky and John Thornhill, "Russia 'Bust' Says Rating Agency," *Financial Times,* September 24, 1999.

15. For a recent example of such problems, see Alan Cullison, "Russia Closes Bank Vexing Western Investors Who Were Set to Gain from Restructuring Deal," *Wall Street Journal,* June 30, 1999. See also Andrew Jack, "Russian Sales of Fake Goods Cost $1 Billion," *Financial Times,* February 22, 2000.

16. For an analysis of Russian arms sales, see Richard F. Grimmett, *Conventional Transfers to Developing Nations, 1992–1999* (Washington, D.C.: Congressional Research Service of the Library of Congress, August 18, 2000), 6. These figures include Russian arms sales to China and India, which are now Russia's main customers.

17. Andrei Musatov, "Putin to Use Defense Industry to Bolster Country's Economy," *Russia Journal,* December 21–27, 1999.

18. *Rossiskaya Gazeta,* May 13, 1998; translated in Johnson's Russia List 3277, May 14, 1998.

19. *Izvestia,* February 14, 1998; translated in *CDSP* 50, no. 7 (1998): 17.

20. Reuters report, cited in Johnson's Russia List 4391, July 9, 2000. See also Michael Wines, "Putin Describes an Ill Russia and Prescribes Strong Democracy," *New York Times,* July 9, 2000.

21. Ostrovsky, "Russia to Cut Military." Russia also hopes to join the World Trade Organization but has a difficult road ahead. See Andrew Jack and Frances Williams, "Russia Sets Its Heart on Quick WTO Accession," *Financial Times,* December 15, 2000. *The Economist,* in an article in November 2000, rated Russia last on corporate governance among key emerging market economies, after Turkey, the Philippines, Indonesia, Thailand, and the Czech Republic. See "Boris the Belligerent: Is Boris Fedorov a Self-interested Gadfly, or a Champion of Investors' Rights and Economic Reform in Russia?" *The Economist* (November 18, 2000), 80.

22. For a description of Soviet-Iranian relations during this period, see Robert O. Freedman, *Moscow and the Middle East: Soviet Policy since the Invasion of Afghanistan* (Cambridge: Cambridge University Press, 1991).

23. Russian arms sales, particularly the supply of missile technology to Iran, had become a sore point in U.S.-Russian relations and drew strong congressional protests and the threat of sanctions. On this issue see Freedman, "Russian-Iranian Relations under Yeltsin," 265–84.

24. Ibid.

25. See Yuri Merzliakov, "Legal Status of the Caspian Sea," *International Affairs* (Moscow) 45, no. 1 (1999): 37, and Dr. Shirazi, "The Caspian Sea and Its Strategic Challenges," *Kar va Kargae* (Tehran), September 23, 2000, translated in FBIS-NES-2000–1211 (December 14, 2000).

26. Viktor Vishniakov, "Russian-Iranian Relations and Regional Stability," *International Affairs* (Moscow) 45, no. 1 (1999): 152.

27. The Russian-Iranian interaction over Chechnya is discussed in Freedman, "Russian-Iranian Relations under Yeltsin."

28. Cited in RFE/RL Iran Report 3, no. 7 (February 7, 2000).

29. This was clearly the concern of some of Russia's Iranian specialists. See N. M. Mamedova, "Novii Etap Politischeskoi Zhizni Irana" (New stage in the political life of Iran), in *Blizhnii Vostok i Sovremennost,* ed. Vladimir Isaev (Moscow: Institute for the Study of Israel and the Near East, 2000), 132.

30. Cited in Elaine Sciolino, "Skipping the Charm, President of Iran Chastises His Country's Reformers and the U.S.," *New York Times,* September 8, 2000. See also Mollie Moore and John Anderson, "Iran's Khatami Is Caught in the Middle," *Washington Post,* November 28, 2000.

31. Cited in David James, "Iranian President Wants Strong Ties with Russia," *Washington Times,* September 8, 2000. For his part Putin had singled out Iran for special mention in his new foreign policy doctrine.

32. Colum Lynch, "Albright, Iranian Minister Meet in Silence," *Washington Post,* September 16, 2000.

33. Cited in RFE/RL Newsline 4, no. 232, part 1 (December 1, 2000).

34. Itar-Tass, November 24, 2000, cited in FBIS-SOV-2000–1124 (November 24, 2000).

35. Reuters report, "Russia Says No Arms for Teheran," *New York Times,* December 6, 2000.

36. On this point, see Freedman, *Moscow and the Middle East.*

37. Soviet policy during the Gulf War is discussed in Robert O. Freedman, "The Soviet Union, the Gulf War, and Its Aftermath," in *The Middle East and the United States,* 2d ed., ed. David W. Lesch (Boulder: Westview Press, 1999), 365–92.

38. Interfax, February 2, 1995, cited in *Commonwealth of Independent States and the Middle East (Jerusalem)* (hereafter *CIS/ME*) 20, nos. 2–3 (1995): 37.

39. *Krasnaya Zvezda,* August 3, 1995, in FBIS-FSU (August 4, 1995), 9.

40. Interfax, August 24, 1995, in FBIS-FSU (August 25, 1995), 13.

41. See the report by Robert Corzine, "Saddam Casts Shadow over Oil Market," *Financial Times,* January 26, 1996.

42. See the report by David Hearst, "Russia Signs 'Giant' Oil Deal with Iraq," *Manchester Guardian Weekly,* February 18, 1996.

43. Cited in Charles Truehart and David Hoffman, "France and Russia Differ from U.S. in Agendas on Iraq," *Washington Post,* November 13, 1997.

44. *Nezavisimaya Gazeta,* November 28, 1997. Translated in *CDSP* 49, no. 48 (1997): 11.

45. Yelena Suponina, "U.N. Sanctions Cramp Lukoil," *Moscow News,* July 7–13, 1999.

46. For the text of UN Security Council Resolution 1284, see the UN website. The resolution was clearly a compromise. Initially Russia wanted only a period of 60 days for Iraq to show compliance, while the United States had demanded 180 days. See Colum Lynch, "U.S. Eases Stance on Iraq Arms Monitors," *Washington Post,* December 11, 1999.

47. "Russia, Iraq Sign Deal on Power Plant," *Washington Times,* December 22, 1999. The equipment for the plant, however, would have to be approved by the United States, which continued to have a concern about the importing to Iraq of "dual-use" equipment.

48. Barbara Crosette, "U.N. Names Ex-head of Atomic Energy Agency to Lead Iraq Monitoring," *New York Times,* January 27, 2000. See also Crosette, "Iraqis Seem Less Hostile to New Weapons Inspector," *New York Times,* January 28, 2000.

49. "Top Arms Inspector to Rely on U.N. in Iraq," *New York Times,* February 5, 2000.

50. Colum Lynch, "U.N. Arms Inspectors Back Down," *Washington Post,* August 31, 2000.

51. Agence France Press, "Moscow Pushing U.N. on Regular Baghdad Flights," December 5, 2000; interview by the author, Russian diplomat, Washington, D.C., December 18, 2000; Moscow Radio, November 30, 2000, cited in FBIS-SOV-2000–1130 (November 30, 2000).

52. The importance of the United Nations to Russia was reiterated by Foreign Minister Ivanov in presenting Russia's new foreign policy doctrine to reporters in July 2000: "The organization of the United Nations must remain the main center of regulating international relations in the twenty-first century. Russia will resolutely oppose any attempts to lower [the United Nation's] role and that of its Security Council" (Reuters, July 10, 2000, cited in Johnson's Russia List 4395, July 11, 2000).

53. Interviews by the author with Turkish scholars and officials in Istanbul and Ankara, Turkey, June 14–28, 1996, and the *Turkish Times,* June 23, 1996.

54. On this point, see Duygu Bazoglu Sezer, "Turkish-Russian Relations: From Adversity to 'Virtual Rapprochement,'" in *Turkey's New World,* ed. Alan Makovsky and Sabri Sayari (Washington, D.C.: Washington Institute for Near East Policy, 2000), 96–98.

55. The author flew on Turkish Air from Istanbul to Tashkent in September 1993, a far better experience than a similar flight on Aeroflot from Moscow to Tashkent he had taken during the Soviet era.

56. *Pravda,* February 19, 1992, in FBIS-FSU (February 20, 1992), 43.

57. Vladimir Kulistikov, "Turks from the Adriatic to the Great Chinese Wall Are a Threat to Russia," *New Times* (Moscow), no. 20 (1992): 3.

58. See Sezer, "Turkish-Russian Relations," 95.

59. Cited in Stephen J. Blank, "Turkey's Strategic Engagement in the Former USSR and U.S. Interests," in *Turkey's Strategic Position at the Crossroad of World Affairs,* ed. Stephen Blank, Stephen C. Pelletiere, and William T. Johnsen (Carlisle Barracks, Pa.: U.S. Army War College, 1993), 56.

60. See Maksim Yusin, "Teheran Declares 'Great Battle' for Influence in Central Asia," *Izvestia,* February 7, 1992, translated in *CDSP* 44, no. 6 (1992): 18.

61. Interview by the author of the deputy foreign minister, Uzbek Foreign Ministry, Tashkent, Uzbekistan, September 30, 1993. See also Islam Karimov, *Building the Future: Uzbekistan Its Own Model for Transition to a Market Economy* (Tashkent, 1993).

62. Turkish correspondent Semih Idiz called 1993 a year that forced Turkish diplomats into a "crisis management mode." *Turkish Times,* February 1, 1994, 1.

63. During her visit to Moscow in early September 1993, Turkey's new prime minister, Tansu Çiller, was quoted as saying, "President Yeltsin has agreed to cooperation between Turkey and Russia to lift the anti-Iraqi embargo." *Washington Times,* September 10, 1993.

64. *Izvestia,* July 21, 1994.

65. See Elizabeth Fuller, "Turkish-Russian Relations, 1992–1994," RFE/RL Report 3, no. 18 (May 16, 1994): 9.

66. Interviews by the author in Turkey in June 1996 indicated that while the Turkish government was apparently not directly aiding the Chechen rebels, private groups in Turkey, especially Islamic groups, were assisting the Chechens.

67. Moscow scored a partial success on the CFE issue in late May 1996 when it was given an additional three years to reduce its heavy equipment (AP report, *Boston Globe,* June 2, 1996). See also Sezer, "Turkish-Russian Relations," 107.

68. The Laleli district in Istanbul is a center of Russian-Turkish "suitcase trade," and it was primarily merchants from this district who sent the money to aid Yeltsin's campaign. See the report by Dogu Ergil, "Russian Elections and the Future of Turco-Russian Relations," *Turkish Times,* June 23, 1996. So many Russian tourists now come to the Turkish resort of Antalya that by 1996 there was a special Russian newspaper for them there, *Antalya Dlya Vas* (Antalya for you).

69. Cited in Gligori@aol.com, November 12, 1997.

70. Cited in Sanubar Shermatova, "Gas Brings Turkey and Russia Closer," *Moscow News,* nos. 51–52, 1997 (December 25, 1997–January 8, 1998), 6.

71. See Lionel Barber, "Russia Stands by Missile Sale," *Financial Times,* January 28, 1998.

72. Toni Marshall, "Greece to Deploy Russian Missiles in Crete to Ease Turkish Concerns," *Washington Times,* November 19, 1998.

73. See R. Jeffrey Smith, "Earthquakes Aid Relations between Greeks, Turks: Goodwill Eases Tensions: Cyprus Still Sticking Point," *Washington Post,* November 10, 1999.

74. "Greece Now Supports Turkey Joining EU," *Washington Post*, September 6, 1999.

75. Cited in Kerin Hope, "Aegean Military Tensions: Ankara and Athens Agree to Defense Talks," *Financial Times*, January 21, 2000. See also Stephen Kinzer, "Turkey Considers Scaling Back Military Challenge to Greece," *New York Times*, June 8, 2000. In October 2000, however, there was a brief Turkish-Greek contretemps over the Aegean that was quickly brought under control. See Douglas Frantz, "Despite Turkish-Greek Thaw, Cyprus Quarrel Is Not Melting," *New York Times*, December 18, 2000.

76. See Peter Preston, "How the Earth Moved for Athens and Ankara," *Manchester Guardian Weekly*, January 27–February 2, 2000.

77. Sezer, "Turkish-Russian Relations," 106.

78. Ibid., 107.

79. Ibid., 107–8.

80. Andrew Jack and Leyla Boulton, "Russia Paves Way for Pipeline," *Financial Times*, December 4–5, 1999.

81. Hugh Pope, "Russia Takes Lead in Race to Supply Gas to Turkey," *Wall Street Journal*, February 17, 2000. Meanwhile, Iran was also a competitor in the Turkish natural gas market, and an agreement to extend for three years the existing 22-month contract was negotiated in February 2000. amboll@aol.com, August 24, 2000.

82. Quoted in *Rossiskaya Gazeta*, October 25, 2000, in FBIS-SOV-2000–1025 (October 25, 2000).

83. Itar-Tass Press Review, October 26, 2000, in FBIS-SOV-2000–1026 (October 26, 2000).

84. Moscow Interfax (in English), October 25, 2000, in FBIS-SOV-2000–1025 (October 25, 2000).

85. Itar-Tass Press Review; "Russia to Increase Gas Sale to Energy-Hungry Turkey," Agence France Press, October 28, 2000.

86. David Buchan and Stephen Fuller, "Summit Seals New Security Charter," *Financial Times*, November 20–21, 1999.

87. Ibid.

88. Amberin Zaman, "Deal Looms for Building Oil Pipeline via Turkey," *Washington Post*, November 6, 1999. Nonetheless, serious security problems with the pipeline remained, although they may be partially overcome if the feasibility study, authorized in October 2000, is done properly. For a Russian view of the threat that the Turkish pipeline system would pose to Russia, see Vladimir Yuratev and Anatoly Sheshtakov of the Russian Ministry of Foreign Economic Relations, "Asian Gas Will Flow East: New Alliance Infringes on Russian Interests," *Nezavisimaya Gazeta*, May 13, 1993, in *CDSP* 45, no. 14 (1993): 16–18. For a Western view arguing that Moscow is practicing economic warfare over the pipeline issue, see Stephen Blank, *Energy and Security in Transcaucasia* (Carlisle, Pa.: U.S. Army War College, 1994).

89. Cited in *Turkistan Newsletter* 4, no. 197, November 7, 2000.

90. "Turkey Wants New Rules on Passage in Straits," *Washington Times,* February 16, 2000.

91. These events are discussed in detail in Robert O. Freedman, "Russian and Israel under Yeltsin," *Israel Studies* 3, no. 1 (spring 1998): 140–69.

92. See Viktor Belikov and Viktor Litovkin, "Russian Arms Business Will Grow through the Addition of Israel," *Izvestia,* June 20, 1997; translated in *CDSP* 49, no. 25 (1997): 28.

93. Reuters report, *Washington Post,* August 21, 1997.

94. Akiva Eldar, "Netanyahu Asked IMF to Give Russian $4.8 Billion Loan: In Washington, Sharon Calls Russian Israelis 'Key to Vote,'" *Ha'aretz,* April 9, 1999. See also Ze'ev Schiff, "Israel's Dangerous Dance with Russia," *Ha'aretz,* April 9, 1999; Leonid Gankin, "Israel Will Help Russia Get IMF Loan," *Kommersant* (Moscow), March 23, 1999, in *CDSP* 51, no. 12 (1999): 24.

95. Eldar, ibid.

96. Yelena Suponina, "Russia Tells Palestinians to Hold Off," *Vremya,* April 7, 1999, in *CDSP* 51, no. 14 (1999): 22.

97. For an excellent analysis of this issue, see Oded Eran, "Russian Immigrants, Russia, and the Elections in Israel," *Analysis of Current Events* (ACE) 11, nos. 5–6 (May/June 1999): 13–15.

98. Michael Wines, "Putin Making Gesture to Jews Slips into a Factional Morass," *New York Times,* September 19, 2000.

99. S. A. Greene, "Police Raid Moscow Shul [synagogue] in Probe of Mogul," *The Forward,* October 22, 2000; Reuters, "Israeli Speaker Wants Spain to Release Gusinsky," *Ha'aretz,* December 15, 2000.

100. Interviews with Russian diplomat, Washington, D.C., May 2000, with Israeli Foreign Office, Jerusalem, June 2000, and with Russian Embassy in Tel Aviv, June 2000.

101. Pavel Felgengauer, "Israel Drops Out of Moscow-Beijing Axis," *Moscow News,* no. 30 (August 1–7, 2000), in *CDSP* 52, no. 31, 19–20.

102. Interview with Russian diplomat, Washington, D.C., May 2000.

103. Interfax (in English), October 13, 2000, in FBIS-NES-2000–1013 (October 13, 2000) and RFE/RL Newsline 4, no. 200, part 1 (October 16, 2000).

104. Reuters, "Russia's Putin Calls for End to Mid-East Violence," October 14, 2000.

105. William A. Orme, Jr., "Barak and Arafat Agree by Phone to Keep Security Link," *New York Times,* November 25, 2000.

106. AP/Reuters, "Israel Welcomes U.N. Rejection of Observer Force," *Ha'aretz,* December 19, 2000.

107. For a recent review of Russian-Israeli economic ties, see Andrei Fedorchenko, "Rossiisko-Israil'skie Ekonomicheskie Sviazi" (Russian-Israeli economic ties), in *Mirovaya Ekonomika i Mezhdunarodnie Otnosheniya,* no. 2 (2000): 62–69. In December 2000, Moscow also put into orbit an Israeli spy satellite.

The Impact of September 11

The Bush Administration, the European Union, and the Arab-Israeli Conflict

ROBERT O. FREEDMAN

The terrorist attacks on the United States on September 11 have caused the Bush administration to change its foreign policy orientation from one of unilateralism to multilateralism as it has sought to build a world-wide coalition against terrorism in general and against the terrorist al-Qaeda network based in Afghanistan in particular. It is, of course, too early to tell whether this new multilateralism will be limited to the fight against terrorism or whether it will be extended to other diplomatic arenas. Nonetheless, in the post–September 11 atmosphere of coopera-tion between the United States and its European allies in the fight against Osama Bin Laden, it is useful to ask whether Euro-Atlantic cooperation can be extended to the quest for an Arab-Israeli peace settlement. This chapter examines Euro-Atlantic cooperation—or the lack thereof—dur-ing the Clinton administration and beginning of the Bush administra-tion. Initially, the Bush administration chose not to get seriously involved as Israeli-Palestinian violence, precipitated by the al-Aqsa intifada, esca-lated in the period up to September 11, 2001. European efforts to fill the diplomatic vacuum during that period will be discussed. The chapter will then examine U.S. and European policy from September 11 until January 20, 2002, the end of the Bush administration's first year in of-fice.

The Legacy of the Clinton Administration

The Rabin-Peres Period

While the Arab-Israeli conflict was an important issue for both the United States and the European Union during the Clinton administration, it was not the only Middle East issue that preoccupied leaders on both sides of the Atlantic, and just as there were Euro-Atlantic differences in both emphasis and substance on the Arab-Israeli conflict, so too were there differences on other Middle East issues. Thus, for example, the United States pushed hard to get its NATO ally, Turkey, admitted to the European Union, while members of the EU were, to a greater or lesser degree, resistant. By the end of the Clinton administration, though, Turkey had been invited to apply for membership. Second, in the case of Iraq, not only were there differences between the United States and the European Union, there were differences among EU members as well, with Britain providing solid backing for the U.S. anti–Saddam Hussein strategy while France was increasingly critical of it. In the case of Iraq, therefore, a common European Union foreign and defense policy was not very much in evidence as the Clinton administration came to an end. By contrast, in the case of Iran, the United States was alone in seeking to isolate the Islamic regime as the European Union pursued a policy of constructive engagement with the Islamic Republic. While the EU states pointed to the election of Mohammad Khatami, a moderate, as Iran's president as evidence of the success of its policy, the United States argued that the continued domination of Iranian policymaking by hard-liners, led by supreme religious leader Ayatollah Khameini, and Iran's continued support of terrorism justified the American policy of sanctions against Iran.[1]

In sum, while the United States cooperates with the European Union, or at least with some EU countries on several Middle East issues, it is in conflict with the EU on others, and the lack of Euro-Atlantic harmony on such issues as Iran, Iraq, and Turkey would appear to have a negative effect on the U.S. willingness to cooperate with the European Union on other Middle East issues, first and foremost the Arab-Israeli conflict.

When Clinton took office in January 1993, the Arab-Israeli peace process had received a major boost from the Madrid Conference; this conference brought the Arab states and Israel together for the first time since the Geneva Conference following the 1973 Arab-Israeli war. The Madrid Conference set up two separate tracks of peacemaking. The first dealt with bilateral talks between Israel, Syria, Lebanon, and a joint Palestinian-Jordanian delegation. The second dealt with multilateral issues such as economic cooperation, water sharing, refugees, and security. The concept behind the multilateral track was that progress in multilateral areas such as economic cooperation would contribute to progress in the bilateral talks. While the United States supervised the bilateral talks, the European Union was given responsibility for running the multilateral talks on economic cooperation, called the Regional Economic Development Working Group (REDWG).[2] Syria refused to participate in the REDWG, which reduced its effectiveness—the Syrians claimed they did not want to "reward" Israeli hard-liners by participating.[3] There is no evidence that EU states such as France, which had a closer relationship with Syria than did the United States, pressured Syria to participate, a move that could have enhanced the peace process as a whole.

While the Madrid process stagnated when Yitzhak Shamir was Israel's prime minister, it received a major boost when Yitzhak Rabin became Israel's prime minister in July 1993. Rabin supported "back-channel" talks with the Palestine Liberation Organization, which took place with the support of Norway, a European, albeit non-EU state, and the talks were crowned with success in September 1993, when the Oslo I agreement, called the Declaration of Principles, was signed on the White House lawn. Here it is important to note that the Oslo I agreement was directly negotiated between Israelis and Palestinians, with the United States primarily serving as a cheerleader once the agreement had been signed. Second, the fact that the Oslo process was facilitated by Norway, a non-EU state, rather than by the EU or an EU member state, reflects Israel's deep distrust of the organization, highlighted by the 1980 Venice Declaration when the European Community, the EU's predecessor, called for the PLO's "association" with the Middle East peace process—at a time when the PLO was still openly calling for Israel's destruction.[4] The United States also took a dim view of the Venice Declaration and of initial European unwillingness to serve in the multinational force in the Sinai following the Israeli-Egyptian peace treaty of 1979.[5] Once Oslo I had been signed, U.S. president Bill Clinton called for a donors' conference to help pay for the developmental needs of the emerging Palestinian entity. The EU became the primary economic supporter of what became known as the Palestinian Authority, although the aid was never made conditional on the development of genuine democratic institutions or financial transparency, omissions that were to have increasingly severe consequences as the years wore on.

Following the Oslo I agreement, the peace process continued to make progress as Jordan and Israel signed a peace treaty in October 1994, with President Clinton again serving as a cheerleader as the treaty was signed on the border between the two countries. There was also progress on the Israeli-Palestinian front as the Oslo II agreement was signed in September 1995, despite a rising crescendo of terrorist attacks by Palestinian groups such as Hamas and Islamic Jihad seeking to sabotage the peace process, and the murder in February 1994 of Muslims praying in the Tomb of the Patriarchs in Hebron by an Israeli terrorist. Here again the United States served as a cheerleader in support of the agreement, rather than playing a major role in its negotiation.[6]

Meanwhile, for its part, the European Union appeared to be working on a parallel track to aid the peace process with the establishment of a Euro-Mediterranean partnership, called the Barcelona process, in November 1995. The true origins of the Euro-Med partnership are clouded in debate, with some analysts claiming that it was primarily a German sop to the key Mediterranean members of the European Union—France, Spain, and Italy—in return for support for EU expansion eastward (something that would be to Germany's advantage), and others asserting that France, in pushing the Barcelona process, was primarily interested in spurring economic development in North Africa so as to prevent a mass migration from its former colonies to France. Whatever the motivations for the establishment of the Barcelona process (officially it was to create a free trade zone by 2010, a common area of peace and stability, and the development of a set of institutions to foster cooperation between the civil societies in the Euro-Med region),[7] it did have potential to enhance the Arab-Israeli peace process. First and foremost it provided another area where Israel could meet with its Arab neighbors, especially Syria and Lebanon, which continued to boycott the multilateral talks despite the fact that Syrian-Israeli bilateral negotiations, under U.S. auspices, had become quite serious by the time the Barcelona process began,[8] and despite the fact that first the dovish Yitzhak Rabin and then the dovish Shimon Peres, rather than the hawkish Yitzhak Shamir, were the Israeli prime ministers.

The peace process, however, was soon to receive a series of blows. First, Rabin was assassinated in early November 1995 by a Jewish religious fanatic. Rabin's successor, Shimon Peres, quickly moved to implement the Oslo II agreement, enabling the Palestinians to gain control of all the major Palestinian-populated cities on the West Bank except Hebron, and this in turn facilitated Palestinian elections for the Palestinian Authority's parliament and executive (Arafat was elected as the PA's executive). Then, however, another round of Palestinian terrorist attacks struck a nearly mortal blow to the peace process. After Peres had arranged for elections to be held in May 1996, four Hamas and Islamic Jihad terrorist attacks, killing scores of civilians in Jerusalem and Tel Aviv, undermined Israeli public support for the peace process, thus enabling Likud hard-liner Benjamin Netanyahu to be elected Israel's prime minister in the May 1996 elections—despite Clinton's efforts to support Peres by convening an international antiterrorism conference on March 13, 1996. Compounding the problem was the support given by Syria's official radio station for the terrorist attacks[9]—and Syria's boycott of the antiterrorism conference— developments that effectively ended the Syrian-Israeli bilateral talks.

The Netanyahu Period

Following the Israeli elections, the personal conflict between Netanyahu and Arafat all but froze the peace process that, according to the Oslo I agreement, was to begin discussion of the final-status issues of boundaries, Jewish settlements, security, refugees, and Jerusalem by May 1996. Netanyahu exacerbated the problem later in September 1996 by secretly opening the ancient Hasmonean tunnel, which was close to but not attached to the Temple Mount/Haram, holy to both Jews and Muslims. This sparked severe rioting by the Palestinians, leading to seventy deaths (55 Palestinians and 15 Israelis). It took the personal intervention of Bill Clinton, with the help of Jordan's King Hussein (but not the European Union) to bring an end to the rioting. Perhaps more important, the deep suspicion that had developed between Netanyahu and Arafat forced the United States for the first time to take direct control of the Israeli-Palestinian peace process with the goal of securing an agreement over the divided city of Hebron, where the massacre of Jews by Arabs in 1929 and of Arabs by a Jew in 1994 had embittered relations. Dennis Ross, the chief American negotiator, worked intensively between October 1996 and January 1997 to secure an agreement. In the midst of his negotiations, the European Union appointed its own special envoy to the peace process, Miguel Angel Moratinos. While EU members may have seen Moratinos's appointment as a means of increasing their influence in a peace process that had appeared to stagnate under Netanyahu, the appointment was negatively perceived by Dennis Ross. In the words of Ross, "I think that it is important when you are in a delicate stage of a negotiating process for all those who want to be helpful to be supportive. Right now, I think that it is generally agreed not only by the party [sic] but by others that the effort that we [the U.S.] are making is the one they support."[10]

The Palestinians, however, welcomed the appointment of Moratinos, hoping to exploit the EU presence as a lever against both Israel and the United States. The PLO representative in Brussels, Leyla Shaheed, stated,

"The U.S. and Europe have different opinions about how to develop and support the peace process. The European position concerning the Palestinian issue and other matters in the region, is far more advanced than that of America. . . . Israel prefers to deal with the Arabs through the Americans and therefore does not want a European role because the European position toward peace is similar to the Arab and Palestinian one."[11]

Moratinos was to make, at most, a minor contribution to the negotiations leading to the January 1997 Hebron Agreement that split the city of Hebron between Israelis (20 percent) and Palestinians (80 percent) and stipulated three additional Israeli withdrawals on the West Bank, although no stipulation was reached as to the size of the withdrawals. However, following the Hebron Agreement the Palestinian-Israeli peace process again stagnated. In part this was due to Netanyahu's policy of continuing to build Jewish settlements on the West Bank and also his authorization of the construction of a Jewish housing development on a hill in disputed East Jerusalem called Har Homa. A second cause of the stagnation in the peace talks was yet another outburst of Palestinian terrorism, beginning with a bomb in a Tel Aviv café in March 1997 that killed three Israelis and additional bombs in Jerusalem on July 30 and September 4 that killed twenty-one Israelis and wounded hundreds more. Netanyahu reacted to the bombings by imposing a border closure that prevented Palestinians on the West Bank and Gaza from working in Israel (a tactic that had also periodically been used by Rabin), by withholding tax payments collected from Palestinians working in Israel and owed to the Palestinian Authority (a tactic also to be used by Ehud Barak, Netanyahu's successor, following the outbreak of the al-Aqsa intifada in September 2000), and by threatening to send Israeli forces into Palestinian areas to root out the terrorists (a tactic to be employed by Barak's successor, Ariel Sharon). Ironically, with continued Palestinian terrorism (here defined as the killing of Israeli civilians), which Arafat either could not or would not prevent, the European Union in 1997 undertook the responsibility to train Palestinian security forces to prevent terrorist activities, a program that by the time of this writing (January 2002) has yet to prove its effectiveness.[12]

In September 1997, after appearing to withdraw from the Middle East peace effort because of its concentration on NATO expansion, the United States again intervened, this time with the peace process on the verge of total collapse after the two Hamas bombings. The new U.S. secretary of state, Madeleine Albright, who had been sworn in on January 23, 1997, but had not yet made an official visit to the Middle East, came to Israel in an effort to jump-start the stalled peace process. She appealed to Arafat to take unilateral action to root out the terrorist infrastructure and called on Netanyahu for a time-out in settlement construction in the occupied territories, a plea Netanyahu rejected. The peace process continued to stagnate until November, when the Israeli cabinet voted in principle in favor of another troop withdrawal but specified neither its extent nor its timing. Meanwhile, Clinton had grown exasperated with what his administration perceived as stalling by Netanyahu, and he publicly snubbed the Israeli prime minister during Netanyahu's November 1997 visit to the United States to talk to Jewish organizations. Netanyahu's ties to the Republicans in Congress and to their allies on the religious right of the American political spectrum (such as Jerry Falwell, whose Liberty University students regularly make pilgrimages to Israel)[13] helped insulate the Israeli leader from U.S. pressure, a process that would continue into 1998 as a weakened Clinton got bogged down in the Lewinsky scandal.

Despite his growing weakness, Clinton, acting through Secretary of State Albright, again sought in May 1998 to salvage the peace process whose apparent demise was badly damaging the U.S. position in the Middle East. Arab friends of the United States, as well as its Arab enemies, increased their complaints about a U.S. double standard of pressuring Iraq while not pressuring Israel. Albright, in an effort to reverse this situation, following meetings with Netanyahu and Arafat in London, issued an ultimatum for Israel to accept a 13 percent withdrawal. This, however, failed due to the support Netanyahu received from Republicans in the U.S. Congress, the pro-Israeli lobby in the United States led by the American-Israel Public Affairs Committee (AIPAC), and the Christian religious right.[14] Interestingly enough, American Jewry was badly split over Netanyahu's policy. Reform and Conservative Jews, already angry at Netanyahu for his favoritism to Israel's Orthodox Jews, called for Netanyahu to engage more energetically in the peace process, while Orthodox Jews (a clear minority in the American Jewish community) tended to support the Israeli prime minister.[15]

During the summer of 1998 the U.S. effort took on a new focus: seeking to get Israeli approval by linking the Israeli withdrawal in stages to Palestinian action to combat terrorism and assure Israeli security. Meanwhile a new element had been added to the Israeli-Palestinian conflict: Yasser Arafat's threat to unilaterally declare a Palestinian state upon the expiration of the Oslo I agreement on May 4, 1999. While Netanyahu issued a counterthreat of a unilateral Israeli response, which many interpreted as annexation of large parts of the West Bank if Arafat went ahead to declare a state, the Palestinian leader's threat may have been enough to get Netanyahu to agree to meet Arafat in late September 1998 in Washington when both leaders were in the United States to address the United Nations At his first meeting with Arafat in a year, Netanyahu finally agreed in the presence of Clinton to the 13 percent withdrawal figure stipulated by the United States, but only on condition that 3 percent of the area would be a "nature reserve" on which the Palestinians would be prohibited from building, a condition to which Arafat agreed.[16] The 13 percent figure was a considerable concession for Arafat, who had initially demanded a 30 percent withdrawal, and the Palestinian leader also toned down his speech at the UN, where he refrained from threatening to declare a state on May 4, 1999. But other issues continued to raise questions about the ultimate success of the negotiations even as Netanyahu and Arafat agreed to return to Washington in mid-October. First and foremost were the security agreements that Israel demanded in return for its phased 13 percent withdrawal. These included the specifics of Palestinian action to dismantle terrorist cells, extradite prisoners, confiscate excess guns, and stop what the Israelis called "incitement" of citizens through anti-Israeli speeches, sermons, and propaganda.[17] Other issues included the opening of an airport in Gaza, safe passage for Palestinian officials traveling between the West Bank and Gaza, and a clear repudiation by the PLO of its charter calling for the destruction of Israel. Then, of course, there were final-status issues such as Jerusalem, borders, water, refugees, and the future of Israeli settlements that were supposed to be negotiated by May 4, 1999. Clinton met with Arafat separately the next day to urge him to work effectively to combat terrorism. The Central Intelligence Agency, an organization with the confidence of both Israel and the Palestinian Authority, was proposed as a compromise institution to monitor Palestinian efforts to curb terrorism. Indeed, as far back as March 1998, the Hamas spokesman, Ibrahim Ghawsah, had noted the effectiveness of the CIA when he complained that military operations against Israel had become difficult because of security cooperation between Arafat's Palestinian Authority and Israel, "especially after the CIA joined in this coordination."[18]

However, besides the security questions involved in a Palestinian-Israeli agreement, there were real concerns among both Israelis and Palestinians as to whether Clinton was strong enough to broker an agreement, given the Lewinsky affair. Despite the skepticism and the illness of King Hussein, Clinton was able to move the peace process several steps forward in mid-October as Netanyahu, Arafat, and King Hussein (who left the Mayo Clinic to play an important mediating role) gathered with U.S. officials at the conference center of the Wye Plantation on Maryland's Eastern Shore. After eight days of intense bargaining, including the threat of a walkout by Netanyahu, a modest agreement was achieved between Netanyahu and Arafat. The agreement involved Israeli withdrawal in three stages from 13.1 percent of West Bank land (3 percent of which would become a nature preserve), transferring an additional 14.2 percent of land jointly controlled to sole Palestinian control, releasing 750 prisoners, and agreeing to the opening of a Palestinian airport in Gaza and of two corridors of safe passage between Israel and Gaza. In return, Arafat agreed to changing the Palestine National Charter to clearly eliminate the twenty-six articles calling for Israel's destruction, although the manner in which the change was to take place was a bit vague (reference was made to an assembly of Palestinian notables). Clinton's promise to be present during the Palestinian action, however, would serve to dramatize the event. Arafat also agreed to issue a decree prohibiting all forms of incitement to violence, to cut the number of Palestinian police to 30,000 (from 40,000), to arrest and confine thirty terrorism suspects wanted by Israel, and to collect illegal weapons and suppress terrorism, with the CIA attesting to the fact that the Palestinian Authority was making every effort to crack down on terrorism. The two sides also agreed to resume negotiations on final-status issues.[19]

Initially, the Wye Agreement appeared to restore a modicum of confidence between Arafat and Netanyahu. Israeli troops, in the first stage of the agreement, withdrew from 2 percent of the occupied West Bank, and Israel released 250 Palestinian prisoners and allowed the opening of the Palestinian airport in Gaza. However, the momentum for peace was quickly reversed. Palestinians, complaining that the prisoners who were released were only "car thieves," not the political detainees they wanted, carried on violent protest activities.[20] These protests, together with a series of Palestinian terrorist attacks against Israelis, including the attempt to set off a bomb in the Mahane Yehudah market in Jerusalem and an attack on an Israeli soldier in Ramallah (actions that Arafat proved unwilling or unable to prevent), led Netanyahu, under heavy pressure from right-wing elements in his governing coalition, to freeze additional troop withdrawals on December 2. The Israeli prime minister conditioned the resumption of the withdrawals on Arafat halting what he called a campaign of incitement against Israel, foregoing his intention to declare a Palestinian state on May 4, 1999, and acceding to Israel's selection of the prisoners who were to be released.[21]

For its part, the Clinton administration, despite the ongoing impeachment process, was making major efforts to keep the peace process going.

On November 29, speaking at a Palestinian donor conference he had convened in Washington, President Clinton pledged $400 million in additional aid to the Palestinians, on top of the $500 million he had pledged in 1993. All told, some $3 billion in aid was pledged to the Palestinians (the European Union pledged 400 million ECU),[22] an amount that would greatly help the beleaguered Palestinian economy, although questions were raised at the conference about corrupt Palestinian officials siphoning off previous aid for their own personal use.[23] The United States also sought to downplay the conditions Netanyahu had placed on further Israeli troop withdrawals under the Wye Agreement, with State Department spokesman James P. Rubin stating on December 2, 1998, "The agreement should be implemented as signed. We do not believe it is appropriate to add new conditions to implementation of the agreement."[24] The most important effort to restore momentum to the Israeli-Palestinian peace process was taken by Clinton himself when he journeyed to Gaza in mid-December to witness the Palestinians formally abrogating the clauses in the Palestine National Charter calling for Israel's destruction, an action the Netanyahu government had long demanded. Clinton's visit resulted in a warming of relations between the United States and the Palestinian Authority, which received increased international legitimacy as a result of the U.S. president's visit—an outcome that Israeli critics of Netanyahu blamed on Netanyahu.[25]

While U.S.-Palestinian relations, at least on the level of the Palestinian "street," were to suffer a serious blow when the United States bombed Iraq two days after Clinton's visit to the Palestinian Authority,[26] Clinton's personal relationship with Arafat was to remain strong, as Arafat was to meet Clinton and Albright in Washington in early February 1999. In any case, Clinton's summit with Arafat and Netanyahu following the visit to Gaza proved unsuccessful despite the U.S. president's claims of reviving the stalled Middle East peace talks. Netanyahu held fast to his position that no further withdrawals would take place until the Palestinians met his conditions. This position proved the death knell for his coalition government, as members from within Netanyahu's ruling Likud Party, led by Defense Minister Yitzhak Mordechai, threatened to pull out of the government because of Netanyahu's obdurate position on the peace process. Suffering a major political blow when his finance minister, Ya'acov Ne'eman, resigned, Netanyahu moved to call for new elections before his government would fall on a no-confidence vote.[27] With elections scheduled for May 17, 1999, the peace process was in effect frozen, leaving the United States somewhat nervously on the diplomatic sidelines, hoping that Arafat would not prematurely declare a Palestinian state and thus strengthen the chances for Netanyahu's reelection.

Meanwhile, as the Israeli elections neared, the European Union provided another example of what might be termed "declaratory diplomacy" as the European Council, meeting in March 1999 in Berlin, issued a declaration that it was reaffirming "the continuing and unqualified Palestinian right to self-determination including the option of a state, and looks forward to the early fulfillment of this right."[28] The May 1999 Israeli elections initially appeared to bear out this hope as Labor Party leader Ehud Barak, a highly decorated soldier and a disciple of Yitzhak Rabin, running on a peace platform, decisively defeated Netanyahu 56 percent to 44 percent, a far larger margin than that by which Netanyahu had defeated Peres (50.5 percent to 49.5 percent). Following his defeat Netanyahu withdrew both from the Knesset and from the leadership of the Likud Party, to be replaced by Ariel Sharon. Yet while Barak began his period as prime minister amid great hope, less than two years later he ended it in political disgrace, defeated in the election for prime minister by Ariel Sharon by a two-to-one margin, with the peace process all but destroyed by the al-Aqsa intifada that erupted in September 2000 while he was prime minister.

The Barak Interlude

When Barak took office he switched the direction of Israel's peace policy from the Palestinian track to the Syrian track, and received positive signals from Syria. Barak may have thought that peace with Syria, which basically involved only territorial issues, would be easier to achieve than peace with the Palestinians, where negotiations had yet to deal with the highly sensitive issues of Jerusalem and the plight of Palestinian refugees. Needless to say, the Palestinian leadership took a dim view of the shift in priorities, as well as Barak's decision to allow the continued expansion of Jewish settlements on the West Bank. Barak permitted expansion of the settlements in order to keep the National Religious Party, whose constituency included the West Bank settlers, in his coalition. The expansion took place primarily in areas around Jerusalem, in cities like Maaleh Adumim that Barak hoped to annex. For his part Clinton went along with Barak's peace process priority and invested a great deal of his personal prestige, including a meeting with Hafiz al-Assad in Geneva in March 2000, to try to obtain a peace process breakthrough.[29] Despite Clinton's best efforts, however, an agreement with Syria was not achieved, in part because of a dispute over Syria's claim to territory on the northeast shore of the Sea of Galilee, and in part because of Hafiz al-Assad's rapidly deteriorating health (he was to die a few months after meeting Clinton in Geneva).

Barak then sought to politically outflank the Syrians by arranging a unilateral pullout from southern Lebanon in May 2000. Assad had been manipulating Hizballah attacks against Israeli forces in southern Lebanon, and occasional rocket attacks into Israel proper, as a means of pressuring Israel to be more flexible in its negotiations with Syria. Indeed, just such an escalation of fighting had occurred following the collapse of the Syrian-Israeli talks in February 1996. By unilaterally withdrawing from southern Lebanon, even without a peace treaty, Barak may have hoped to avoid a repetition of these events while gaining support in the international community, including the United States, which had long pressed for such a pullback. Unfortunately for Barak, while he may have received support from the international community, he set a precedent for withdrawing under fire and without an agreement, from a territory occupied by Israeli troops. This lesson was not lost on a number of Palestinians who felt that if Israel could be made to withdraw from Lebanon under fire, it could also be made to pull out of at least the West Bank and Gaza under similar pressure.

Following the failure of the Syrian talks, Barak turned back to the Palestinian track. After initial discussions between the two sides in May, Barak pushed for a summit in July in the United States where, at one stroke, all the remaining final-status issues, including those that had not yet been seriously discussed, such as Jerusalem and the refugee problem, could be settled and a peace agreement achieved. Clinton went along with Barak's plan and devoted two weeks of scarce presidential time to the summit, which became known as Camp David II. There have been many different explanations for the failure of the Camp David II summit with even members of the same delegation disagreeing as to the causes of the failure. Those sympathetic to Arafat blame Barak's negotiating style, his "take it or leave it" attitude, and his unwillingness to meet what they felt were even the minimum needs of the Palestinians. Those sympathetic to Barak note that he offered unheard-of Israeli concessions that threatened the viability of his coalition government, especially on Jerusalem, which hitherto Israel had contended was to remain united under Israeli control. Barak's supporters asserted that Arafat, by rejecting the Israeli concessions, demanding the return of the more than three million Palestinian refugees to Israel proper (which would have destroyed Israel as a Jewish state), and making no counteroffers, had demonstrated that he was not a serious partner for peace.[30] Following the failed summit, Clinton took Barak's side in the debate over who was responsible for the failure, thereby alienating Arafat, who lost badly in the court of Western opinion, including Western Europe where the Palestinian leader was also blamed for the summit failure. Following the failed summit, Arafat also came under criticism from Palestinians for his heavy-handed authoritarian ways and the corrupt practices within the Palestinian Authority. Arafat counterattacked, claiming he had defended the interests of the world's Muslims at Camp David by not making concessions on the Temple Mount/Haram. He also stepped up the military training given to Palestinian youth in special military camps, perhaps assuming that in the aftermath of the failure of the negotiations, the only alternative was renewed conflict.

Conflict was to come in late September 2000, following the visit of the new Likud leader, Ariel Sharon, to the Temple Mount/Haram. This move was linked to internal Israeli politics as Netanyahu had begun to challenge Sharon's leadership of the Likud Party. Palestinian rioting broke out, for which the Israeli police were ill prepared. As Palestinian casualties rose, the intifada spread and soon both the West Bank and Gaza erupted. The causes of the intifada are as much in dispute as the causes of the failure of Camp David II, as Palestinians and Israelis have very different narratives on the issue. For the Palestinians the uprising was the result of rising frustration over continued Israeli settlement expansion and the failure of the Oslo process to give them what they demanded; the visit of Sharon to the Temple Mount/Haram was the straw that broke the camel's back. Israelis saw the uprising as an attempt by Arafat to get by force what he could not get by negotiations, an effort to win back international public opinion by again becoming the David to Israel's Goliath as Palestinian casualties rose more quickly than Israeli. The Israelis perceived that Arafat intended to apply the lesson of Lebanon to force Israel to withdraw through the use of violence. Now, though, the Palestinians would not be limited to stones as in the first intifada; they would fight with gunfire and mortar attacks as the Palestinians turned the weapons given by the Israelis under the Oslo process against their one-time peace partners.[31] There was also the suspicion that whether or not Arafat himself precipitated the intifada, he was exploiting it to divert attention from Palestinian criticism of his authoritarian and corrupt practices.

Whatever the cause of the intifada, President Clinton sought to quell it, much as he had sought to end the violence in 1996 following Netanyahu's opening of the Hasmonean tunnel. Consequently he convened an Arafat-Barak summit at Sharm el-Sheikh on October 16 and proposed an investigatory commission to analyze the causes of the conflict. Attending the summit, in addition to Barak, Arafat, and Clinton, were Egypt's president Hosni Mubarak, Jordan's new king Abdullah II, UN secretary-general

Kofi Annan, and a representative of the European Union, as the United States for the first time included the EU in the politics of Middle East peacemaking (or, perhaps, peace salvaging). The Commission of Inquiry, headed by former U.S. senator George Mitchell, also had an EU representative, Javier Solana, the representative of the EU's newly established Common Foreign and Security Policy Institution, along with two other Europeans (albeit not representatives of EU states), Süleyman Demirel, former president of Turkey, a country with a defense agreement with Israel and one that had sought to follow an evenhanded policy in the Israeli-Palestinian conflict; and the foreign minister of Norway, the country that had facilitated the Oslo I agreement.

Unfortunately for Clinton, despite Arafat's pledge at Sharm el-Sheikh to stop the violence,[32] the task proved either beyond his will or beyond his ability to achieve, and the intifada not only continued, the violence escalated. Clinton tried again in December, preparing with the help of Dennis Ross and his colleagues an American plan to settle all the final-status issues, including the most heavily disputed ones over Jerusalem and the so-called right of return of Palestinian refugees. Essentially Clinton proposed some major trade-offs, urging Israel to withdraw from 95 percent of the West Bank while also compensating the Palestinians with Israeli territory near Gaza, making East Jerusalem the capital of the new Palestinian state, dividing the Temple Mount/Haram area, with the Palestinians getting the Temple Mount/Haram and Israel the Jewish quarter of the Old City, the Western Wall, and a passage to both through the Armenian quarter. On the issue of the Palestinian right of return, Clinton's plan called for the vast majority of refugees to go to the new Palestinian state.[33] Barak was willing to accept the plan even though he knew that with Israeli elections looming on February 7, he would run into problems with the Israeli electorate. For his part Arafat added so many conditions to his acceptance of the plan that he in fact rejected it, once again confirming to most Israelis that the Palestinian leader was not really interested in peace. To make matters worse several of his entourage made disparaging comments about Clinton, rather poor payment for the president's almost Herculean efforts he had made to settle the Israeli-Palestinian conflict and his personal support for Arafat.

The Bush Administration

Incoming U.S. president George W. Bush had witnessed the immense political capital that Clinton invested in trying to secure an Arab-Israeli peace agreement, and the very meager return on that investment. Even if

Bush had had the inclination to actively pursue an Arab-Israeli settlement, looking at Clinton's record he would have had pause. Adding to
Bush's hesitation was the fact that he entered the presidency with a minimum of political capital, having lost the popular vote for president to Al
Gore and only eking out a minimal victory over Gore in the electoral
college because of a hotly disputed vote count in Florida. In addition, the
Republicans had suffered major losses in the U.S. Senate in the fall 2000
election, controlling it in January 2001 only by a one-vote margin and
then losing control several months later when a liberal Republican defected from the ranks of his party. In addition Bush faced an economic
downturn. In sum, even if he had been inclined to undertake a major new
Middle East peace initiative, which he was not, the overall domestic
political situation in the United States appeared to preclude any such
initiative.

The Bush administration's policy toward the Arab-Israeli conflict
evolved through five stages in its first year. The stages were (1) the inauguration until the Powell visit to the Middle East in February 2001; (2) the
Powell visit to the Middle East until the Sharon, Mubarak, and Abdullah
visits to the United States in March and early April 2001; (3) the temporary reoccupation of Gazan land by Israeli forces in mid-April 2001 until
the issuance of the Mitchell Report in mid-May 2001; (4) the period between the suicide bombing of the Dolphinarium in Tel Aviv in June to the
suicide attacks on the World Trade Center and Pentagon in September;
and (5) the period since the September 11 suicide attacks.

From Bush's Inauguration to Powell's Middle East Trip

January–February 2001

When the Bush administration took office on January 20, 2001, it took a
long time to get its senior-level executives in place, especially with regard
to Middle Eastern affairs, where an assistant secretary of state was not
approved until late May. In addition, the administration was initially beset
by an extraordinary number of public disagreements over such policy issues as whether to strengthen sanctions against Iraq (Secretary of State
Colin Powell) or weaken them (Vice President Richard Cheney); whether
to take a more aggressive military stance against Iraq (Secretary of Defense
Rumsfeld and Deputy Secretary of Defense Wolfowitz—yes; Powell—no);
whether to pull U.S. peacekeeping forces out of the multinational force in
the Sinai (Rumsfeld—yes; Powell—no); whether to support negotiations
with North Korea (Powell—yes; Bush—no); whether to pull U.S. forces
out of Balkan peacekeeping missions (Powell—no; Rumsfeld—yes); and

whether to drill in the Arctic National Wildlife Refuge (Environmental Protection Agency head Christy Whitman—no; Bush—yes), to mention only a few of the disputes. In addition, the Bush administration faced a significant degree of optimism in the Arab world, especially among Palestinians, that Bush, following in the steps of his father, who had clashed openly with then Israeli prime minister Yitzhak Shamir, as well as with Sharon, would take a much tougher stance toward Israel than Clinton had done. In this they were to be sorely mistaken. Initially, Bush followed essentially a "not Clinton" policy and refused to get personally involved in trying to settle the conflict. Secretary of State Powell repeatedly emphasized the primary responsibility of the parties themselves to solve the conflict. "We will facilitate, but at the end of the day, it will have to be the parties in the region who will have to find the solution."[34]

In this, perhaps, the administration was hoping for a return to the situation that prevailed during the Oslo I and Oslo II agreements, which were negotiated directly between Israelis and Palestinians without significant U.S. intervention. The Bush administration followed up its words with deeds that emphasized the new hands-off policy. Thus when Special Middle East Envoy Dennis Ross retired in January 2001, no replacement was named, and it was not until late May, with the Israeli-Palestinian conflict rapidly escalating, that a "special assistant" for the Middle East, William Burns, was appointed. Second, the United States did not send a representative to the Israeli-Palestinian negotiations at Taba, which took place at the end of January, just before the February 7, 2001, Israeli elections.[35] Here the European Union stepped in with its special representative, Miguel Moratinos, attending. Third, the United States ended CIA mediation efforts between Israel and the Palestinians, which had begun as part of the Wye Plantation agreement of October 1998. Finally, and much to the displeasure of the Palestinians, Bush supported the Israeli position that the offers made by Israel at Camp David II and at Taba were off the table once the new Israeli government, headed by Likud leader Ariel Sharon, was elected on February 7, 2001.

Policy Making: Powell's Middle East Trip and the Visits of Sharon, Mubarak, and Abdullah

February–March 2001

Despite the effort to play down the U.S. role in the Arab-Israeli conflict, the first foreign trip undertaken by the newly appointed U.S. secretary of state was to the Middle East. Powell's purpose, however, was not to deal directly with the al-Aqsa intifada but rather to convince the Arab states to support his plans for "smart sanctions" against Iraq. However, his Arab hosts, including not only Egypt and Jordan, Kuwait, and Saudi Arabia but also Syria, had a different priority. They urged the Bush administration to become actively involved in settling the Arab-Israeli conflict. Evidently prepared for this eventuality, Powell, even before his arrival in the Middle East, had urged Israel to hand over $54 million in taxes owed to the Palestinian Authority (Israel had refused to do so as long as the PA was fomenting violence) and to lift the siege on the West Bank and Gaza, which Israel had imposed for security reasons. Secretary of State Powell repeated these points during his visit and also called for a renewal of peace talks after a reduction in violence—not the total cessation of violence demanded by Sharon.[36] However, Powell was to move closer to the Israeli position several weeks later.

On the eve of the Sharon visit to Washington in mid-March, Powell gave a major speech on the Middle East to a conference of the pro-Israeli AIPAC lobbying organization. In it, he moved to support Sharon's position on the violence, noting that the starting point for talks had to be the end of violence. In a clear slap at Arafat, Powell publicly stated that "leaders have the responsibility to denounce violence, strip it of legitimacy [and] stop it." Powell also repeated the Bush administration's position that the United States would assist, but not impose a peace agreement: "The U.S. stands ready to assist, not insist. Peace arrived at voluntarily by the partners themselves is likely to prove more robust . . . than a peace widely viewed as developed by others, or worse yet, imposed."[37]

When Sharon met with Bush several days later, he was again reassured that the United States would facilitate, not force, the peace process. Bush also sought to enlist Sharon in his campaign to develop a national missile defense system, something the Israeli leader, whose country was a prime target of such rogue states as Iran and Iraq, was only too happy to agree to. Sharon, for his part, pressed Bush not to invite Arafat to the White House unless Arafat publicly called for an end to the violence, a request endorsed by nearly 300 members of Congress (87 Senators and 209 House members), who also called on Bush to close the PLO's Washington office and cut U.S. aid to the PA if the violence did not cease.[38]

Yet the Sharon visit, as successful as it was, was not without its problems. On the eve of the visit, Sharon authorized the construction of more Jewish housing in the East Jerusalem suburb of Har Homa, near Bethlehem, a development criticized by State Department spokesman Richard Boucher as a unilateral act "not contributing to peace and stability."[39] In

addition, Secretary of Defense Rumsfeld, apparently oblivious to the escalating conflict between Israel and the Palestinians that had caused a result-
ant deterioration in Israeli-Egyptian relations, told Sharon that the United
States wanted to withdraw U.S. forces serving as peacekeepers in the
multinational force in the Sinai Desert.[40]

Still, the Sharon visit was clearly a success and marked a high point in
the U.S.-Israeli relationship for the new Israeli leader, who had been
severely criticized by previous U.S. administrations. At the end of March,
the United States vetoed a UN Security Council resolution calling for a
UN observer force on the West Bank and Gaza as "unbalanced and un-
workable,"[41] and Bush, in a news conference, took the strongest anti-
Palestinian position of the administration to this point: "The Palestinian
Authority should speak out publicly and forcibly in a language that the
Palestinian people (understand) to condemn violence and terrorism. . . .
The signal I am sending to the Palestinians is stop the violence and I can't
make it any more clear."[42]

During their visits to Washington in late March and early April, Egyptian president Mubarak and Jordan's King Abdullah II called for a more
active U.S. role. The Bush administration continued to insist that the Israelis and Palestinians had to bear the primary responsibility for coming to an
agreement. Unfortunately for Bush, however, an upsurge of Israeli-Palestinian fighting was to call into question the U.S. strategy.

From Israel's Incursion into Gaza to the Mitchell Report

Mid-May

Following the Sharon visit to Washington and the U.S. veto of the UN
Security Council resolution, the Palestinians escalated the fighting in an
apparent attempt to precipitate an Israeli reprisal that would force both
the United States and the European Union (Israel's primary trade partner)
to take action. Thus the Palestinians began to fire mortars not just at
Israeli settlements in Gaza but also into Israel proper. This indeed brought
a major Israeli response, with Israeli forces in April invading the section of
Gaza from which the mortars had been fired into Israel. Israeli brigadier
general Yair Naveh stated that Israel would stay there "as long as it
takes—days, weeks, months." Powell termed the Israeli action "excessive
and disproportionate," and the Israeli forces soon withdrew, seemingly
under U.S. pressure. Nonetheless, Powell also blamed the Palestinians for
precipitating the Israeli attack with "provocative" mortar attacks on Israeli territory.[43] The United States also disappointed Israel when the State

Department's annual terrorist report did not brand the PA as a terrorist organization for its role in fostering the intifada (and the terrorist bombings that were a part of it). Instead, the report only noted that the Israeli government had accused the PA of facilitating terrorist attacks.[44]

Meanwhile, as Palestinian mortar and other attacks against Israel continued to increase, Israel stepped up its retaliatory raids into territories in Gaza controlled by the Palestinian Authority, although it quickly withdrew each time. The United States condemned the attacks and Israel's retaliatory efforts, with State Department spokesman Boucher noting that the Israeli responses represented "a serious escalation that causes concern that makes it harder to resolve this." Boucher also criticized the Palestinians, who "have to immediately end provocative acts of violence."[45] Meanwhile, possibly as a response to Palestinian actions, Sharon once again began to push settlement expansion, claiming that the West Bank and Gaza were not "occupied" territory, but "disputed" territory.[46] This prompted the expected denunciation from the State Department (which mirrored criticism on the left of the Israeli political spectrum) with State Department spokesman Phillip Reeker denouncing the expansion as he stated, "This activity risks further inflaming the already volatile situation in the region and is provocative."[47]

The fighting escalated further, as terrorist attacks by Palestinians were met by increasingly severe Israeli reprisals, including the use, for the first time, of Israeli jet fighters to bombard Palestinian positions. The Bush administration seemed hard pressed to respond to the situation; its only hope appeared to be the publication of the Mitchell Report in mid-May. The report gave the administration a diplomatic framework on which to base its Middle East position.

Conceived at the Sharm el-Sheikh summit in October 2000 as a device to determine the causes of the al-Aqsa intifada and find ways to bring the fighting to a halt, the report was delivered by a commission headed by former U.S. senator George Mitchell, who had been President Clinton's special envoy to the conflict between Protestants and Catholics in Northern Ireland. The report did not assign blame to either side for starting the intifada; instead, it described each side's reasons for blaming the other for the outbreak and continuation of the intifada. It also listed a series of steps the Israelis and Palestinians should take to resume negotiations. These included, in sequential order: (1) a 100 percent effort to stop the violence; (2) the immediate resumption of security cooperation; (3) the exchange of confidence-building measures; and (4) the speedy return to serious negotiations.[48] In many ways the Mitchell Report was supportive of the Israeli position in the conflict and far more favorable to Israel than the peace plan proposed earlier by Egypt and Jordan. Thus it called for a cease-fire before negotiations; and it called for the PA to condemn incitement and denounce terrorism, to arrest terrorists, and to prevent gunmen from using Palestinian populated areas to fire upon Israeli populated areas and Israeli military positions. It also did not blame Sharon's visit to the Temple Mount/Haram for precipitating the intifada. On the negative side, as far as Israeli prime minister Sharon was concerned, was the call to freeze all settlement activity, including "natural growth," as a necessary confidence-building measure. (Israel has always held to the position that the future of the settlements was a final-status issue to be negotiated by the two sides.) Still, on balance, it was a report that was quite sympathetic to the Israeli position, and Sharon, while having reservations about the settlement issue, agreed to order a cease-fire and called on Israeli forces not to fire upon Palestinians unless fired upon. For their part the Palestinians, while also accepting the report in principle, made cooperation contingent on a halt to the building of settlements. Palestinian deeds, however, did not follow their words as a series of terrorist attacks were mounted against Israel in Hadera and Jerusalem along with the killing of Jews in the West Bank and Gaza, activities that the PA could not, or would not, stop. Meanwhile, Powell, who warmly praised the Mitchell Report, appointed a special assistant to help implement it. William Burns, the U.S. ambassador to Jordan, who had been nominated to become the assistant secretary of state for Near Eastern affairs, was given the task of trying to establish a time line of Israeli and Palestinian confidence-building measures that might bring about the unconditional cease-fire deemed an absolute necessity by the Mitchell Report.[49] Still, despite Burns's appointment and subsequent efforts to secure a resumption of security cooperation between the Israelis and Palestinians, Powell continued to echo the administration theme that the United States would not directly intervene, as had the Clinton administration, to put forth its own solution to the conflict. Powell asserted that the United States was neither ready to get involved in shuttle diplomacy nor was it ready to get involved in sensitive final-status issues. This was to change with the Dolphinarium suicide bombing in June 2001.

U.S. Policy from a Tel Aviv Disco Suicide Bombing to the Suicide Attacks on the World Trade Center and the Pentagon

June–September 2001

The United States was to become more involved, albeit only briefly, following the suicide bombing of the Tel Aviv beachfront disco, the Dolphinarium, that killed twenty-one people, mostly teenagers, on June 1, 2001. With Israeli prime minister Sharon under heavy pressure not only to terminate the cease-fire initiated by the Mitchell plan but also to launch a massive attack on the Palestinian leadership, Arafat, who had held back from accepting a cease-fire, finally endorsed it. In part this was due to pressure from Bush, who strongly condemned the bombing, stating, "I condemn in the strongest terms the heinous terrorist attack in Tel Aviv this Sabbath evening. There is no justification for senseless attacks against innocent civilians. This illustrates the urgent need for an immediate, unconditional cessation of violence." Bush also called on Arafat "to condemn this act and call for an immediate cease-fire."[50] Arafat's condemnation of the terrorist act and his call for a cease-fire was also due to heavy pressure from German foreign minister Joshka Fischer, who indicated that the terrorist act had cost the Palestinians dearly in public opinion not only in the United States but also in Europe.[51] Bush followed Arafat's call for a cease-fire by sending CIA chief George Tenet to the Middle East to consolidate the cease-fire, something that was achieved, on paper at least, on June 13. Almost immediately, however, the cease-fire began to break down. Neither Hamas leader Abdel Aziz Rantisi nor Fatah leader Marwan Barghouti supported the cease-fire, and Arafat either could not or would not prevent further attacks on Israel. To prevent the situation from deteriorating further, Bush sent Secretary of State Powell to the Middle East several weeks later. Powell's visit came after an open disagreement between Sharon, who was visiting the United States, and President Bush, with Bush, perhaps accenting the positive, stating "progress had been made toward controlling the violence" and Sharon saying that mediation would not work as long as the shooting continued.[52] In any case, the Powell trip proved to be a failure, as violence not only continued but escalated during the summer with drive-by shootings of Israeli settlers, mortar firing into Jewish settlements in Gaza and into Gilo, a suburb of Jerusalem occupied after the 1967 war, and several suicide bombings including one in a pizza parlor in Jerusalem that killed fifteen Israelis along with the suicide bomber. As these events transpired, Sharon responded both militarily and diplomatically. On the diplomatic front, he went to France, Italy, and Germany in early July seeking to convince the Europeans to pressure Arafat to halt the attacks on Israel, much as Fischer had pressured the Palestinian leader to agree to a cease-fire after the Dolphinarium bombing. He was not successful in his quest, hearing from Gerhard Schroeder, chancellor of Germany and Israel's best friend in Europe, that the Mitchell Report should be implemented, even if the violence had not come to a halt.[53] With the United States again taking a hands-off policy following the failure of the Powell mission, and Europe unwilling to bring the desired diplomatic pressure on Arafat, Sharon stepped up Israel's military reaction as a war of attrition intensified between Israelis and Palestinians. The Israeli actions included not only incursions into Palestinian territory and the takeover of Orient House, the de facto Palestinian headquarters in East Jerusalem, but also assassinations of Palestinians suspected by Israel of planning terrorist attacks, including, at the end of August, the leader of the Popular Front for the Liberation of Palestine, Abu Ali Mustafa. There was a mixed U.S. reaction to the Israeli assassination policy. State Department spokesman Richard Boucher condemned it, stating, "Israel needs to understand that targeted killings of Palestinians don't end the violence but are only inflaming an already volatile situation and making it much harder to restore calm."[54] Taking an opposing view was U.S. vice president Dick Cheney, who had stated on Fox TV in early August, "If you've got an organization that has plotted or is plotting, some kind of suicide bomber attack, for example, and they have hard evidence of who it is and where they're located, I think there's some justification in their trying to protect themselves by preempting."[55] Meanwhile, President Bush, who had used U.S. influence at the United Nations to prevent an anti-Israeli resolution on international monitors from being approved, remained adamant that Arafat must "put 100 percent effort into stopping the terrorist activity" before the beginning of peace talks and "do a better job of quashing violence."[56] With diplomacy frozen, the Palestinian-Israeli conflict intensified. America's Arab allies, including Egypt, called for the United States to take a more active role because Arafat could not stop the violence on his own and "America is the only sponsor of the peace process."[57] The outspoken French foreign minister, Hubert Vedrine, caustically compared Bush to Pontius Pilate, washing his hands of the Middle East. Despite all the pressure to become involved, the United States remained on the diplomatic sidelines. This was to change after the terrorist attacks on the World Trade Center and the Pentagon on September 11, 2001.

After the Terrorist Attacks of September 11

Immediately after the terrorist attacks on the World Trade Center and the Pentagon, the United States changed its hands-off policy toward the Israeli-Palestinian conflict and sought to build a coalition including Muslim states against Osama Bin Laden and his al-Qaeda terrorist organization. In an effort to gain Arab support, the United States announced its support of a Palestinian state and put a considerable amount of pressure on Sharon to agree to a meeting between Israeli foreign minister Shimon Peres and Arafat to establish yet another cease-fire, despite the fact that Palestinian violence had not stopped as Sharon had demanded as the price for talks. Since the violence continued after the cease-fire, including a terrorist bombing in Jerusalem and an attack on a Jewish settlement in Gaza, there was some question as to the long-term effect of the Peres-Arafat meeting— and the U.S. strategy. Meanwhile, European states also became active in trying to build the coalition with Muslim states, with European leaders visiting states such as Iran with which the United States did not have diplomatic relations. The initial activities of the European states raised questions as to their impartiality—and their future ability to serve as me-diators—in the Arab-Israeli conflict. Thus, trying to curry the favor of Iran (a policy that was, at least initially, to backfire, when Iran's supreme reli-gious leader Ayatollah Khameini repudiated cooperation with the United States), British foreign minister Jack Straw issued a statement that "One of the factors that helps breed terrorism is the anger many people in the region feel at events over the years in Palestine."[58] This statement was perceived as legitimizing Palestinian terrorism, with some Israelis wonder-ing if Straw's use of the term "Palestine" and his visit to Iran, a supporter of terrorism and a nation that called for Israel's destruction, indicated that Britain had demonstratively tilted to Israel's enemies. While a call from Prime Minister Blair to Sharon assuaged the Israeli prime minister, what appeared to be British pandering to the Iranian government (still number one on the U.S. terrorist list) left a very bad impression on the Israelis. Similarly, France angered Israel when its ambassador to Israel, Jacques Huntziger, appeared to legitimize Palestinian terrorism by stating there could be no comparisons between the terrorism in the United States and Palestinian terrorism in Israel because "terror here is connected to the Israeli-Palestinian situation" and "it is completely irresponsible, politi-cally, to make such a comparison."[59] Israel complained that Britain and France were legitimating some acts of terrorism while deploring others. The United States, by putting some terrorist organizations on its frozen-funds list, while conspicuously omitting others, such as Hamas, Islamic Jihad, and Hizballah, appeared to be doing the same thing. Interestingly enough, India, facing terrorist attacks from Pakistani-based terrorist orga-nizations that were also omitted from the list, had the same complaint as Israel: it appeared that the United States and its European allies, in trying to win over the Muslim world, were legitimating some kinds of terrorism but not others, and thereby seemingly encouraging some terrorists—all in the name of building a coalition against Osama Bin Laden. Frustrated by this policy, Sharon called it the equivalent of British and French policy at the 1938 Munich Conference when Czechoslovakia was sold out to the Nazis. His comments drew a retort from the White House press secretary, Ari Fleischer, calling them "unacceptable."[60] While Sharon was later to apologize, claiming his words were misinterpreted, the basic issue remained unresolved and was a cause of growing friction in U.S.-Israeli relations.

Meanwhile, Palestinian attacks on Israel escalated and so did retaliation by the Israeli army. In the latter part of October, Israeli cabinet minister Rehavam Zeevi was assassinated in a Jerusalem hotel, and this precipitated a move by the Israeli army into six major Palestinian cities to search for the assassins because, as Sharon asserted, Arafat continued to refuse to arrest Palestinians who attacked Israelis. The Israelis also stepped up their policy of killing or capturing suspected terrorists. Israelis compared their actions to that of the United States in Afghanistan, arguing that just as the United States was justified in attacking the Taliban for harboring terrorists, so too was Israel in invading the Palestinian areas looking for terrorists.[61]

The U.S. State Department, however, had a different view—at least at that time. State Department spokesman Philip Reeker, noting the Palestinian casualties resulting from the Israeli incursions, stated that Israeli forces "should be withdrawn immediately from all Palestinian-controlled areas. We deeply regret and deplore Israeli defense force actions that have killed numerous Palestinian civilians over the weekend."[62] He also stated that Israel should abstain from further incursions. President Bush was a bit milder in his criticism, noting, "I would hope the Israelis would move their troops as quickly as possible." Bush balanced the criticism of Israel, however, with criticism of Arafat: "We continue to call upon Chairman Arafat to do everything he can to bring the killer to justice. It is very important that he arrest the person who did this act—and continue to arrest those who would disrupt and harm Israeli citizens. He must show the resolve necessary to bring peace to the region."[63]

This, however, was to be the low point in the U.S.-Israeli relationship through the end of 2001. Beginning in November the United States scored a series of military victories in Afghanistan (the bombing had begun, albeit in a limited way, in October) as Secretary of Defense Donald Rumsfeld's military activities took precedence over Colin Powell's limited success in coalition building.[64] Hitherto the United States had gotten, at best, very limited support, except for some intelligence cooperation from its main

Arab allies in the Middle East, Saudi Arabia and Egypt, whose media were filled with anti-American rhetoric. Indeed the majority of the hijackers in the September 11 terrorist attacks came from Saudi Arabia, but the Saudis refused to permit the United States to use its bases on Saudi soil to launch attacks against Taliban targets in Afghanistan, although the Saudis did break diplomatic relations with the Taliban regime, as did the UAE. The Saudi and Egyptian religious establishments also did not condemn the September 11 suicide attacks as contrary to Islam, until the Taliban had already been defeated.[65] The only Arab leader who expressed strong support for the United States was King Abdullah II of Jordan, who was rewarded with the rapid passage of the U.S.-Jordanian free trade agreement.

By contrast the United States received a great deal of assistance from Pakistani leader Pervez Musharraf, who exploited the September attacks to crack down on the Pakistani religious groups that were both supporting the Taliban and threatening his regime. He also could justify his policy as preventing a U.S.-Indian alliance aimed at Pakistan, given India's rapid endorsement of the U.S. antiterrorism campaign.

In any case as the Taliban fled one city after another in Afghanistan, often leaving operational equipment such as tanks behind, they became increasingly discredited. The same was true for Osama Bin Laden, whose call for the Moslem world to rise up against the United States received little active support from Muslims except for some Pakistani youth, whose efforts to join his jihad against the United States proved to be a disaster as many were killed or captured or returned embittered to Pakistan.[66]

In this atmosphere of military victory, the United States embarked on a twofold strategy. The first, to try to reinvigorate the Israeli-Palestinian peace process, was warmly greeted by its European allies and by pro-U.S. governments in the Arab world. The second strategy, to threaten to carry the war from Afghanistan to other supporters of terror such as Iraq, met with far less support. Britain, America's closest ally in the anti-Taliban war, opposed an attack on Iraq, as did Russia, America's new ally in the war against terrorism, which had endorsed the establishment of U.S. bases in Central Asia.

The U.S. effort to invigorate the Israeli-Palestinian peace process began with a speech by President Bush at the United Nations, where he said, "We are working for the day when two states—Israel and Palestine—live peacefully together within secure and recognized boundaries." However, in a clear warning to Arafat to crack down on terrorists, he also noted, "Peace will come when all have sworn off forever incitement, violence and terror. There is no such thing as a good terrorist."[67] Bush also pointedly did not meet Arafat at the United Nations. As Condoleezza Rice, his national security adviser, noted, "You cannot help us with al-Qaeda, and hug Hizballah or Hamas. And so the President makes that clear to Mr. Arafat."[68] The United States backed up Rice's words by adding Hamas, Islamic Jihad, and Hizballah to the post–September 11 terrorist list.

The next step in the U.S. peace effort came on November 19 with a major speech by Secretary of State Colin Powell on the U.S. view of a solution to the Israeli-Palestinian conflict.[69] In his speech Powell strongly condemned Palestinian terrorism, noting that the al-Aqsa intifada was now mired in "self-defeating violence." He also stated that, while the United States believed that there should be a two-state solution to the conflict, with two states, Palestine and Israel, living side by side in secure and recognized borders, the Palestinians must make a 100 percent effort to stop terrorism, and for this actions, not words, were required, and terrorists must be arrested. He emphasized that "no wrong can ever justify the murder of the innocent," that terror and violence must stop now, and Palestinians must realize their goals by negotiations, not violence. He further asserted, possibly in response to Arafat's call for the return of the more than 3 million Palestinian refugees to Israel, something that would have upset Israel's demographic balance, that the Palestinians must accept the legitimacy of Israel as a Jewish state.

As far as Israel was concerned, while emphasizing the close ties between the two countries, "bound together by democratic tradition," and the "enduring and iron-clad commitment [of the United States] to Israeli security," Powell indicated that Israel too had to make concessions for peace to be possible. These included a stop to settlement activity and an end to the occupation of the West Bank and Gaza that "causes humiliation and the killing of innocents." In conclusion he stated that the United States would do everything it could to facilitate the peace process "but at the end of the day the peoples have to make peace"—a position very similar to the one Powell held when he took office almost a year before.

In order to implement the U.S. vision of peace, Powell announced, in addition to promises of economic aid, the dispatch of Assistant Secretary of State William Burns and the former marine general Anthony Zinni to meet with Israeli and Palestinian delegations to reach a cease-fire that would lay the basis for the resumption of peace negotiations. In an effort to facilitate the Zinni mission, Bush put his personal prestige on the line by writing to five important Arab leaders, King Abdullah II of Jordan, Egyptian president Hosni Mubarak, King Mohammed VI of Morocco,

Saudi Arabia's Crown Prince Abdullah (who had publicly praised Powell's speech), and President Bin 'Ali of Tunisia, asking for their help in persuading "the Palestinian leadership to take action to end violence and get the peace process back on track."[70] For his part, Zinni stated that his goal was achieving a cease-fire that would allow for the implementation of the Mitchell plan. The former marine general asserted that he would stay in the region "as long as needed" to complete his mission.[71] Unfortunately for Zinni it was to be a most ill-fated mission and one that left not only the peace process but also U.S.-Palestinian relations close to collapse.

Almost as soon as Zinni arrived he had to confront Palestinian terrorism—the terrorism that both Bush and Powell had asked Arafat to prevent. Thus on November 27 two Palestinian terrorists, one of whom was a member of Arafat's Fatah organization (the other was from Islamic Jihad), killed three Israelis and wounded thirty others in Afulah, a town in northern Israel. Zinni responded to the violence in a balanced way, stating, "This is why we need a cease-fire. Both sides have suffered too much."[72] Zinni then met with Arafat, asking him to end the violence, but even as they were meeting, Palestinian gunmen fired at the Israeli Jerusalem neighborhood of Gilo from the neighboring Palestinian suburb of Beit Jala—despite an explicit promise by Palestinian leaders not to do so in October.[73] The next day three more Israelis were killed as a suicide bomber exploded a bomb on a public bus near the Israeli city of Hadera.[74] This time Zinni's response was much stronger, as he asserted, "The groups that do this are clearly trying to make my mission fail. There's no justification, no rationale, no sets of conditions that will ever make terrorist acts a right way to respond."[75] Zinni's words, however, did not stem the tide of terrorism as two days later suicide bombers killed ten Israeli teenagers who had gathered at the Ben Yehudah pedestrian mall in Jerusalem. This time Arafat condemned the attacks, stressing not the loss of life by Israel but the negative political effect the suicide bombers were having on the Palestinian world image: "The goal of the attacks has been to destroy the American peace efforts. These attacks cause great damage to our people in international public opinion and the Palestinian Authority will do everything in its power to catch those responsible. It pays its condolences to the Israeli people."[76]

Zinni, however, by now was furious as he saw his mission literally going up in flames. He demanded that "Those responsible for planning and carrying out these attacks must be found and brought to justice. This is an urgent task and there can be no delay or excuses for not acting decisively. The deepest evil one can imagine is to attack young people and children."[77] President Bush, whose prestige had been put on the line by the Zinni mission, also responded strongly. "Now more than ever chairman Arafat and the Palestinian Authority must demonstrate through their actions and not merely their words, their commitment to fight terror."[78]

Even Bush's words, however, did not suffice to stop the terrorism; one day later fifteen Israelis were killed in a suicide bomber attack on an Israeli bus in Haifa. While Powell, Bush, and Zinni had asserted that nothing justified such terrorist attacks, Hamas, the organization responsible for the bus bombing, justified it as "the natural retaliation by a people slaughtered day and night, whose dignity is humiliated by the Zionist enemy."[79] The Hamas justification was directly contrary to the U.S. position that nothing justified terrorism, and it is not surprising that this time when Israel retaliated against the Palestinian Authority, the United States did not respond critically. Sharon ordered the destruction of Arafat's helicopters and the airport runway in Gaza—in a symbolic blow to Arafat's position as a leader who traveled the world—and also attacked PA security headquarters on the West Bank and Gaza. Israel also reimposed closure on the major Palestinian West Bank cities from which Israel had withdrawn as a gesture to the United States when Zinni began his visit. Presidential spokesman Ari Fleisher noted, "Obviously Israel has the right to defend herself, and the President understands that clearly."[80] In addition, in reinforcing the U.S. demand that Arafat imprison the terrorists and keep them in jail, Fleisher noted, "The President thinks it is very important that Palestinian jails not only have bars on the front, but no longer have revolving doors at the back."[81] Dennis Ross, the former U.S. envoy to the Arab-Israeli conflict, who had devoted more than a decade of his life to the peace process, was far more caustic in his criticism of Arafat: "Mr. Arafat must act. For 15 months he has allowed his territory to be a haven for those who attack Israelis. They have been free to plan and organize, to build their bombs and recruit their bombers. Despite every commitment he has made to renounce violence and terror he has shown a complete tolerance for both, releasing suicide bombers from jail and lying about it. This has to stop. . . . He must decide that the Palestinian Authority will not be a safe haven for terrorists. He must stop glorifying suicide bombers by calling them martyrs. . . . A Palestinian war on Palestinian terrorists is the only way to save the Palestinian Authority."[82]

Bush stepped up the pressure on Palestinian terrorism by freezing the assets of the Holy Land Foundation for Relief and Development, which the United States contended was linked to Hamas.[83] At the same time a

U.S. Senate resolution was introduced that added to the pressure on Arafat by calling on President Bush to suspend relations with Arafat if he failed to "destroy the infrastructure of Palestinian terrorist groups."[84] Meanwhile, the European Union (under pressure from influential Americans like Richard Perle to cut aid to the Palestinian Authority),[85] although seeking to maintain a balanced position, also stepped up the pressure on Arafat. While calling on Israel to stop destroying the infrastructure of the Palestinian Authority, it also called on the Palestinians to take concrete steps to arrest those involved in recent terrorist attacks and to dismantle Hamas and Islamic Jihad.[86] At the end of December it took a further step by expanding the EU list of terrorist organizations to include, among others, Islamic Jihad and the Izzedine al-Qassam Brigade, a wing of Hamas.[87] The United States and the European Union split, however, on a UN Security Council resolution in mid-December calling for a monitoring mechanism to ease conditions in the West Bank while also condemning all terrorist acts, executions without trial, excessive use of force, and the destruction of property. Calling the resolution unbalanced and aimed at isolating Israel politically, the United States vetoed the resolution, while France voted for it and Britain abstained.[88]

As the pressure built, Arafat began to arrest some terrorists, but far fewer than either the United States or Israel demanded. Meanwhile, yet another Palestinian suicide bomber struck in Haifa, blowing himself up before boarding a bus,[89] and three days later ten Israelis were killed when Hamas detonated bombs under a bus traveling in the West Bank and shot passengers trying to flee. An exasperated Israeli government announced that "Chairman Arafat has made himself irrelevant as far as Israel is concerned" and that it was breaking all contact with him.[90] Then, as a further blow to Arafat, Israeli tanks surrounded his compound in Ramallah, and Israeli troops blew up the main transmission tower of the Palestine Broadcasting Company while also hitting offices of Arafat's Fatah organizations in Gaza, Ramallah, and Jenin.[91] Meanwhile, it was clear that the United States, and especially President Bush, was also thoroughly exasperated by Arafat, who had done nothing to prevent Palestinian terrorists from destroying the mission of General Zinni on which he had staked his personal prestige.[92] U.S. secretary of state Colin Powell stated diplomatically that the United States "really can't give up hope, we can't walk away from this, the stakes are too high." Nonetheless, Powell also warned that Hamas was "more likely to destroy the Palestinian cause than to destroy the State of Israel" and stated that the "burden" was on Arafat to stop the spiral of violence.[93]

Arafat seemed belatedly to get the message from U.S. and EU political pressure and from Israeli military pressure. On December 16 he called for an immediate cease-fire, condemning both suicide attacks and the launching of mortar attacks.[94] Nonetheless the Palestinian leader did not root out the Hamas and Islamic Jihad organizations from Gaza and the West Bank but rather negotiated a tenuous truce with them, something that was clearly unsatisfactory to the Israeli government, which kept him penned up in Ramallah and, in a further blow to his prestige, prohibited him from leaving Ramallah to attend Christmas services in Bethlehem. Meanwhile, while saying that the United States would remain involved in trying to mediate the Israeli-Palestinian conflict, Powell returned Zinni to the United States (so much for Zinni saying he would stay as long as necessary to solve the crisis),[95] while Powell himself began to devote his time to trying to prevent a war between India and Pakistan, both of which had nuclear weapons, following an attack on the Indian legislature on December 13 by Muslim terrorists who India claimed were backed by Pakistan.[96] After intense U.S. mediation President Musharraf agreed to ban a number of Islamic terrorist groups, including Lashkar-e-Taiba and Jaish-e-Mohammed, the two organizations India blamed for the December 13 attack, and the two countries stepped back from the brink of war.[97] As part of its efforts to prevent an Indian attack on Pakistan, the United States belatedly put the two Islamic groups on its post–September 11 terrorist list, much as it had earlier done to Hamas and Islamic Jihad.[98]

Meanwhile, Arafat's tenuous truce began to break down less than three weeks after it had begun. In early January 2002 Israeli forces captured a ship, the *Karine-A,* with fifty tons of weapons including C-4 explosives and Katusha rockets—clearly weapons of terrorism. Arafat's initial denial that the Palestinian Authority had anything to do with the vessel further undermined his credibility, both in the United States and in Israel, although, under heavy U.S. pressure, he was later to arrest several of the Palestinian officials involved, including a major general in his own security forces and an officer in the Palestinian Authority's naval police.[99] Meanwhile Hamas broke the truce by attacking an Israeli military outpost in Gaza, killing four Israeli soldiers and claiming it was in retaliation for Israel's seizure of the weapons ship.[100] Israel's retaliation was not long in coming. First it hit a series of Palestinian naval targets, setting a fuel depot and a barracks on fire and destroying a number of boats docked in Gaza. It also destroyed a series of Palestinian homes in a refugee camp that it claimed gave cover to the Hamas attackers. Finally, it ripped up the runway of the Palestinian airport in Gaza as yet another symbolic act against

Arafat, although the action drew criticism from EU officials because the European Union had paid for construction of the airport.[101] By contrast Powell called the Israeli actions defensive in nature and warned Arafat that failure to take action against those involved in the arms smuggling would "complicate enormously" relations between Arafat and the United States.[102]

Following the Hamas attack and the Israeli reprisal, violence began to escalate. Israeli forces killed Raed Karmi, a Palestinian Fatah militia leader who had killed a number of Israelis in the previous few months.[103] Palestinian terrorists linked to Arafat's own Tanzim militia responded by killing six Israeli civilians and wounding more than thirty at a Bat Mitzvah party in the Israeli town of Hadera.[104] The Israeli response was to move its tanks to within 100 meters of Arafat's compound in Ramallah and then to destroy the main Palestinian radio transmitter.[105] Meanwhile, Colin Powell, sensing the atmosphere was not ripe for another visit by General Zinni, had already called off his visit to the Middle East.[106]

Thus ended the first year of the Bush administration's on-and-off efforts to end the Israeli-Palestinian conflict. The terrorist attacks by Arafat's Tanzim militia and the Israeli responses in mid-January 2002 serve as a useful point of departure for drawing some conclusions about the Bush administration's initial year of effort to end Israeli-Palestinian violence, and the role, if any, the European Union could play to aid the U.S. effort.

Conclusions

In looking at the course of U.S. policy toward the Arab-Israeli conflict under both President Clinton and President Bush and the very limited role of the EU so far in the peace process, several conclusions can be drawn. First, the greatest progress was made when the parties themselves, Israelis, Palestinians, and Jordanians, negotiated directly, securing the Oslo I (September 1993) and Oslo II (September 1995) agreements, as well as the Jordanian-Israeli peace treaty (October 1994). In all three cases the United States was essentially a cheerleader on the sidelines. When relations broke down between Israelis and Palestinians, however, the United States stepped in, with Special Envoy Dennis Ross playing the major role in securing the Hebron agreement in January 1997. Following a further deterioration of Israeli-Palestinian relations, it became necessary for President Clinton himself to be personally involved, and after hard negotiations he managed to secure another agreement in October 1998 at the Wye Plantation. The Wye Agreement, however, fell apart several months later, and the Israeli government collapsed soon afterward. When Ehud Barak became Israeli prime minister, he initially chose to give priority to the Syrian track, and President Clinton sought unsuccessfully to mediate an Israeli-Syrian agreement. Unfortunately for Clinton, when he and Barak then turned to the Palestinian track, his efforts again failed despite a two-week effort at Camp David II. When the al-Aqsa intifada broke out, Clinton again sought to use his influence, this time to quell the violence. In October, he convened the sides at Sharm el-Sheikh, but to no avail, and his December 2000 peace plan was contemptuously rejected by the Palestinians—despite all of Clinton's efforts to bring about a Palestinian state.

Given President Clinton's record of failure despite his major personal involvement, it is not surprising that President Bush, who came into office with a weak political mandate and with other political priorities, was initially wary of getting heavily involved in the Israeli-Palestinian conflict. Bush's position, as articulated by Secretary of State Powell, was that the two sides should settle the conflict themselves, with the United States *assisting*, not *insisting*. Perhaps to the surprise of many Arab observers, Bush also tilted toward the Israeli side, calling for an end to the violence before substantive negotiations could begin. As the United States adopted a hands-off attitude, violence mounted, and the United States warmly endorsed the May 2001 Mitchell Report as a way to stop the violence and return to negotiations. While Israeli prime minister Sharon proved willing to have a cease-fire, Palestinian Authority chairman Yasser Arafat was not, until a Palestinian suicide bomber killed more than twenty young Israelis at the Dolphinarium on Tel Aviv's seafront at the beginning of June 2001. Under heavy pressure from both Bush and German foreign minister Joshka Fischer, Arafat acceded to the cease-fire but proved unwilling or unable to enforce it as both Hamas and Arafat's own Tanzim militia refused to agree to stop fighting. In an effort to salvage the situation, Bush sent first CIA director George Tenet and then Colin Powell to resuscitate the cease-fire, to no avail. Consequently, having gotten heavily involved in the Israeli-Palestinian conflict despite his initial reluctance to do so, and having had no more success in stopping the violence than President Clinton had had, Bush pulled back. With the United States moving into the background, the European Union stepped forward to try to reach an Israeli-Palestinian agreement, but its efforts proved no more successful than those of the United States, and by September 10, the day before the terrorist attacks in New York and Washington, violence between Israelis and Palestinians had risen sharply.

Following the terrorist attacks, the United States became reengaged in the Israeli-Palestinian conflict, this time appearing to tilt to the Palestinian side as the United States sought to build a Muslim and Arab-supported coalition against Osama Bin Laden and his charges that the United States was waging war against Islam. Thus high-ranking American officials began to talk about a Palestinian state, and the United States initially refused to put Hamas and Islamic Jihad—deemed to be terrorist organizations by Israel but "national liberation movements" by the Arabs—on the new U.S. terror list. However, U.S. policy changed once the United States, beginning to win the war in Afghanistan militarily in November, observed that the Muslim world was not heeding Bin Laden's call to join his jihad against the United States and saw the at best tepid support by most Arab regimes (Jordan a conspicuous exception) for the U.S. antiterrorist effort. Thus Hamas and Islamic Jihad were placed on the new terrorist list along with Hizballah, and while still calling for a Palestinian state, U.S. officials began to demand more aggressively that Arafat crack down on Palestinian terrorism. Thus President Bush, speaking at the United Nations, called for a two-state solution to the Israeli-Palestinian conflict, with "two states—Israel and Palestine—living peacefully together within secure and recognized boundaries." Bush followed up this statement by denouncing terrorism as he asserted "there is no such thing as a good terrorist" and conspicuously refrained from meeting Arafat at the United Nations because the Palestinian leader, in the words of Bush's national security adviser, Condoleezza Rice, was still hugging Hizballah and Hamas, despite denouncing al-Qaeda. Secretary of State Colin Powell, in an impassioned speech on November 19, echoed the twofold message of President Bush, calling for a two-state solution to the Israeli-Palestinian conflict while demanding an end to terrorist attacks on Israel. Powell also announced the dispatch of a special assistant, former marine general Anthony Zinni, to the Middle East to work out a cease-fire, and President Bush put his prestige on the line as well by asking five Arab leaders, including Egyptian president Hosni Mubarak, King Abdullah II of Jordan, and Saudi Arabia's Crown Prince Abdullah, to persuade Arafat to end the violence.

Unfortunately for both Zinni and Bush, the American special representative's trip to the Middle East proved to be a disaster as a series of Palestinian terrorist attacks made a mockery of the visit, attacks that Arafat either could not or would not prevent. By mid-December, not only the United States but also the European Union had lost faith in Arafat. To prevent himself from being totally isolated, the Palestinian leader belatedly denounced terrorism on December 16 and announced yet another cease-fire. Yet, by negotiating an agreement with Hamas and Islamic Jihad which left them able to strike in the future, instead of destroying the two organizations and cracking down on his own Tanzim militia as well, Arafat left himself open to the Israeli charge that he was not serious about fighting terrorism. The Israelis, having destroyed his helicopters and blockaded him in his office compound in Ramallah, declared him to be "irrelevant" to the peace process. When, two weeks later, the Israelis captured a ship with fifty tons of arms headed to the Palestinians, including Katusha rockets and C-4 explosives—weapons in clear violation of the Oslo agreements—and Arafat denied any Palestinian Authority connection to the weapons, despite the testimony of a Palestinian Authority naval officer captured on board the ship, Arafat's credibility hit a new low point. When Hamas then resumed attacks on Israel, citing the capture of the arms ship as a pretext for breaking the cease-fire, violence quickly escalated and on the eve of President Bush's first anniversary in office, there appeared little he, or the EU, could do to stop the violence.

In sum, while U.S. military and diplomatic power had succeeded in destroying both the Taliban regime in Afghanistan and the al-Qaeda terrorist network based there, in the aftermath of the terrorist attacks of September 11, the Israeli-Palestinian conflict proved to be a much more difficult problem to resolve, despite President Bush's major efforts. Whether President Bush and U.S. diplomacy, with or without the cooperation of the European Union, will be any more successful in Bush's remaining time in office is a question that only the future can resolve.

In looking to a possible role for the European Union in helping to resolve the Arab-Israeli conflict, the outlook does not appear bright. First, the EU states, despite having proclaimed a common security and defense policy, remain divided, with France and England tending to back the Arab side in the Arab-Israeli conflict, and Germany the Israeli side. Furthermore disputes between the EU and the United States on policy toward Iran and Iraq tend to present barriers to greater cooperation in dealing with the Arab-Israeli conflict. Finally, the EU, as a whole, is not yet a factor of importance in world politics, despite its growing economic strength. Essentially, as one EU official recently noted, EU policy is one of "damage limitation" and "waiting until Washington is on board." Given the experience of the Bush administration in its first year of trying to mediate the Israeli-Palestinian conflict, it may be a while until the Bush administration is again "on board" in a serious way.

Notes

1. For a discussion of U.S.-EU interaction in the cases of Iraq and Iran, see Robert O. Freedman, "American Policy toward the Middle East in Clinton's Second Term," in *Mediterranean Security in the Coming Millennium,* ed. Stephen J. Blank (Carlisle Barracks, Pa.: Strategic Studies Institute of the U.S. Army War College, 1999), 384–405.

2. On the European role, see Joel Peters, "Europe and the Arab-Israeli Peace Process: The Declaration of the European Council of Berlin and Beyond," in *Bound to Cooperate: Europe and the Middle East,* ed. Sven Behrendt and Christian-Peter Hanelt (Gutersloh, Germany: Bertelsmann Foundation Publishers, 2001), 164.

3. Interview, Syrian deputy ambassador to the United States, February 1992, Baltimore, Maryland.

4. For a critical Israeli view of EU diplomacy, see Joseph Alpher, "The Political Role of the EU in the Middle East: Israeli Aspirations," in Behrendt and Hanelt, *Bound to Cooperate,* 193–206.

5. See Robert E. Hunter, "Western Europe and the Middle East since the Lebanon War," in *The Middle East after the Israeli Invasion of Lebanon,* ed. Robert O. Freedman (Syracuse, N.Y.: Syracuse University Press, 1986), 93–113.

6. For a useful survey of U.S. policy during this period, see William B. Quandt, *Peace Process: American Diplomacy and the Arab-Israeli Conflict since 1967* (Berkeley: University of California Press, 2001), chap. 11.

7. For an overview of the challenges facing the Euro-Med partnership, see Alvaro Vasconcelos and George Joffé, ed., *The Barcelona Process: Building a Euro-Mediterranean Community* (London: Frank Cass, 2000).

8. See Itamar Rabinovich, *The Brink of Peace: The Israeli- Syrian Negotiations* (Princeton, N.J.: Princeton University Press, 1998).

9. Ibid., 227.

10. Cited in Rodolfo Ragioneri, "Europe, the Mediterranean, and the Middle East," in Blank, *Mediterranean Security,* 436.

11. Cited ibid.

12. Peters, "Europe and the Arab-Israeli Peace Process," 161.

13. David Coven, "Liberty U. to Send 3,000 Students on a Study Tour of Israel," *Chronicle of Higher Education,* September 25, 1997, 51.

14. For an analysis critical of U.S. strategy at this time, see Robert Satloff, "Shifting Sands: The U.S.'s Disturbing New Israel Policy," *New Republic,* June 1, 1998.

15. These divisions are discussed in Robert O. Freedman, "The Religious-Secular Divide in Israeli Politics," *Middle East Policy* 6, no. 4 (June 1999).

16. Martin Sief, "Arafat Accepts Israeli Land Deal for West Bank," *Washington Times,* September 30, 1998.

17. Steven Erlanger, "U.S., Israel, and Arafat Inch toward Pact," *New York Times,* September 29, 1998.

18. Vernon Loeb, "CIA Emerges to Resolve Middle East Disputes," *Washington Post,* September 30, 1998.

19. For a description of the Wye Agreement, see Barton Gellman, "Netanyahu, Arafat Sign Accord," *Washington Post,* October 24, 1998.

20. Lee Hockstader, "Attacks Kill Arab; Injure 3 Israelis," *Washington Post,* December 1998.

21. Ann LeLordo, "Israel Issues Ultimatum, Halts West Bank Pull-Out," *Baltimore Sun,* December 3, 1998.

22. Peters, "Europe and the Arab-Israeli Peace Process," 162.

23. Philip Shenon, "U.S. and Other Nations Plan More Aid for Palestinians," *New York Times,* December 1, 1998; Martin Sieff, "Palestinians Get More U.S. Aid," *Washington Times,* December 1, 1998.

24. Hockstader, "Attacks Kill Arab."

25. Judy Dempsey, "Palestinians Turn the Tables on Israelis: Arafat Poses as Clinton's Friend as Netanyahu Sulks," *Financial Times,* December 16, 1998.

26. Toni Marshall, "Clinton Goes from Cheers to Jeers in Two Days," *Washington Times,* December 18, 1998.

27. Judy Dempsey, "Deep Freeze in Jerusalem," *Financial Times,* December 23, 1998.

28. Cited in Peters, "Europe and the Arab-Israeli Peace Process," 157.

29. For a description of U.S. efforts to achieve a Syrian-Israeli peace agreement, see Quandt, *Peace Process,* 358–61.

30. For analyses of the failure of Camp David II, see Quandt, 362–68; Ari Shavit, "End of a Journey [Interview with former Israeli foreign minister Shlomo Ben-Ami]," *Ha'aretz* (English), October 3, 2001; Robert Malley and Hussein Agha, "Camp David: The Tragedy of Errors," *New York Review of Books,* August 9, 2001, 59–65; Ehud Barak, "It Seems Israel Has to Wait for New Palestinian Leadership," *International Herald Tribune,* July 31, 2001; Alain Gresh, "The Middle East: How the Peace Was Lost," *Le Monde Diplomatique,* September 2001, 1, 8–9; Barry Rubin, "The Region," *Besa@mail.biu.ac.il* (June 25, 2001); and Bassam Abu-Sharif, "A Call to Israel to Understand What the Palestinians Want," *www.ipcri.org* (September 14, 2001).

31. For a different view of the "Lessons of Lebanon," see Roula Khalaf, "Misleading Ghosts of Lebanese Resistance," *Financial Times,* August 16, 2001.

32. Quandt, *Peace Process,* 370.

33. Ibid., 371.

34. Cited in Dana Milbank, "Powell Vows U.S. Will Match Foes," *Washington Post,* December 17, 2000.

35. See Mathew Burger, "Middle East Talks Held in Taba—without the United States," *Washington Jewish Week,* January 25, 2001.

36. "Colin Powell's Conversion," *Washington Times,* editorial, February 28, 2001; Alan Sipress, "Powell Urges Cooperation in Ending Middle East Violence," *Washington Post,* February 26, 2001.

37. Cited in Roula Khalaf, "Powell Sets Out Bush Line on Middle East," *Financial Times,* March 20, 2001.

38. Alan Sipress, "Lawmakers Criticize Palestinians," *Washington Post,* April 6, 2001.

39. Alan Sipress, "Bush Assures Sharon on U.S. Role in Talks," *Washington Post,* March 21, 2001.

40. Cited in Jane Perlez, "Rumsfeld Seeks to Withdraw American Troops from Sinai," *New York Times,* April 19, 2001.

41. Barbara Crosette, "U.S. Vetoes UN Council Bid on Palestinian Force," *New York Times,* March 29, 2001.

42. Cited in Ben Barber, "Bush Presses Arafat to Stop Violence," *Washington Post,* March 30, 2001. See also AP report, "Mubarak to Meet Bush, Gauge President's Support," *Baltimore Sun,* April 1, 2001.

43. Alan Sipress, "Worried U.S. Issues Rebuke to Israelis," *Washington Post,* April 18, 2001.

44. Marc Lacey, "Attacks Were Up Last Year U.S. Terrorism Report Says," *New York Times,* May 1, 2001.

45. Cited in Ben Barber, "Israel Refuses to Halt Settlement Building," *Washington Times,* May 8, 2001.

46. Cited in Mike O'Connor, "Sharon Promises to Continue Expansion in West Bank, Gaza," *Washington Post,* May 9, 2001.

47. Cited in AP report, "Settlement Allocation Cut after U.S. Protests," *Jerusalem Post,* May 10, 2001.

48. For the text of the Mitchell Report, see *Ha'aretz* (English edition), May 6, 2001.

49. Jane Perlez, "U.S. Widens Role in Mideast Crisis, Sending an Envoy," *New York Times,* May 22, 2001.

50. Cited in Lee Hockstader, "Bombing Kills at Least 17 at Tel-Aviv Club," *Washington Post,* June 2, 2001.

51. Cited in Deborah Sontag, "Arafat Calls for Cease-Fire, Deploring Tel-Aviv Attacks," *New York Times,* June 3, 2001.

52. Cited in William A. Orme, Jr., "Shockwave in Israel over Bush's Comment," *New York Times,* June 28, 2001.

53. Herb Keinon, "Playing Europe," *Ha'aretz* (English), July 6, 2001.

54. Jane Perlez, "U.S. Says Killings by Israel Inflame Middle East Conflict," *New York Times,* August 28, 2001.

55. Cited in Mark Lavie, "Cheney Backs Israel Assassination Policy," *Sydney Morning Herald* (Australia), August 4–5, 2001.

56. Cited in Melissa Radler, "U.S. Backs Israel at U.N., Opposes International Monitors," *Jerusalem Post,* August 21, 2001.

57. Cited in Reuters report, "Egypt Leader Joins Arab Chorus Pressing U.S. on Its Middle East Role," *New York Times,* August 27, 2001.

58. Cited in Aluf Benn, "Blair: No Apologies Were Made for Straw," *Ha'aretz* (English), September 26, 2001.

59. Cited in Dalia Shehari, "French Ambassador: Cannot Compare Terror in U.S., Israel," *Ha'aretz* (English), September 14, 2001.

60. Cited in Aluf Benn, "Sharon Calls Powell after White House Blasts PM comments," *Ha'aretz* (English), October 5, 2001.

61. See Eli Kintosh, "U.S. vs. Israel: Blip Say Jewish Groups," *Forward,* October 26, 2001.

62. Daniel Milbank and Lee Hockstadter, "Israeli Incursion Strains Relations," *Washington Post,* October 24, 2001.

63. Tim Weiner, "Israel Rebuffs U.S. Demand to End Its West Bank Raids," *New York Times,* October 24, 2001.

64. For an analysis of U.S. military progress in Afghanistan, see Thom Shanker, "Conduct of War Is Redefined by Success of Special Forces," *New York Times,* January 21, 2002.

65. For analyses of U.S.-Saudi relations during the war, see David B. Ottaway and Robert G. Kaiser, "Saudis May See U.S. Exit: Military Presence Seen as Political Liability in Arab World," *Washington Post,* January 18, 2002, and Robert G. Kaiser, "Powell: Saudis Have Not Mentioned U.S. Withdrawal," *Washington Post,* January 19, 2002. See also Phillip Smucker, "Egypt Draws Line on U.S. War: Says Arabs Will Fight Terror on Own Terms," *Christian Science Monitor,* reprinted in *Washington Times,* January 2, 2002. For an overview of Middle East reactions to the September 11 terrorist attacks, see Cameron S. Brown, "The Shot Seen around the World: The Middle East Reacts to September 11th," *Middle East Review of International Affairs 5,* no. 4 (December 2001): 1–32. The denunciations of suicide bombing came only in early December. By contrast the mufti of Jerusalem, Sheikh Akrameh Sabri, said suicide bombings were justified, and he condemned the religious leaders in Egypt and Saudi Arabia for giving in to "international pressure." See Daniel Sobelman, "Suicide Bombings Are Justified, Jerusalem Mufti Sabri Tells Paper," *Ha'aretz,* December 9, 2001.

66. While it is too early to determine the lasting effect on Pakistan of the Taliban collapse, there are some preliminary indications. See Doug Struck, "Religious Radicals Facing Backlash in Pakistan," *Washington Post,* January 28, 2002, and John F. Burns, "Bin Laden Stirs Struggle on Meaning of Jihad," *New York Times,* January 27, 2002.

67. For the text of Bush's speech, see the *New York Times,* November 12, 2001. See also Serge Schmemann, "Arafat Thankful for Bush Remark about 'Palestine,'" *New York Times,* November 12, 2001.

68. Cited in Bill Sammon, "Bush Will Not Meet with Arafat," *Washington Times,* November 9, 2001.

69. For the text of Powell's speech, see "United States Position on Terrorists and Peace in the Middle East," U.S. Department of State web site, *www.state.gov/secretary/rm/2001/6219.htm* (November 19, 2001).

70. Janine Zacharia, "Bush Asking Arab Nations to Pitch In for a Secure Peace," *Jerusalem Post,* November 25, 2001.

71. Aluf Ben, "Zinni to PM: I Will Stay as Long as Needed to Fulfill My Mission," *Ha'aretz,* November 27, 2001.

72. Cited in *New York Times,* November 28, 2001.

73. See James Bennet, "U.S. Envoy Meets Arafat and Asks for End to Violence," *New York Times,* November 29, 2001.

74. Avi Machlis, "Israeli Bus Blast Casts Shadow on Peace Process," *Financial Times,* November 30, 2001.

75. Joel Greenberg, "Envoy to Middle East Assails Palestinian Militants," *New York Times,* December 1, 2001.

76. Cited in Lee Hockstadter, "Bomber in Bus Kills 15 in Israel," *Washington Post,* December 3, 2001.

77. Ibid.

78. Cited in Peter Herman, "Terrorists Kill at Least 10 in Israel," *Baltimore Sun,* December 2, 2001.

79. Cited in Hockstadter, "Bomber on Bus."

80. Cited in James Bennet, "Israelis Strike Arafat's Bases," *New York Times,* December 4, 2001.

81. Cited in Bill Sammon and Ben Barber, "U.S. Takes Harder Line on Arafat," *Washington Times,* December 4, 2001.

82. Dennis Ross, "Can Arafat Stop the Violence?" *New York Times,* Op Ed, December 4, 2001.

83. See David Sanger, "Bush Freezes Assets of Biggest U.S. Moslem Charity," *New York Times,* December 5, 2001, and Bill Sammon, "Bush Freezes Hamas's Assets," *Washington Times,* December 5, 2001.

84. Cited in Harvey Morris, "Israel Reaps the Rewards of Lobbying Drive in U.S.," *Financial Times,* December 6, 2001.

85. See Francis Elliott, "Bush Advisor Asks EU to Cut Aid to 'Corrupt' Arafat Regime," *London Sunday Telegraph,* reprinted in *Washington Times,* December 10, 2001.

86. Herb Keinon, "EU: Arafat Must Dismantle Hamas, Islamic Jihad," *Jerusalem Post,* December 11, 2001.

87. Donald McNeil, Jr., "European Union Expands Its Lists of Terrorist Groups, Requiring Sanctions and Arrests," *New York Times,* December 29, 2001.

88. See Judy Dempsey, "U.S. Pressure on EU over Middle East Resolution," *Financial Times,* December 17, 2001, and Edith M. Lederer, "U.S. Vetoes Palestinian-backed U.N. Resolution," *Jerusalem Post,* December 16, 2001.

89. Joel Greenberg, "More Violence Jolts ME Truce Efforts," *New York Times,* December 10, 2001.

90. James Bennet and Joel Greenberg, "Israel Breaks with Arafat after Palestinian Assault on Bus in West Bank Kills 10," *New York Times,* December 13, 2001.

91. Tracy Wilkinson, "Israel Pounds Palestinian Authority," *Los Angeles Times,* December 14, 2001.

92. See Elaine Sciolino, "U.S. Jewish Leaders Call President Blunt in Assailing

Arafat," *New York Times,* December 14, 2001. The author's interview with a participant in Bush's meeting with Jewish leaders confirmed the Sciolino report.

93. Cited in *Ha'aretz Service and Agencies,* "Powell: U.S. Will Not Abandon Its Role in Mideast Mediation," December 13, 2001; Peter Slevin and Lee Hockstadter, "U.S. Hangs On in Middle East: 'Stakes Are Too High' to Pull Out, Powell Says," *Washington Post,* December 13, 2001.

94. Clyde Haberman, "Arafat Demands Halt in Attacks against Israelis," *New York Times,* December 17, 2001.

95. Aluf Benn, "U.S. Envoy Recalled to Washington; Meets Egypt's Mubarak," *Ha'aretz,* December 16, 2001.

96. Alan Sipress, "Musharaf Urged to Calm South Asia: U.S. Asks Pakistani Leader to Act against Islamic Militants," *Washington Post,* January 12, 2002.

97. Rajiv Chandrase Karan, "India and Pakistan Step Back: New Delhi Welcomes Anti-Terror Vow but Wants Action," *International Herald Tribune,* January 14, 2002.

98. "Designation of Foreign Terrorist Organizations," U.S. State Department web site, *www.state.gov/secretary,* December 26, 2001.

99. Lee Hockstadter, "Arafat Arrests Three in Arms Incident," *Washington Post,* January 12, 2002.

100. Mary Curtius, "Hamas Takes Responsibility for Attack," *Los Angeles Times,* January 10, 2002.

101. Margot Dudkevich, "Navy Destroys PA Boats and Installations," *Jerusalem Post,* January 13, 2002.

102. Cited in "Powell: IDF Actions Are Defensive Response," *Jerusalem Post News Agencies,* January 13, 2002.

103. David Rudge, "Defense Minister Ben-Eliezer: Tanzim Terrorist Had Been Planning More Murders," *Jerusalem Post,* January 16, 2002.

104. David Rattner, "Hadera Victims Buried on Friday," *Ha'aretz,* January 20, 2002.

105. Amos Harel, "IDF Plans to Hit More PA Targets, Voice of Palestine Radio Torched in Ramallah, Police Bombed in Tulkarm," *Ha'aretz,* January 20, 2002.

106. Aluf Benn, "U.S. Decides to Postpone Zinni's Return: Sources Cite Failures to Implement Full Cease-Fire," *Ha'aretz,* January 15, 2002.

Bibliography

Books

Abdo, Geneive. *No God but God: Egypt and the Triumph of Islam.* New York: Oxford University Press, 2000.

Abrahamian, Ervand. *Tortured Confessions: Prisons and Public Recantations in Modern Iran.* Berkeley and Los Angeles: University of California Press, 1999.

Abu Odeh, Adnan. *Jordanians, Palestinians, and the Hashemite Kingdom in the Middle East Peace Process.* Washington, D.C.: United States Institute of Peace, 1999.

Ahmad, Feroz. *The Turkish Experiment in Democracy: 1950–1975.* Boulder, Colo.: Westview Press, 1977.

Amuzegar, Jahangir. *Iran's Economy under the Islamic Republic.* Rev. ed. London: I. B. Tauris, 1997.

Ayubi, Nazih N. *Overstating the Arab State.* London: I. B. Tauris, 1999.

Bakhash, Shaul. *Reign of the Ayatollahs: Iran and the Islamic Revolution.* Rev. ed. New York: Basic Books, 1990.

Baram, Amatzia. *Building toward Crisis: Saddam Husayn's Strategy for Survival.* Washington Institute for Near East Policy Paper no. 47. Washington, D.C., 1998.

Bianchi, Robert. *Unruly Corporatism: Associational Life in Twentieth-Century Europe.* New York: Oxford University Press, 1989.

Bill, James, and Robert Springborg. *Politics in the Middle East.* New York: Longman, 2000.

Binder, Leonard. *In a Moment of Enthusiasm: Political Power and the Second Stratum in Egypt.* Chicago: University of Chicago Press, 1978.

Blank, Stephen. *Energy and Security in Transcaucasia.* Carlisle Barracks, Pa.: U.S. Army War College, 1994.

Brubaker, Rogers. *Nationalism Reframed: Nationhood and the National Question in the New Europe.* Cambridge: Cambridge University Press, 1996.

Brumberg, Daniel. *Reinventing Khomeini: The Struggle for Reform in Iran.* Chicago and London: University of Chicago Press, 2001.

Cantori, Louis J., and Andrew Ziegler, eds. *Comparative Politics in the Post-behavioral Era.* Boulder, Colo.: Lynne Rienner, 1988.

Chubin, Shahram, and Charles Tripp. *Iran and Iraq at War.* Boulder, Colo.: Westview Press, 1988.

Clawson, Patrick. *Unaffordable Ambitions: Syria's Military Buildup and Economic Crisis.* Washington, D.C.: Washington Institute for Near East Policy, 1989.

Cobban, Helena. *The Israeli-Syrian Peace Talks, 1991–1996 and Beyond.* Washington, D.C.: United States Institute of Peace Press, 1999.

Crystal, Jill. *Oil and Politics in the Gulf: Rulers and Merchants in Kuwait and Qatar.* Cambridge: Cambridge University Press, 1990.

Deeb, Marius. *The Lebanese Civil War.* New York: Praeger, 1980.

Ehteshami, Anoushiravan, and Raymond A. Hinnebusch. *Syria and Iran: Middle Powers in a Penetrated System.* New York: Routledge, 1997.

Fandy, Mamoun. *Saudi Arabia and the Politics of Dissent.* New York: St. Martin's Press, 1999.

Feldman, Shai. *The Future of U.S.-Israeli Strategic Cooperation.* Washington, D.C.: Washington Institute for Near East Policy, 1996.

Freedman, Lawrence, and Efraim Karsh. *The Gulf Conflict, 1990–1991.* Princeton, N.J.: Princeton University Press, 1993.

Freedman, Robert O. *Moscow and the Middle East: Soviet Policy since the Invasion of Afghanistan.* Cambridge: Cambridge University Press, 1991.

———, ed. *The Middle East and the Peace Process.* Gainesville: University Press of Florida, 1998.

———, ed. *Israel's First Fifty Years.* Gainesville: University Press of Florida, 2000.

Fuller, Graham E. *Algeria: The Next Fundamentalist State?* Santa Monica, Calif.: Arroyo Center, Rand Corporation, 1996.

Garfinkle, Adam. *Israel and Jordan under the Shadow of War.* New York: St. Martin's Press, 1992.

Gause, F. Gregory, III. *Oil Monarchies: Domestic and Security Challenges in the Arab Gulf States.* New York: Council on Foreign Relations Press, 1994.

Ghareeb, Edmund. *The Kurdish Question in Iraq.* Syracuse, N.Y.: Syracuse University Press, 1981.

Grimmett, Richard F. *Conventional Arms Transfers to Developing Nations, 1992–1999.* Washington, D.C.: Congressional Research Service of the Library of Congress, 2000.

Grossman, David. *The Yellow Wind.* New York: Farrar, Straus, Giroux, 1988.

Gunther, Michael M. *The Kurds and the Future of Turkey.* New York: St. Martin's Press, 1997.

Harris, George S. *Troubled Alliance: Turkish-American Problems in Historical Perspective, 1945–1971.* Washington, D.C.: American Enterprise Institute for Public Policy Research, 1972.

Harris, William. *Faces of Lebanon.* Princeton, N.J.: Marcus Wiener, 1997.

Hinnebusch, Raymond. *Egyptian Politics under Sadat.* New York: Cambridge University Press, 1985.

Hiro, Dilip. *Iran under the Ayatollahs*. London: Routledge and Kegan Paul, 1985.

Hunter, Shireen, ed. *Iran and the World*. Bloomington: Indiana University Press, 1990.

Ibn Khaldun. *The Muqaddimah: An Introduction to History*. Translated by Franz Rosenthal. Princeton, N.J.: Princeton University Press, 1989.

Jiryis, Sabri. *The Arabs of Israel*. Beirut: Institute of Palestine Studies, 1969.

Jreisat, Jamil E. *Politics without Process: Administering Development in the Arab World*. Boulder, Colo.: Lynne Rienner, 1997.

Khadduri, Majid. *The Gulf War: The Origins and Implications of the Iraq-Iran Conflict*. New York: Oxford University Press, 1988.

Kirisci, Kemal, and Gareth Winrow. *The Kurdish Question and Turkey: An Example of a Trans-State Ethnic Conflict*. London: Frank Cass, 1997.

Klieman, Aaron. *Statecraft in the Dark: Practice of Quiet Diplomacy*. Boulder, Colo.: Westview Press, 1982.

Kretzmer, David. *The Legal Status of the Arabs in Israel*. Boulder, Colo.: Westview Press, 1990.

Levey, Zach. *Israel and the Western Powers, 1952–1960*. Chapel Hill: University of North Carolina Press, 1997.

Lijphart, Arend. *Democracy in Plural Societies: A Comparative Exploration*. New Haven, Conn.: Yale University Press, 1977.

Linn, Ruth. *Conscience at War: The Israeli Soldier as a Moral Critic*. New York: State University of New York Press, 1996.

Lukacs, Yehuda. *Israel, Jordan, and the Peace Process*. Syracuse, N.Y.: Syracuse University Press, 1999.

Lustick, Ian. *Arabs in the Jewish State: Israel's Control over a National Minority*. Austin: University of Texas Press, 1980.

Lynch, Mark. *State Interests and Public Spheres*. New York: Columbia University Press, 1999.

Makiya, Kanan. *Republic of Fear*. Berkeley and Los Angeles: University of California Press, 1989.

———. *Cruelty and Silence*. Berkeley and Los Angeles: University of California Press, 1993.

Marr, Phebe, ed. *Egypt at the Crossroads*. Washington, D.C.: National Defense University, 1999.

———. *The Modern History of Iraq*. Boulder, Colo.: Westview, 1985.

Menashri, David. *Revolution at a Crossroads: Iran's Domestic Politics and Regional Ambitions*. Washington, D.C.: Washington Institute for Near East Policy, 1999.

Migdal, Joel. *Strong Societies and Weak States*. Princeton, N.J.: Princeton University Press, 1988.

Mufti, Malik. *Sovereign Creations: Pan-Arabism and Political Order in Syria and Iraq*. Ithaca, N.Y.: Cornell University Press, 1996.

Munson, Henry, Jr. *Religion and Power in Morocco*. New Haven: Yale University Press, 1993.

Nachmani, Amikam. *Israel, Turkey, and Greece: Uneasy Relations in the East Mediterranean*. London: Frank Cass, 1987.

Nakhleh, Emile. *The Gulf Cooperation Council: Policies, Problems, and Prospects*. New York: Praeger, 1986.

Neff, Donald. *Fallen Pillars: U.S. Policy toward Palestine and Israel since 1945*. Washington, D.C.: Institute for Palestine Studies, 1995.

Nonneman, Gerd. *Iraq, the Gulf States, and the War*. London: Ithaca Press, 1986.

Peleg, Ilan. *Human Rights in the West Bank and Gaza: Legacy and Politics*. Syracuse, N.Y.: Syracuse University Press, 1995.

Perthes, Volker. *The Political Economy of Syria under Assad*. London: I. B. Tauris, 1995.

Posusney, Marsha Pripstein. *Labor and the State in Egypt*. New York: Columbia University Press, 1997.

Quandt, William B. *Between Ballots and Bullets: Algeria's Transition from Authoritarianism*. Washington, D.C.: Brookings Institution Press, 1998.

———. *The Peace Process: American Diplomacy and the Arab-Israeli Conflict since 1967*. Berkeley: University of California Press, 2001.

Rabinovich, Itamar. *The Brink of Peace: The Israeli-Syrian Negotiations*. Princeton, N.J.: Princeton University Press, 1998.

Ramazani, R. K. *Revolutionary Iran: Challenge and Response in the Middle East*. Baltimore, Md.: Johns Hopkins University Press, 1986.

Richards, Alan, and John Waterbury. *A Political Economy of the Middle East*. 2d ed. Boulder, Colo.: Westview Press, 1996.

Robins, Philip. *Turkey and the Middle East*. London: Royal Institute of International Affairs/Pinter Publishers, 1991.

Rouhana, Nadim. *Palestinian Citizens in an Ethnic Jewish State*. New Haven, Conn.: Yale University Press, 1997.

Safran, Nadav. *Saudi Arabia: The Ceaseless Quest for Security*. Cambridge: Harvard University Press, 1985.

Said, Edward. *The End of the Peace Process: Oslo and After*. New York: Pantheon, 2000.

Salem, Elie. *Violence and Diplomacy in Lebanon: The Troubled Years, 1982–1988*. London: I. B. Tauris, 1995.

Sandler, Samuel, and Hillel Frisch. *Israel, the Palestinians, and the West Bank*. Lexington, Mass.: Lexington Books, 1984.

Savir, Uri. *The Process: 1,100 Days That Changed the Middle East*. New York: Random House, 1998.

Sela, Avraham. *The Decline of the Arab-Israeli Conflict: Middle East Politics and the Quest for Regional Order*. Albany: State University of New York Press, 1998.

Sharon, Ariel, and David Chanoff. *Warrior: An Autobiography*. New York: Simon and Schuster, 1989; rev. ed., 2001.

Shevtsova, Lilia. *Yeltsin's Russia: Myth and Reality*. Washington, D.C.: Carnegie Endowment for International Peace, 1999.

Theroux, Peter. *The Strange Disappearance of Imam Moussa Sadr*. London: Weidenfeld and Nicolson, 1987.

Waterbury, John. *The Egypt of Nasser and Sadat: The Political Economy of Two Regimes*. Princeton, N.J.: Princeton University Press, 1983.

Wiarda, Howard. *Corporatism and Development*. Amherst: University of Massachusetts Press, 1977.

Wilson, Rodney. *Economic Development in the Middle East*. London: Routledge, 1995.

Wright, Robin. *The Last Great Revolution: Turmoil and Transformation in Iran*. New York: Knopf, 2000.

Zakheim, Dov S. *Flight of the Lavi: Inside a U.S.-Israeli Crisis*. Washington, D.C.: Brassey's, 1996.

Articles and Chapters in Books

Abu Jaber, Faleh. "Shaykhs and Ideologues: Detribalization and Retribalization in Iraq, 1968–1998." *Middle East Report* 215 (summer 2000).

Alnajjar, Ghanim. "The Challenges Facing Kuwaiti Democracy." *Middle East Journal* 54, no. 2 (spring 2000).

Aronoff, Myron J., and Pierre M. Atlas. "The Peace Process and Competing Challenges to the Dominant Zionist Discourse." In *The Middle East Peace Process: Interdisciplinary Perspectives,* edited by Ilan Peleg. New York: State University of New York Press, 1998.

Bahry, Louay. "The Opposition in Bahrain: A Bellwether for the Gulf?" *Middle East Policy* 5, no. 2 (May 1997).

Bakhash, Shaul. "Iranian Politics since the Gulf War." In *The Politics of Change in the Middle East,* edited by Robert B. Satloff. Boulder, Colo.: Westview Press, 1993.

———. "Iran since the Gulf War." In *The Middle East and the Peace Process: The Impact of the Oslo Accords,* edited by Robert O. Freedman. Gainesville: University Press of Florida, 1998.

Baram, Amatzia. "Neo-Tribalism in Iraq: Saddam Hussein's Tribal Policies, 1991–96." *International Journal of Middle East Studies* 29, no. 1 (February 1997).

Barkey, Henri J. "Under the Gun: Turkish Foreign Policy and the Kurdish Question." In *The Kurdish Nationalist Movement in the 1990's,* edited by Robert Olson. Lexington: University Press of Kentucky, 1996.

Barnett, Michael, and F. Gregory Gause III. "Caravans in Opposite Directions: Society, State, and the Development of Community in the Gulf Cooperation Council." In *Security Communities,* edited by Emmanuel Adler and Michael Barnett. Cambridge: Cambridge University Press, 1998.

Blank, Stephen J. "Turkey's Strategic Engagement in the Former USSR and U.S. Interests." In *Turkey's Strategic Position at the Crossroad of World Affairs,* edited by Stephen J. Blank, Stephen C. Pelletiere, and William T. Johnsen. Carlisle Barracks, Pa.: U.S. Army War College, 1993.

Brand, Laurie. "The Effects of the Peace Process on Political Liberalization in Jordan." *Journal of Palestine Studies* 28, no. 2 (winter 1999).

Bronson, Rachel. "United States Policy toward the Persian Gulf: A New Focus for a New Administration." *Orbis* (spring 2001).

Cantori, Louis J. "Egypt at the Crossroads: Domestic, Economic, and Political Stagnation and Foreign Policy Constraints." In *The Middle East and the Peace Process,* edited by Robert O. Freedman. Gainesville: University Press of Florida, 1998.

Cantori, Louis J., and Peter Benedict. "Local Leadership in Urban Egypt: Leader, Family, and Community Perceptions." In *Local Politics and Development in the Middle East,* edited by L. Cantori and Peter Benedict. Boulder, Colo.: Westview Press, 1984.

Cobban, Helena. "The Nature of the Soviet-Syrian Link under Assad and Gorbachev." In *Syria: Society, Culture, and Polity,* edited by Richard T. Antoun and Donald Quataert. Albany: State University of New York Press, 1991.

Deeb, Marius K. "Libya." In *Political Parties of the Middle East and North Africa,* edited by Frank Tachau. Westport, Conn.: Greenwood Press, 1994.

———. "Militant Islam and Its Critics: The Case of Libya." In *Islamism and Secularism in North Africa,* edited by John Ruedy. New York: St. Martin's Press, 1994.

———. "Lebanon in the Aftermath of the Abrogation of the Israeli-Lebanese Accord." In *The Middle East from the Iran-Contra Affair to the Intifada,* edited by Robert O. Freedman. Syracuse, N.Y.: Syracuse University Press, 1991.

Deeb, Mary-Jane. "Tunisia." In *Religion in Politics,* edited by Stuart Mews. Essex, U.K.: Longman Group UK Limited, 1989.

———. "Militant Islam and the Politics of Redemption." *ANNALS, AAPSS* 524 (November 1992).

———. "Political and Economic Developments in Libya." In *North Africa in Transition,* edited by Yahia Zoubir. Gainesville: University Press of Florida, 1999.

Deeb, Mary-Jane, and Marius Deeb. "Internal Negotiations in a Centralist Conflict: Lebanon." In *Elusive Peace: Negotiating an End to Civil Wars,* edited by I. William Zartman. Washington, D.C.: Brookings Institution, 1995.

Dekmejian, R. Hrair. "The Rise of Political Islamism in Saudi Arabia." *Middle East Journal* 48, no. 4 (autumn 1994).

Dunn, Michael Collins. "The Al-Nahda Movement in Tunisia: From Renaissance to Revolution." In *Islamism and Secularism in North Africa,* edited by John Ruedy. New York: St. Martin's Press, 1994.

Eran, Oded. "Russian Immigrants, Russia, and the Elections in Israel." *Analysis of Current Events* (ACE) 11, nos. 5–6 (May/June 1999).

Fakhro, Munira A. "The Uprising in Bahrain: An Assessment." In *The Persian Gulf at the Millennium,* edited by Gary G. Sick and Lawrence G. Potter. New York: St. Martin's Press, 1997.

Fedorchenko, Andrei. "Rossiisko-Israil'skie Ekonomicheskie Sviazi" (Russian-Israeli economic ties). *Mirovaya Ekonomika i Mezhdunarodnie Otnosheniya* 2 (2000).

Felgengauer, Pavel. "Israel Drops Out of Moscow-Beijing Axis." *Moscow News* 30 (2000).

Freedman, Robert O. "Russia and Israel under Yeltsin." *Israel Studies* 3, no. 1 (spring 1998).

———. "Russian-Iranian Relations under Yeltsin." *The Soviet and Post-Soviet Review* 25, no. 3 (1999).

———. "The Soviet Union, the Gulf War, and Its Aftermath." In *The Middle East and the United States,* edited by David W. Lesch. 2d ed. Boulder, Colo.: Westview Press, 1999.

Gause, F. Gregory III. "Gulf Regional Politics: Revolution, War, and Rivalry." In *Dynamics of Regional Politics: Four Systems on the Indian Ocean Rim,* edited by W. Howard Wriggins. New York: Columbia University Press, 1992.

———. "The Gulf Conundrum: Economic Change, Population Growth, and Political Stability in the GCC States." *Washington Quarterly* 20, no. 1 (winter 1997).

———. "Saudi Arabia Over a Barrel." *Foreign Affairs* 79, no. 3 (May/June 2000).

Ghabra, Shafeeq. "Kuwait and the Dynamics of Socio-Economic Change." *Middle East Journal* 51, no. 3 (summer 1997).

Ghanem, Asad, Nadim Rouhana, and Oren Yiftachel. "Questioning 'Ethnic Democracy': A Response to Sammy Smooha." *Israel Studies* 3, no. 2 (1998).

Ghareeb, Edmund. "New Media and the Information Revolution in the Arab World: An Assessment." *Middle East Journal* 54, no. 3 (summer 2000).

Hale, William. "Turkey, the Middle East, and the Gulf Crisis." *International Affairs* 68, no. 4 (October 1992).

Hamarneh, Mustafah. "The Opposition and Its Role in the Peace Process: A Jordanian View." In *Palestine, Jordan, Israel: Building a Base for Common Scholarship and Understanding in the New Era of the Middle East.* Research Studies no. 105. Jerusalem: PASSIA, 1997.

Heydemann, Steven. "The Political Logic of Economic Rationality: Selective Stabilization in Syria." In *The Politics of Economic Reform in the Middle East,* edited by Henri Barkey. New York: St. Martin's Press, 1992.

Hinnebusch, Raymond. "Revisionist Dreams, Realist Strategies: The Foreign Policy of Syria." In *The Foreign Policies of Arab States: The Challenge of Change,* edited by Bahgat Korany and Ali E. Hillal Dessouki. Boulder, Colo.: Westview Press, 1991.

———. "Does Syria Want Peace: Syrian Policy in the Syrian-Israeli Negotiations." *Journal of Palestine Studies* 26, no. 1 (autumn 1996).

Joffe, George. "Islamic Opposition in Libya." *Third World Quarterly* 10, no. 2 (1988).

Karpat, Kemal H. "Turkish-Soviet Relations." In *Turkey's Foreign Policy in Transition: 1950–1974,* edited by Kemal H. Karpat. Leiden: E. J. Brill, 1975.

———. "Turkish and Arab-Israeli Relations." In *Turkey's Foreign Policy in Transition: 1950–1974,* edited by Kemal H. Karpat. Leiden: E. J. Brill, 1975.

Kedar, Alexandre. "A First Step in a Difficult and Sensitive Road: Preliminary Observations on Quaadan v. Katzir." *Israel Studies Bulletin* 16, no. 1 (March 2000).

Khashan, Hilal. "Arab Attitudes toward Israel and Peace." *The Washington Institute Policy Focus.* Research Memorandum no. 40, August 2000. Washington, D.C.: Washington Institute for Near East Policy, 2000.

Kirisci, Kemal. "Turkey and the Kurdish Safe-Haven in Northern Iraq." *Journal of South Asian and Middle Eastern Studies* 19, no. 3 (spring 1996).

Kostiner, Joseph. "Shia Unrest in the Gulf." In *Shiism, Resistance, and Revolution,* edited by Martin Kramer. Boulder, Colo.: Westview Press, 1987.

Landau, Jacob. *The Arab Minority in Israel, 1967–1991: Political Perspectives.* Tel Aviv: Am Oved, 1993. In Hebrew.

Lesch, David W. "Is Syria Ready for Peace?: Obstacles to Integration in the Global Economy." *Middle East Policy* 6, no. 3 (February 1999).

Lewin, Anat. "Turkey and Israel: Reciprocal and Mutual Imagery in the Media, 1994–1999." *Journal of International Affairs* 54, no. 1 (fall 2000).

Lustick, Ian. "Stability in Deeply Divided Societies: Consociationalisation vs. Control." *World Politics* 31, no. 3 (April 1979).

Ma'oz, Moshe. "Changes in Syria's Regional Strategic Position vis-à-vis Israel." In *Modern Syria: From Ottoman Rule to Pivotal Role in the Middle East,* edited by Moshe Ma'oz, Joseph Ginat, and Onn Winckler. Brighton, U.K.: Sussex Academic Press, 1998.

Makovsky, Alan. "Israeli-Turkish Relations: A Turkish Periphery Strategy?" In *Reluctant Neighbor: Turkey's Role in the Middle East,* edited by Henri J. Barkey. Washington, D.C.: United States Institute of Peace Press, 1996.

Mamedova, N. M. "Novii Etap Politischeskoi Zhizni Irana" (New stage in the political life of Iran). In *Blizhnii Vostok i Sovremennost,* edited by Vladimir Isaev. Moscow: Institute for the Study of Israel and the Near East, 2000.

Merzliakov, Yuri. "Legal Status of the Caspian Sea." *International Affairs* (Moscow) 45, no. 1 (January 1999).

Milani, Mohsen M. "Reform and Resistance in the Islamic Republic of Iran." In *Iran at the Crossroads,* edited by John L. Esposito and R. K. Ramazani. New York: Palgrave, 2001.

Mortimer, Robert. "Islam and Multiparty Politics in Algeria." *The Middle East Journal* 45, no. 4 (autumn 1991).

Mufti, Malik. "The United States and Nasserist Pan-Arabism." In *The Middle East and the United States: A Historical and Political Reassessment,* edited by David W. Lesch. Boulder, Colo.: Westview Press, 1999.

Nachmani, Amikam. "The Remarkable Turkish-Israeli Tie." *Middle East Quarterly* 5, no. 2 (June 1998).

Peleg, Ilan. "Otherness and Israel's Arab Dilemma." In *The Other in Jewish Thought and History,* edited by Laurence J. Silberstein and Robert L. Cohn. New York: New York University Press, 1994.

———. "The Arab-Israel Conflict and the Victory of Otherness." In *Books on Israel.* Vol. 3, edited by Russell Stone and Walter Zenner. New York: State University of New York Press.

———. "Israel's Constitutional Order and Kulturkampf: The Role of Ben-Gurion." *Israel Studies* 3, no. 1 (1998).

———. "Culture, Ethnicity, and Human Rights in Contemporary Biethnic Democracies: The Case of Israel and Other Cases." In *Negotiating Culture and Human Rights,* edited by Lynda Bell, Andrew Nathan, and Ilan Peleg. New York: Columbia University Press, 2001.

Ram, Uri. "The Promised Land of Business Opportunities: Liberal Post-Zionism in the Golden Age." In *The New Israel: Peacemaking and Liberalization,* edited by Gershon Shafir and Yoav Peled. Boulder, Colo.: Westview Press, 2000.

Robins, Philip. "Turkish Policy and the Gulf Crisis: Adventurist or Dynamic?" In *Turkish Foreign Policy: New Prospects,* edited by Clement H. Dodd. Huntingdon, U.K.: Eothen Press, 1992.

Seale, Patrick, and Linda Butler. "Assad's Regional Strategy and the Challenge from Netanyahu." *Journal of Palestine Studies* 26, no. 1 (autumn 1996).

Sezer, Duygu Bazoglu. "Turkish-Russian Relations: From Adversity to 'Virtual Rapprochement.'" In *Turkey's New World,* edited by Alan Makovsky and Sabri Sayari. Washington, D.C.: Washington Institute for Near East Policy, 2000.

Shahin, Emad Eldin. "Secularism and Nationalism: The Political Discourse of 'Abd al-Salam Yassin." In *Islamism and Secularism in North Africa,* edited by John Ruedy. New York: St. Martin's Press, 1994.

Shermatova, Sanubar. "Gas Brings Turkey and Russia Closer." *Moscow News* 51–52 (1997).

Simon, Rita J., and Jean M. Landis. "Trends in Public Support for Civil Liberties and Due Process in Israeli Society." *Social Science Quarterly* 71, no. 1 (spring 1990).

Smooha, Sammy. "Minority Status in an Ethnic Democracy: The Status of the Arab Minority in Israel." *Ethnic and Racial Studies* 13, no. 3 (1990).

Soysal, Ismail. "Turkish-Arab Diplomatic Relations after the Second World War (1945–1986)." *Studies on Turkish-Arab Relations* 1 (1986).

———. "The 1955 Baghdad Pact." *Studies on Turkish-Arab Relations* 5 (1990).

Steinberg, Gerald. "The Poor in Your Own City Shall Have Precedence: A Critique of the Katzir-Qaadan Case and Opinion." *Israel Studies Bulletin* 16, no. 1 (2000).

Vishniakov, Viktor. "Russian-Iranian Relations and Regional Stability." *International Affairs* (Moscow) 45, no. 1 (1999).

Wheeler, Deborah. "New Media, Globalization, and Kuwaiti National Identity." *Middle East Journal* 54, no. 3 (summer 2000).

Yavuz, M. Hakan. "Turkish-Israeli Relations through the Lens of the Turkish Identity Debate." *Journal of Palestine Studies* 27, no. 1 (autumn 1997).

Yesilada, Birol A. "Turkish Foreign Policy toward the Middle East." In *The Political and Socioeconomic Transformation of Turkey,* edited by Attila Eralp, Muharrem Tünay, and Birol A. Yesilada. Westport, Conn.: Praeger, 1993.

Yiftachel, Oren. "The Ethnic Democracy Model and Its Applicability to the Case of Israel." *Ethnic and Racial Studies* 15 (1992).

Zunes, Stephen. "The Strategic Functions of U.S. Aid to Israel." *Middle East Policy* 4, no. 4 (October 1996).

Contributors

Shaul Bakhash is Clarence Robinson Professor of History at George Mason University. A native of Iran, he has written extensively on Iranian politics and served on a mission of American Middle East specialists to the Soviet Union in 1988. Among his many publications are *Iran: Monarchy, Bureaucracy and Reform under the Qajars, 1848–1896* and *The Politics of Oil and Revolution in Iran.*

Louis Cantori is professor of political science at the University of Maryland, Baltimore County, and is also a consultant to numerous agencies of the U.S. government, including the AID project in Egypt and the Directorate of Planning of the Middle East headquarters of the Air Force. Among his many publications are *Local Politics and Development in the Middle East* and *Comparative Politics in the Post-behavioral Era.*

Marius K. Deeb is professor of Islamic and Middle Eastern studies at the School of Advanced International Studies at Johns Hopkins University. Among his many publications are *Political Parties in Egypt* and *The Lebanese Civil War.* He also coauthored, with his wife, Mary-Jane Deeb, the book *Libya since the Revolution: Aspects of Social and Political Development.* He also has a book forthcoming on Syria's war on Lebanon and the peace process.

Mary-Jane Deeb is the Arab world area specialist at the Library of Congress. Until the summer of 1998 she was the editor of the *Middle East Journal,* a professor of international relations and Middle East politics at American University in Washington, D.C., and director of the Algeria Working Group at the Corporate Council on Africa. She is the author of *Libya's Foreign Policy in North Africa* and coauthor with her husband, Marius Deeb, of *Libya since the Revolution: Aspects of Social and Political Development.*

Robert O. Freedman is Peggy Meyerhoff Pearlstone Professor of Political Science at Baltimore Hebrew University and visiting professor of political science at Johns Hopkins University. A former president of the Association for Israel Studies, he is the author of four books dealing with the Soviet Union and Russia, most recently *Moscow and the Middle East,* and the editor of thirteen books, the most recent *Israel's First 50 Years* and *The Middle East and the Peace Process.*

F. Gregory Gause III is an associate professor of political science at the University of Vermont and director of the university's Middle East Studies Program. He was on the faculty of Columbia University in the years 1987–95 and was Fellow for Arab and Islamic Studies at the Council on Foreign Relations in New York in 1993–94. He has published two books, *Oil Monarchies: Domestic and Security Challenges in the Arab Gulf States* and *Saudi-Yemeni Relations: Domestic Structures and Foreign Influence.*

David W. Lesch is associate professor of history at Trinity University in San Antonio. He has written *Syria and the United States: Eisenhower's Cold War in the Middle East* and *1979: The Year That Shaped the Modern Middle East* and edited *The Middle East and the United States: A Historical and Political Reassessment.*

Yehuda Lukacs is director of the Center for Global Education, George Mason University, where he directs international educational programs in over fifty countries. He is the author of *Arab-Israeli Conflict: Two Decades of Change; Israeli-Palestinian Conflict: A Documentary Record;* and *Israel, Jordan, and the Peace Process.*

Malik Mufti is associate professor in the Department of Political Science at Tufts University, where he has taught since 1992. He is the author of *Sovereign Creations: Pan-Arabism and Political Order in Syria and Iraq,* as well as numerous journal articles and book chapters on the domestic and foreign policies of Jordan, Egypt, Israel, and Turkey.

Ilan Peleg is the Charles A. Dana Professor of Government and Law at Lafayette College. He is the author or editor of six books, including *Human Rights in the West Bank* (1995). His most recent book, *Negotiating Culture and Human Rights,* is forthcoming from Columbia University Press. Professor Peleg is the editor of the *Israel Studies Bulletin* and has served as president of the Association for Israel Studies.

Don Peretz is professor emeritus of political science, SUNY–Binghamton, where he taught from 1966 to 1992. He also served as professor and lecturer at Williams, Vassar, Dropsie, Hofstra, and Hunter Colleges from 1954 to 1961 and as representative of the American Friends Service Committee with UN Relief for Palestine Refugees in 1949. He has published twelve books, including *The Middle East Today; Israel and the Palestine Refugees; Government and Politics of Israel;* and *Palestinians, Refugees, and the Middle East Peace Process.*

Barry Rubin is director of the Global Research in International Affairs (GLORIA) Center of the Interdisciplinary Center (IDC) and editor of the *Middle East Review of International Affairs* (MERIA). His latest books include *The Tragedy of the Middle East; Revolution until Victory? The Politics and History of the PLO;* and *From Revolution to State-Building: The Transformation of Palestinian Politics.*

Judith S. Yaphe is senior research professor and Middle East project director in the Institute for National Strategic Studies at the National Defense University at Ft. McNair, Washington, D.C. Some of her recent publications include "U.S. Policy towards Iraq," "Iraq: Human Rights in the Republic of Fear," and "Do No Harm," a study of Arab perspectives on NATO's Mediterranean initiatives, published in *The Mediterranean Quarterly* in November 1999.

Index